"*The Chicago Freedom Movement* is ̲ ̲.̲ ̲ ̲ ̲ ̲ ̲ ̲ ̲ ̲ ̲ ̲ ̲.on to the literature about this era in the city's and the country's history. The compelling first-person narratives also remind us of the historical roots of today's activists in cities like Chicago, who continue the fight against racial and economic injustice."

—Peter T. Alter, historian and director,
Studs Terkel Center for Oral History, Chicago History Museum

"*The Chicago Freedom Movement* should be a handbook for present-day human rights activists. Through the eyes of a diverse group of seasoned civil rights leaders, it weaves a fabric that connects the actions and lessons of summer 1966, through decades of Chicago history, to inform reinvigorated grassroots movements today."

—Philip Nyden, professor of sociology and director of the
Center for Research and Learning, Loyola University Chicago

"*The Chicago Freedom Movement* brings together a unique collection of voices that help to shine a light on an important set of northern-based struggles and a powerful chapter in the larger movement history."

—Barbara Ransby, historian and author of *Ella Baker and the Black Freedom Movement: A Radical Democratic Vision*

"*The Chicago Freedom Movement* is an exciting new treatment that explains the movement from a variety of points of view, including narratives from both historians and participants. The book presents voices and documentation in a fresh way that helps us to better understand the movement's goals, successes, and failures, as well as its legacy for us today. Both scholars and general readers will gain new perspectives from this story."

—Michael Honey, author of *Going Down Jericho Road: The Memphis Strike, Martin Luther King's Last Campaign*

"This book makes a significant contribution to the understanding of the Chicago movement. It contains details about the Chicago Freedom Movement (tenant organizing, the North Shore project, the role of women, the role of nonviolence training with youth, the role of music, the lead poisoning campaign, etc.) that are usually left out or glossed over. Essential reading for historians, classrooms, and community activists."

—Tracy E. K'Meyer, author of *Civil Rights in the Gateway to the South: Louisville, Kentucky, 1945–1980*

The Chicago Freedom Movement

THE
CHICAGO
FREEDOM
MOVEMENT

Martin Luther King Jr.
and Civil Rights Activism
in the North

Edited by
Mary Lou Finley, Bernard LaFayette Jr.,
James R. Ralph Jr., and Pam Smith

Foreword by Clayborne Carson

UNIVERSITY PRESS OF KENTUCKY

Scholarly publisher for the Commonwealth,
serving Bellarmine University, Berea College, Centre College of Kentucky, Eastern
Kentucky University, The Filson Historical Society, Georgetown College, Kentucky
Historical Society, Kentucky State University, Morehead State University, Murray
State University, Northern Kentucky University, Transylvania University, University
of Kentucky, University of Louisville, and Western Kentucky University.
All rights reserved.

Editorial and Sales Offices: The University Press of Kentucky
663 South Limestone Street, Lexington, Kentucky 40508-4008
www.kentuckypress.com

Library of Congress Cataloging-in-Publication Data

Names: Finley, Mary Lou, 1943- editor. | LaFayette, Bernard, Jr., editor. |
  Ralph, James R. (James Richard), 1960- editor. | Smith, Pam (Consultant),
  editor.
Title: The Chicago Freedom Movement : Martin Luther King Jr. and civil rights
  activism in the north / edited by Mary Lou Finley, Bernard LaFayette Jr.,
  James R. Ralph Jr., and Pam Smith ; foreword by Clayborne Carson.
Description: Lexington, Kentucky : University Press of Kentucky, 2016. |
  Series: Civil rights and the struggle for Black equality in the twentieth
  century | Includes bibliographical references and index.
Identifiers: LCCN 2015047420| ISBN 9780813166506 (hardcover : alk. paper) |
  ISBN 9780813166520 (pdf) | ISBN 9780813166513 (epub)
Subjects: LCSH: African Americans—Civil
  rights—Illinois—Chicago—History—20th century. | Civil rights
  movements—Illinois—Chicago—History—20th century. | King, Martin
  Luther, Jr., 1929-1968. | Chicago (Ill.)—Race relations.
Classification: LCC F548.9.N4 C465 2016 | DDC 323.1196/073077311—dc23
LC record available at http://lccn.loc.gov/2015047420

ISBN 978-0-8131-7500-3 (pbk. : alk. paper)

This book is printed on acid-free paper meeting
the requirements of the American National Standard
for Permanence in Paper for Printed Library Materials.

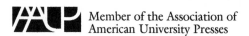

Member of the Association of
American University Presses

Contents

Photographs follow page 206

Foreword

When Martin Luther King Jr. arrived in Chicago late in July 1965 to deliberate with leaders of the city's civil rights organizations, he realized that he was coming to the end of one stage of his life and commencing another. He was confident that Congress would soon pass the major new legislation that would become the Voting Rights Act. Along with the Civil Rights Act of 1964, this victory signaled a decisive triumph over the southern Jim Crow system of legalized racial segregation and discrimination. Although few Americans recognized it at the time, the Selma to Montgomery voting rights march would be the final sustained display of unified black-white protest in pursuit of national civil rights goals.

Because King was a visionary leader gifted with global and historical perspective, he recognized the enormous significance as well as the limitations of what had been achieved during the two decades following the end of World War II. Black Americans had overcome a viciously obdurate system of oppression, and elsewhere in the world more than fifty nations had freed themselves from colonialism. South African apartheid would endure for another quarter century, and other forms of invidious discrimination would persist even longer, but for the first time in history, a majority of humanity had gained basic constitutional rights in the nations where they resided.

Even as King acknowledged how much had been achieved during his adult life, he was aware of the challenges that still lay ahead as he pushed the freedom movement beyond civil rights reforms. Indeed, although King's broad awareness of class as well as racial oppression was often not prominent in his civil rights oratory, it had always been a central aspect of his ministry. During his first year as a student at Crozer Theological Seminary, King became infatuated with the social gospel of early-twentieth-century American theologian Walter Rauschenbusch. In a paper written for one of his classes at Crozer, he foreshadowed the concerns of his final years when he announced, "I must be concerned about unemployment, [slums], and economic insecurity." In 1952 he confided to his future

ix

wife, Coretta Scott, about "the gospel that I will preach to the world" in even more expansive terms, mentioning "a warless world, a better distribution of wealth, and a brotherhood that transcends race or color."

In 1955, after Rosa Parks refused to give up her seat on a segregated Montgomery bus, King was unexpectedly drafted into the role of civil rights leader rather than social gospel minister. For the next decade, he devoted himself to the civil rights cause while downplaying his more controversial views regarding economic justice, but once King received the Nobel Peace Prize in 1964, his social gospel perspective became more evident. In his Nobel lecture he insisted that "what is happening in the United States today is a relatively small part of a world development." While recognizing that the problem of racial injustice remained unsolved in many nations, King asserted that the world faced two other major "evils"—that is, poverty ("the time has come for an all-out world war against poverty") and war ("it is as imperative and urgent to put an end to war and violence between nations as it is to put an end to racial injustice").

Thus, by the time King led a march to Chicago City Hall and then addressed a rally sponsored by the city's Coordinating Council of Community Organizations, he already felt restricted by the label of civil rights leader. In a 1965 *Ebony* magazine article he insisted that, "in the quiet recesses of my heart, I am fundamentally a clergyman, a Baptist preacher. This is my being and my heritage for I am also the son of a Baptist preacher, the grandson of a Baptist preacher and the great-grandson of a Baptist preacher." Few of his admirers or critics understood that his ministerial mission was actually more far-reaching and controversial than his civil rights agenda. At the Chicago rally he referenced his earlier social gospel perspective when he announced that his primary objective was "to bring about the unconditional surrender of forces dedicated to the creation and maintenance of slums."

When King returned to Chicago early the next year, he, like earlier social gospel ministers, made a commitment to "live in the very heart of the ghetto." Along with Coretta and their children, he moved to a rundown apartment in the Lawndale neighborhood. "I would not only experience what my brothers and sisters experience in living conditions, but I would be able to live with them," King explained. As had Rauschenbusch and many of his followers, King concluded that slums and poverty were the product of deeply rooted problems associated with capitalism. He was convinced that the nonviolent strategies he had used successfully in the South would also prove effective in the northern cities.

The Chicago campaign therefore became a starting point for King's final years of leadership. In subsequent speeches his biblical point of reference was no longer the story of the Exodus from Egypt—"even after you've crossed the Red Sea, you have to move through a wilderness with prodigious hilltops of evil and gigantic mountains of opposition." King increasingly referred to Jesus's Good Samaritan parable about the Levite and the priest who refused to help a man injured by thieves along the road from Jericho to Jerusalem.

In Chicago and later in Memphis, King risked damaging the acclaim he had received as a civil rights leader in order to confront problems that were even more intractable than racial oppression in the Jim Crow South. "We look back at 1966 as a year of beginnings and of transition," he later wrote. "For those of us who came to Chicago from Georgia, Mississippi, and Alabama, it was a year of vital education." He admitted he had little success in his initial confrontation with urban racial and economic problems—"in all frankness, we found the job greater than even we imagined."

In November 1966, after King reached an agreement with Chicago officials that achieved only some of his goals, he retreated briefly from the protest campaign there to complete his last book, *Where Do We Go from Here: Chaos or Community?* By then, it was becoming clear that the new stage of the African American freedom struggle might last longer than the long struggle for equal citizenship rights. "We found ourselves confronted by the hard realities of a social system in many ways more resistant to change than the rural South," King reflected. Some of his critics attributed his lack of success in Chicago to the folly of a southern civil rights leader who failed to recognize the limits of his competency. Seen, however, from King's overriding social gospel perspective, he was returning to his deepest convictions as a social gospel minister after a decade-long detour into civil rights leadership. He had accomplished much during his swift rise to international prominence, but the most prophetic period of his life still lay ahead. King was confident that oppressed people throughout the world had finally freed themselves from bondage, but he was less certain that he could lead them to a Promised Land.

The story of the Chicago campaign is a crucial part of King's life and of this nation's long struggle to realize its egalitarian and democratic ideals. King did not overcome the complex global problems he confronted during his final years, but that failure is not his alone; it is also the failure of those of us who have outlived him. It has been a half century since he asked, "Where do we go from here?" We still have not fully answered him, but the contributions to this book tell the story of many who were committed to carrying on King's work over many decades, both in Chicago and elsewhere. These essays provide helpful suggestions for those who are now prepared to carry it forward in the current era.

When King addressed striking sanitation workers in Memphis on the day before his assassination, he famously ended his oration by noting that he had "seen the Promised Land. I may not get there with you. But I want you to know tonight, that we, as a people, will get to the Promised Land." Earlier in his speech, King less famously elaborated on the Good Samaritan parable, with its theme of dangerous unselfishness in response to those in need. King noted that the Samaritan "got down from his beast, decided not to be compassionate by proxy. But he got down with him, administered first aid, and helped the man in need. . . . The first question that the Levite asked was, 'if I stop to help this man, what will happen to me?' But the Good Samaritan came by, and he reversed the question. 'If I do not stop to help this man, what will happen to him?'"

Clayborne Carson

Abbreviations

ACLU	American Civil Liberties Union
AFSC	American Friends Service Committee
AME	African Methodist Episcopal
CAPCC	Chatham–Avalon Park Community Council
CBL	Contract Buyers League
CCCO	Coordinating Council of Community Organizations
CCELP	Citizens Committee to End Lead Poisoning
CDC	community development corporation
CETA	Comprehensive Employment and Training Act
CFM	Chicago Freedom Movement
CFS	Chicago Freedom School
CHA	Chicago Housing Authority
CORE	Congress of Racial Equality
CRA	Community Reinvestment Act
CUCA	Coalition for United Community Action
FHA	Federal Housing Administration
GIU	Gang Intelligence Unit
HELP	Hospital Employees Labor Program
HOME	Home Opportunities Made Equal
HUD	US Department of Housing and Urban Development
IFHR	Immigrants Fair Housing Roundtable
IUD	Industrial Union Department (of AFL-CIO)
JOIN	Jobs or Income Now
KOCO	Kenwood-Oakland Community Organization
LCDC	Lawndale Christian Development Corporation
LCMOC	Leadership Council for Metropolitan Open Communities
LISC	Local Initiative Support Corporation
MLK	Martin Luther King Jr.
NAACP	National Association for the Advancement of Colored People

NSSP	North Shore Summer Project
PTA	Parent-Teacher Association
RWDSU	Retail, Wholesale, Department Store Union
SCLC	Southern Christian Leadership Conference
SCOPE	Summer Community Organization and Political Education project
SDS	Students for a Democratic Society
SNCC	Student Nonviolent Coordinating Committee
SOUL	Students Organized for Urban Leadership
TIF	tax increment finance
TWO	The Woodlawn Organization
UAW	United Automobile Workers
UCC	United Church of Christ
UIC	University of Illinois–Chicago
UNCAT	United Nations Committee against Torture
UPWA	United Packinghouse Workers of America
URLTA	Uniform Residential Landlord-Tenant Act
UWL	United We Learn
WCG	We Charge Genocide
WHOA	Winnetka Home Owners Association
WSCP	West Side Christian Parish
WSF	West Side Federation
WSO	West Side Organization

Introduction

Mary Lou Finley, Bernard LaFayette Jr., James R. Ralph Jr., and Pam Smith

> To make Chicago a beautiful city, a city of brotherhood.
> —Martin Luther King Jr., August 26, 1966

In September 1965 a dozen or so members of Dr. Martin Luther King Jr.'s southern field staff moved into the West Side Christian Parish's Project House in the heart of Chicago's Near West Side, joining other volunteers already living there. Black and white, male and female, most of them still in their early twenties, they had already been tested by civil rights struggles in the South. It was just weeks after passage of the Voting Rights Act and six months after Selma—where civil rights demonstrators had overcome brutal beatings to cross the Edmund Pettus Bridge and march to Montgomery, Alabama, in the struggle to obtain voting rights in the South. They came to Chicago to work for James Bevel, himself fresh from Selma, where he had been director of direct action for King. Bevel was serving as the parish's program director, and he would soon be appointed director of the Chicago Project of the Southern Christian Leadership Conference (SCLC) as well, an "elder" at the age of twenty-eight.[1]

Among these SCLC staffers were James Orange, age twenty-two, who had joined the movement in Birmingham and helped the Selma-to-Montgomery marchers persevere in the rain with his inspired song-leading; eighteen-year-old Dorothy Wright (later known as Dorothy Tillman), who had joined the SCLC staff after organizing a student walkout at her Montgomery, Alabama, high school on the day the Selma march arrived; and Lynn Adler, twenty-two, a recent University of Pennsylvania graduate who had spent the summer in Hale County, Alabama, working for

1

SCLC's Summer Community Organization and Political Education project (SCOPE).[2]

Some were Chicagoans who had headed south and were returning to their home territory: Claudia King had been active with the Chicago chapter of the Congress of Racial Equality (CORE); Jimmy Wilson, a former gang leader from Chicago's Lawndale community, had been helping the West Side Christian Parish organize youth before going south. Suzi Hill and Jimmy Collier were Chicago students who had been drawn south by the excitement of the campaign in Selma; Jimmy would soon be writing new freedom songs for the Chicago movement.

Others came from afar: Charlie Love from San Francisco, Eric Kindberg and Anne Gillie from elsewhere in the Midwest. Many came dressed in blue work shirts and overalls, the signature uniform for southern civil rights workers organizing rural farmers, ready to meet Chicago head-on. Twenty-five-year-old Bernard LaFayette Jr., a veteran of the Nashville movement and the Freedom Rides and a former college roommate and compatriot of James Bevel's, was already established on Chicago's West Side, on the staff of the American Friends Service Committee (AFSC). LaFayette had arrived a year earlier, invited by AFSC to develop a nonviolent approach to the West Side's problems.[3]

The Project House where these new arrivals settled was just half a block from the famed Maxwell Street Sunday market, an old immigrant community bustling with peddlers, shopkeepers, and families selling wares from the backs of trucks. Even more popular were Chicago's Polish sausages, sold at a vending stand on the corner. And there was music everywhere; in fact, many a Chicago blues musician first found an audience at the Sunday market. Residents of the Project House were awakened at 6:30 a.m. on Sunday morning by the vibrant sounds of tambourine and gospel music wafting in the windows from a market street band just outside. They had indeed arrived in Chicago.[4]

The new arrivals soon moved from the Maxwell Street neighborhood to shared apartments in East Garfield Park, farther out on the West Side and closer to the Warren Avenue Congregational Church, which would be their headquarters. There, they discovered Edna's, a tiny, newly opened soul-food restaurant on Madison Street, just a block away. Edna's one-dollar fried chicken dinners—served by Edna and cooked by her father—became a mainstay. As the staff became better acquainted with Edna, she and her father often served them free dinners when paychecks were late or money was short.[5]

The staff's arrival in Chicago was the first concrete step in Dr. King's move to join forces with that city's civil rights movement in what would soon become the Chicago Freedom Movement (CFM), a coalition of King's SCLC and the Chicago-based Coordinating Council of Community Organizations (CCCO). And so it began. Meetings took place and an official organizational structure emerged as autumn unfolded and relationships between SCLC and CCCO were formalized. By the time their collaboration went public, the staff's work was well under way. The movement that grew out of this collaborative effort soon declared its intention to end the slums in Chicago.

This volume draws its inspiration from "Fulfilling the Dream: SCLC-CCCO Fortieth Anniversary Three Day Commemoration and Action Conference," held in Chicago at the Harold Washington Cultural Center in July 2006. The conference brought together hundreds of Chicago Freedom Movement veterans, historians, youth activists, and engaged citizens to revisit the stories of the movement and reexamine its impact and contemporary relevance. Some of the essays in this book began as presentations at the conference, and our collaboration in organizing the commemoration brought the four of us together as the editors of this volume.

The primary goal of this book is to investigate the deep impact of the Chicago Freedom Movement. Histories of the civil rights movement often fail to fully discuss the Chicago Freedom Movement, or they dismiss it as a "defeat" for Dr. King and for nonviolence. Even some of its participants hold similar views. This book calls for a reconsideration of that verdict now that nearly fifty years have passed, giving us a fresh perspective. We argue that the Chicago Freedom Movement *did* have a substantial impact, and we show how the ripples of that impact had significant consequences in many areas: tenants' rights, black political power, fair housing, and community development in poor communities, to name a few.

Sometimes nonviolent direct action campaigns lead to immediate, visible victories, such as the Selma campaign, which led to passage of the Voting Rights Act in 1965. But the victories achieved by social movements often emerge much later, long after the major campaigns have ended, as activist and nonviolence trainer Bill Moyer points out in his "Eight Stages of Social Movements" model.[6] Successful campaigns put the issue on the public agenda, but legal, institutional, and cultural changes may come years later, as other groups and their political allies keep forging ahead in different, less visible arenas. Thus, as we explore the impact of the Chicago Freedom Movement, we need to pay attention to how the work started in the 1960s was carried on in the years and decades that followed.

We recognize that the issues raised by the Chicago movement—slum housing, housing discrimination, racial and economic injustice—are far from resolved even today. Though we argue that the movement had a significant impact, it did not "end slums in Chicago in eighteen months," as Bevel proclaimed it would. Nor did it lead to the immediate desegregation of housing in Chicago. Furthermore, we have experienced a decades-long backlash against the gains of the 1960s, and this has slowed—or even reversed—some of the progress from that era. Nonetheless, we maintain that changes *have* come and that the ripples spreading out from the Chicago Freedom Movement changed Chicago and the nation.

The book's second goal is to relate some of the untold and less familiar stories from the movement. We begin by presenting a brief history of key moments in the movement, as recounted by some of the participants—an oral history of the movement itself. We hope this both serves readers who are not familiar with the movement's history and provides insight into the experiences of the movement's participants.[7]

In exploring the impact of the Chicago Freedom Movement, we take a larger, more capacious view of its activities, discussing not just the well-known story of the open-housing marches against housing segregation but also the stories of tenant union organizing, the campaign against childhood lead poisoning, youth organizing, and the selective buying campaigns and economic development projects of Operation Breadbasket, as well as the music of the movement and women's contributions.

We also take a more expansive view of nonviolent social movements in general. Although social movements are often associated in the public eye with protests, or what some scholars call "contentious politics," most movements have "constructive program" projects as well. "Constructive program" is a concept from Mohandas K. Gandhi's work in the Indian independence movement; this type of project engages large numbers of people in activities of daily living in which they conduct themselves as liberated human beings and in accordance with their vision of a transformed society. The classic symbol of this type of program is the spinning wheel: Gandhi encouraged the Indian people to spin and weave their own cloth rather than buy cloth from Britain because British laws and tariffs had destroyed the Indian textile industry and impoverished many Indians. In villages across India, millions took up the spinning wheel and in this way became part of the independence movement. More recent examples of constructive program projects include ethnic studies programs at universities, Freedom Schools and citizenship education classes conducted during the civil rights movement, the free breakfast programs for children operated by the Black Panthers in the late 1960s, nonsexist children's books, and rape crisis centers developed by activists in the women's movement. Some of the projects described in this book are clearly protests, while others, such as the campaign against childhood lead poisoning and the Dr. King Legacy Apartments in Chicago, can best be described as constructive programs. As a movement matures, these constructive programs often proliferate as activists invent creative new ways to manifest their vision.[8]

Finally, we hope this book provides a portrait of the Chicago movement as an experiment in nonviolence that is relevant to students and practitioners of nonviolence today. The Chicago Freedom Movement was arguably the first large-scale nonviolent civil rights campaign in a major metropolis in the United States. And contrary to many opinions at the time, the Chicago movement did not signify the death knell for nonviolence. Nonviolence has been taken up by people around the world over the past five decades. At a secret peace movement meeting in East Germany in the 1980s, a photograph of Martin Luther King hung on the wall where the forbidden meetings were held, acting as a source of inspiration for those activists, according to one account. Chinese students holding pro-democracy protests in Tiananmen Square in 1989 were singing the civil rights anthem "We Shall Overcome," translated into Chinese, as they faced down the tanks. A 1950s "comic book"—graphic novel—about the Montgomery bus boycott that circulated secretly throughout the South during the 1950s and early 1960s was translated into Arabic and distributed in many Arab countries, just in time for the Arab Spring in 2011. People from many lands and many cultures are inspired by the stories of nonviolent action from the American civil rights movement as they continue their own efforts to effect change in oppressive situations. Further, nonviolence training continues. Bernard LaFayette and his many colleagues and students are teaching Kingian nonviolence throughout the United States and in many international settings.[9]

What was the Chicago Freedom Movement? The answer to this question is more complex than it first appears. Most visibly, the Chicago Freedom Movement was the organizational collaboration between Martin Luther King's Southern Christian Leadership Conference and Chicago's Coordinating Council of Community Organizations headed by Al Raby. This collaboration began with James Bevel's arrival in Chicago in September 1965 and lasted until CCCO was dissolved in the fall of 1967, marking the formal end of the Chicago Freedom Movement. This book focuses primarily on the activities of that period, 1965 to 1967, and the legacy of that time. But that is not the whole story.

Before 1965, important groundwork was laid, including CCCO's organizing for better schools and AFSC's organizing on the West Side. We consider these activities critical precursors to the Chicago Freedom Movement, and CCCO's work involving schools was an important movement in itself. (See Christopher Reed's chapter 3 for additional stories about earlier civil rights activism in Chicago.) Further, CCCO's demise in 1967 did not end SCLC's work in Chicago. The center of that work moved to Operation Breadbasket, led by Jesse Jackson, and addressed important economic issues over the decades—first as an arm of SCLC until 1971 when it was reformulated as Operation PUSH, and later evolving into the Rainbow PUSH Coalition in 1996. Early on, Operation Breadbasket developed voter registration as another aspect of its agenda. Nor did the end of the Chicago Freedom Movement spell an end to tenant union work, which continued for many years as local Chicagoans carried on that struggle.

In addition to being an organizational alliance between SCLC and CCCO, the Chicago Freedom Movement was simply a social movement, and like any social movement, activists near and far picked up on the

CFM's momentum and ideas and pursued them in their own ways. Sometimes those activists working at a later date or in other locales did not even realize they were building on the work of the Chicago Freedom Movement, a common phenomenon in social movement history. Sometimes, though, the use of common symbols, language, or personal networks linked those efforts back to Chicago.[10]

We recognize that the Chicago Freedom Movement occurred at a critical juncture in the history of the civil rights movement. Cries of "Black Power" were beginning to resound across the nation, raised to dramatic visibility by Stokely Carmichael as members of both SCLC and the Student Nonviolent Coordinating Committee (SNCC) marched across Mississippi in June 1966 to continue James Meredith's 220-mile "march against fear." This movement happened at a moment when dramatic shifts in perspective led to declarations that "black is beautiful" and to a growing Pan-African consciousness. The mood of many in the African American community was also shifting, leading to the adoption of more assertive approaches to change. This shift in mood, the increasingly rapid rate of change in American culture, and the exhaustion of patience at the grassroots level led some to see the Chicago Freedom Movement's nonviolent strategies and interracial coalitions as relics of an era whose time was past, and this may have played a role in the tendency to underestimate its impact. We want to revisit this movement's story and uncover the significant changes it brought about, even if those achievements fell short of the hopes of participants and contemporary observers.

This book builds on several recent works that have identified a "new civil rights historiography," focusing on both a longer historical time frame and a wider geographic lens, making visible what one historian has called "the forgotten struggle for civil rights in the North." By reexamining the work of the Chicago Freedom Movement and illuminating some of its lesser-known contributions, this book challenges the traditional civil rights narrative and expands its scope to include a deeper analysis of movements in the North, thus planting itself firmly within this new historiography.[11] At the same time, this book invites other scholars and researchers to dig deeper into the rich history of the Chicago Freedom Movement and its legacy. Many of the chapters herein are exploratory probes of topics that deserve further investigation.[12]

In this collection we present a variety of voices, including both oral histories and analyses by scholars and activists. We recognize that oral histories are based on the recollections of participants and that individuals experience and remember events differently. This, in our view, adds richness to the layered story we are endeavoring to tell.

We also want to acknowledge that two of us were deeply involved with SCLC and its role in the Chicago Freedom Movement, and this may be reflected in the book's perspectives and the contributors included. Mary Lou Finley worked on the SCLC staff as James Bevel's secretary, and as noted earlier, Bernard LaFayette Jr. worked with AFSC and was Bevel's longtime colleague.

This book stresses the importance of the actions of ordinary people in bringing about change. It is a story of strategic fighters using the tools of nonviolence creatively to change their city and their country and, in so doing, to make history. It is this social agency, the active shaping of the community's collective experience, that we hope to make more visible. It is also a story of a black-led collaboration of African Americans, progressive whites, and some Latinos—a collaboration that contributed significantly to multiracial coalition building in Chicago.

Notes

1. The West Side Christian Parish was founded in 1952 by the Chicago City Missionary Society—now the Community Renewal Society—and ministers from a sister group, the East Harlem Protestant Parish, a liberal Protestant ministry in New York City dedicated to advocating for the disadvantaged and oppressed. The parish had four storefront churches and a thrift shop in addition to the Project House, where the volunteers, many of them from the Brethren Volunteer Service, lived. Don Benedict, executive director of the Chicago City Missionary Society, was instrumental in supporting the movement and served on the Agenda Committee, a key leadership group for the Chicago Freedom Movement. See Don Benedict, *Born Again Radical* (New York: Pilgrim Press, 1982), 92–93.

2. Willy Siegel Leventhal, *The SCOPE of Freedom: The Leadership of Hosea Williams with Dr. King's Summer '65 Student Volunteers* (Montgomery, AL: Challenge Publishing, 2005), 520.

3. Other SCLC staff arriving from the South included Sherie Land, Bennie Luchion, and Chicagoans LaMar McCoy, Earless Ross, and Maurice Woodard. They were later joined by the Reverend Charles Billups, a key leader in the 1963 Birmingham campaign; Stoney Cooks, aide to executive director Andrew

Young in Atlanta; and Al Sampson from the executive staff in Atlanta. Others from the Chicago area who joined the staff shortly thereafter included Chicago Theological Seminary student Jesse Jackson, former Students for a Democratic Society member Julian Brown, journalist Carolyn Black, student organizer Patti Miller, and Melody Heaps, who served as liaison to the labor movement. Louis Andrades from East Harlem also joined the staff in Chicago, as did Billy Hollins, Brenda Travis, Candy Dawson, Felix Valluena, Monroe Walker, and Meredith Gilbert. West Side Christian Parish volunteers Molly Martindale, Mary Lou Finley, and David Jehnsen and staff members Diana Smith and Colia Liddell LaFayette worked with the SCLC staff. (Mary Lou Finley joined the SCLC staff shortly after she began working as Bevel's secretary.) There were, of course, numerous volunteers, among them Prexy Nesbitt, a student intern from Antioch College. See James R. Ralph Jr., *Northern Protest: Martin Luther King, Jr., Chicago, and the Civil Rights Movement* (Cambridge, MA: Harvard University Press, 1993), 254 n. 7, 261 n. 59, 205; "North and South: Southern Christian Leadership Conference Staff News," March 1967, http://www.crmvet.org/sclc/6703_sclc_ns.pdf.

4. The Maxwell Street market began in the 1880s, and in 1912 it became Chicago's official open-air market. It served as an entry point for many generations of immigrants, who often got their start in business by operating peddler carts there. It had long been a Jewish neighborhood, but in the 1950s and 1960s there were both Jewish and African American business owners, and many connections between them. The market was known for its music, especially jazz and blues; Muddy Waters, Howlin' Wolf, and Hound Dog Taylor reportedly played there on Sunday mornings. The market on Maxwell Street was closed in 1994 to make room for the expansion of the University of Illinois's Chicago campus and was moved to an indoor facility nearby. See Carolyn Eastwood, *Near West Side Stories: Struggles for Community in Chicago's Maxwell Street Neighborhood* (Chicago: Lake Claremont Press, 2002), 19–21, 202–3.

5. Edna's Restaurant later moved to a larger space a few doors down on Madison Street. Edna Stewart became one of Chicago's most famous soul-food cooks, and the restaurant long served as a meeting place for Chicago politicians, a place to find out what was happening on the West Side. Sadly, Edna passed away in June 2010 at age seventy-two. However, the restaurant reopened a few months later, with Edna's former produce manager, Henry Henderson, at the helm and head chef Lillie Joiner running the kitchen. It is now called Ruby's, after Henderson's mother. The Warren Avenue Congregational Church building now houses the New Greater St. John Community Missionary Baptist Church.

6. See Bill Moyer with JoAnn McAllister, Mary Lou Finley, and Steven Soifer, *Doing Democracy: The MAP Model for Organizing Social Movements* (Gabriola Island, BC: New Society Publishers, 2001), and Sidney Tarrow, *Power in Movement: Social Movements and Contentious Politics* (Cambridge: Cambridge University Press, 1998), 199–200.

7. For a more detailed history of the Chicago Freedom Movement, see Ralph, *Northern Protest.* Additional sources are listed in the notes for chapter 2.

8. On contentious politics, see Tarrow, *Power in Movement.* On Gandhi's ideas, see Gene Sharp, "The Theory of Gandhi's Constructive Program," in *Gandhi as a Political Strategist with Essays on Ethics and Politics* (Boston: Extending Horizons Books/Porter Sargent Publishers, 1979), 77–86.

9. Gandhi referred to his work as experiments with truth. See Mohandas K. Gandhi, *Gandhi, an Autobiography: The Story of My Experiments with Truth,* trans. Mahadev Desai (Boston: Beacon Press, 1957). The story about East Germany is from Bill Moyer, personal communication, 1986. On the singing of "We Shall Overcome" in China, see Dean McIntyre, "Music Musing #89: We Shall Overcome," General Board of Discipleship, United Methodist Church, www .gbod.org/worship/default.asp?act=reader&item_id=15797&loc_id=17,1003 (accessed September 22, 2009). The graphic novel is *Martin Luther King and the Montgomery Story* (Nyack, NY: Fellowship of Reconciliation, n.d). For more information on international uses of nonviolence, see Jonathan Schell, *The Unconquerable World: Power, Nonviolence, and the Will of the People* (New York: Henry Holt, 2003); Gene Sharp, Joshua Paulson, Christopher A. Miller, and Hardy Merriman, *Waging Nonviolent Struggle: 20th Century Practice and 21st Century Potential* (Manchester, NH: Extending Horizons Books/Porter Sargent Publishers, 2005); Stephen Zunes, Lester R. Kurtz, and Sarah Beth Asher, eds., *Nonviolent Social Movements: A Geographic Perspective* (Malden, MA: Blackwell Publishers, 1999); Peter Ackerman and Jack Duvall, *A Force More Powerful: A Century of Nonviolent Conflict* (New York: St. Martin's Press, 2000).

10. See Moyer et al., *Doing Democracy.* See Patrick D. Jones, *The Selma of the North: Civil Rights Insurgency in Milwaukee* (Cambridge, MA: Harvard University Press, 2009), and Tracy E. K'Meyer, *Civil Rights in the Gateway for the South: Louisville, Kentucky, 1945–1980* (Lexington: University Press of Kentucky, 2009), 111–44, for how housing movements in Milwaukee and Louisville borrowed from the Chicago movement.

11. Jeanne F. Theoharis and Komozi Woodard, eds., *Freedom North: Black Freedom Struggles outside the South, 1940–1980* (New York: Palgrave Macmillan, 2003), vii; Thomas J. Sugrue, *Sweet Land of Liberty: The Forgotten Struggle for Civil Rights in the North* (New York: Random House, 2008).

12. The past is necessarily interpreted through the lens of the present. As the present emerges, new angles of insight into past episodes open up. Further research, beyond what we were able to include here, is needed on the perspectives of black women. New sources, such as the Kale Williams Papers at the Chicago History Museum and the Al Pitcher Papers at the University of Chicago Special Collection Research Center, will bring new evidence to bear on the question of the significance of the Chicago Freedom Movement.

Part 1

Living the Chicago Freedom Movement

Part 1

Living the Chicago Freedom Movement

1

In Their Own Voices

The Story of the Movement as Told by the Participants

Edited by James R. Ralph Jr. and Mary Lou Finley

American popular culture likes to simplify complex issues. The Chicago Freedom Movement has often been depicted as a contest of wills between Martin Luther King Jr. and Mayor Richard J. Daley, with Daley "winning" and King "losing." That depiction is misleading. The Chicago Freedom Movement was a mass movement driven by inspired leadership and with the broad involvement of a community fed up with decades of entrenched inequity and abuse.

The strength of the Chicago Freedom Movement came from people seeking to make lasting changes in their communities. In this opening section, the story of the Chicago Freedom Movement is told in the words of those who were present and made numerous personal sacrifices to better the lives of current and future black Chicagoans. The recollections of a few are offered here as representative of the many who gave their time and energy to make the Chicago Freedom Movement what it was. While most of the voices here belong to Chicago Freedom Movement activists, the perspectives of others who were involved in the broader upheaval the movement caused are also included. As editors, we have added material to contextualize the participant accounts.

The Chicago Freedom Movement stood on the shoulders of earlier generations of activists in Chicago. And that is a long list of people, starting with John W. E. Thomas's pursuit of civil rights in the Illinois legislature in the aftermath of the Civil War, Ida B. Wells-Barnett's fight against lynching in the early 1900s, Earl Dickerson's quest to end restrictive covenants in the 1930s and 1940s, James Farmer's and Bernice Fisher's vision for the Congress of Racial Equality (CORE) in the early 1940s, and Charles Hayes's and Addie Wyatt's broad vision for civil rights unionism in the 1940s and 1950s. When the Southern Christian Leadership Conference (SCLC) arrived in 1965, Chicago activists were not wringing their hands and waiting for a rescuer. The struggle was already under way to end inadequate schools, horrible housing conditions, and the pernicious, predatory practices of the real estate industry.

Two struggles in particular laid the groundwork for the Chicago Freedom Movement: the schools campaign and the campaign to improve poor housing conditions on the West Side.

Prelude I: Organizing for Better Schools

This critical phase of the 1960s Chicago civil rights movement sprang from the mounting distress of black parents and their children over unequal education in Chicago's public schools. In the aftermath of the famous *Brown v. Board of Education* decision, the Chicago NAACP claimed that Chicago's schools suffered from deliberate segregation. Unlike in the American South, that segregation resulted not from formal Jim Crow laws but from administrative policies. In early 1962, on the city's Far South Side, black parents and students expressed the depth of their frustration by organizing protests at the Burnside School. Alma Coggs was a leader in the fight for better education at Burnside:

> We were living in public housing and [had] three children. We looked for a house, and we found one on Vernon Avenue. That was in 1951; that's when we moved to Vernon Avenue from way out in Altgeld Gardens at about 130th; and this was 9330 Vernon. It was a very stable neighborhood, but in the area around it, a little further away, all of the white families were just moving, hastening to move because of the school situation. The Burnside School became overcrowded, after not being crowded at all. We had another school about five blocks away, and that school was actually underused. It had ten empty rooms, while Burnside was

built for 800 and had close to 3,000 students. That is how over-crowded it was! They would not admit any of the kids from our area to the other school, Perry Elementary.

That is how that got started. We had asked the school district as parents, we had asked them as a community, and we had asked them as the school. The Burnside School had asked to place some of the kids over there; they just said "no," and we felt that was really what you call gerrymandering.

Instead of 9 a.m. to 3 p.m. our school had to go into something like 8 a.m. to 1 p.m. and 1 p.m. to 4 p.m. shifts: double shifts. Most of the parents were very upset about that. They just thought that that was terrible. It was hard on the teachers because you had many more students than they could handle; then the discipline became pretty bad, the kids started acting ugly, and the teachers could not handle them.

For the parents and others in the community it just got to be too much. We'd had it. It wasn't something that was planned outside. It was something that was kind of spontaneous because it was so logical. And two or three people suggested—of course, you know, when you get the NAACP and those different groups involved—the first thing they said was "let's picket." . . . We had a very good PTA and it just happened that I was president of the PTA; that is how I became the spokesman for the actions. So we actually sat down and planned it, and the parents really took part. We were just protesting the fact that they ignored us, and we felt that if they allowed our students to go to school over there it would alleviate some of the problems we were having.

A lot of the parents said that we will be there, we will come out, and we will support it. We are not going to let you do it by yourselves. So not only did the parents come, but the ministers in the area also came.

The initial group was largely women, but there were quite a few men that supported us. They were apprehensive, especially once the police got involved when the Board of Education was ordering the parents out of the school. At first we were just pick-eting in hallways and in the school building and they asked us to leave. A lot of the folks said, "Don't leave." The police just told them that "it's our duty—we've been ordered—to put you out; and if you don't go peacefully we will have to arrest you." And so that is what they did. Some of the people decided that they could not afford to be arrested. And we said, "Well, why not? Let's see if that will accomplish anything." But it did not, really. They did actually lock up about fifteen of us. We decided we would not go back and be locked up again. We would do our picketing outside. And so that continued for two to three weeks.

In the meantime, in the evenings afterwards, there would be meetings, and different groups wanted to meet with us and see what they could suggest. And so they had a big community meeting, and they decided on trying to sue the Board of Education. With the help of the NAACP and other outside groups, we actually sued the Board of Ed for the right to transfer our children.[1]

Protests erupted in other city neighborhoods, and legal action was pursued in support of equal opportunity in public education. The ferment led to the founding of the Coordinating Council of Community Organizations (CCCO) in late 1962. Meyer Weinberg was a professor at Wright Junior College in the late 1950s and early 1960s and a member of Teachers for Integrated Schools, one of the first groups to join CCCO. He recalls how he learned about the extent of segregation in the Chicago public schools:

I really didn't know much about the history of segregation in Chicago so I had to learn it. And my teacher was Faith Rich of CORE. She had been active on the school issue starting in the 1950s. She had also coauthored an article in *Crisis* in 1958 with Rita Phillips called "De Facto Segregation in the Chicago Public Schools."[2] It was news to me. It became clear, at least to me, that this whole distinction between de facto segregation and de jure segregation was a fake kind of distinction, a distinction without a difference, and that segregation in the North was a conscious creation of the school system working along with city government.[3]

Al Raby entered the Chicago civil rights movement through Teachers for Integrated Schools. He describes his early involvement:

> Meyer Weinberg called together a group of teachers and said essentially that some segment of every profession in the country had taken a position on integrated education. He had been unsuccessful in getting the teachers' union to take a position and thought that we ought to form an organization speaking to those issues. That organization was called Teachers for Integrated Schools. In the early 1960s he and I, then, became delegates to the Coordinating Council of Community Organizations, which was a broadly based civil rights, civic, community umbrella started by the Urban League and The Woodlawn Organization. So it was as a delegate to the Coordinating Council of Community Organizations that I first became involved in the movement of the 1960s.[4]

Despite the protestations of black Chicagoans, superintendent Benjamin Willis and the Board of Education refused to acknowledge the existence of a problem in the public schools. CCCO leaders decided they had to make an even more dramatic plea for change, so they organized a boycott in October 1963 in which more than 225,000 black youths stayed home from school. More than 175,000 black students participated in a second boycott in February 1964. Meyer Weinberg recalls the first school boycott in the fall of 1963:

> It was not spontaneous in any sense. It was well thought out. For instance, I remember getting a phone call from the PTA at Marshall High School which has been a black school since the late fifties, early sixties. I got called because I was chairman of the Education Committee of CCCO—this was less than a week, maybe three days before the first boycott. And they had a lot of questions to ask about whether they should keep their kids out. So I went there and I told them I graduated from this school [in 1938], and that when I went to it, it was a first-rate school, really a fine school, and that there is no reason why it can't be for your

children too. They were worried about the legal situation. There was a state law in Illinois that if you kept your child out of school for three consecutive days for reasons other than sickness you could be arrested for abandoning your children. [The boycott lasted one day.] It was a mass sort of thing. A quarter of a million kids were kept out, and that's as many as there were on the March on Washington.[5]

David Jehnsen, organizer of the West Side Christian Parish's youth group, gives this account of another action on the school issue:

In 1963 we changed the name of the Parish's youth group from the Loyal Hearts to the Parish Youth Action Committee, and I worked with Alan Howe, another Parish volunteer, to train them in nonviolence and civil disobedience. We used the Nashville Sit-in Movement White Paper, Dr. King's *Stride toward Freedom*, my notes from a nonviolence workshop Bayard Rustin had given in preparation for the March on Washington, and a few pamphlets on Gandhi's philosophy and the steps [in a nonviolent campaign].

In 1963 and early 1964 Chicago civil rights organizations were boycotting segregated schools to try to get rid of Ben Willis, the Superintendent of Schools. While even at this early stage we knew that simply removing the superintendent couldn't solve the problem, we also thought we needed to be involved with the civil rights organizations in their efforts. The Parish Youth Action Committee leaders essentially took over the Crane High School Student Government and on one occasion led a five- to six hundred student march to downtown Chicago to support a demonstration at City Hall. The civil rights groups hadn't seen this type of student involvement before and there was new credibility for the work we were doing on the West Side of Chicago.[6]

Rosie Simpson, one of those who boycotted and led demonstrations against Superintendent Willis, recalls the grassroots flavor of the early Chicago demonstrations:

I'd already been wrestling with the school district on severe over-crowding and segregation issues when I started going down to the Board of Education to find out what the plans were for our kids. And I found out that they were going to set up a bunch of "Willis Wagons" [portable classrooms] between the railroad tracks and the alley, and that's where they planned to send our kids to school. We decided as parents we were not going to allow that to happen. We decided that when they came out to build that school we were going to lay down in front of the bulldozers, we were going to do whatever was necessary to stop that. And that is what we proceeded to do.

We laid down in front of the bulldozers and when the paddy wagons came to take us to jail, we chained ourselves to the paddy wagons and threw the keys away after we'd locked the locks. That went on for a couple of months and Ben Willis did not decide to change. However, we kept protesting, we got the community involved, Dick Gregory came out there with us, the Reverend John Porter was there with us. The city came together. We went to CCCO of course, and they came out to support us.[7]

In 1964 Al Raby became the CCCO's convener. Here, he describes the dynamics in the organization: "In the broad coalition that we had in the CCCO there were what were generally identified as radical, impatient activists, and I guess I fell into that spectrum. . . . On the other side of the spectrum, there were conservative people, the most prominent one was Bill Berry, who had the most respect across the board of anybody in that group, but certainly he had the respect of that element which tended to be more conservative."[8]

Edwin "Bill" Berry, then the executive director of the Chicago Urban League and a CCCO founder, sizes up the nature of political power faced by civil rights activists in Chicago: "This town was still suffering from plantation politics. Our representation in the City Council was by six black aldermen who were referred to opprobriously but very accurately as the 'Silent Six,' who simply carried out Massa Daley's orders, for what he wanted done on the plantation. And that gave us almost no representation."[9]

Despite all the protests by citizens like Alma Coggs, Rosie Simpson, and Al Raby, city authorities did not change school policies on race and public education. In the summer of 1965 CCCO, led by Raby, staged daily marches through downtown Chicago asking Superintendent Willis to resign.

The Reverend John Porter of Christ United Methodist Church in Englewood, on the city's South Side, joined the struggle for equal education early on and was one of the leaders of the open-housing marches in the summer of 1966:

I was introduced to the movement by my college philosophy professor, Dr. Warren Steincross, who had been a colleague of Dr. King's at the Boston School of Theology in the early 1950s. In August 1962, when I'd finished graduate studies at Garrett Seminary at Evanston, Dr. King sent me a telegram, inviting myself, and certainly hundreds of others across the country, to join him in SCLC's first mass demonstration in a southern city—Albany, Georgia.

After spending six days there I came back on fire to Chicago's Englewood community, where I was pastor of the Christ United Methodist Church. We began agitating, organizing, picketing, demonstrating, so that by 1963 we'd formed the first Freedom School, taking 100 kids out of the B-level entry school because of racism. And we joined Rosie Simpson and their protest at Seventy-Fifth and Lowell. And we protested police brutality, slum landlords, merchants who sold bad meat, and those who would not hire blacks at Sixtieth and Halsted [a shopping district on the South Side].

We also petitioned SCLC for membership, and Rev. Dr. C. T. Vivian, who was SCLC's chapter director, told us that if we formed an active group, were chartered in Illinois, and were very active, involved in teaching nonviolent tactics, and paid the $100 fee, we could become an affiliate. So we became SCLC's first affiliate in Chicago, which was housed in Christ Methodist Church. We were in the papers, particularly in Englewood, every week, and from there we were part of CCCO's foundation for inviting Dr. King to Chicago for the 1966 marches.

We also marched in 1965, from City Hall to communities on the South Side fourteen miles away: Hyde Park, Englewood, Chatham, all over. Fourteen miles from City Hall to the South Side. We marched almost every day. We marched with Dick Gregory, Ma Houston, Al Raby, myself, and others. And one of the things that is a lasting memory was the spirit. That spirit. That's what got us: the spirit. We marched, and didn't know we'd marched fourteen miles, because every step along the way we sang songs like "We Shall Not Be Moved," and that theme song of the movement, "We Shall Overcome." That was part of the spirit of the movement, and laid the foundation for SCLC to come to Chicago, joining CCCO, to form the Chicago Freedom Movement.[10]

Billy Hollins, who later served on the SCLC-Chicago staff, also participated in the demonstrations against Willis: "We used to march fourteen miles a day. We'd march seven days a week. At one point Dick Gregory took over the marches. He used to fly all the way from California, every day. He worked at the 'hungry i' in San Francisco at night, and he would fly every day and march with us all day, and fly back at night. He used to tell us, 'Don't come with no cute shoes, because we're going to march.'"[11]

Don Rose, who served on the CCCO's staff, also remembered the protests against Superintendent Willis:

It was June 8, 1965, when Ben Willis was rehired by the Board of Education. The CCCO called two demonstrations, one to be held on June 10 and one to be held on June 11, where we'd march from Balbo Street over to City Hall to express the political nature of the rehiring of Ben Willis. The first march—a couple of thousand people—went through flawlessly. The second march, as we went down Balbo—named, interestingly, after an Italian fascist—right at the intersection of Columbus and Balbo the cops hit us all. There was a huge sit down, and they arrested some 250 people, including Dick Gregory, who, when he sprung himself out of jail the next day announced, "We are going to march from this spot, Balbo and Columbus to City Hall. Every day, forever and ever." And as the movement went those days, you couldn't say Dick Gregory was wrong, and you couldn't say "well, let's reconsider," so we started marching every day.

This was really a precursor to Dr. King's decision to come to Chicago.[12]

Prelude II: Organizing on the West Side

The work of the American Friends Service Committee (AFSC) on Chicago's West Side was another important, though less heralded, dimension of the groundwork for the Chicago Freedom Movement. Early on, AFSC was hoping to build on the momentum of the southern civil rights movement.

Tony Henry helped launch these efforts on Chicago's West Side and recalls:

We were very concerned about the northern oppression of people of color, and black people in particular. There was discussion within AFSC among people of color and others, particularly in the Community Relations Division, about bringing to the surface the type of oppression that occurs in the North. We needed to have some kind of campaign like the southern campaigns.

Meanwhile, in Chicago, Chicago CORE . . . was working on housing as an issue. . . . We picked housing as an issue . . . in a fairly classic style, in which we went around the neighborhood and surveyed people: "What is the biggest issue in this neighborhood which you thought we ought to be concerned about: is it housing, is it education, is it police brutality or what?" And the issue that came up on top was housing, and so Chicago CORE decided to focus on housing, and even organized a summer campaign one year to focus in on housing. That then gave the impetus to the AFSC creating a housing program.[13]

In the summer of 1964 Kale Williams, executive director of AFSC, brought Bernard LaFayette on staff. As LaFayette explained it, "They deliberately wanted to find someone with extensive work with nonviolence in the

South to come to Chicago to experiment with how nonviolence could work in the North."[14] LaFayette recalls one of those early organizing efforts:

> This campaign focused on the condition of slum housing in the area where people of color lived. In addition to the lack of trash pick-up and unswept streets, the physical housing was in disrepair: broken windows, busted door locks, unpainted surfaces, crumbling steps, and of most concern was the lead-based paint peeling from the walls.
>
> In the process of organizing tenants, we discovered that young children were experiencing severe health problems. Young children suffered from swollen stomachs, blindness, damaged internal organs, vomiting and paralysis due to ingestion of peeling lead-based paint chips from the interior walls of the slum housing. The peeling paint chips fell from the interior walls of the ceiling onto the floors and sometimes even in the babies' cribs. Toddlers sometimes gnawed on the window sills as they peered out the windows. The lead from the paint could cause irreversible damage to the children's brain cells, which could result in a permanent physiological impairment.
>
> Rather than organize a protest march to address the problem, which is always an appropriate method after gathering information, educating the constituents, and preparing oneself for the campaign, we decided to address the problem directly, working with youth in the community.[15]

SCLC Decides to Target Chicago

According to the Reverend Dr. C. T. Vivian, who served on SCLC's executive staff, the success of the southern voting rights campaign in the spring of 1965 was a turning point for the civil rights movement: "The truth is, I woke up one day after Selma. It was really over but we were still there. I woke up one day and I was saying to myself, 'The movement as we have been doing it is over.' Once we had won the voting rights bill, I figured things were gonna be over and I was right."[16]

Bill Berry, an influential figure in Chicago civil rights circles, recalls:

"Martin [Luther King Jr.] said frequently that he was enticed into coming to Chicago because of the movement that we had going. And Chicago was a major city and a laboratory with all the problems, and we all
felt like if we could do the thing here we'd pretty well have a formula for
doing it anywhere. We told Martin, if he didn't already know, we had a
tough town. It was hard to crack, but if we did crack it in a political sense
we had a mayor who could deliver."[17]

Raby was in close contact with King as he decided on the next step
for SCLC:

During the summer of 1965 Martin was invited back to support
our efforts to oust Benjamin C. Willis. Now he had been thinking about and was looking about for a northern city, and had
been to Chicago on three occasions: once for the '64 rally; once
immediately after that to do a voter registration drive in Chicago
as part of a national effort; and then again when he was supporting our activities in Chicago. He decided to come to Chicago for
a variety of reasons: one, there was a broad coalition; two, he was
familiar with the leadership and had worked with it before; three,
he had friends in Chicago like [attorney] Chauncey Eskridge,
who had worked with him in the South, and Mahalia Jackson was
here, plus the fact that Jim Bevel and Bernard LaFayette were
here. We didn't make a formal request until we informally knew
the decision had been made.

There was some controversy within SCLC about whether or
not it was appropriate to go north. And it had a very fundamental and legitimate basis. Those who argued that it was premature
to go north foresaw that the kind of coalition and support that
one got in the North for the civil rights struggle in the South—
some of those supporters would be confronted with their own
racism and that confrontation would make it difficult and in some
instances impossible [for them] to continue to support the southern movement as well.[18]

Andrew Young, executive director of SCLC, remembers there was
disagreement within the organization about heading north:

After Selma, we had the Voting Rights Act; really, shortly after the Voting Rights Act, the Watts riots started. It was Bobby Kennedy who was saying the reason why they were having these riots in the North was because southern leaders had neglected the North. And I got upset; I said, "What do you mean? We have no more than fifty people, we have a budget of about $500,000–$600,000 a year, and we're running voter registration drives, we're desegregating the South, we had sit-ins, Freedom Rides. We're doing everything we could think of where we had been placed. And, he's got the National Guard, the Justice Department, the FBI . . . and why is it our problem to go north?" So, I was against going north.

I think Dr. King felt guilty about not doing anything in the North, and Bevel and Bernard, whom he respected a great deal, played on his guilt, saying, "You have to prove that nonviolence will work in the North, that this isn't just a southern phenomenon." And, I said, "You all stay up there and prove it. Our job is registering voters."[19]

The End-the-Slums Campaign

When James Bevel and a dozen or so SCLC field staff arrived on Chicago's West Side in September 1965, they started by educating themselves on conditions in the slums. They gathered staff members from a number of Chicago community organizations—about eighty people in all. This Wider Community Staff met on Tuesday and Thursday mornings for education on urban issues and training in nonviolence. The topics discussed were wide ranging: welfare rights, the Chicago political machine, slum housing conditions, people who were unable to get bank loans to buy houses and had to rely on contracts, falling plaster, rats attacking babies, and an analysis of the resources drained from the community from every direction. The SCLC staff joined with the staff of the West Side Christian Parish and worked together on organizing tenant unions and then the Union to End Slums, focusing on East Garfield Park and later Lawndale and the Near North Side. They were joined in this work by other Chicago organizations.

Bevel comments on the purpose of the Wider Community Staff meetings:

And what happened was the SCLC staff here in the city became more scientifically knowledgeable about Chicago than almost any black person in this city. For instance, our staff had to take maps and ride the whole bus system, so that you get a visual picture of Chicago. Then they would have to come to lectures twice a week . . . on what is Chicago, how it grew, what are the dynamics of it, and when did this pattern start, when did that pattern start, when did this ethnic group come, and what science and industry did these guys bring, what were the inner dynamics in this particular community?

You see, you have to know what you are talking about, you can't shoot bullets into the air.

Then we had to ground people from Chicago, the Chicago Freedom Movement and a lot of Chicago staff people, in the principles of nonviolence so that the issue would really be resolved. Nonviolence is potent; it is a science. And if you are going to get anything done it is because you used nonviolence. Violence cannot bring individual or social consciousness, nor can it solve the problem. It transfers and defers problems, but it does not solve problems. So those meetings had to ground people in that because we had a lot of Christian people but they were not grounded in using Christian principles to solve problems. They profess Christianity, but when they start trying to solve problems, they go back to using violent methods.[20]

The Chicago Freedom Movement

The SCLC-CCCO's joint project, the Chicago Freedom Movement, was officially launched in January 1966, and shortly thereafter Dr. King demonstrated his solidarity with the inner-city poor by moving into a decrepit apartment at 1550 South Hamlin Avenue in North Lawndale, on Chicago's West Side.

Raby, cochair of the Chicago Freedom Movement, reflects on the focus on the West Side:

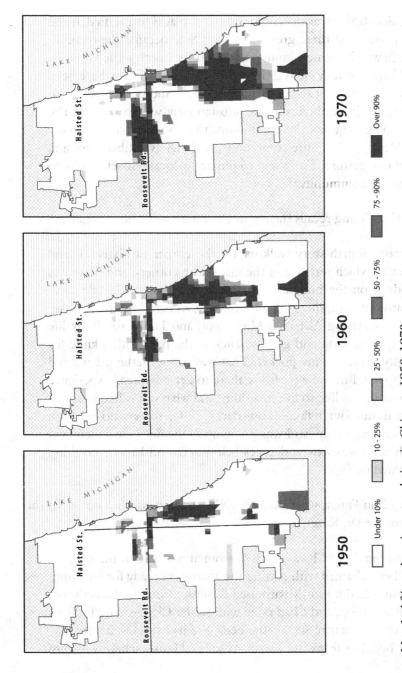

Map 1. African American population in Chicago, 1950–1970

1950

1960

1970

LAKE MICHIGAN

Halsted St.

Roosevelt Rd.

Under 10%   10 - 25%   25 - 50%   50 - 75%   75 - 90%   Over 90%

The South Side was the community that blacks first settled in and the population there grew. The West Side became the community in which the new immigrants from the South settled into, by and large. So they viewed themselves, and I think may have been viewed, as kind of secondary importance. And what Martin was trying to do symbolically and substantively was to say that I'm not going to ignore this community, that I'm concerned with the problems of the entire community, and that as a substantive and symbolic gesture, I'm going to physically locate myself here—to unite the community.[21]

Andrew Young recalls staying in Dr. King's apartment in Lawndale:

It was a fourth-story walk-up on the corner of Sixteenth and Hamlin, which was one of the main drug corners, and there was no door on the building. The policemen would say, "Be careful around here, there are a lot of drug addicts." I could just see myself surviving Alabama, Mississippi, and Louisiana all my life and then coming and getting stuck in the back with a knife for twenty dollars in my pocket. That was not something I wanted to happen. But, we were living there to get a firsthand experience of what it was like to live in a slum, and what it was like was, you were in this fourth floor, it was dark. . . . There were no lights on the steps going up, so I was going up in the dark. And there was no heat; it was sixteen degrees below zero and I had everything I owned on.[22]

Mary Lou Finley, working as Bevel's secretary, had helped set up the apartment for Dr. King:

Diana Smith and I—as the two women working in the office—had been charged with getting the apartment ready for Dr. King. We furnished it mostly with used furniture from the Parish's secondhand shop, and I had gone with staffer Charlie Love to Sears to buy new mattresses for the beds. We had stocked it with surplus bedding from the Parish's Project House, where we were living. Finally the day came when Martin Luther King was moving in.

It was very cold that day—January, Chicago cold—and so, at the end of the day, I telephoned Andrew Young (who always accompanied Dr. King on his Chicago sojourns) and asked if they needed more blankets. I worried that we hadn't supplied enough for the January cold. He said, yes, they might need some more blankets, and furthermore, could I stop somewhere and get some good Chicago barbecued ribs and bring them over for dinner. "Bring some for you and Bill, too," he said. Bill Moyer, then on the staff of the American Friends Service Committee, had a car, and he had offered to help with this venture. A short while later Bill and I found ourselves sitting on the new linoleum floor in the living room, with our paper plates of ribs on the orange crates serving as end tables, laughing over barbecue with Dr. King and Andrew Young.

Then, the doorbell rang. In came a young man from the neighborhood, accompanied by the Chicago policeman sitting guard outside Dr. King's new Chicago home. "Are you really Martin Luther King?" he asked when he arrived inside the apartment. Dr. King let out a rich, deep laugh. "Yes, I certainly am," he replied. "I couldn't believe you were moving into my neighborhood!" the young man replied. The warm, joshing conversation continued for a bit, then the young man departed.

A half hour later the doorbell rang again. The same young man returned this time accompanied by a half dozen others. "I went back and told my buddies that Dr. King had moved in here, but nobody believed me," he said. "They all wanted to come see for themselves." Dr. King welcomed them all into the cramped living room, where he sat on the stately but faded gold couch—clearly delighted—and after everyone had been introduced to him, talked with them of housing and neighborhoods and young people and the movement. "We hope you will all join us in this movement in Chicago," he called to them as they began to leave, trooping down the long dark staircase to the cold night outside.[23]

Lawrence Johnson, leader of the Conservative Vice Lords of Lawndale, was one of those young men who met with Dr. King in his apartment:

> We were labeled a gang. But we always considered ourselves protectors of the community. I know you've heard of Bobby Gore. He was my hero, my mentor. That's something that's very well known, still to this day, very well known. Bobby had a vision for the things we were doing. There were various groups, called gangs, in the area—the Roman Saints, the Cobras, others. Bobby's vision was they are not our enemies. The concept was to cease the fighting among one another and to seize the trade of the Twenty-Fourth Ward. It was about jobs in the neighborhood.
>
> If we control the stores, the restaurants, the taverns, the pool halls, the money stays within our community. If some lady's house catches on fire, we can aid and assist her. If somebody loses his or her job and can't pay the bills, we can get his or her lights turned back on. Where there's glass we're going to have grass. Give us the paint, we'll correct the deplorable situations in our community.
>
> The building where Dr. King lived wasn't very far from what you might call a boys' club. Our office was there along with the pool room we owned. Later on, next to that was the African Lion, an Africa shop we developed around 1967.
>
> I've been to Dr. King's apartment numerous times. Some of my first memories were going there to see Dr. King, thinking that the great civil rights leader was in Chicago, and in our 'hood, on our turf! When we gathered to see him, there were a range of us; I was one of the younger guys, peewees we were called. I was still in school. At the time it was Peppilow, the founder; Bobby Gore, the president; and some others going to see if it's really him, and what he wants to do in the 'hood. It was basically determined that the guys with rank would go.
>
> The times when we went to see Dr. King, those were one of the most fascinating times of my life. There were a lot of conversations on the back porch as well as in the hall. We had ideological

struggles—well, you could call them respectful arguments—with Dr. King about what was the best method, was it violence or non-violence, and what was the problem in the community. We would say, "We respect what you're saying, but if someone hits me, I'm going to hit him back." Sometimes it was fascinating, unbelievable. I didn't have a great deal of knowledge about Dr. King myself. I could read, so I learned more about him in the newspapers. I knew I was around someone who was different. I didn't have enough sense at that time to attribute it to his educational background. I just knew he was different.

One time, he told us, you're no match for the police. Not because you're not as tough, or not as intelligent or not as vigilant, but because police represent the establishment. They've got three weapons you don't have. We thought he meant guns, various types of guns. But he said: "You don't have information, you don't have communication, and you're missing mobilization."

At first, we thought it was a put-down. But then he would search for a way and a means to explain to us. He'd just knock it down: he would say, you're no match, and piece by piece, describe to us, tell us and educate us as to why we were not a match. Hearing this, seeing him, being young, living a depressive life in America, you couldn't help but to fall in love with him, to admire him, want to protect him.

We did protect him. This was our 'hood. Several guys would be out, hanging out on the corner, at his apartment building, 24/7. It was a directive that was given, because this brother was about some of the same things we were about.

We thought we could protect him better than the Chicago Police Department. I think he thought that too.

Dr. King influenced me and some of the other guys, too; he was encouraging us to get an education. "If you can't read or write or keep books how do you expect to maintain a business?" he said.[24]

In February 1966, the Chicago Freedom Movement underscored the desperate condition of many inner-city residents by taking over a run-down apartment building at 1321 South Homan Avenue. Andrew Young remembers the intervention:

> Dr. King came up there and we went around to visit some people. One place we went had no heat, it's still sixteen degrees outside, and they had a new baby wrapped in newspaper and a bath towel. We said, "You can't do this!" That's what started a rent strike. We sent somebody to get some coal to fire the furnace and so, almost on the spot, with a lawyer by the name of [William] Kunstler, we decided that people who didn't get heat and didn't get lights and services, shouldn't pay rent. We decided to get them to pay it to us. And we created an escrow account, and we decided, first of all, to fix up the furnace and buy them coal and provide them with heat.[25]

Tony Henry, the director of Housing Opportunities, saw a direct connection between the AFSC housing program and the Union to End Slums: "They decided to start off in the housing program we were working on. People were gravitating toward the idea of Dr. King. And so when it came true that he did come north, we set up rallies for him to speak to; and we organized meetings where people would come and testify as to the nature of housing discrimination in the North, and how their landlords were so unfair to them, and he agreed to listen. He drew large throngs of people."[26]

The creation of the Union to End Slums ultimately led to rent strikes. Billy Hollins recalls the effort necessary to organize a rent strike:

> That was part of organizing folk, to make them understand. Once you cause people to be able to see where they can receive a benefit, you can almost call on those people to do all kinds of stuff. "You['re] going to end up in a better apartment. . . ." I'm just taking their own strengths and causing them to use their own strengths to understand where they are. It's not like I had to beat them over the head, it's not like a vision somewhere; they were living it.
>
>   And when you talk about the children: it wasn't just the

slums, it was also that the children didn't have recreation areas. It wasn't just the buildings; what's the chance of their kid running out in the street because they were playing with a ball? There's not space, not stuff to play on.

You take people where they are. You know that mothers care about their children. So when you start talking about their children, they say, "All right, we're going to go with you." What I try to do in organizing is to try to find out where people are, and give that back to them. It's like repackaging it.[27]

Teenager Jim Keck participated in the Jenner School boycott on Chicago's North Side in 1966, for which the Chicago Freedom Movement offered support. He came to the Chicago Freedom Movement through the West Side CORE and the Christian Student Movement. Here, he recalls an episode that occurred during an attempt to organize tenants in a building near Douglas Park in North Lawndale in the summer of 1964:

We're organizing, going door-to-door, and one of the families agrees to let us use their apartment for the meeting. So the day of the meeting comes and there's close to thirty-five people in her apartment, which is really crunched. We came up with this agreement . . . the list of demands. One of the big problems in the building was rats. They often say in organizing that you dream for a moment like this. So as we show the tenants the demands, they go, "Geez, we're gonna get thrown out of here, I don't know." We told them that they have the option to control their rent; we could put it in escrow. It was an actual method in those days, in how you could do a rent strike, as long as you had the money in escrow and you paid, you showed that you paid for repairs or whatever. So as we are talking to them saying, "This is what you have to do; you have to withhold your rent," some people started getting cold feet. And they start saying, "Well, the guy is bad, what if we get thrown out?" So this kind of downer thing is going on and people start getting cold feet. Now, the woman that hosted the party had put out little saltines with American cheese. So on the coffee table are these little saltines. A rat jumps up on the coffee table, picks up a piece of the cheese, and he starts eating it like a squirrel and looking at everybody. No fear!

At that point people were like, "Damn it, we have to." So the rat turned the whole meeting around![28]

Later, in 1966, Keck was organizing tenants in East Garfield Park with the Union to End Slums:

They wanted a meeting with Dr. King and the pastor there, and several other pastors. They wanted to have a meeting where he listened to the people's concerns. So we brought the people from that building to a meeting with Dr. King. They went one by one and said there were rats and roaches; there was lead paint, which there was; there were no screens. Everybody came up with a "Dr. King, please help us" kind of thing.

While this was going on the landlord shows up with some white guy with a cigar in his mouth. And he's standing by the door where everybody could see him. Then five people jump up behind our people to speak. We organizers were thinking, "Who the hell are these people? They're not people we work with." Four of them were painters and they all get up and say they never use lead paint, that the people are lying. They were all African American guys. The last one was a middle-aged black woman and she said she was the rent collector. She apparently was, because people were really scared of her. She proceeded to say that the tenants are a bunch of liars, they're filthy, they're a problem, they've been reported to the police, and that the landlord is the greatest thing that's happened since Wonder Bread.

Then what happens is the audience starts siding with the landlord like, "That's right, we're not probably where we should be . . . yeah, we probably don't take care of. . . ." You know, it was all this whining and whimpering. Dr. King was stuck with this.

Many of us on the staff didn't even realize he could think on his feet, because we would hear him give standard speeches that he gave all over the place. But he got up there and dealt with the situation. What he did was—you know how wonderfully he

spoke—he said to the five people who testified against the tenants, "I can understand how you might feel this way. I understand we're not a perfect people, but we've come through." He
basically did a thing where he kind of brought them in, like, "I
understand where you're coming from. I understand why you
would say this." And then he gets into this thing, implying that
maybe they were put up to it. He says, "I forgive you because you
have families too." And lo and behold the five people who testified against the tenants get up there and apologize to him and
say that they were lying and that they did use lead paint. Dr. King
turned the whole meeting around!

And I'll never forget standing in the back, as most organizers do, and watching as the landlord took off like you wouldn't
believe. 'Cause the whole place was going crazy like you wouldn't
believe. He built to a crescendo. So what he said was, "We can't
be bothered with this infighting; we have a nation to save. We
can't be bothered; this country needs our experience to get past
this." He just had everybody so fired up![29]

According to Jimmy Collier, a member of the SCLC team organizing
on the West Side, nonviolence guided their efforts, but there were many
different currents in Chicago:

Generally speaking the staff was very loyal. We were careful
about the people we recruited. This was a very disciplined group
because of James Bevel.

On a practical level, we were dealing with the Muslims, who
were growing in visibility. Malcolm X was a factor on the West Side
of Chicago. There were organized elements of people who either
had a Muslim or a separatist or an isolationist political approach,
or a religious political approach, or just a violent approach, self-
defense or violence. And there were also people who were part of
the resurgence of Back to Africa movements. And of course you
had in Chicago, as you would have in urban centers, you had an
intellectual group. So there were lots of different community elements that had different ideas about what to do. And that also

was a little bit different from in the South where, generally speaking, it was simpler to tell who the bad guys were.[30]

The relationship between SCLC and CCCO, between the West Side movement and the rest of the Chicago civil rights movement, was not without some tension. David Jehnsen was one West Side organizer who discerned the differences pulsating through the Chicago coalition:

> There were two different philosophies and that produced two different types of leadership functions. One type of leadership function is the power leader, the person who wants a piece of the action. And Al [Raby] certainly wanted a piece of the action. And then [there was James] Bevel, who characterized our philosophy that we need to be influence leaders, catalysts, and gadflies and work with the power leaders like Al Raby's more local leadership. And the catalyst, the gadfly, the influence leader philosophy is that we want to change the conditions, we don't just want a piece of the action. And I think during that period a lot of these kinds of problems between certain personalities emerged because people weren't as distinct about how both leadership patterns are important and make contributions to the movement.[31]

Coalescing the leadership on the West Side was another part of the work. As Jehnsen explained: "Since I was living on the West Side and working with the West Side Christian Parish, I organized, with the help of a very famous pastor, Woodrow Wilson Taylor, a Seventh Congressional District clergy alliance. . . . We had never been able to bring the African American pastors and Catholic priests and white Protestants together on the West Side; so we started a process that ended up, before the middle of 1964, with something called the West Side Federation."[32]

Operation Breadbasket

While activists in the Chicago Freedom Movement helped organize the Union to End Slums on the West Side and the Near North Side, Jesse Jackson organized the Kenwood-Oakland Community Organization on the South Side. In addition, Jackson organized a coalition of ministers who wanted their own project.

Gary Massoni, then a student at Chicago Theological Seminary, worked with Jackson from the first days of Operation Breadbasket:

Breadbasket had learned some lessons from the movement in the South, and one of those was that the church was tremendously important. In fact, the church was central to activism in the black community. And so, the work that began before Breadbasket was introduced was to gather a group of black ministers, develop their sense of ethics around social issues, and introduce them to a little bit of social gospel theology.

Jesse Jackson brought together several black ministers, including the Reverend Arthur Brazier, the Reverend John Porter, the Reverend Clay Evans, and others, to meet weekly with a couple of the members of the faculty from the Chicago Theological Seminary and a social ethics professor from the Divinity School of the University of Chicago, Al Pitcher, who had been very active in CCCO before all this started. So, many of these circles kind of came together. When Dr. King came back to Chicago in January 1966, he introduced to these ministers the concept of SCLC's program called Operation Breadbasket, which had been operating successfully in Atlanta. They had had a little background in theology and ethics and the social issues facing their communities, and they hoped that some activism could make a difference.

The black community, and certainly the black ministers, were not united in welcoming Dr. King to Chicago. There were divisions, and there was opposition to his coming. Several ministers, several black ministers, held a press conference and said that he should not come. Others supported his coming and welcomed him into their pulpits. When Jesse Jackson was appointed to be the director of Operation Breadbasket, there was already this group, a core group of ministers who became the negotiators for Operation Breadbasket. The premise here was to build respect between the community and the businesses that were operating

in that community. The idea was that you could have an economic withdrawal from a company if they refused to respect their
customers, if they refused to hire people from the community;
that was the basic starting point: to open up jobs and to build
respect.

Our first campaign was with a dairy company—Country
Delight Dairy—which at that time sold [its products] only in
High-Low stores. High-Low and Red Rooster were other targets. But we took on the dairy products just before Easter. We
followed the Gandhian-King process of doing some research,
gathering the information, doing some education, starting the
negotiations. The negotiations were very, very hostile. We met
with essentially racist comments from the president of the company. Another person from the company was hostile towards
those of us who were white on the negotiating team. And before
long it all broke down and we decided we had to go hit the
streets. We began picketing the weekend before Easter. And as
you know, dairy products don't last all that long, and you can't
send them back to the cow. So, they began to think seriously
about what was happening with a major, major shopping weekend coming up and products sitting on their shelves, spoiling.

By the end of the week before Easter, we were able to reach
an agreement: the Country Delight Dairy people decided that
they could hire some black drivers for their trucks and that they
could influence High-Low grocery stores to hire more black
cashiers in their stores. This was the beginning of the negotiations with High-Low.[33]

Obstacles

The Chicago Freedom Movement faced many obstacles as it organized
its campaign to end slums, including from within the black church and
from Mayor Daley's political machine. The most well-known black clergyman in Chicago was Joseph H. Jackson, head of the National Baptist Convention. He had a long history of opposing Martin Luther King
and his approach to social change within the church; in fact, a group

of pastors—including Dr. King—had broken with the National Baptist Convention to form the Progressive National Baptist Convention due to these differences.

Hattie Williams recalls the degree to which Joseph H. Jackson and other prominent leaders frowned on King's Chicago efforts:

> That was the surprising horror of the years of the civil rights movement, to see politicians that were black, like our alderman, Claude Holman, who would get on TV or anywhere and say, "Wild horses wouldn't take me from the side of the mayor." Mayor Daley was alive then, and his lackey was the alderman of this ward. So what I'm saying is that Daley didn't want Dr. King in Chicago, and many of the black ministers who were straight Democratic people—they were part of the Democratic machine, for the rewards, for the concessions, for the patronage jobs— they would go to their parishioners in the church—and they all rejected Dr. King.[34]

Williams's father was a member of Reverend Jackson's Olivet Baptist Church on Chicago's South Side, and she recalls that one day, during a break in a recital at the church, she tried to spread news about an upcoming rally featuring Dr. King: "I was passing out a flyer saying that Dr. Martin Luther King Jr. would be at Soldier Field. We were going to have a rally. During the intermission I just happened to be giving people these flyers and then Dr. Jackson's wife said, 'I'm going to tell your father what you're doing down here, and we don't allow this mess at Olivet.' And she pulled all the [flyers] right out of people's hands and people were just standing there aghast."[35]

Al Raby reflected on how the use of power and patronage by the Daley administration could limit support in the black community for civil rights initiatives:

> One classic example of the extent to which the politicians opposed Martin was Clay Evans's church. Clay Evans appeared in a picture in the *Chicago Defender* with Martin and was in the process of building a church—had the foundation laid for it. The finan-

cier called up and said essentially that if he continued to be active with Martin, he could not rely on the financier. And that church basement, the foundation, remained there for a number of years.

When you realize that every businessman was subject to inspections and every church, during the War on Poverty, had programs financed by the federal government going through the city for administration, you had an awesome amount of power against you. During that time you had the Red Squad, police spies, and a whole variety of things. You are asking people to put themselves out on the line, to jeopardize things, to not be anonymous and to stand up and be counted, to put their investment on the line. It's not a small thing to do.[36]

David Jehnsen, one of the chief organizers of the Union to End Slums, recalls how officials from the mayor's office were constantly responding to the organizing effort on the West Side. In the winter of 1966 the Daley administration announced a plan to exterminate rats:

They had this flurry of activity to kill the rats. The guy from the Urban Progress Center [Chicago's federally funded War on Poverty program] was really uninformed as to who Bevel was, or any of us. So we organized a whole bunch of community people—Reverend Bill Briggs probably organized part of it—basically men that this guy wanted to speak to, and enlist their help, and in some cases, wanted to hire. So we convened twenty-five or thirty people, and Bevel was in the meeting; when he spoke he gave this eloquent statement about how people needed to clean up the rats in their backyard and so on. And the guy from the Urban Progress Center, from the mayor's program, said, "That was a really good talk that you just gave. Would you be interested in a job working with us?" Bevel sat there with his mouth open, and the rest of us got a laugh.

There was one thing after another. Starting in late fall '64 and winter '65, when Bernard and I started convening groups of people to do the West Side movement, we were constantly producing projects that would pop up like this. These projects were out of the control of the city fathers, so they were continually reacting to us, which gave us confidence that we were on the right track.[37]

Vietnam

In May 1966, as plans for the summer direct action campaign were getting under way, Martin Luther King had a meeting in Chicago that drew his attention to world events, particularly the war in Vietnam. Thich Nhat Hahn, a famed Zen Buddhist monk and peace activist, later told the story of that meeting:

> In 1965, I wrote a letter to Martin Luther King to tell him about the suffering in Vietnam and the struggle we were leading for human rights and peace. Exactly one year later I met the Reverend King in Chicago and we talked a lot about the future of the world, of America, Europe, Asia. We were hosted by an organization called the Fellowship of Reconciliation. We spoke of community and Sangha; Reverend King spoke of Sangha in terms of a Beloved Community. We discussed how we could spread the ideas of truth and right thinking, how we could practice right speech to educate people about peace, human rights and social justice.

Although it was nearly a year later, on April 4, 1967, when Dr. King made his famous antiwar speech at Riverside Church in New York City, the escalating war was on his mind while the Chicago campaign was in progress. The meeting with Thich Nhat Hahn had a significant impact on King; one year later he nominated the Buddhist monk for the Nobel Peace Prize, noting in his nomination, "I am privileged to call him my friend."[38]

A Focus on Open Housing

While parents and civil rights groups under the CCCO umbrella were organizing for better schools, another organizing effort was emerging from the American Friends Service Committee. In response to crises resulting from efforts to integrate Chicago housing in the 1950s, AFSC had developed a program to help African Americans find housing in the suburbs. Although this was separate from CCCO's work, it later proved important to the Chicago Freedom Movement and its campaign in the summer of 1966.

Bert Ransom, one of the staff members of AFSC's fair-housing initiative, recalls:

After having taught in the Chicago Public Schools for five years, in June of 1964, I was accepted to do an internship with the Eleanor Roosevelt Memorial Foundation for one year. I chose to do my internship with the American Friends Service Committee. I was assigned to work in the Housing Opportunities Program, designed to creatively encourage the Chicago area real estate industry to consider abandoning discriminatory real estate practices and make housing opportunities equal for all people. Within the Housing Opportunities Program was a unit called HOME (Home Opportunities Made Equal), where I worked full time. Recognizing the racially segregated housing market, HOME operated as a real estate office to serve African American people in the market for housing in nontraditional African American neighborhoods. The housing and rental stock was made available by willing White persons who sold or rented their properties to African Americans, thereby bypassing the city's real estate system. HOME had a monthly listing service and provided services free of charge.[39]

Bill Moyer, the director of HOME, was a pivotal figure in the Chicago Freedom Movement's decision to launch open-housing demonstrations. Moyer had organized fair-housing groups in many western and North Shore suburbs and served as director of the North Shore Summer Project in 1965 (see chapter 6 for additional information). In early 1966 he began a program in Oak Park. Here is his description of the links between this work and the Chicago open-housing marches:

The Oak Park project was a plan to have a direct action campaign focusing: one, on the real estate offices, and two, on getting a fair housing ordinance passed by the city government in a community where a number of black families wanted to move. We had four or five black families from our program who had already moved to Oak Park. HOME Inc. had maybe ten more black families that wanted to move to Oak Park and who were willing to be involved in a direct action campaign similar to those in the South. We had meetings, and the first thing we did was send pairs of couples, a white family and a black family, or even two white families. We would have a white family go into a real estate office and ask for the kind of housing that their paired black family want[ed], and then they would get all of the information and leave. And then a few minutes later the black family would go in and ask for the same information, and they would be told there wasn't anything. And then we either had the first white family go back and talk with them again about the housing, just to show it was still available, or have a second white family ask for the same thing. We documented the discrimination there and wrote that up.

Then, every [Saturday] for a number of months, we'd have a meeting in a church or something and then a march through town, and show up at the one or two or three real estate offices in the center of Oak Park. They would just go in and ask for service, and if they were refused they would stay in the office and we would stay outside and have a rally with the rest of the people for the rest of the afternoon. It was like a sit-in. A number of times the real estate office would close on Saturday, and we would just stay outside and the black families would line up for service. Each Saturday I would invite one of the movement leaders from SCLC; Jesse Jackson was there a few times, and Bernard LaFayette and Bevel came and maybe Andy Young. We just repeated these marches each week.

Actually we had started earlier in the year with a black family—the man worked out that way—who lived in a tent in front of the real estate office on a flatbed truck for a while. That got some national publicity when they were refused service at Baird and Warner.

I really chose this project totally separately. It had nothing to do with SCLC at the time.[40]

A Focus on Housing Discrimination

By late spring, the Chicago Freedom Movement had decided to target housing discrimination as the main focus of its summer direct action campaign. Bill Moyer had attracted the attention of SCLC's leadership with his open-housing work, especially in Oak Park. He was asked to prepare a position paper on the merits of an open-housing thrust:

> We got massive publicity—and I think what happened is that it was such a clear analogy to the restaurants. Even most white people in that area were agreeing that restaurants should be open, and they were open in the North on a nondiscriminatory basis. We made that analogy with the real estate offices.
>
> And I think at the same time, that SCLC had begun seeing that they did not have a real handle on a direct action strategy. I think that they probably were looking for something that would really point out the basic racism in the North and in Chicago, just trying to have some kind of clear violation of basic principles of civil rights. I think they couldn't quite get the same handle on it (in their other work, a handle) where they could demand that the government pass laws and change things. The real estate offices were a centralized system, licensed by the state and organized, so you had a much clearer resolution possibility, but also a much clearer, more focused definition, handle on the problem.[41]

James Bevel was impressed by Moyer's analysis and the merits of targeting housing discrimination:

> Coming up here in 1965, when they were telling me you can't live here, there, I would not stand for that. That is more of an affront to me, and a violation of me, than not eating at a lunch counter, not going to the theater, or having to go to the back of the bus, and can't vote. You can't just tell a man he can't live

somewhere. Suppose a man is working at the airport. He can't live near the airport, where he can walk if he wanted to. A man has a right to live where he can work. People work on vocation and not on race; you can't penalize a man because of his color in the housing market! You have to have a housing market based on economic law, not dispositions toward people.

Now in demonstrations you can't have some obscure issue that is cloudy in the minds of people. Should a man have a right to rent and buy a house in the city if he works or lives in that city and he is a citizen of that city? You have to pick a target so that when the opposition is arguing, he makes a fool of himself.

The other thing we had to do: nobody had ever been able to force Daley into negotiations. He had his six Negro aldermen and they spoke to the community, said what he said. So we had to force what is called a dialogue. The black community felt powerless to have a meeting with the mayor, so we had to break up that feeling of powerlessness. We'll have to create enough havoc in the community so that he can't stop us.[42]

Both Moyer and Bevel saw the connection between the slums and open housing, and they pointed out this link to the staff and to the larger community. Because African Americans were trapped in certain neighborhoods, and because those neighborhoods were overcrowded, landlords in the African American neighborhoods could get higher rents and did not have to keep up the buildings. Open housing would help those who moved out of the traditionally African American neighborhoods, and by giving people more choices, it would pressure the landlords to make their buildings attractive to renters.

Rally at Soldier Field

The kickoff for the summer direct action campaign came on July 10, 1966, when more than 30,000 supporters flowed into Soldier Field for a rally and then a march to City Hall, where Martin Luther King (much like his namesake Martin Luther) posted a long list of demands on the door. Among those demands was this: "For our primary target we have chosen housing. As of July 10 we shall cease to be accomplices to a housing system of discrimination, segregation and degradation. We shall begin to act as if Chicago were an open city. We shall act on the basis that every man is entitled to full access of buying or renting housing that is sound, attractive, and reasonably priced."

Al Raby spoke at the Soldier Field rally on July 10. Here are excerpts from his speech:

Good afternoon, Ladies and Gentlemen—and welcome to the long hot summer.

It's been two years since we met here in Soldier Field, and we've seen many changes, many significant changes, and many victories. But we are the first to recognize that the revolution for human rights in Chicago is far from over—in fact it has just begun. Nonetheless, we can justly be proud of the victories that have been achieved through the banding together and determination of those of us who are seeking positive social change.

Certainly the fact that Dr. Willis is leaving at the end of this summer is a major victory, in that it means the greatest stumbling block to quality, integrated education has been removed. But that does not mean any of the fundamental problems of this school system have been solved. . . .

We are on the move.

We have seen as well the banding together and organizing of new kinds of groups constructively acting to solve their own problems, to determine their own destinies and to declare themselves a part of the democratic process. We saw the JOIN Community Union organize a tenants union and gain, for the first time in this country's history, a collective bargaining contract with building management and affirm the rights of tenants to deal with landlords.

In recent weeks the East Garfield Union to End Slums picketed and sat in for days on one of the city's biggest slumlords. When that slumlord sought an injunction against the direct action, the court wisely directed him to sit down and negotiate with the union. . . . In a few weeks we expect to see the East Gar-field group gain its collective bargaining contract. We are on the move. . . .

. . . I look forward to the day . . . when we develop a new breed of political leader that will more positively represent the constituency of impoverished and dispossessed people of this city. . . . Those of us who have fought for independent political can-didates who will do just that can take heart in the victories of our two new state senators, Dick Newhouse and Charlie Chew. . . . From the new atmosphere I feel in this city I am certain that we will see many new independent aldermanic candidates challenge this machine and win for more people the kind of representation they need. . . .

We saw, too, in an unfortunate but predictable kind of inci-dent, the first revolt of our oppressed Latin American commu-nity. . . . The grievances of our Spanish-speaking amigos are the same as ours, and we joined hands with them and here we are together today to say both "we shall overcome" and "nos otros vinceamos." . . .

Now the Mayor has proclaimed himself in favor of open occupancy, but he says the City Council can't write the kind of effective law we need. Many of us believe that the city can write a better law than the phony one we've got. But even as a first step the Mayor and the City Council must put themselves on record in favor of President Johnson's original open occupancy law, without any crippling amendment. And the Mayor can see to it that his 13 Congressmen not only vote for the law, but give it the kind of leadership that we in Chicago deserve and demand. . . .

Now we are going to be involved in much direct action this summer, and one action will be a rent strike by the Tenants Action Council at Old Town Gardens. . . .

That's just one form of direct action—and there will be more. In the past our direct action programs have been criticized. I maintain they are necessary. It is only through direct action—or its threat—that we have gained our small victories thus far. . . .

We believe that people in this city do care, and will act when the message is made clear.

We must, each of us, end finally the slave psychology that is the breeding ground for the denial of our manhood. We must reject the bill of goods we have been sold that makes us conk our hair and measure our women by the length of their hair and the lightness of their skins and the delicacy of their noses. We must stand up and proclaim our negritude, and ask the world to recognize it, instead of acting as if this is our shame.

I would rather suffer and if necessary die here in Chicago to end the slave psychology and the pathology of racism that is at the root of most war, than to be a hero in some foreign land fighting a war against a faceless enemy in support of a dubious democracy.

In the name of CCCO and SCLC, we declare Chicago an open city, and we enlist you into the nonviolent army to end racism in Chicago.[43]

Hattie Williams, who had been involved in the earlier campaign for equal education, attended the Soldier Field rally:

I took part in the rally at Soldier Field and my participation was to be there, to bring people there and also to distribute the flyers, throughout this neighborhood and anywhere else that I could.

I just remember that Dr. King as usual, had that charisma, and he gave a speech. He explained his presence in Chicago, why he was here. And I noticed—the reason I guess that I participated, even at that small level, is I noticed such hostility coming from unlikely places, such as outstanding civic leaders and politicians; in fact, they were in opposition to Dr. King's even coming. They made these statements that he was okay in the South, but he had no business coming up here north. And so I felt that I had to defend that position because I felt that he had every right to be here.[44]

The Chicago Freedom Movement called for an open city and presented a rich list of demands addressing open housing. These demands involved the Real Estate Board, financial institutions, the Chicago Housing Authority, the governor, the federal government, the mayor, and the City Council. In addition to fair housing, the Chicago Freedom Movement called for open employment, improvements in the welfare system, and a citizens' review board for the police.[45]

Rioting, Preparation, and Action

Two days after the Soldier Field rally, there was a confrontation between police and African American youths on the Near West Side. The young people had opened a fire hydrant to provide some respite from the sweltering heat—a common practice in many Chicago neighborhoods. The confrontation sparked four days of rioting that spread to Lawndale and into the Garfield Park area.

Bernard LaFayette describes how the organizers of the Chicago Freedom Movement responded to the rising fury in black communities:

> It turned attention away from what we were doing. We were there having a meeting on the West Side when the riots first started. We were out there on the streets—Jesse Jackson, Bevel, myself, and others. That was one of the reasons that no one got killed in that first riot.
>
> I was running through the alley with the gangs. We had different assignments. My assignment was to catch up with the gangs and divert them away from confrontation with the policemen. I was glad I was there to try to at least prevent a lot of unnecessary bloodshed.
>
> We saw it as the natural course of events; it was still another demonstration of what happens when you have a hot, overcrowded situation, and people feel trapped in the ghetto communities. It reaffirmed what we were saying: that tensions build up because of the conditions.[46]

The rioting on the West Side did not stop the multidimensional work of the Chicago Freedom Movement. College students came to Chicago to spend the summer working with the movement. James Godsil recalls:

> I lived with about ten or fifteen college students from all over the country in the Project House on Peoria Street, in the 1200 block between Maxwell Street and Roosevelt Road. Most of us taught in Freedom Schools during the workweek and were on the marches during the evenings and weekends of July and August.
>
> My experience with SCLC and its Chicago partners that summer radically changed my life and, quite possibly, the lives of the other students of the Project House.
>
> The Freedom Summer contact person I remember being most involved with the Project House students was Gloria Shapiro, who lived in a suburb north of Chicago and who had a couple of parties with some of the top leadership. I had a couple of brief conversations with Reverend Bevel. During the Chicago riot of summer 1966 we were sent to live with families in the North Shore suburbs, including a man named Harper and a woman named Smith, whose daughters, Diana and Leslie, respectively, were Project House students. Carolyn Black was another local college student living at Project House.
>
> I taught in a storefront Freedom School on Roosevelt that summer. We were taught by a Berkeley anthropologist how to play mind games that advanced children's analytic skills. I also taught black history and developed a theatrical production, which my eight-year-old pupils put on at a local church, with a very young Jesse Jackson in attendance, speaking, with the help of notes.[47]

The Union to End Slums achieved a milestone when in mid-July, after months of pressure, it compelled the landlord of many run-down buildings in East Garfield Park to sign a collective bargaining agreement with its tenants. Gilbert Cornfield was the attorney who helped the East

Garfield Park Union to End Slums negotiate with the real estate firm of Condor and Costalis:

> I got to the site and there were people all around. They were picketing and so forth. They were waiting for me to get there because Condor and Costalis wanted to meet. And Jim [Bevel] and the others were uncertain, now that they wanted to meet, what it is that we want[ed].
>
> That Sunday we had them recognize the Garfield Park Union to End Slums as the exclusive bargaining representative for the tenants in all those buildings and commit themselves to start collective bargaining for a contract, which would be, in effect, the elimination of the old lease arrangement.
>
> We went in to their offices and came out sometime afterwards and announced the agreement to the people. It was a very thrilling moment.[48]

Open-Housing Marches

Within a week after the rally at Soldier Field, the neighborhood direct action campaign began. It stared quietly, with the testing of real estate offices in a targeted Southwest Side neighborhood, followed by an integrated picnic in a park, a shop-in at neighborhood grocery stores, attendance of African Americans at white churches, and a prayer vigil outside a Catholic church. After an overnight vigil at a real estate office was called off due to the hostile response, the first march was held in a Southwest Side neighborhood. By late July, hundreds of volunteers were marching for open housing. On August 5 Dr. King was struck in the head by a rock as he led a march through Marquette Park on the Southwest Side. Some of the picket signs carried by the marchers declared: "Negroes are people; people need houses."

The first big march took place on the Southwest Side on Sunday, July 31. Bernard Kleina, a teacher and photographer and later the longtime director of a Fair Housing Center in metropolitan Chicago, wrote about his experience:

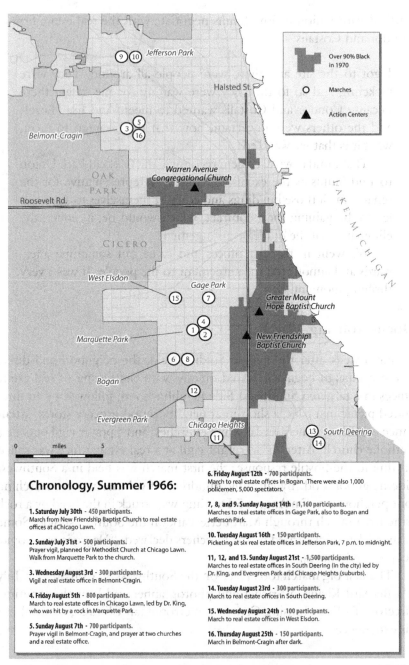

Chronology, Summer 1966:

1. Saturday July 30th - 450 participants.
March from New Friendship Baptist Church to real estate offices at aChicago Lawn.

2. Sunday July 31st - 500 participants.
Prayer vigil, planned for Methodist Church at Chicago Lawn. Walk from Marquette Park to the church.

3. Wednesday August 3rd - 300 participants.
Vigil at real estate office in Belmont-Cragin.

4. Friday August 5th - 800 participants.
March to real estate offices in Chicago Lawn, led by Dr. King, who was hit by a rock in Marquette Park.

5. Sunday August 7th - 700 participants.
Prayer vigil in Belmont-Cragin, and prayer at two churches and a real estate office.

6. Friday August 12th - 700 participants.
March to real estate offices in Bogan. There were also 1,000 policemen, 5,000 spectators.

7, 8, and 9. Sunday August 14th - 1,160 participants.
Marches to real estate offices in Gage Park, also to Bogan and Jefferson Park.

10. Tuesday August 16th - 150 participants.
Picketing at six real estate offices in Jefferson Park, 7 p.m. to midnight.

11, 12, and 13. Sunday August 21st - 1,500 participants.
Marches to real estate offices in South Deering (in the city) led by Dr. King, and Evergreen Park and Chicago Heights (suburbs).

14. Tuesday August 23rd - 300 participants.
March to real estate offices in South Deering.

15. Wednesday August 24th - 100 participants.
March to real estate offices in West Elsdon.

16. Thursday August 25th - 150 participants.
March in Belmont-Cragin after dark.

Map 2. Chicago Freedom Movement open-housing marches, summer 1966

Remember Why You're Here, Brother

Sometimes it pays to be late. On July 31, 1966, I intended to meet up with civil rights marchers at a South Side Church who were going to march in Marquette Park for open housing. As with the demonstrations in Selma, Alabama, and elsewhere, the purpose of meeting at a church was to mentally and spiritually prepare for a nonviolent response to what could be a violent afternoon. As I was driving east toward the church the demonstrators were driving west, so instead of going to the church, I fell in behind and was the last car in the procession as we approached Marquette Park.

The cars filled all the spaces in the small parking lot on the southeast corner of the park, so I was left to park between two police cars near the entrance. I went to this march with the intention of photographing the demonstration, but seeing the size of the opposition and the less than 400 marchers, I put my camera back in the car and joined the march.

As we started marching, angry whites started spitting on me and the other marchers. Not being mentally prepared to accept this kind of degrading abuse, I told someone in the mob, "I wouldn't do that if I were you," as if I were ready to take on the whole mob. Then an older African American man in front of me turned around and said, "Remember why you're here, brother." From that point on, I remained silent and walked in solemn procession while rocks, bottles, and cherry bombs were thrown at us over the heads of the police who were "escorting" the marchers through the park.

Escorted by reluctant police officers, it turned out to be the most brutal march in which I had ever been involved. When we returned to our cars, we saw several that were pushed into the lagoon and others that were set on fire, turned over, or damaged in some way. Ironically, only three cars remained untouched. One was mine, and the other two were the police cars I had parked between. Had I arrived earlier, my car would have been damaged or destroyed like the others. The *Chicago Tribune* reported, "At least 25 persons were injured, most of them being hit with bottles, stones, and broken glass thrown by white hecklers . . . cherry bombs and firecrackers were tossed among the marchers; bottles and bricks flew through the air . . . police said at least 15 cars were set on fire, two were pushed into a lagoon; windows and windshields were smashed on at least 30 cars. Dozens of tires were slashed."[49]

Due to the condition of our cars and the hostility of the angry white mob, it was impossible to return to our vehicles. Instead, the marchers headed east on 71st Street, where, for a period of time, police protection broke down completely. Before reaching 71st Street, when the police were still walking alongside the demonstrators, the mob came close enough to spit on us. When we reached 71st Street, our police escort disappeared and the mob moved further away from us, to the other side of the street. However, without the police presence, the mob threw the rocks much harder and windows broke above and around us. Despite the rocks hitting us, we had to just keep walking. Even if the police escort had been there, little would have been done to protect the marchers. The police took action only when one of the mob hit a police officer. Then the police clubbed him down to the ground.

It wasn't until we approached Ashland Avenue that the mob retreated. At that time Ashland was the "dividing line" between black and white neighborhoods. The white mob seemed to lose its "courage" as it approached Ashland Avenue. Later that night, a police officer escorted me back to my car, which had remained undamaged throughout the entire demonstration.

Sometimes it pays to be late.[50]

A broad coalition of people participated in the open-housing demonstrations—men and women, blacks and whites, people of all faiths. One of the organizers was Bert Ransom, who directed the South Side Action Center:

We had the South Side Action Center, as well as the West Side Action Center. . . . We had a diverse staff of about nine people in the South Side Action Center who were dedicated, committed, and energetic for the movement cause. And I can distinctly remember some highlights of my role with that staff, and how we were up in the middle of the night—three thirty and four o'clock in the morning, going through these areas that were planned to be marched on, making certain that we had a working map of where the marchers would go. And we would go in advance of their gathering, so that we would have a plan that was very clear, and very definitive about the marches. We also participated in readying the community through mass meetings, which was very important; I had learned very much of that in Montgomery as well. People had to know what the nature of the movement was, the philosophy, and what it was that was expected. We worked very diligently on that, and so when the marchers came, they were psychologically prepared, and ready to go into action.

The other part was getting those in the community who were committed to going to jail, recognizing that we would have bail money to get them out—but that part of the demonstration was very necessary, that people were committed to being locked up for freedom, and for what they believed in. I like to think that the role that we had was really in the boiler room of the movement. Someone had to do the everyday work to keep it moving towards the goals which it had set.[51]

Nancy Jefferson, a longtime activist on the West Side, participated in the march in Marquette Park on August 5:

I was right there when Dr. King was hit in that march in Marquette Park, when he felt that this was the most racist town that he had been in. Having come from the South—I grew up in Tennessee—I don't think we saw as much hatred out of Bull Connor and all of them as we saw in Marquette Park in Chicago.

Dr. King used to say to us, "The people are afraid of anything they don't know." And he says, "People or things, conditions or housing or whatever it is that they don't know, they are afraid of that." So we tried to demonstrate with the nonviolent attitude, with love.

It was frightening, it was really frightening because we felt, first of all, that this town itself was not willing to accept non-racial housing either. That wasn't the tune of this town. They couldn't accept that. And we felt that the Marquette people felt that they had the sanction of the power structure of this town, Mayor Daley and the rest of them. And so they felt very strongly that they had a right to do what they had to do. And if it was killing or whatever they had to do to make sure that housing stayed segregated, that's what they were going to do. That was just frightening.

Dr. King had taught us, and we felt like Jesus going to the cross; somebody had to bear the burden. And although, you know, it was frightful, and you were afraid, but you felt that you had to have the courage. And that somehow some of those people would never know, but there were others that we might show and demonstrate that it was the right thing to do, and that they too would be free by educating themselves to live with each other.[52]

Andrew Young recalls the sense of danger during the early marches into the Southwest Side:

I parked [my car] down the street by a lake. When we came back, they had set my car on fire and pushed it into the lake. It was a brand new Ford. The mobs in the South were usually male and usually poor. And they ran in the one to two hundreds. The mobs in the North were all ages and fairly well dressed and they ran in the thousands. There could have been eight to ten thousand people out there at any of those marches. And so, just the unknown . . . not knowing who was in the mob.[53]

Ed Vondrak, publisher of the *Southwest News-Herald,* was out of town with his family, having breakfast at Starved Rock on the Illinois River, when he saw the morning headlines: "King Marches Today in Marquette Park." He saw trouble coming and quickly returned to Chicago, going straight to Marquette Park:

> So I went back to the office and I called the editor at home. I said, "There is trouble in the park, and I'm too old to get mixed up with it. It is going to be bad." And I'll tell you why I thought so. I saw the Southwest ministerial group out there . . . and I saw these people lined up. I saw the whites on one side and the blacks on the other, the priests and ministers, including a couple of women ministers. And I said, "I can't believe this. These are Lithuanians, a deeply religious people, and they are throwing rocks at their nuns and they are spitting on their priests, and this is hard to believe. There is going to be chaos before the day is over."[54]

James Godsil attended one of the mass meetings held in the evenings before the marches:

> I vividly remember a speech by Dr. King at a small church on the South Side. There were two young men standing in the center aisle, challenging Dr. King's vision and demanding the right to speak. Dr. King gave the podium over to them for five or ten minutes. They passionately presented the "Black Power, segregation from white activists" position. When they were finished Dr. King summoned up his immense spirit and transcendent mind, but also his bottomless compassion, to respond with an oration that, after about five minutes, resulted in the young critics cheering intensely, and the air in the church [was] so thick that I thought I could literally walk into midair, right off the balcony. I still feel that power.[55]

Bernard LaFayette comments on recruiting local gang members as marshals for the marches:

> We had to train the marshals. The marshals for the most part were West Side gang members and people like that which we

had mobilized. We had gotten to know them through the riots. If they were not involved in some kind of meaningful role, then they would take their own traditional kind of action in those situations. So we had to get them involved, which obligated them. And besides, they were ideal because they weren't afraid of violence and physical injury. So they played a very noble role. They were actually the vanguard, in a sense. They were the border between the hostile crowds and the demonstrators, and they knocked down broken bottles and firecrackers when people were throwing them toward the marchers. They were there to protect us. So they felt they had a really important, major role.[56]

After these dramatic demonstrations on the Southwest Side, the marches moved to other white neighborhoods to show that the problem existed across Chicago, not just in one neighborhood. Sometimes several marches took place in different neighborhoods on the same day. And after the major marches on the Southwest Side, the Chicago police increased their protection, and the demonstrators were no longer in such jeopardy.

John McDermott was executive director of the Chicago Catholic Interracial Council, which had long been a member of CCCO and had mobilized scores of demonstrators for the open-housing marches. He recalls the draining experience of mounting marches, week after week, in the heat of July and August, and the overall strategy of the campaign:

You went to meetings day and night. You were exhausted. You had some people get arrested. And you didn't really have a lot of time or energy to think globally.

But the basic strategy was this: we were in a northern city which had lots of laws against discrimination, where the problem was not the same as in the South. How do you deal with de facto segregation and discrimination? That is what we were confronting. How to develop a national policy on that was very unclear at that time.[57]

Tony Henry was one of those who wondered whether the focus

on open housing sapped energy from the West Side organizing effort. According to Henry, the open-housing campaign caused a split among the movement staff:

> I was skeptical about going [to the Southwest Side] myself because it did not have the foundation of community organizing of the type that we were doing with tenants on the West Side; but, unfortunately, SCLC staff and Dr. King saw that the press focused in on the uproar, and it grew bigger, and there was a lot of public attention on the issue of the hostility of whites to the idea of black people coming to march in their neighborhoods demanding the right to live there. There was a dynamic of the marches in Marquette Park, attracting the hostility that exposed the nature of racism in the North.[58]

Summit Negotiations and the Summit Agreement

The open-housing demonstrations alerted Chicagoans and the nation to the extent of housing discrimination in the North. They also caused the city's civic and political leadership to seek a resolution of the mounting crisis. On August 17 Mayor Richard J. Daley and other influential Chicagoans convened with representatives of the real estate industry and leaders of the Chicago Freedom Movement at the behest of the Chicago Conference on Religion and Race. This gathering at the downtown St. James Cathedral led to the appointment of a subcommittee chaired by Thomas Ayers, head of Commonwealth Edison, to pursue further negotiations.

When an injunction by the City of Chicago limited the scope of the protests, the open-housing demonstrations moved to the suburbs, staging marches in Chicago Heights and Evergreen Park. The Chicago Freedom Movement even pledged to march on Cicero on August 28. Cicero had been the site of a fierce antiblack riot in 1951, and only weeks earlier, black teenager Jerome Huey had been killed there while job hunting on his bicycle. On August 26 the summit participants gathered at the Palmer House for final negotiations. All endorsed an agreement that brought an end to the open-housing demonstrations in exchange for a long list of commitments, including the city's commitment to promote fair housing, the Chicago Real Estate Board's pledge to drop its opposition to the state open-occupancy law, and the commitment by political, business, and religious leaders to support the creation of an organization to fight for open housing throughout the Chicago metropolitan area (this organization would become the Leadership Council for Metropolitan Open Communities). The planned march to Cicero was called off as a result of the Summit Agreement.

Al Raby, one of the leaders in the Chicago Freedom Movement's delegation at the summit negotiations, reflects on the decision to negotiate:

> The general position of the major church leadership, the politicians, and the newspapers, etc., was that the point had been made, had been heard and understood, and the time had now come to see if there could be a resolution of some of the issues. They proposed a summit meeting. Our concern with the summit meeting and the problem of movements in general is that movements have a momentum, and once they have lost their momentum it is difficult if not impossible to re-create. A movement is always vulnerable to its opposition, and particularly if its opposition is an institution and has an institutionalized capacity. Where the movement has been most successful, it has institutionalized its demands. In the movement for voting rights, the institutionalized enforcement of that rested with the Justice Department, and it had the capacity to carry on and to hold to account people who violated that.
>
> So the fear was that this was all a game, that the opposition players understood the vulnerability of the movement, and that there wouldn't be any substantive agreements or institutionalization of responsibility. That was always the big question.[59]

John McDermott was a member of the Agenda Committee, the leadership group that negotiated the Summit Agreement. According to him, the movement leadership could have been better prepared when the call for negotiations was sounded:

We didn't take it seriously at first. We thought it was going to be a public relations ploy on the part of the mayor and the establishment. [We didn't] draw up demands or proposals until the night before. [We were] not fully aware of our power and impact on these [people] and not fully aware until we got into the room that they wanted to deal. And then we had to negotiate, but it is pretty hard to change your list of demands in the middle of negotiations. It could have been done more effectively. But that doesn't mean it was done badly.[60]

Gordon Groebe, a member of the delegation representing the real estate industry at the summit negotiations, remembers that the moral dimension of the open-housing crisis placed great pressure on Chicago's Realtors to accept change: "We felt that [Mayor Daley] was concerned about the people in the community and stopping the marches. He had found a way to get it on the table. And we felt we were part of that process. We did not see [the summit negotiations] as part of the solution to stopping the marches. We went there probably with self-interest, to give them a position which we could live with."[61]

Ed Marciniak of the Chicago Commission on Human Relations notes the political pressures generated by the open-housing marches: "So the question [for the summit negotiations] is sorting out the [agenda items] we don't agree upon and see if we can get an agreement. That was the whole point of the summit. Once the Conference on Religion and Race decided to move ahead, we saw light at the end of the tunnel. We saw an opportunity to end the confrontation that had developed. So what we did was we pushed with it as much as we could. And we twisted arms of people to get involved."[62]

Kale Williams, executive director of the American Friends Service Committee, was on the subcommittee that developed the Summit Agreement:

A number of consultations began to take place among various leaders of religion, government, labor in the city and this resulted in a meeting August 17 of what came to be called a Summit Conference of the leaders of business, industry, labor, religion and government in the city of Chicago, a group of about seventy people, including thirteen from the Chicago Freedom Movement—to confer about what might be done. It was obvious that something needed to be done. The city was at a point of severe tension. It seemed that city officials thought that all that needed to be done was for them to say they would do something about the problem of housing and that then the marches ought to stop. This didn't satisfy the people in the movement. That first meeting ended without a resolution, but with the agreement that a small subcommittee which turned out to be 17 people would work to resolve the issues. If they could come up with some results then the larger group would be reconvened. That group of 17 people including 5 from the Freedom Movement did meet for a total of 60 hours in the next 9 days. This was the most intensive mutual education and negotiation that I have ever experienced. . . . At the end of that time there was an agreement that the marches would end for a time on the basis that each of these leadership groups would commit themselves to specific steps to help make Chicago a truly open city and to end the discrimination in housing that existed. On August 26 the larger group was reconvened, the agreements were discussed and accepted by all the people there. The marches were ended, including one that had been planned for the following Sunday in perhaps the most resistant community of all, the suburb of Cicero. The city breathed a collective sigh of relief.

[The] dramatic and intense activity was ended, and most people, in the movement and in the leadership groups, began to organize for the next phase, that of implementation of the agreement.[63]

John McKnight of the US Commission on Civil Rights recounts his reaction to the second summit meeting at the Palmer House on State Street in downtown Chicago:

I went to the second summit meeting not knowing what had been decided, and when I saw what had been decided I was very disappointed.

I thought it was a very weak agreement. It all depended on process. It was to set up mechanisms to try to reach something with best efforts, good faith—something Dr. King was given to accept, incidentally. It was actually almost unbelievable to me that the major outcome would be an agreement to create an organization to try to do something about the problem.

I was hip to the process "scam" as a problem in terms of reaching an agreement on a civil rights issue. I had been involved for four years in that struggle. Here it seemed to me that those people had not gotten an agreement to a single tangible thing.[64]

Ed Marciniak, in contrast, was pleased that the agreement focused on the entire metropolitan area, not just the city: "We had originally gone down to Springfield for a statewide fair-housing law so it would include the metropolitan area; that was our strategy. We did not want it just applying to the city and not to the suburbs. We lost. Ultimately we passed the Chicago ordinance [1963], a weak one. But it was a first step. It was the city's victory that [the Summit Agreement] said 'Metropolitan Open Communities.' This idea was involved in the conversations we had in preparing the actual agreement, and it started to sink in there."[65]

Two months after the agreement was signed, the AFSC's Kale Williams offered a different analysis of its significance:

First, what did it accomplish for opening housing in the city? Well, one has to be an optimist to say that it accomplished very much. Others would say that nothing has been accomplished: not one more Negro family has been enabled to move to a white area in the two months since that time. And that is true. But I am an optimist. What was accomplished is that for the first time in any major northern city all of the leadership groups did publicly commit themselves to a policy of open housing and to specific actions that they would take to make this real. Some of those actions have been taken. Some are being taken. It is not moving fast enough for those of us who had the concern originally. It is perhaps moving too fast for some people and whether it moves enough is a matter to be decided in the future. . . . The problem is one of keeping alive the sense of urgency that is sufficient to meet the real problem that exists. There has been created a continuing organization with the president of one of our largest utilities as the chairman of it and with the continuing participation of these major leadership groups. One might say that what until now has been the concern only of the American Friends Service Committee and a few other people in fair housing committees and some of the churches has now been accepted as a major concern at the top of the agenda of substantial leadership groups in the community. . . .

. . . I think the most important way to look at this drama is to look at it in relation to the much larger problem of racial conflict in our time. After more than 100 years we are still trying to eliminate the racism that poisons so much of all that is good in our nation. . . . I think the real alternatives are between a revolution, a pace of change we could only regard as revolutionary, which is guided and led by people who are committed to nonviolence or a struggle which is likely, by design or default to become violent, defeating the ends of justice in the process. . . . I think we cannot sit on the sidelines believing that nonviolence is the fullest expression of the Quaker tradition and say, "Go to it, Dr. King." I think that we have got to join this revolution, strengthen its nonviolent leadership, and take our full role beside that leadership to make the best witness we can as Friends and the American Friends Service Committee for our concept of justice built on love and expressed through community.[66]

Bob Lucas, chairman of Chicago CORE, was not pleased with the Summit Agreement:

We came up with the open-housing marches and it got real. Cars were burned, people were stoned and all that kind of thing—which is great for us because I guess all the tensions in Chicago were trained in the white and black communities. It got really tense. It almost felt like you could cut the tension with your hand.

Anyway, there were four or five very important people working to convince Dr. King to stop marching. And that was the
so-called Summit Agreement. The agreement was to figure out
some way to stop the marches, because it was beginning to affect
the mayor politically.[67] At CORE we had more troops in the
movement in Chicago than any other group at that time. And
I wasn't invited [to the meeting]. I didn't really feel too badly
about it then, because I understood why they didn't invite me:
mainly because they didn't believe—and they were right—that I
would go along with any compromise.

They had the second summit meeting in the Palmer House
and at that time our office was downtown. I got a call from a newspaper reporter who knew me, and he said, "Bob, did you know
that the freedom movement is now negotiating with King and all
the big shots in the city around the open-housing marches?" And
I said, "No, I didn't know it."

And so I jumped up and ran to the Palmer House and I
went to the door of the meeting room. They had a policeman at
the door, and he said, "Where are you going?" I said, "Into the
meeting." He looked, and my name wasn't on the list. King just
happened to glance toward the door and he saw me, and he sent
Bevel over to tell the policeman to let me in. The policeman was
a very decent fellow, and he let me in, but it so happened that
that time, they had just completed the motion to stop the open-
housing marches! When I learned that, I guess I said in a rather
loud voice, "We're not going along with the agreement, and to
show them we're not going with the agreement, we're going to
march to Cicero."[68]

Others agreed with Lucas's assessment, and although the Chicago
Freedom Movement withheld its support, more than 250 demonstrators
marched into Cicero on September 4, under the protection of the Illinois
National Guard. Lucas recalls: "The odd thing was when we were making
plans to go, we were criticized by Jesse Jackson and Jim Bevel and Andy
Young. The day we went to Cicero, King called me from the airport,
and he says, 'Bob, we were hoping you wouldn't go to Cicero, but since

you're going, I just want you to know that you have my support and we hope nothing happens to you.'"[69]

After the Summit Agreement

With the Summit Agreement, the dramatic direct action campaign of the Chicago Freedom Movement came to an end. In the months that followed, however, the Union to End Slums carried on its work; Operation Breadbasket's Saturday morning meetings continued to grow, and its negotiations with businesses proceeded; and the Freedom Movement Follow-up Committee tracked the ongoing progress of the Summit Agreement's commitments. Mary Lou Finley reports on the committee's work:

> Bill Moyer of the American Friends Service Committee chaired the Follow-up Committee; I served on it along with six or so others. We understood that if the commitments in the Summit Agreement were not kept, there could be more marches the following summer, so it was important to track the progress.
>
> We decided to focus our work on the commitments of city and county departments: the Chicago Commission on Human Relations, the Chicago Housing Authority, the Department of Urban Renewal—Relocation Department, and the Cook County Department of Public Aid. We gathered data over the next nine months. My job was to report on what was happening with the Chicago Housing Authority; I gathered statistics from the CHA, interviewed CHA staff, and went out to public housing projects in white neighborhoods, knocking on tenants' doors asking if any African Americans had recently moved in. Not surprisingly, I found no evidence of new black tenants in those buildings. In May 1967 we finished our work and prepared an 80-page report, providing our evidence that real change was virtually nonexistent. Some agencies, like the Chicago Commission on Human Relations, had made a superficial change with a "checking program," which they claimed met their commitments, but we did not view this [as] an effective solution. However, by the time we con-

cluded this work, Martin Luther King Jr. had already announced that no more marches were necessary. The report was shelved.[70]

There was, however, at least one concrete result of the Summit Agreement during that year. The Leadership Council for Metropolitan Open Communities, an organization charged in the Summit Agreement with "responsibility for the education and action programs necessary to achieve fair housing," had been established in December 1966 and was beginning to get organized.[71]

In January 1967 SCLC sent another team to Chicago, under the leadership of Hosea Williams, to conduct a voter registration campaign. This work continued for several months but made little headway. (A few years later, Jesse Jackson's Operation Breadbasket conducted much more successful voter registration campaigns.)

As work on the tenant unions continued, a range of open-housing efforts took place, some of which were reported in the SCLC staff newsletter. Meredith Gilbert was serving as a key organizer of the Lawndale Union to End Slums, and in March 1967 Gilbert and his young family moved to an apartment in the all-white Belmont-Cragin area on the North Side. Gilbert reported that some of the neighbors were friendly, but a brick had been thrown through his window; he also reported holding a "workshop" in the local tavern with some white residents of the neighborhood. As other activists continued to advance open housing in Chicago, SCLC went to the aid of open-housing activists in Louisville, Kentucky.[72] During late 1966 and 1967 Al Raby, Meredith Gilbert, and others continued to work on tenant union issues, at one point testifying before an Illinois legislative committee on housing, making a strong case for changes in landlord-tenant law.

The "End" of the Chicago Freedom Movement

By the spring of 1967, many of Dr. King's team had dispersed. James Bevel was in New York City, organizing for the Spring Mobilization against the War in Vietnam, and many of the field staff had left Chicago or turned to other pursuits. Dr. King himself was increasingly preoccupied with opposing the Vietnam War. On April 4, 1967, he made his

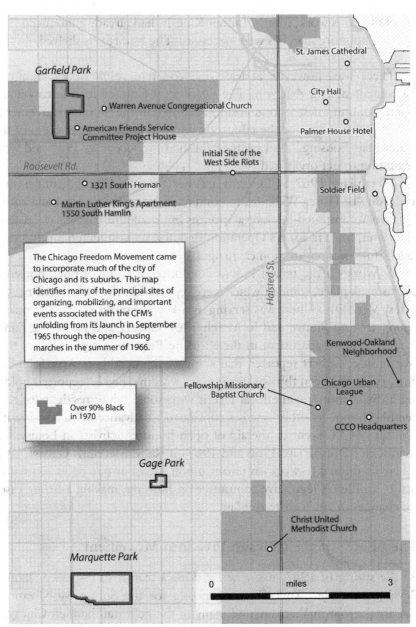

Map 3. Important sites of the Chicago Freedom Movement, September 1965–August 1966

famous "Beyond Vietnam" speech at Riverside Church in New York City, calling for an end to the "triple evils" of poverty, racism, and militarism. He would soon turn to preparations for the Poor People's Campaign, a national effort.

Meanwhile, CCCO was becoming increasingly fragmented and had lost its sense of purpose once Superintendent Willis finally resigned. In September 1967 Al Raby resigned as convener, and CCCO itself dissolved a few weeks later. This marked the end of the Chicago Freedom Movement as an organizational alliance between CCCO and SCLC, but not the end of the initiatives and impulses unleashed by that movement.

Raby reflects on King's decision to focus his energies elsewhere after the spring of 1967, and he comments on the change in civil rights work in Chicago:

> Martin had been criticized in some quarters for not staying in one place. Well . . . I wonder if the critics would have left him in the first place that he got bogged down until he accomplished what he had set out to accomplish. Martin's primary role was a national role; it was a role to inspire and support local groups. He couldn't be a substitute for that local movement. That is not to say that in every instance Martin made the best decision, even in times of competing responsibilities. But there is no way in hell that I would have set Martin down in Albany, Georgia, and said, "You stay here until you succeed." And there is no way in which he should have stayed in Chicago until there was the end to segregation in this city.
>
> The Coordinating Council of Community Organizations diminished in its importance and Operation Breadbasket became more important, in the way that the school issue was for several years the major issue and then the housing issue became the major issue. What in fact occurred was the creation of a new organization, and that [organization] took on the remnants of the activist movement.[73]

SCLC continued to have a strong presence in Chicago with Operation Breadbasket, which won important victories in 1967. Breadbasket continued as an SCLC project until 1971, when it became a separate organization, Operation PUSH. Gary Massoni reports on Operation Breadbasket's work in late 1966 and 1967:

> The ministers of Operation Breadbasket signed a covenant with National Tea Company on December 9, 1966. The format of this agreement was similar to the one with High-Low Foods (regarding commitments for jobs), except that the demands for the distribution of black-manufactured products and for banking in black-owned banks were expanded. In two more covenants with supermarket chains, the employment demands remained essentially on the same basis, but the business demands were further elaborated. . . . [In] the Jewel Food Stores agreement, announced on April 28, 1967, Jewel agreed not only to transfer some store accounts to black banks and to distribute the black products, they also agreed to establish a "market advisory council" within their management group to advise Negro businessmen on ways to improve their marketing and general business skills. Jewel also agreed to use the services of Negro businessmen in the areas of garbage collection, pest exterminating, and janitorial maintenance, and in the construction of new stores. . . . National Tea . . . broke ground on May 11, 1967, for the first major chain store in Chicago to be built by black contractors.
>
> Dr. King attended the groundbreaking ceremonies and announced the nationwide significance of this event: it was the first such major construction job by black contractors anywhere in the country. . . . While business development was the central focus of Operation Breadbasket's activities early in 1967, the theme of national expansion began to dominate the program by the end of the year.[74]

Postscript I: The Poor People's Campaign, 1968

The Chicago campaign directly influenced the launching of the next major initiative of Dr. King and SCLC—the Poor People's Campaign.

Bernard LaFayette became the national director, and Tony Henry of AFSC in Chicago was appointed associate director and head of the Washington, DC, office. Over the course of the campaign, Jesse Jackson and Herman Jenkins served terms as "mayor" of Resurrection City, the tent city built on the National Mall that stood for more than two months. Al Sampson organized in Newark with Jenkins.

Tony Henry explains how the Chicago effort and the Poor People's Campaign were linked by more than just shared personnel:

> The idea of trying to do something in the North, and not just the South, which had been Dr. King's focus, was very much in the air. People like James Bevel and Bernard LaFayette played a big role in helping to shape some of these ideas. The concept of a campaign of poor people from all over the country attacking racial discrimination and other types of oppression finally began to take root and blossomed. What came out of that finally was the decision to bring poor people from all over the country to Washington, DC.[75]

Raby had this to say about the connection between Chicago and the Poor People's Campaign:

> I think that Chicago was an education for Martin, and in some ways was an education for those of us in Chicago who believed we were very sophisticated and knowledgeable. It was an education in terms of the conquerability of poverty in northern areas. He was certainly familiar with poverty in the South; I think it was an education in terms of resistance. You should remember that at the same time we were in the midst of the rhetoric of Black Power, and Martin, I think, was trying to say to the activists, that as a leader of the Poor People's March I am going to bring forward and make visible the rainbow nature of poverty in this country.[76]

But then tragedy struck. In April 1968, just as preparations for the Poor People's Campaign were about to come to fruition, Dr. King was called to Memphis, Tennessee, to lead a march of striking garbage workers. On April 4 he was assassinated while standing on the balcony of the Lorraine Motel. Riots broke out in more than 100 cities across the country.

At the massive funeral for Dr. King, his casket moved through the streets of Atlanta in a cart pulled by mules, symbolic of the mule trains already bringing Mississippi farmers to Washington for the Poor People's Campaign. After the funeral, SCLC staff insisted that the Poor People's Campaign must go on. Bernard LaFayette settled down in Washington to continue the preparations, along with Tony Henry, Bill Moyer, and others.

SCLC Chicago staffer Billy Hollins, who served as the Midwest regional coordinator for the Poor People's Campaign, recalls:

I went up to Michigan and found some Native Americans; I went to Indiana and found some poor white folks. I went to churches, I went to organizations, and I talked about the Poor People's Campaign. We're going to have some buses leaving, we're going to Washington, DC. This is Martin Luther King's movement— we always used Martin Luther King's name—you need to get on this bus—you need to be part of this thing! I was able to organize those people. And then I would get other people to organize people. I didn't do all this on my own. I would find people who would work.

First we sent eighteen buses, then fourteen more buses, and in the last group we sent twelve buses. The buses cost $1,000 apiece, and then you had to give people some money and make sure we had food, and we had to give something to the people in charge so they had a little stash if something went wrong. I did a lot of fund-raising for all of this, too. When it was time to go, I sent all the buses over to Jesse Jackson's place and let him kick it off![77]

Jimmy Collier, returning to the SCLC staff after a sojourn in California, served as one of the New York City organizers for the Poor People's Campaign:

The Poor People's Campaign was great because the issue of poverty was so important, but it didn't get completed. King wanted to connect that there were poor people in DC and every other city, and then go to Wall Street to show civil rights supporters how the whole system worked. The campaign happened, with people living on the Mall in front of the White House in a tent city called Resurrection City, but it fizzled before we got to Wall Street. After Dr. King was killed, people were in shock and grief and it was a miracle that the campaign happened at all.[78]

Postscript II: Opening up the Building Trades, 1969

In 1969 the Reverend C. T. Vivian and the Reverend Jesse Jackson played central roles in the Chicago demonstrations aimed at opening up the building trades unions to African Americans. Vivian reports:

So, the city burns down [after Martin Luther King was killed] and we come down to a meeting to see what we're going to do with this. We joined together with a number of men that were heads of major businesses, like Sears and Roebuck, Wards, First National Bank, and Continental Bank—about thirteen guys. After the town was just about burned down, they wanted to create something and make a difference. So I came in with the plan that we create something for the South Side. Archie Hargraves wrote it up, but I laid it out for them. We created a plan for a whole organization. We needed about $8 million, so that had to come from the businesses downtown. (Later we saw that the $8 million could come from the federal government.) We brought together sixty-one nongovernmental organizations and formed the Coalition for United Community Action.

But the real players, the big-time players, were the gangs. Our concern was, how do you move them from their usual way of thinking? If you could get them involved, then they become the force you need to go after the biggies. If you don't have any force that's not already bought by City Hall or the businessmen, what force are you going to use to change Chicago? This is where we came in.

We also gathered together another group which we called the Roundtable. The Roundtable was made up of black adults that everybody could appreciate who worked downtown in the big companies, as vice presidents and things like that. By the time we had everything going smoothly, the gangs came to the position that if any of their guys got in a fight with another, what they would do is ask for a group of these community leaders. They became kinds of uncles to the group. We created a group that made decisions so that the gangs wouldn't have to shoot each other and fight each other all the time. We would decide who was right and who was wrong.

The first thing we did was to close down the Red Rooster stores. They were all over the South Side of Chicago, and they sold bad meat or nearly bad, and bad vegetables, at the same price as if they were good. So we wanted to stop those Red Rooster stores from selling bad stuff. Jeff Fort, head of the Blackstone Rangers, had people working at the Red Rooster, so he pulled his people out and demonstrated with us at the Red Rooster. This was one of the things that connected us with the gangs. The YMCA also had someone working with the gangs, and he said they wanted to meet me. So we had an evening of it.

We needed the power of the really poor and left-out to be the force that would demand jobs from the city in spite of City Hall. What do you have to break into to show that these young men are an important part of the city and got jobs? The building trades unions had all kinds of jobs, but if you were black you didn't become a full member of any of them. So we had to take on the unions.

We organized demonstrations at the building sites. We were confronting them. We weren't just standing there looking at them and saying we're hungry. We were saying, "You're not giving us jobs, so it's time you get out of here." We did it nonviolently, but all those guys in those unions were afraid; we weren't. They would leave the work and the work would stop. We stopped half a billion dollars of work right downtown in the middle of the city!

The mayor called me and said we needed a meeting. We met at City Hall because nothing was going to happen unless the mayor said it was going to happen. Monsignor Egan was my friend, and he knew the mayor very well. We finally convinced the mayor that I wasn't against Chicago; I was for Chicago. And little by little he came to settle it. We were talking about union jobs where we would demand not only the wages but the union cards to go along with it. It was called the Chicago Plan, and later that became the Boston Plan, the New York Plan, the Newark Plan; it moved all over the country. In fact, the national administration had to come our way. We got the 20,000 jobs and the administration gave us the money: 5,000 jobs a year for four years or 4,000 jobs a year for five years. You can only win in Chicago once, and here we did, we won.[79]

Meyer Weinberg points to the deep repercussions the Chicago civil rights struggle had on Chicago's subsequent history:

The greatest triumph of the civil rights movement in Chicago was the people it educated, black and white, and I might say especially black women. That in part was a matter of King, but also more so of the CCCO as a whole. I mention women because a lot of them became active through the school issue, because many of them were on the PTA. . . . A lot of them became active and now many of them are lawyers and such. I don't mean those were the good old days. I think that Thoreau said that anyone who speaks of the golden age is wrong, because to have a golden age you had to have golden people. And we didn't have golden people, but we had very many good people, and I think that much of the success of Harold Washington [Chicago's first black mayor] has come from that milieu. It is hard for me to think of Harold Washington without the civil rights movement going as it did.[80]

After 1969, the impact of the Chicago Freedom Movement was felt in a multitude of ways. Part 3 of this book discusses the ripples that moved outward from the Chicago Freedom Movement—from these stories—as the work continued over the next years and decades. Though there were many challenges, there were also important victories.

Notes

Passages from the following have been published elsewhere and are reprinted here with permission:

Mary Lou Finley, "Welcome," in *Injustice/Injustica: Chicago Freedom Movement Literary Journal, 1966–2006, Voices Then and Now* (Chicago: Chicago Freedom Movement 40th Anniversary Commemoration, 2006), 26–27. Copyright by author. Used with permission.

Bernard Kleina, "Remember Where You Are, Brother," in *Injustice/Injustica: Chicago Freedom Movement Literary Journal*, 9–11. Copyright by author. Used with permission.

Bernard LaFayette, "End-the-Slums Movement," in *America's Growing Inequality: The Impact of Poverty and Race*, ed. Chester Hartman (Lanham, MD: Lexington Books, 2014), 519–20. Used with permission of the publisher.

Gary Massoni, "Perspectives on Operation Breadbasket," in *Chicago, 1966: Open Housing Marches, Summit Negotiations, and Operation Breadbasket*, ed. David Garrow (Brooklyn, NY: Carlson Publishing, 1989), 210–11, 217. Copyright by author. Used with permission.

Al Raby, speech at the July 10 rally at Soldier Field, box 4-21, Al Raby Speeches, 1965–1966, CCCO Papers, King Center Library and Archives, Atlanta, Georgia. Used with permission from the King Center Library and Archives.

Elbert C. (Bert) Ransom, "Action Excerpts of the Chicago Freedom Movement," in *Injustice/Injustica: Chicago Freedom Movement Literary Journal*, 23–25. Copyright by author. Used with permission.

1. Alma P. Coggs, telephone interview by James Ralph, October 14, 1988.

2. "De Facto Segregation in the Chicago Public Schools," *Crisis*, February 1958, 87–93, 126–27. Many persons contributed to this report.

3. Meyer Weinberg, interview by James Ralph, Chicago, December 30, 1986.

4. Al Raby, interview by James Ralph, Chicago, September 12, 1986.

5. Weinberg interview.

6. David Jehnsen, "Introduction to the Third Generation of Kingian Nonviolence Faculty and Certified Trainers" (unpublished manuscript, June 2013), 7.

7. Rosie Simpson, presentation at "Fulfilling the Dream: The Chicago Freedom Movement 40th Anniversary Commemoration and Action Conference," Harold Washington Cultural Center, Chicago, July 23, 2006.

8. Raby interview.

9. Edwin C. (Bill) Berry, interview by Bob Jordan, Chicago, July 28, 1986.

10. The Reverend John R. Porter, presentation at "Fulfilling the Dream," July 23, 2006.

11. Billy Hollins, presentation at "Fulfilling the Dream," July 23, 2006.

12. Don Rose, presentation at "Fulfilling the Dream," July 23, 2006.

13. Tony Henry, interview by Keith Harvey, Chicago, ca. 2007.

14. Bernard LaFayette, telephone interview by Mary Lou Finley and Pam Smith, June 27, 2011.

15. Bernard LaFayette, "The End-the-Slums Movement," *Poverty & Race* 15 (May/June 2006): 12, republished in *America's Growing Inequality: The Impact of Poverty and Race,* ed. Chester Hartman (Lanham, MD: Lexington Books, 2014).

16. C. T. Vivian, interview by Mary Lou Finley, Atlanta, January 4, 2011.

17. Edwin C. (Bill) Berry, personal communication with Kale Williams, ca. 1972.

18. Raby interview.

19. Andrew Young, interview by Mary Lou Finley, Atlanta, January 3, 2012.

20. James Bevel, interview by James Ralph, Chicago, August 11, 1988.

21. Raby interview.

22. Young interview.

23. Adapted from Mary Lou Finley, "Welcome," in *Injustice/Injustica: Chicago Freedom Movement Literary Journal, 1966–2006, Voices Then and Now* (Chicago: Chicago Freedom Movement 40th Anniversary Commemoration, 2006), 26–27.

24. Lawrence Johnson, telephone interview by Mary Lou Finley, February 15, 2015.

25. Young interview.

26. Henry interview.

27. Billy Hollins, interview by Mary Lou Finley, Atlanta, January 7, 2012.

28. Jim Keck, interview by Pam Smith and Mary Lou Finley, Chicago, September 2011. For other accounts of Keck's experiences, see Pete Seeger and Bob Reiser, *Everybody Says Freedom: A History of the Civil Rights Movement in Songs and Pictures* (New York: W. W. Norton, 2009), 229–30, and Ben Joravsky, "A Moment of Truth," *Chicago,* August 1986, 99–100.

29. Keck interview.

30. Jimmy Collier, telephone interview by James Ralph, January 31, 1992.

31. David Jehnsen, telephone interview by James Ralph, August 20, 1991.

32. David Jehnsen, presentation at "Fulfilling the Dream," July 23, 2006. The Reverend Shelvin Hall was the key leader for the West Side Federation for many years, and Lewis Kreinberg was its director. The Reverend Randall Harris is the current executive director.

33. Gary Massoni, presentation at "Fulfilling the Dream," July 23, 2006.

34. Hattie Williams, interview by Olin Eugene Myers, Chicago, June 13, 1986.

35. Ibid.

36. Raby interview.

37. Jehnsen interview.

38. Thich Nhat Hahn, "Support President Obama's Sangha," *Mindfulness Bell,* Summer 2009, www.mindfulnessbell.org/wp/tag/martin-luther-king; "Thich Nhat Hanh and Martin Luther King's Dream Comes True in Mississippi," Plum Village press release, September 25, 2013, http://plumvillage.org/press-releases/thich-nhat-hahn-and-martin-luther-kings-dream-comes-true-in-mississippi/.

39. Elbert C. (Bert) Ransom, "Action Excerpts of the Chicago Freedom Movement," in *Injustice/Injustica: Chicago Freedom Movement Literary Journal,* 23–25.

40. Bill Moyer, telephone interview with James Ralph, 1988.

41. Ibid.

42. Bevel interview.

43. Demands from "Program of the Chicago Freedom movement," in *Chicago, 1966: Open Housing Marches,* ed. David Garrow (Brooklyn, NY: Carlson Publishing, 1989), 104–9; Al Raby's remarks from his speech at the July 10 rally at Soldier Field, box 4-21, Al Raby Speeches, 1965–1966, CCCO Papers, King Center Library and Archives, Atlanta.

44. Williams interview.

45. For a statement of the demands, see Garrow, "Program of the Chicago Freedom Movement."

46. Bernard LaFayette, interview with James Ralph, Chicago, September 19, 1987.

47. James Donnelly Godsil, personal communication to Mary Lou Finley and Pam Smith, June 2006. Also see http://www.milwaukeerenaissance.com/CulturalProjects/JamesDonnellyGodsilStories.

48. Gilbert Cornfield, interview by Pam Smith and Mary Lou Finley, Chicago, November 2010.

49. *Chicago Tribune,* August 1, 1966.

50. Adapted from Bernard Kleina, "Remember Why You're Here, Brother," *Injustice/Injustica: Chicago Freedom Movement Literary Journal,* 9–11.

51. Elbert C. (Bert) Ransom, presentation at "Fulfilling the Dream," July 23, 2006.

52. Nancy Jefferson, interview by Robert Jordan, Chicago, 1986.

53. Young interview.

54. Edward Vondrak, interview by James Ralph, Chicago, August 14, 1986.

55. Godsil, personal communication.

56. LaFayette interview. On gangs, see also chapter fourteen by Pam Smith.

57. John McDermott, interview by James Ralph, Chicago, July 7, 1988.

58. Henry interview.

59. Raby interview.

60. McDermott interview.

61. Gordon Groebe, interview by James Ralph, Chicago, August 27, 1991.

62. Edward Marciniak, interview by James Ralph, Chicago, July 5, 1991.

63. Kale Williams, "The Open Housing Campaign—Chicago 1966: A Report Presented to the Annual Meetings of the American Friends Service Committee, November 5, 1966," 6–7, author's files.

64. John McKnight, interview by James Ralph, Evanston, Illinois, August 19, 1986.

65. Marciniak interview.

66. Williams, "Open Housing Campaign," 8–9.

67. The marches pitted two of the mayor's major constituencies—the black community and the working-class white community—against each other.

68. Robert Lucas, interview by Pam Smith and Mary Lou Finley, November 3, 2010.

69. Ibid.

70. Mary Lou Finley, unpublished manuscript, June 2014.

71. Subcommittee to the Conference on Fair Housing, "The 'Summit Agreement,'" in Garrow, *Chicago, 1966*, 153.

72. "North and South: Southern Christian Leadership Conference Staff News," March 1967, http://www.crmvet.org/docs/sclc/6703_sclc_ns.pdf; Tracy E. K'Meyer, *Civil Rights in the Gateway for the South: Louisville, Kentucky, 1945–1980* (Lexington: University Press of Kentucky, 2009), 111–44.

73. Raby interview.

74. Gary Massoni, "Perspectives on Operation Breadbasket," in Garrow, *Chicago, 1966*, 210–11, 217. See also Martin Deppe, *Operation Breadbasket: An Untold Story of Civil Rights in Chicago, 1966–1971* (Athens: University of Georgia Press, 2017).

75. Henry interview.

76. Raby interview.

77. Hollins interview.

78. Jimmy Collier, interview by Pam Smith and Mary Lou Finley, Oakhurst and Fresno, California, March 2011.

79. Vivian interview.

80. Weinberg interview.

Part 2

Background and History

2

Interpreting the Chicago Freedom Movement

The Last Fifty Years

James R. Ralph Jr.

Martin Luther King Jr. never quite knew how to judge the Chicago Freedom Movement. Shortly after the high-level negotiations that brought the open-housing campaign to a close in late August 1966, King told his congregation in Atlanta that the Summit Agreement "will probably stand out as a most significant and far-reaching victory that has ever come about in a Northern community on the whole question of open housing." He believed, moreover, that the Chicago accord would do more than right the city's racial wrongs, for it would "serve as inspiration for us to carry on in the days ahead."[1] But several months later, King was not so certain about the impact of the Chicago Freedom Movement. He privately questioned the wisdom of some of the decisions made.[2]

King's uncertainty reflected the slow implementation of the Summit Agreement and the troubles facing the nonviolent civil rights movement. It also dovetailed with a growing consensus among journalists and pundits that the Chicago Freedom Movement was, ultimately, a failure. The first generation of historians writing on the Chicago campaign seconded that verdict, and this negative assessment has dominated popular and historical perceptions of the Chicago Freedom Movement ever since.

When the major direct action phase of the Chicago Freedom Movement came to a close in late August 1966, a number of observers hailed its impact. The National Committee against Discrimination in Housing extolled the Chicago campaign. "Still King," declared the *Christian*

Century.[3] But other commentators took the opposite position. The *New Republic* called it "a very short-term compromise" that was "obviously no major victory for King's Chicago Freedom Movement."[4] Increasingly, commentators adopted the position of some Chicago activists, particularly those who had forged ahead with the canceled march into Cicero, that the Daley administration had bested the movement leadership in the summit negotiations by producing a weak agreement.[5]

A long feature in the *New York Times* in January 1967 captured the growing negative consensus. Entitled "Dr. King Plagued by Resistance and Apathy in Chicago Slums," the article highlighted the difficulties the Chicago Freedom Movement faced in implementing the Summit Agreement and in making headway in other initiatives. Hosea Williams, one of King's chief lieutenants, offered a number of vivid but gloomy reflections on progress in Chicago—including his comments about "hopelessness" and "powerlessness"—that would be quoted by many subsequent chroniclers of the Chicago Freedom Movement.[6]

The first round of historical examination of the Chicago Freedom Movement built on this critical assessment. "The Chicago debacle" was how David Levering Lewis categorized it in his important biography of King, published in 1970.[7] In *America in Our Time,* published in 1976, Godfrey Hodgson stated, "Martin Luther King went to Chicago and was routed."[8] This bleak reading was echoed in later major studies of the civil rights movement and surveys of modern American history. In the mid-1980s Alonzo Hamby concluded in *Liberalism and Its Challengers* that the Chicago Freedom Movement "undeniably was more failure than success," and Manning Marable labeled it a "failure."[9] At roughly the same time, Adam Fairclough included a chapter titled "Defeat in Chicago" in his study of the Southern Christian Leadership Conference (SCLC), *To Redeem the Soul of America.*[10] A few years later, in his survey of the civil rights movement, Robert Weisbrot argued that "in many respects, the Chicago freedom movement had emerged as a debacle to rival the Albany movement."[11]

The chroniclers of the history of Chicago, especially its political history, have largely dismissed the impact of the Chicago Freedom Movement. Mike Royko's *Boss: Richard J. Daley of Chicago* offered an early and remarkably vivid picture of a cynical mayor toying with civil rights activists. William J. Grimshaw's more scholarly study, *Bitter Fruit: Black Politics and the Chicago Machine,* also highlighted the frustrations of advocates of racial justice.[12]

A negative judgment of the Chicago Freedom Movement persists in more recent historical writings. In *The House I Live In: Race in the American Century,* Robert Norrell discusses the Chicago Freedom Movement at length and then writes, "As soon as [King] had left the city, official Chicago ignored its promises and returned to segregation as usual."[13] In another recent overview, *Unfinished Business: Racial Equality in American History,* Michael J. Klarman contends that "Mayor Richard Daley proved a more formidable adversary to King than had Bull Connor or Jim Clark." In the end, Klarman writes, "King's Chicago campaign was widely judged a disaster, and one of his lieutenants, Hosea Williams, bleakly concluded, 'The Negroes of Chicago have a greater feeling of powerlessness than any I ever saw. . . . [T]hey're beaten down psychologically.'"[14] Finally, in his ambitious synthesis *We Ain't What We Ought to Be: The Black Freedom Struggle from Emancipation to Obama,* Stephen Tuck contends that "the Chicago campaign had floundered in the face of hostility from Democratic politicians (black and white) and grassroots white violence."[15]

Certainly, the Chicago Freedom Movement did not have the catalyzing effect of King's earlier campaigns in Birmingham and Selma, Alabama. The campaign against Jim Crow segregation in Birmingham in the spring of 1963 captured the world's attention and helped pave the way for the momentous Civil Rights Act of 1964. The 1965 campaign for access to the ballot box in Selma prompted passage of the Voting Rights Act of 1965. By these high standards, the Chicago Freedom Movement has been found wanting by many observers.[16]

A number of scholars have questioned the approaches to social change adopted by the Chicago Freedom Movement. In *Mean Streets: Chicago Youths and the Everyday Struggle for Empowerment in the Multicultural City,* Andrew J. Diamond argues that the efforts of Chicago activists to recruit gang members were generally ineffectual. "The SCLC-CCCO," he concludes, "was surely somewhat out of touch with the reality of many gang members," and he contends that Black Power currents had much more resonance with them.[17] Beryl Satter argues in *Family Properties:*

Race, Real Estate, and the Exploitation of Black Urban America—a fascinating story of the exploitation of African Americans in their search for housing on Chicago's West Side—that the focus on open occupancy was misplaced. "The key to fixing the dual housing market," she writes, "was ending the structural, industry-wide blockage of credit to African Americans." An effective effort to aid African Americans, according to Satter, was the Contract Buyers League. Established in 1968, after the end of the Chicago Freedom Movement, it fought against destructive mortgage arrangements and worked to make conventional mortgages accessible to black homeowners.[18]

This general sense of the shortcomings of the Chicago Freedom Movement no doubt helps explain its modest place in American popular memory. Even as major museums have opened to commemorate important landmarks in the battle for racial justice, the Chicago Freedom Movement remains largely orphaned. The Birmingham Civil Rights Institute opened in 1992 and is located on ground zero of the civil rights campaign. The Lorraine Motel in Memphis, Tennessee, where Martin Luther King was assassinated in 1968 as he led a campaign in support of local sanitation workers, is now the site of the National Civil Rights Museum. By contrast, the North Lawndale apartment building where King lived for a time, immersing himself in the experiences of African Americans confined to Chicago's West Side ghetto, was torn down, and until recently the site remained a vacant lot—a metaphor for the Chicago campaign.[19]

History textbooks—custodians of what is deemed important in American history—also largely neglect the Chicago Freedom Movement. In their well-received survey *The African-American Odyssey*, Darlene Clark Hine and her coauthors state, "The Chicago strategy was a dismal failure."[20] But this treatment—however critical—at least acknowledges the Chicago Freedom Movement. Most American history textbooks simply ignore it. The sixth edition of *The Enduring Vision: A History of the American People* does not mention it at all. Nor does the fourth edition of *Liberty, Equality, and Power* or the sixth edition of *America's History*.[21]

That the Chicago Freedom Movement has generally been characterized as a defeat helps explain its diminished stature in the public's memory, but on its own, this verdict is not decisive. After all, Pearl Harbor was a staggering setback for the United States, but it is well remembered by ordinary Americans and historians. A tighter comparison is the valiant yet ultimately unsuccessful strike by Eugene Debs and fellow unionists to support Pullman workers in the 1890s, which is now recognized as a decisive moment in the history of organized labor.[22] At least as telling is the fact that the conventional narrative of the modern civil rights movement has had difficulty handling the Chicago campaign. That narrative is generally bounded by the *Brown v. Board of Education* decision and the Montgomery bus boycott in the mid-1950s to the successful Selma campaign in 1965. This was, as Bayard Rustin once put it, the "classic" phase of the civil rights movement, when the central dramas took place in the American South and the enemies—legalized segregation and exclusion—were clear.[23] The first installment of the memorable documentary *Eyes on the Prize* framed its reading of the movement in this fashion.[24] Early surveys of the modern civil rights movement, such as Howard Sitkoff's *The Struggle for Black Equality*, concentrated on developments between *Brown* and Selma. Only one of its seven chapters covers the period after 1965.[25] The Chicago campaign, meanwhile, followed the Selma victory and unfolded in the more ambiguous racial terrain of the North.

The conventional narrative of African American protest recognizes that activism did not stop in 1965, but it shifts attention to the advocates of Black Power and those who took to the city streets in anger. All the general history textbooks previously mentioned feature sections on urban rioting and the emergence of the Black Power movement. They cover the violent uprisings in Newark and Detroit in 1967 and those that occurred after the assassination of Martin Luther King in 1968, as well as the rise of Black Power spokesmen and the Black Panther Party. The nonviolent Chicago Freedom Movement does not fit comfortably into such coverage.

Recently, a growing number of historians have challenged this conventional reading of the Black Power movement. Led by Peniel Joseph, these historians have criticized this portrayal's truncated temporal perspective and its triggering role in the demise of the civil rights movement. They reveal the deep roots of Black Power and how Black Power currents intersected with civil rights forces to create "a complex mosaic rather than mutually exclusive and antagonistic movements."[26]

This new trend in historical scholarship is unlikely, however, to draw greater attention to the Chicago Freedom Movement. The emphasis in Black Power studies is on excavating the roots of black radicalism, uncovering the international cross-currents that shaped Black Power, and tracing the influence of Black Power well beyond the 1960s. The main agenda of this new work is "to critically engage an ongoing conversation about the uses and abuses of the black freedom movement (sometimes boiled down to civil rights) that has, up until recently, largely excluded Black Power."[27] The unfolding of the Chicago Freedom Movement was influenced by the rising prominence of Black Power, but it is difficult to imagine how the Chicago campaign, with its promotion of interracialism and nonviolent discipline, is likely to figure prominently in this new wave of scholarship.

An equally exciting trend in scholarship is the growing interest in the African American freedom struggle in the North. Until recently, historians had barely explored this topic. There were some pioneering journal articles and monographs, yet they hardly constituted a field.[28] But that changed in 2003 with the publication of Jeanne Theoharis and Komozi Woodard's *Freedom North: Black Freedom Struggles outside the South*, a collection of essays about northern activism.[29] At roughly the same time, a series of highly regarded local studies emerged—Martha Biondi's *To Stand and Fight: The Struggle for Civil Rights in Postwar New York City*, Matthew Countryman's *Up South: Civil Rights and Black Power in Philadelphia*, Clarence Lang's *Grassroots at the Gateway: Class Politics and the Black Freedom Struggle in St. Louis*, and Patrick Jones's *The Selma of the North: Civil Rights Insurgency in Milwaukee*, to name just a few.[30]

The place of the Chicago Freedom Movement in this new field is ambiguous, however. Putting a spotlight on the Chicago campaign deflects attention from the wide array of local movements in the North and the rich and varied history of activism in that region. In her introduction to *Freedom North*, Theoharis takes aim at scholars like Adam Fairclough who cite the Chicago Freedom Movement as "the first and only real attempt by the Civil Rights Movement to mount a major campaign of nonviolent direct action in the North." She decries "recent studies of racial politics in the postwar urban North" that "have either ascribed Northern protest solely to the influence of Martin Luther King and other

Southern leaders or focused primarily on the course of white backlash against racial reform."[31]

The energetic exploration of northern activism is, however, shaking up the conventional framing of the modern civil rights movement. Future surveys will overlook developments outside the South at their peril. Thomas J. Sugrue's sweeping 500-page study *Sweet Land of Liberty: The Forgotten Struggle for Civil Rights in the North*, published in 2008, will not be easily ignored. Sugrue covers the Chicago Freedom Movement in detail, even though he fails to explore the civil rights groundwork laid by Al Raby and the Coordinating Council of Community Organizations that helped bring King and SCLC to Chicago. Moreover, he views the Chicago Freedom Movement as something of an oddity in the northern freedom struggle of the 1960s because of its interracial, coalitionist quality. He stresses instead the rise of black radicalism, with a Black Power emphasis.[32]

Biographers of Martin Luther King and analysts of his public career are the one group of scholars who have generally not downplayed the Chicago Freedom Movement. In his Pulitzer Prize–winning biography of King, *Bearing the Cross*, David Garrow devotes more than 100 pages to developments surrounding the Chicago campaign. He stresses that the Chicago experience was essential to King's evolution as a leader.[33] In the final installment of his massive, three-volume study of King and the modern civil rights movement, Taylor Branch contends that his experience in Chicago was central to his maturation as a leader for social justice. "Chicago nationalized race," he insists, "complementing the impact of Watts. Without it King would be confined to posterity more as a regional figure." He also argues that the Chicago Freedom Movement accomplished more than is generally acknowledged. He even notes that the Summit Agreement was a stronger accord than those King and SCLC had achieved in their other single-city campaigns. "What sharply distinguished the movement," he writes, "was the disparity in their wider impact. The weaknesses of the Birmingham settlement disappeared in a rippling tide that dissolved formal segregation by comprehensive national law. The Selma campaign itself never defeated or converted Sheriff Jim Clark, but the nation democratized voting rights to make segregationists such as him relics of the past. No corresponding shift enhanced the

Chicago settlement in outcome or reputation, and all its shortcomings remained an eyesore."[34]

King's biographers have drawn on memoirs by the civil rights leader's close associates. Ralph Abernathy and Andrew Young both saw the Chicago campaign as a seminal experience for King and SCLC. "Chicago marked a turning point for SCLC," Young writes in *An Easy Burden: The Civil Rights Movement and the Transformation of America.* "Our work there forced Martin and me and other creative thinkers within our circle to concern ourselves more directly with the multifaceted implications of urban poverty and to direct our attention more pointedly to its underlying causes."[35]

Garrow's and Branch's biographies and the perspectives of King's old colleagues emphasize a more radical King than is commonly depicted in popular culture. In a recent study, *From Civil Rights to Human Rights: Martin Luther King, Jr., and the Struggle for Economic Justice,* Thomas F. Jackson develops the theme of economic justice in King's vision and highlights the significance of his time in Chicago. "Martin Luther King drew important lessons from the Chicago marches and concurrent efforts at community empowerment," Jackson writes. "Chicago renewed his sense of social ministry to the poor, his empathy for their plight, and his appreciation of their capacities." The Chicago Freedom Movement, Jackson argues, "became a central prelude in King's decision to build a nationwide coalition capable of empowering all poor people and moving the nation toward democratic socialism."[36]

The Chicago campaign was decisive in shaping the last years of King's public ministry. As Michael K. Honey notes, King "envisioned 'a planetary movement' [King's own phrase] for economic justice and human rights, and an end to war, racism, and poverty." His final days were devoted to supporting a sanitation workers' strike in Memphis. It was during the Chicago movement that King and his team sought to build—albeit with difficulty—a more dynamic partnership with the progressive elements of the American labor movement.[37]

The latest scholarship on Martin Luther King affirms the perspective of the relatively rare studies that have argued for the centrality of the Chicago Freedom Movement in understanding the course of the African American freedom struggle and modern American history. Thirty years ago, Allen Matusow placed the Chicago campaign at the center of his history of the 1960s. In *The Unraveling of America,* Matusow pointed to the uneven record of accomplishment of the Chicago movement, but more significantly, he viewed its unfolding as illustrative of the challenge of confronting northern racial inequality. "Civil Rights in the North," he wrote, "was a drama in three parts—schools, housing, and jobs—played out in Chicago and featuring Mayor Richard J. Daley, Lyndon Johnson, and Martin Luther King."[38]

My own study, *Northern Protest: Martin Luther King, Jr., Chicago, and the Civil Rights Movement,* built on Matusow's reading (and on Alan Anderson and George Pickering's *Confronting the Color Line: The Broken Promise of the Civil Rights Movement in Chicago*) to argue that the Chicago Freedom Movement was a telling episode not just in the history of Chicago but also in the trajectory of the country in the 1960s. "The Chicago Freedom Movement," I wrote in 1993, "did not recast the American racial scene as had the Birmingham and Selma campaigns. It did, however, signal the coming of a new era of contentious debate over national policy to right racial wrongs."[39]

In the past decade or so, it has become more likely for general histories of modern America or of race relations to reference the Chicago Freedom Movement. Eric Foner did so in *The Story of American Freedom,* as did Maurice Isserman and Michael Kazin in *America Divided.*[40] More recently, prize-winning historian Leon Litwack acknowledged the importance of the Chicago Freedom Movement in his overview of the struggle for racial equality in America. Litwack prefaces *How Free Is Free? The Long Death of Jim Crow* with two scenes—the first set after the Civil War, when former slaves in the low country of South Carolina confront a Union general and question why the Union is not committed to distributing land to the newly freed people, and the second set in Chicago in the summer of 1966. Litwack follows the conventional critique of the Chicago Freedom Movement, noting, "The old tactics of nonviolence, street marches, and mass rallies no longer achieved the desired results." But he balances this assessment with the recognition that developments in Chicago mattered. "If nothing else . . . Chicago nationalized the Civil Rights Movement and confirmed for [Martin Luther King] the endemic, intractable, infinitely varied and resourceful racism of white America."[41]

Litwack's analysis reveals an emerging interpretation of the Chicago Freedom Movement—that it is significant precisely because it revealed how thoroughly embedded racism was in the entire country. Some scholars have even turned a frequent criticism of the Chicago Freedom Movement in 1966—the choice of open housing as its major target—into a prescient insight. In *American Apartheid: Segregation and the Making of the Underclass,* Douglas S. Massey and Nancy A. Denton insist that housing segregation is the "Forgotten Factor" in understanding "racial inequality" and "the plight of the urban poor in America." Moreover, Massey and Denton state that "probably no fair housing group in the country has been more energetic than the Leadership Council for Metropolitan Open Communities and its allies." The Leadership Council, which finally closed its doors in 2006, was the direct outgrowth of the Summit Agreement of August 1966.[42]

Over the years, a few studies have recognized the creative approaches to economic injustice that flowed out of the Chicago Freedom Movement. The Chicago chapter of Operation Breadbasket, with the Reverend Jesse Jackson at its helm, was established in 1966 as one front of the Chicago campaign. It turned to selective buying campaigns to break racial barriers in employment. For the past five decades, Jackson and his supporters—subsequently as Operation PUSH and today as the Rainbow PUSH Coalition—have fought to open up the American economy to minorities. The best biographies of Jackson, such as Marshall Frady's *Jesse: The Life and Pilgrimage of Jesse Jackson,* develop the context from which this charismatic and creative activist sprang.[43]

Recently, Gordon Mantler placed Chicago at the center of the broader story of early efforts to mobilize a wide coalition against inequality. In *Power to the Poor: Black-Brown Coalition and the Fight for Economic Justice,* he argues that the Chicago campaign "represented the first time that SCLC tried to reach Latinos as part of its mobilization, both because of the city's growing Puerto Rican and Mexican American presences in or near many black neighborhoods and because the campaign needed every possible ally." Then he covers Jesse Jackson's later work to build this broader coalition.[44]

There are signs in contemporary Chicago of a growing recognition of the good fight waged against entrenched inequality by King and his supporters in the mid-1960s. Recently, for example, the Lawndale Christian Development Corporation (LCDC) opened a beautiful complex of affordable housing on the site where King rented an apartment during the Chicago campaign. The new complex is called the Dr. King Legacy Apartments. In the fall of 2013 the LCDC opened a small museum in this complex dedicated to King and fair housing.[45]

Accounts of new strategies to fight housing segregation, the work of Jesse Jackson and his organization, and the stirring story of the Dr. King Legacy Apartments have not, however, shaken the gloomy assessment shared by scholars and the general public alike that the Chicago Freedom Movement was a failure, albeit a revealing one. But the historic election and then reelection of Barack Obama—in concert with a fuller appreciation of the Chicago campaign in its totality—will ultimately, I predict, raise the reputation of the Chicago Freedom Movement.

Up until now, explorations of Chicago politics and its legendary political figures—Royko's *Boss*, Grimshaw's *Bitter Fruit*, and, more recently, Adam Cohen and Elizabeth Taylor's *American Pharaoh: Mayor Richard J. Daley*—have minimized the local reverberations of the Chicago Freedom Movement.[46] But now, with almost fifty years of hindsight, the cracks in the patron-client political rule that contained black Chicagoans for decades—cracks triggered by the Chicago movement—loom larger. In 1983 Harold Washington, an African American politician who had broken free of the Chicago political establishment, was elected as a reform mayor, largely because of a tidal wave of support among black voters. A number of the Chicago-based leaders in the Chicago Freedom Movement, including Al Raby, played important roles in Washington's election. Furthermore, a number of the black ministers, who had exposed themselves to retaliation by supporting King's work in Chicago in the mid-1960s, rallied behind Washington's candidacy.[47]

It was this vibrant sense of possibility occasioned by Harold Washington's mayoralty that led a recent graduate of Columbia University to move to Chicago to become a community organizer. Though born in Hawaii, Barack Obama was attracted to the Midwest metropolis in part because of the forces unleashed more than twenty years earlier by the Chicago Freedom Movement. In 2000 Obama acknowledged this connection in a tribute to Martin Luther King. "The proliferation of black elected officials throughout the Deep South, and the birth of the black independent political movement in Chicago grow out of the risks he took," Obama wrote.[48] Over time, the full story of Barack Obama's political ascent in Chicago and the role played by Jesse Jackson's two runs for the presidency in 1984 and 1988 will be combined, I anticipate, with the achievements of the forty-fourth president and with a greater recognition of the new ideas and initiatives developed and set in motion by the 1965–1967 campaign, leading to a fundamental reconsideration of the Chicago Freedom Movement and its legacy.[49]

Notes

This chapter expands on themes I first developed in my 2006 essay "Assessing the Chicago Freedom Movement," which was recently reprinted in Chester Hartman, ed., *America's Growing Inequality: The Impact of Poverty and Race* (Lanham, MD: Lexington Books, 2014), 509–13. Used with permission of the previous publishers.

1. Martin Luther King Jr. (MLK) speech, August 28, 1966, MLK speech file, King Center Library and Archives, Atlanta.

2. MLK to Stanley Levison, FBI 100-111180-9-1345a, June 24, 1967; MLK speech, May 29–31, 1967, MLK speech file, King Center Library and Archives.

3. *Trends in Housing,* October 1966, 5; *Christian Century,* September 7, 1966, 1071.

4. *New Republic,* September 17, 1966, 9–10.

5. *Chicago Daily Defender,* September 7, 1966; John McKnight, interview by James Ralph, August 19, 1986.

6. "Dr. King Plagued by Resistance and Apathy in Chicago Slums," *New York Times,* January 16, 1967, 22.

7. David Levering Lewis, *King: A Critical Biography* (New York: Praeger, 1970), 354.

8. Godfrey Hodgson, *America in Our Time* (Garden City, NY: Doubleday, 1976), 269.

9. Alonzo L. Hamby, *Liberalism and Its Challengers: From F.D.R. to Reagan* (New York: Oxford University Press, 1985); Manning Marable, *Black American Politics: From the Washington Marches to Jesse Jackson* (London: Verso, 1985), 208.

10. Adam Fairclough, *To Redeem the Soul of America: The Southern Christian Leadership Conference and Martin Luther King, Jr.* (Athens: University of Georgia Press, 1987), 279.

11. Robert Weisbrot, *Freedom Bound: A History of America's Civil Rights Movement* (New York: W. W. Norton, 1990), 184.

12. Mike Royko, *Boss: Richard J. Daley of Chicago* (New York: E. P. Dutton, 1971); William J. Grimshaw, *Bitter Fruit: Black Politics and the Chicago Machine, 1931–1991* (Chicago: University of Chicago Press, 1992). See also Bill Granger and Lori Granger, *Lords of the Last Machine: The Story of Politics in Chicago* (New York: Random House, 1987), 7–8, and Robert G. Spinney, *City of Big Shoulders: A History of Chicago* (De Kalb: Northern Illinois University Press, 2000), 227–31.

13. Robert J. Norrell, *The House I Live In: Race in the American Century* (New York: Oxford University Press, 2005), 246.

14. Michael J. Klarman, *Unfinished Business: Racial Equality in American History* (New York: Oxford University Press, 2007), 185–87.

15. Stephen Tuck, *We Ain't What We Ought to Be: The Black Freedom Struggle from Emancipation to Obama* (Cambridge, MA: Harvard University Press, 2010), 337.

16. See David J. Garrow, *Protest at Selma: Martin Luther King, Jr., and the Voting Rights Act of 1965* (New Haven, CT: Yale University Press, 1978).

17. Andrew J. Diamond, *Mean Streets: Chicago Youths and the Everyday Struggle for Empowerment in the Multiracial City, 1908–1969* (Berkeley: University of California Press, 2009), 265–71.

18. Beryl Satter, *Family Properties: Race, Real Estate, and the Exploitation of Black Urban America* (New York: Metropolitan Books, 2009), 141.

19. On the theme of remembering the civil rights movement, see Renee Christine Romano and Leigh Raiford, eds., *The Civil Rights Movement in American Memory* (Athens: University of Georgia Press, 2006).

20. Darlene Clark Hine et al., *The African-American Odyssey* (Upper Saddle River, NJ: Prentice Hall, 2000), 544.

21. Paul S. Boyer et al., *The Enduring Vision: A History of the American People*, 6th ed. (Boston: Houghton Mifflin, 2009); John M. Murrin et al., *Liberty, Equality, and Power*, 4th ed. (Belmont, CA: Thomson Wadsworth, 2009); James A. Henretta et al., *America's History*, 6th ed. (Boston: Bedford; New York: St. Martin's, 2009).

22. Richard Schneirov et al., *The Pullman Strike and the Crisis of the 1890s* (Urbana: University of Illinois, 1999).

23. Bayard Rustin, "From Protest to Politics: The Future of the Civil Rights Movement," *Commentary*, February 1965, 25–31.

24. *Eyes on the Prize* (Blackside, 1987). Blackside issued an important second series in 1990 that covered developments from 1965 into the 1980s and featured the Chicago Freedom Movement and the northern theater.

25. Howard Sitkoff, *The Struggle for Black Equality, 1954–1980* (New York: Hill & Wang, 1981). It remains to be seen if the recent scholarship on the persistence of civil rights activism beyond the 1960s will lead to a reinterpretation of the Chicago Freedom Movement. See, for example, David L. Chappell, *Wak-*

ing from the Dream: The Struggle for Civil Rights in the Shadow of Martin Luther King, Jr. (New York: Random House, 2014).

26. Peniel E. Joseph, "Introduction: Toward a Historiography of the Black Power Movement," in *The Black Power Movement: Rethinking the Civil Rights–Black Power Era* (New York: Routledge, 2006), 8. See also Peniel E. Joseph, *Waiting 'til the Midnight Hour: A Narrative History of Black Power in America* (New York: Owl Books, 2007), and *Dark Days, Bright Nights: From Black Power to Barack Obama* (New York: Basic Civitas Books, 2010).

27. Joseph, *Black Power Movement*, 10.

28. See, for example, August Meier and Elliott Rudwick, "The Origins of Nonviolent Direct Action in Afro-American Protest: A Note on Historical Discontinuities," in *Along the Color Line: Explorations in the Black Experience*, ed. August Meier and Elliott Rudwick (Urbana: University of Illinois Press, 1976), 307–404, and George Lipsitz, *A Life in the Struggle: Ivory Perry and the Culture of Opposition* (Philadelphia: Temple University Press, 1988).

29. Jeanne F. Theoharis and Komozi Woodard, eds., *Freedom North: Black Freedom Struggles outside the South, 1940–1980* (New York: Palgrave Macmillan, 2003).

30. Martha Biondi, *To Stand and Fight: The Struggle for Civil Rights in Postwar New York City* (Cambridge, MA: Harvard University Press, 2003); Matthew J. Countryman, *Up South: Civil Rights and Black Power in Philadelphia* (Philadelphia: University of Pennsylvania Press, 2006); Clarence Lang, *Grassroots at the Gateway: Class Politics and the Black Freedom Struggle in St. Louis, 1936–75* (Ann Arbor: University of Michigan Press, 2009); Patrick D. Jones, *The Selma of the North: Civil Rights Insurgency in Milwaukee* (Cambridge, MA: Harvard University Press, 2009). For an overview, see "Beyond Dixie: The Black Freedom Struggle outside the South," *OAH Magazine of History* 26 (January 2012). This scholarship is part of what Jacquelyn Dowd Hall has called the "long civil rights movement" framework. See Jacquelyn Dowd Hall, "The Long Civil Rights Movement and the Political Uses of the Past," *Journal of American History* 91 (March 2005): 1233–63. For a vigorous and persuasive critique of this framework, see Sundiata Keita Cha-Jua and Clarence Lang, "The 'Long Movement' as Vampire: Temporal and Spatial Fallacies in Recent Black Freedom Studies," *Journal of African American History* 92 (Spring 2007): 265–88.

31. Jeanne Theoharis, "Introduction," in Theoharis and Woodard, *Freedom North*, 1–4.

32. Thomas J. Sugrue, *Sweet Land of Liberty: The Forgotten Struggle for Civil Rights in the North* (New York: Random House, 2008), 414–19.

33. David J. Garrow, *Bearing the Cross: Martin Luther King, Jr., and the Southern Christian Leadership Conference* (New York: William Morrow, 1986), 431–574.

34. Taylor Branch, *At Canaan's Edge: America in the King Years, 1965–68*

(New York: Simon & Schuster, 2006), 23, 558. For other important studies of King and his evolution as a leader, see James H. Cone, *Martin & Malcolm & America: A Dream or a Nightmare* (Maryknoll, NY: Orbis Books, 1991), and Lewis V. Baldwin, *There Is a Balm in Gilead: The Cultural Roots of Martin Luther King, Jr.* (Minneapolis: Fortress Press, 1991). The King Papers Project, under the direction of Clayborne Carson, has not yet published volumes on King's experiences after Selma. When it does, this will surely transform the study of the Chicago Freedom Movement.

35. Andrew Young, *An Easy Burden: The Civil Rights Movement and the Transformation of America* (New York: HarperCollins, 1996), 421; Ralph David Abernathy, *And the Walls Came Tumbling Down: An Autobiography* (New York: Harper & Row, 1989), 362–99.

36. Thomas F. Jackson, *From Civil Rights to Human Rights: Martin Luther King, Jr., and the Struggle for Economic Justice* (Philadelphia: University of Pennsylvania Press, 2007), 298, 277. See also Thomas F. Jackson, "'Bread of Freedom': Martin Luther King, Jr. and Human Rights," *OAH Magazine of History* 22 (April 2008): 14–16.

37. Michael K. Honey, "Forty Years since King: Labor Rights and Human Rights," *OAH Magazine of History* 22 (April 2008): 18–21; Michael K. Honey, *Going Down Jericho Road: The Memphis Strike, Martin Luther King's Last Campaign* (New York: W. W. Norton, 2007). On the civil rights–labor alliance in the Chicago Freedom Movement, see James R. Ralph Jr., *Northern Protest: Martin Luther King, Jr., Chicago, and the Civil Rights Movement* (Cambridge, MA: Harvard University Press, 1993), 70–72. The literature on the civil rights–labor intersection is vast. For an overview, see Robert H. Zeiger, *For Jobs and Freedom: Race and Labor in America since 1865* (Lexington: University Press of Kentucky, 2007).

38. Allen Matusow, *The Unraveling of America: A History of Liberalism in the 1960s* (New York: Harper & Row, 1984), 198–214.

39. Ralph, *Northern Protest,* 6. See Alan B. Anderson and George W. Pickering, *Confronting the Color Line: The Broken Promise of the Civil Rights Movement in Chicago* (Athens: University of Georgia Press, 1986). For other assessments of the Chicago Freedom Movement, see Lori G. Waite, "Divided Consciousness: The Impact of Elite Black Consciousness on the Chicago Freedom Movement," in *Oppositional Consciousness: The Subjective Roots of Social Protest,* ed. Jane J. Mansbridge and Aldon D. Morris (Chicago: University of Chicago Press, 2001), 170–203; Ronald E. Shaw, "A Final Push for National Legislation: The Chicago Freedom Movement," *Journal of the Illinois State Historical Society* 94 (Autumn 2001): 304–32; "The Chicago Freedom Movement 40 Years Later: A Symposium," in Hartman, *America's Growing Inequality,* 509–25. For an effort to place the Chicago Freedom Movement within the larger story of the northern black freedom struggle, see James R. Ralph Jr., "African-American Activism in

the Midwest," in *Speaking out with Many Voices: Documenting American Activism and Protest in the 1960s and 1970s,* ed. Heather Thompson (Upper Saddle River, NJ: Prentice-Hall, 2010), 5–15. No one has written a sweeping overview of the intersection of the civil rights movement and politics in the Midwest as Jason Sokol recently did for the Northeast in the post–World War II era. See Jason Sokol, *All Eyes Are upon Us: Race and Politics from Boston to Brooklyn* (New York: Basic Books, 2014).

40. Eric Foner, *The Story of American Freedom* (New York: W. W. Norton, 1998), 283; Maurice Isserman and Michael Kazin, *America Divided: The Civil War of the 1960s* (New York: Oxford University Press, 2004), 208–9.

41. Leon F. Litwack, *How Free Is Free? The Long Death of Jim Crow* (Cambridge, MA: Harvard University Press, 2009), 1–4. Even more recently, Carl H. Nightingale places the Chicago Freedom Movement within the global history of segregation. While Nightingale calls King's Chicago campaign a "defeat," he sees it as part of a wider, planetary story. Carl H. Nightingale, *Segregation: A Global History of Divided Cities* (Chicago: University of Chicago Press, 2012), 388–89. The role of organized white resistance to the open-housing marches of the Chicago Freedom Movement has not been fully incorporated into the important story of ethnic, middle-income white Americans in the North in the postwar era. See, for example, Arnold Hirsch, "Massive Resistance in the Urban North: Trumbull Park, Chicago, 1953–1966," *Journal of American History* 82 (September 1995): 522–50; Thomas J. Sugrue, "Crabgrass-Roots Politics: Race, Rights, and the Reaction against Liberalism in the Urban North, 1940–1964," *Journal of American History* 82 (September 1995): 551–78; and Ronald R. Formisano, *Boston against Busing: Race, Class, Ethnicity in the 1960s and 1970s* (Chapel Hill: University of North Carolina Press, 1991). For the intersection of race, housing, and Catholicism, see John T. McGreevy, *The Catholic Encounter with Race in the Twentieth-Century Urban North* (Chicago: University Press of Chicago, 1998).

42. Douglas S. Massey and Nancy A. Denton, *American Apartheid: Segregation and the Making of the Underclass* (Cambridge, MA: Harvard University Press, 1993), 3, 224–25.

43. Marshall Frady, *Jesse: The Life and Pilgrimage of Jesse Jackson* (New York: Random House, 1996), 194–216, 253–62. See especially the essays by Mary Lou Finley and Gary Massoni in David J. Garrow, ed., *Chicago, 1966: Open Housing Marches, Summit Negotiations, and Operation Breadbasket* (Brooklyn, NY: Carlson Publishing, 1989). For a recent reexamination of Jesse Jackson's significance, see Chappell, *Waking from the Dream,* 124–47.

44. Gordon K. Mantler, *Power to the Poor: Black-Brown Coalition and the Fight for Economic Justice, 1960–1974* (Chapel Hill: University of North Carolina Press, 2013), 55.

45. *Chicago Defender,* March 23, 2011, 2; April 6, 2011, 74; August 28, 2013, 20.

46. Adam Cohen and Elizabeth Taylor, *American Pharaoh: Mayor Richard J. Daley: His Battle for Chicago and the Nation* (Boston: Little, Brown, 2000). Dempsey J. Travis is one of the few historians to stress the Chicago Freedom Movement's power to transform local politics. "The current movement for fairness and equity in politics is a legacy of the Chicago Freedom Movement," he writes. Dempsey J. Travis, *An Autobiography of Black Politics* (Chicago: Urban Research Politics, 1987). A recent study by Jeffrey Helgeson continues the traditional assessment of the Chicago Freedom Movement as a "losing encounter with racism, segregation, and the destruction of black communities in Chicago" but adds a more positive accent by noting that the movement also "helped create a great deal of potential political energy." Jeffrey Helgeson, *Crucibles of Black Empowerment: Chicago's Neighborhood Politics from the New Deal to Harold Washington* (Chicago: University of Chicago Press, 2014), 188–90, 242–43.

47. Henry J. Young, ed., *The Black Church and the Harold Washington Story: The Man, the Message, the Movement* (Bristol, IN: Wyndham Hall Press, 1988). See also James R. Ralph Jr., "Black Church Divisions and Civil Rights Activism in Chicago," in *From Every Mountainside: Black Churches and the Broad Terrain of Civil Rights,* ed. R. Drew Smith (Albany, NY: SUNY Press, 2013), 21–38.

48. Barack Obama, "Why Dr. Martin Luther King, Jr., Is Important to Me," *Chicago Defender,* January 15, 2000, 18.

49. David W. Remnick, *The Bridge: The Life and Rise of Barack Obama* (New York: Alfred A. Knopf, 2010), 151–55; Thomas J. Sugrue, *Not Even Past: Barack Obama and the Burden of Race* (Princeton, NJ: Princeton University Press, 2010), 51, 63–64. Sugrue mentions the influence of the Chicago Freedom Movement on Obama's rise as a politician but does not develop the connection at length. He focuses more on the broader civil rights movement. See also the new revision of Gary Rivlin's history of Chicago politics in the 1980s, with new commentary by Clarence Page and Larry Bennett, *Fire on the Prairie: Harold Washington, Chicago Politics, and the Roots of the Obama Presidency,* rev. ed. (Philadelphia: Temple University Press, 2013).

3

Toward the Apex of Civil Rights Activism

Antecedents of the Chicago Freedom Movement, 1965–1966

Christopher Robert Reed

Ever-boastful Chicago—true to its appellation as the boisterous, garru-lous Windy City—could lay claim to a level of civil rights activism in the aftermath of World War II that nearly matched the more famous civil rights revolution of the 1960s. A developing new liberal consensus on race—combined with the Cold War, in which the United States cast itself as the international champion of freedom—generated increased pressure to reduce racial discrimination.[1] Historically underrecognized multira-cial activist groups contributed significantly to the securing of basic citi-zenship rights after 1940. In Chicago the culmination of this process of enlightened activism involved a remarkable demonstration of interracial, interfaith, and interorganizational collaboration and cooperation across the city's neighborhood boundaries. It was ultimately this vibrant local movement that attracted Martin Luther King Jr. and the Southern Chris-tian Leadership Conference (SCLC) to the city in 1965. The framework of a "long civil rights movement," to use Jacquelyn Dowd Hall's term, can appropriately be applied to the story of the pursuit of racial justice in Chicago.

The historical roots of activism in black Chicago run deep. Dating back to Chicago's nineteenth-century frontier past, African Americans had demonstrated both a willingness and an ability to organize effectively to achieve desired ends. During the antebellum era, African American abolitionists John and Mary Jones, with the participation of prominent religious leaders in the community, organized to end discriminatory practices. These activists included the Reverend Richard DeBaptiste and his congregation at Olivet Baptist Church and black women leaders from Quinn Chapel African Methodist Episcopal (AME) Church.[2]

Activism during the Civil War era led to the end of the oppressive Illinois black laws, and participation in governance began with Illinois's reluctant extension of the franchise to black men in 1870. As the black population grew, activists emphasized economic advancement. By the 1890s, attorney Edward H. Morris had become a prominent civil rights advocate in Chicago-area courtrooms and corporate boardrooms. Another activist attorney, John "Indignation" Jones, is better known because of his legendary acerbic personality. By 1895, noted southern antilynching insurgent Ida B. Wells had relocated to Chicago. She married attorney Ferdinand L. Barnett, and together they championed improvements in conditions and opportunities for black people.[3]

As the nineteenth century closed, community spokesperson and journalist Fannie Barrier Williams cited strong social bonds and myriad new community organizations as evidence of greater civic consciousness in black Chicago. This development was consistent with Alexis de Tocqueville's view of the American proclivity for constant organizing in one's own interests.[4]

The First World War and frustration with the oppressive conditions in the Jim Crow South produced the Great Migration of black Americans to Chicago. There was dramatic demographic growth and development, most notably within the increasingly well-defined Black Belt on the city's South Side. There was also heightened community consciousness—led in part by veterans of the war—and a greater willingness to confront racism. Tensions with whites who felt threatened by this growing assertiveness among black people triggered the Chicago Race Riot of 1919. In addition, this era led to employment and business expansion and a desire for independent political action to extend the fullest benefits of citizenship. The immediate consequence of these trends was the heyday of the Black Metropolis during the 1920s, fueled by the conviction that a cohesive African American enclave within the broader city would advance the interests of black residents.[5]

That heyday was relatively short-lived, however. The Great Depression rocked black Chicago, and one unanticipated consequence was increased grassroots activism focused on economic parity and social justice. My book *The Depression Comes to the South Side* details an awakened black population mobilized for social change despite hard times. This period represented a turning point for black Chicagoans. They had once broadly embraced the "Dream of the Black Metropolis," with its voluntary separation; however, a growing segment of the black population began to realize that the dream of living in a segregated, self-contained community was unrealistic. The stress and economic chaos of the 1930s dispelled any notion of a sustainable black-controlled enclave.[6] Full equality was necessary, and in light of broad international, national, and local trends, it was beginning to seem achievable.[7]

"Chicago," Richard Wright once wrote, "is the city from which the most incisive and radical Negro thought has come."[8] St. Clair Drake and Horace Cayton developed this analysis in their classic *Black Metropolis: A Study of Negro Life in a Northern City,* published at the end of World War II. They wrote:

> Brought up sharply against the paradoxes of democracy, the Negro in this initial stage of the development of a line of action could do little more than articulate his discontent. But in the crucible of frustration and despair a new and positive line of thought was forged, which, if it could be implemented, would hold hope for black people and for the institution of democracy. This philosophy of a struggle for *complete equality* was not at variance with the expressed aims of the United Nations. This change in the Negro's mentality came about so rapidly that few people, even Negroes, realized its extent.[9]

The two decades preceding the alliance between the Coordinating Council of Community Organizations (CCCO) and the Southern Christian Leadership Conference provided both the underpinnings and new challenges for the Chicago Freedom Movement and its agenda of securing equality in housing and education. A preexisting level of civic activism, affecting all groups and classes of African Americans, helped accelerate the pace and energy of civil rights protests. A more egalitarian Chicago was envisioned and then demanded through various means, including civil disobedience. The massive effort to defeat the Axis powers coincided with a rising impulse to improve race relations in the United States.

Chicago in the mid-twentieth century began to offer opportunities that black Chicagoans were more than ready to embrace. Drake documented advances in employment, housing, and education in the postwar period in a postscript to *Black Metropolis*.[10] There was, moreover, increasing socioeconomic differentiation in black Chicago. Far South Side communities located beyond the boundaries of the Black Metropolis (designated Bronzeville in the late twentieth century) were growing.

Demands for change began emanating from Park Manor, Chatham, West Chesterfield, Burnside, and other middle-class South Side communities. Residents were raising concerns that went beyond the basic necessities of working- and lower-class life; they were focused on improved police protection and access to public housing as well as decent, affordable private housing.[11] The white power structure dominating all aspects of Chicago life was now forced to face previously ignorable challenges from an increasingly educated and activist African American community.

An energized Chicago Urban League, under the leadership of executive secretary Sidney Williams, along with small community groups and organizations such as the National Negro Congress, aggressively pushed for civil rights. Williams acted in the tradition of John Jones in his commitment to forge ahead in pursuit of emancipation, regardless of any adverse consequences. He targeted segregated housing and discriminatory employment practices before his "radical" activism led to his official dismissal from the Urban League.[12]

The Chicago NAACP was also more assertive in the postwar years. Labor advocates Henry W. McGee (president of the National Association of Postal Employees during the 1940s) and Willoughby Abner (a leader in the United Auto Workers Union during the 1950s) entered the NAACP's leadership ranks. Both men led the fight for a more egalitarian Chicago.[13]

For the NAACP to appeal to blacks, it had to present more than a theoretical concept of what America might become. In its early years, the NAACP's Chicago branch, which was founded in 1910, had to fight the unofficial policy (enforced by the public and private sectors) of black "containment." But racism was not limited to policies and practices. Black Chicago also had to deal with threats of violence and bombings designed to keep black home buyers and apartment dwellers from moving into all-white neighborhoods. Over the years, and despite what was described as the "elitist" attitude of some of its leaders, the branch eventually demonstrated to black working men and women that it existed for their benefit rather than for some unattainable theoretical goal. Support for the branch grew, but very gradually.[14]

One major housing triumph came in 1948, when the US Supreme Court struck down restrictive covenants in the famous *Shelley v. Kraemer* decision. The family of playwright Lorraine Hansberry courageously braved mobs and threats of violence to win a victory for hundreds of other families and individuals seeking better housing outside the confines of the Black Belt. Simultaneously, a handful of middle-class blacks were beginning to break the pattern of restrictive covenants prevalent throughout Chicago by quietly moving into a few white neighborhoods.[15]

Postwar black Chicago witnessed intense confrontation between activists and those who had a stake in the regional Democratic machine. As the city's premier civil rights organization, the Chicago NAACP clashed with the programs and desires of Illinois congressman William L. Dawson's rising Democratic machine. Dawson's plan for hegemony over black life focused on delivering jobs and services to blue-collar black Chicago. This plan offered benefits to the community, but it also accommodated the political wishes of the city's economic establishment and the Democratic machine under the control of Mayor Richard J. Daley. Dawson's reliance on conciliation as a means of racial advancement conflicted, by necessity, with progressive black Chicago's agenda of improved group status as manifested by better and open housing and quality schools.[16]

What emerged was a challenging coexistence between two major forces in Chicago's black community. Both sought black empowerment. In one camp were supporters of an integrationist thrust for civil rights. Their goal was to make the American Dream a reality for black Chicagoans as soon as possible. Among its proponents was the Chicago branch of the NAACP, the Chicago chapter of the National Negro Congress, the Congress of Racial Equality (CORE), and others, which represented a "militant" thrust. They supported doing away with the antidemocratic civic credo, an unofficial blueprint of racist public policy that emphasized maintaining the status quo of white hegemony in all areas of interracial contact.[17] The other notable force was the black political machine that was influenced—some would say directed—by the Cook County Democratic organization. There was a long history of black involvement in party and machine politics. In the early days, Republican Party loyalists had been the primary beneficiaries. After 1933, Democratic mayor Edward Kelly and the Cook County Democratic machine slowly induced the black electorate to abandon its allegiance to the Republican Party. By the late 1940s and early 1950s, Congressman Dawson was tapping this new Democratic bloc of votes. He aligned his powerful ward with the Democratic Daley administration and received the machine's support. These two contending forces sought the hearts and minds of the black community.[18]

The decade of the socially placid and prosperous 1950s was noted for its proliferation of opportunities for white America. Even in light of publicly "accepted" discriminatory practices, this period also brought advancement for the emerging black middle class as its members moved farther south, away from Dawson's political base of operations and his sway in the old Black Metropolis (now the revitalizing, multiracial Bronzeville district).[19] One hard-won success took place on the cusp of the national civil rights revolution. A few black politicians, the Chicago NAACP, the Chicago Urban League, unionists, and myriad other groups had fought for years to pass a fair employment practices bill in the Illinois General Assembly. Illinois finally passed a law in 1961 that outlawed overt discrimination based on race, after years of delay and collusion among Republicans, employers, and some unions.[20]

In the midst of the long struggle, any celebration of progress was tempered. The city's manufacturing base was undergoing dramatic changes. Black Chicago became increasingly distressed as, one by one, the stockyards and then the big meatpackers closed shop and headed to the West or into rural midwestern areas. Blue-collar, family-wage jobs were leaving the area. First, the Wilson Company eliminated its slaughtering operations by 1955 and ceased all activities by 1957. Armour shut down its operations in 1959. Swift followed during the early 1960s.[21]

The demise of the industry did not stop the persistent civil rights activism of the United Packinghouse Workers. And new developments in other parts of the city's economy promised a better future for black Chicagoans. Downtown department stores began to hire African American women to serve the general public from behind their counters, and some African Americans were admitted to the middle ranks of corporate management.[22]

By the mid-1950s, a new wave of civil rights activism had erupted across the South and in the North. In particular, the Chicago NAACP and its sometimes independent-acting Youth Councils challenged northern manifestations of Jim Crow. Beginning in 1953, at the Trumbull Park public housing development on the city's extreme southeastern edge, the NAACP encountered resistance to open housing. Hundreds of Chicago policemen protected a handful of black residents from violence and intimidation. Around the city, black homeowners braved threats and vandalism from resistant white neighbors as they broke free from the confines of the overcrowded Black Metropolis. Individual efforts, sometimes stimulated by ad hoc housing groups, aggressively sought housing opportunities in ownership and renting.[23]

At the same time, the destruction of many housing units within the old South Side's Douglas community (now the northernmost end of the recently designated Bronzeville community straddling King Drive [old South Parkway] from 2600 South to 3500 South) displaced many African American families. Replacing black residents were institutions deemed by downtown political and civic interests to be the salvation of the area immediately south of the Loop. The revitalized Mercy and Michael Reese Hospitals, along with the expanding Illinois Institute of Technology, complemented the construction of the modern Lake Meadows and Prairie Shores apartment complexes along the lakefront. The black-led Property Conservation Commission and smaller ad hoc groups spearheaded the resistance, which was unsuccessful.[24] Unfortunately, urban renewal in Chicago translated into the removal of hundreds of black residents.

In education, the Chicago NAACP led the fight against de facto segregation in the Chicago public schools. The Chicago Board of Education and Mayor Daley held to their commitment to keep the city as white as possible. Empty classrooms in all-white neighborhoods sat within miles and sometimes blocks of overcrowded, predominantly black schools. This spectacle of northern discrimination in public education resulted in double and triple shifts for black students at some of the overcrowded South Side schools. The Chicago branch of the NAACP unofficially investigated the situation school by school, and in 1957 it released its incisive report titled "De Facto Segregation in Chicago Public Schools."[25] This egregious situation made national headlines, and *US News & World Report* carried an analysis of the crisis, much to the embarrassment of Chicago officials.[26] Local hearings ensued, but little was resolved, and almost nothing changed.

In 1961–1962, for the middle-class residents of the Burnside community on the Far South Side, located adjacent to West Chesterfield (twelve miles south of the Loop), overcrowding at the Gillespie School was remedied by having black children attend a white school to the west. There, the pupils encountered segregated seating and classrooms filled with up to forty-nine children each. A protest led by black women was followed by court action. Elsewhere in the city, the construction of mobile classroom facilities for black children, dubbed "Willis wagons" after Superintendent Benjamin Willis, resulted in ire and street-level protests from African American parents.[27]

Blacks and some whites contested the discriminatory management of public recreation space during this period. At Calumet Park on the city's Far South Side, African American picnickers faced violent mobs in 1957 and were warned not to return to established all-white recreational areas. Similar assaults took place at Rainbow Beach on Seventy-Ninth Street around 1958 and again in 1960. The NAACP Youth Councils from the South and West Sides joined with students from the University of Chicago to tackle the problem head-on. Eventually, after some verbal and physical scuffles, the beach was finally opened to the public.[28]

Amid rising racial tensions, riots involving hundreds of persons broke out in black areas of the West and South Sides. Eventually, voices calling for nonviolent activism began to emerge. In 1962 African Americans, along with some white assistance, formed a federated movement under the rubric of CCCO to mount a comprehensive assault on school inequality.[29] Just as the historical roots of protest activism in black Chicago reached back to the previous century, a sense of national solidarity around the issue of equality under the law strengthened in the African American psyche. Whether influenced by the weekly *Chicago Defender*, with its national reach, or the new marvel of television, activist Chicagoans were further stirred by developments in the South. The Supreme Court's 1954 *Brown v. Board of Education* decision encouraged them, and the 1955 murder of fourteen-year-old Chicagoan Emmett Till in Mississippi incensed them. The Montgomery bus boycott influenced local residents to pressure the Chicago-based company that administered the bus lines in Alabama to yield to black demands. Soon afterward, the sit-in explosion of 1960, the Freedom Rides the following year, the Birmingham civil rights demonstrations, the epic 1963 March on Washington (which attracted the support of more than 2,000 black and white Chicagoans), and passage of the Civil Rights Act of 1964 further inspired area activists.[30]

Sensing the enormity of their cause and the need to act decisively, progressive forces focused on inequality in the schools. Following a plan devised by Lawrence Landry of Friends of SNCC (Student Nonviolent Coordinating Committee), CCCO staged two major school boycotts in October 1963 and February 1964—the first involving 225,000 students and the second 175,000. In a celebratory mood on the eve of enactment of the Civil Rights Act of 1964, 75,000 citizens assembled in Chicago's Soldier Field for a civil rights rally that featured Martin Luther King.[31]

But despite this impressive level of activism, Chicago's racist policies and practices seemed impervious to substantial change. In the summer of 1965 CCCO appealed to Dr. King to come to town and bring his SCLC apparatus to bear on local conditions for an intensive campaign. He received a guarantee of support from CCCO, which had expanded into approximately fifty neighborhood, community, civil rights, and other affiliated groups. King's willingness to plunge into Chicago's racial cauldron and stage a campaign in the city raised expectations and sharpened the need for an organizational focus that could directly attack the ruthlessness of localized racism and the Machiavellian tactics of Mayor Daley's political machine.[32]

The story of the Chicago Freedom Movement is the subject of the rest of this book. What is clear here is that the emergence of the Chicago

Freedom Movement in the mid-1960s—with its vision of an egalitarian Chicago—was a logical result of the long fight for full citizenship rights extending back to abolitionist-era Chicago.

Notes

1. Manning Marable, *Race, Reform and Rebellion: The Second Reconstruction in Black America, 1945–1982* (Jackson: University Press of Mississippi, 1984), 13.

2. Christopher Robert Reed, *Black Chicago's First Century*, vol. 1, *1833–1900* (Columbia: University of Missouri Press, 2005), 35–110.

3. Ibid., 110–435; Paula J. Giddings, *Ida: A Sword among Lions: Ida B. Wells and the Campaign against Lynching* (New York: Amistad, 2008).

4. Fannie Barrier Williams, "Social Bonds in the 'Black Belt' of Chicago," *Charities*, October 15, 1905, 40–44. See also Mary Jo Deegan, ed., *The New Woman of Color: The Collected Writings of Fannie Barrier Williams* (De Kalb: Northern Illinois University Press, 2002), and Wanda A. Hendricks, *Fannie Barrier Williams: Crossing the Borders of Region and Race* (Urbana: University of Illinois Press, 2013).

5. Christopher Robert Reed, *The Rise of Chicago's Black Metropolis, 1920–1929* (Urbana: University of Illinois Press, 2011); Christopher Robert Reed, "Black Chicago Civic Organization before 1935," *Journal of Ethnic Studies* 14 (Winter 1987): 65–77; Reed, *Black Chicago's First Century*, 436–44. See also William M. Tuttle Jr., *Race Riot: Chicago in the Red Summer of 1919* (New York: Atheneum, 1970), and James R. Grossman, *Land of Hope: Chicago, Black Southerners, and the Great Migration* (Chicago: University of Chicago Press, 1989).

6. Christopher Robert Reed, *The Depression Comes to the South Side: Protest and Politics in the Black Metropolis, 1930–1933* (Bloomington: Indiana University Press, 2011).

7. St. Clair Drake and Horace R. Cayton, *Black Metropolis: A Study of Negro Life in a Northern City* (New York: Harcourt, Brace, 1945), 754, 759–61, 764–67.

8. Quoted in ibid., xvii.

9. Ibid., 763, emphasis added.

10. St. Clair Drake, as the more academically active coauthor of *Black Metropolis*, updated the conditions under which blacks lived in the two decades after the book's publication by adding three appendices to a two-volume Harper Books paperback edition: *Black Metropolis Updated; Bronzeville 1961* and *Black Metropolis 1969*. The importance of midcentury black Chicago is developed in Adam Green, *Selling the Race: Culture, Community, and Black Chicago, 1940–1955* (Chicago: University of Chicago Press, 2006).

11. Robert Gruenberg, "Dawson of Illinois: What Price Moderation?" *Nation,* September 8, 1956, 197–98. See also James Q. Wilson, *Negro Politics: The Search for Leadership* (New York: Free Press, 1958). Wilson differentiated between the values, status, and training of the black middle class that the postwar era demanded as necessary for them to enjoy their lives fully as first-class citizens and those of the laboring classes. The laboring classes were situated disadvantageously in American society and sought to meet their needs, which Wilson identified as welfare-related needs that could be met through employment, housing, and education. In Congressman William L. Dawson's mind, these latter needs warranted a priority status along both pragmatic and political lines.

12. See Christopher Robert Reed, *The Chicago NAACP and the Rise of Black Professional Leadership, 1910–1966* (Bloomington: Indiana University Press, 1997); Arvarh E. Strickland, *History of the Chicago Urban League* (Urbana: University of Illinois Press, 1967); Erik S. Gellman, *Death Blow to Jim Crow: The National Negro Congress and the Rise of Militant Civil Rights* (Chapel Hill: University of North Carolina Press, 2012); and Rick Halpern, *Down on the Killing Floor: Black and White Workers in Chicago's Packinghouses, 1904–54* (Urbana: University of Illinois Press, 1997), 167–246.

13. Reed, *Chicago NAACP,* 128–91.

14. Ibid., 1–191.

15. See ibid., 100, 120, and James R. Ralph Jr., *Northern Protest: Martin Luther King, Jr., Chicago, and the Civil Rights Movement* (Cambridge, MA: Harvard University Press, 1993), 14–15. See also Lorraine Hansberry, *A Raisin in the Sun* (New York: Random House, 1959), which draws on her family's experience of moving to a white neighborhood.

16. Reed, *Chicago NAACP,* 159–91. See also Christopher Manning, *William L. Dawson and the Limits of Black Electoral Leadership* (De Kalb: Northern Illinois Press, 2009), and Jeffrey Helgeson, *Crucibles of Black Empowerment: Chicago's Neighborhood Politics from the New Deal to Harold Washington* (Chicago: University of Chicago Press, 2014), 248–52.

17. Alan B. Anderson and George W. Pickering, *Confronting the Color Line: The Broken Promise of the Civil Rights Movement in Chicago* (Athens: University of Georgia Press, 1986); interview with militant activist Robert Lucas, discussing CORE, in Dempsey J. Travis, *An Autobiography of Black Chicago* (Chicago: Urban Research Institute, 1981), 247–48. See also Arnold R. Hirsch, *Making of the Second Ghetto: Race and Housing in Chicago, 1940–1960* (Cambridge: Cambridge University Press, 1983), which discusses the race-oriented public policy that stymied progress in open housing in the public and private spheres.

18. Reed, *Chicago NAACP,* 186–91.

19. According to Anderson and Pickering, the years 1957 through 1967 were "the most active" in terms of civil rights in Chicago. *Confronting the Color Line,* 1.

20. Ralph, *Northern Protest*, 11; Duane Lockard, *Toward Equal Opportunity: A Study of State and Local Antidiscrimination Laws* (New York: Macmillan, 1968), 24–27.

21. Rick Halpern and Roger Horowitz, eds., *Meatpackers: An Oral History of Black Packinghouse Workers and Their Struggle for Racial and Economic Equality* (New York: Twayne, 1996), 62.

22. Steven M. Gelber, *Black Men and Businessmen: The Growing Awareness of a Social Responsibility* (Port Washington, NY: Kennikat Press, 1974), 46–51, 83–84.

23. Reed, *Chicago NAACP*, 152–56.

24. Interview with Ida M. Cress, in *Bridges of Memory: Chicago's First Wave of Black Migration*, comp. and ed. Timuel D. Black (Evanston, IL: Northwestern University Press, 2003), 85–86. See also the interview with Bishop Arthur Brazier, ibid., 551.

25. Chicago Branch of the NAACP, "De Facto Segregation in Chicago Public Schools," ca. summer 1957, Papers of the NAACP, Library of Congress, Washington, DC.

26. "NAACP on Local Schools: Segregation Is Increasing," *US News & World Report*, December 13, 1957, 88–89.

27. Ralph, *Northern Protest*, 15–19.

28. Victoria W. Wolcott, *Race, Riots, and Roller Coasters: The Struggle over Segregated Recreation in America* (Philadelphia: University of Pennsylvania Press, 2012), 174–76.

29. Anderson and Pickering, *Confronting the Color Line*, 2.

30. See Green, *Selling the Race*, 179–212; William P. Jones, *The March on Washington: Jobs, Freedom and the Forgotten Years of Civil Rights Struggle* (New York: W. W. Norton, 2013).

31. Ralph, *Northern Protest*, 23, 39.

32. Ibid., 2.

Part 3

The Impact of the
Chicago Freedom Movement

4

The Chicago Freedom Movement and the Federal Fair Housing Act

Leonard S. Rubinowitz

> If out of [the Chicago Freedom Movement] came a fair housing bill,
> just as we got a public accommodations bill out of Birmingham and a
> right to vote out of Selma, the Chicago movement was a success, and
> a documented success.
>
> —Jesse Jackson Sr.

In a 1965 interview Martin Luther King Jr. said: "I don't feel that the
Civil Rights Act has gone far *enough* in some of its coverage. . . . We need
a strong and strongly enforced fair housing section such as many states
already have."[1] By the middle of 1966, the Chicago Freedom Movement
had decided to target racial discrimination and segregation in the city's
housing market. That summer witnessed a direct action campaign aimed
at white neighborhoods that excluded African Americans—starting with
testing for racial discrimination and vigils at real estate offices, and escalating into a series of marches into white neighborhoods to dramatize their
exclusionary character. The leaders hoped their Chicago initiative would
provide a model for similar campaigns in other northern cities.

Here, I focus on another goal of the Chicago Freedom Movement:
to raise the nation's awareness of housing discrimination and to press
Congress to enact the pending corrective legislation—a target Dr. King
had identified a year earlier. I argue that the Chicago Freedom Movement contributed to both the initial failure to secure passage of a federal
fair-housing law in 1966 and the eventual success in 1968. Ironically, the
movement made an unlikely prospect—passage of fair-housing legisla-

tion in 1966—even more unlikely. But when Congress managed to enact a fair-housing law in 1968, the Chicago Freedom Movement, through a series of indirect efforts, contributed to its surprising passage. This chapter shows how that happened.

From the outset of the discussions about targeting housing discrimination, Martin Luther King Jr. and others had viewed national legislation as at least a secondary goal of the movement. When announcing the Chicago plan, King stated, "Our objectives in this movement are federal, state and local. On the federal level we would hope to get the kind of comprehensive legislation which would meet the problems of slum life across the nation."[2] Just as the movement in Birmingham had influenced the introduction of the Civil Rights Act in 1964 and the Selma march had been instrumental in passage of the Voting Rights Act in 1965, King hoped the Chicago movement's shining a light on housing discrimination would lead to federal legislation that specifically addressed open housing.[3]

In an effort to escalate the movement, activists began a series of larger marches into white neighborhoods on the Southwest and Northwest Sides of the city—neighborhoods that were some distance away from the African American community and where African American home buyers and renters were clearly unwelcome. Like the marchers in Alabama—in the cities of Birmingham in 1963 and Selma in 1965—the Chicago marchers were met with violent resistance, but this time the violence came from white bystanders rather than the police. Mayor Richard J. Daley was determined not to turn the demonstrators into martyrs by using the force of the police against them, but marchers in Gage Park (on the city's Southwest Side) and later in Belmont-Cragin (on the Northwest Side) encountered crowds throwing rocks, bottles, cherry bombs, pieces of coal, and even knives. On occasion, white mobs burned, overturned, or pushed marchers' parked cars into nearby bodies of water, such as the lagoon in Marquette Park. King said he had "never seen as much hatred and hostility on the part of so many people."[4] This violence drew the national press to Chicago, and people across the country were once again exposed to the horrific violence encountered by peaceful civil rights demonstrators.

Locally, the marches had serious negative consequences for Mayor Daley—a powerful leader who viewed Chicago as "his" city. For him, the demonstrations represented an unacceptable loss of control of his city and exacted a substantial political cost. Blacks and working-class ethnic whites constituted two of the major voting blocs that had helped bring him to office and kept him there. The marches pitted these two crucial constituencies against each other, with potentially disastrous consequences for the mayor. White homeowners criticized him for permitting the marches to continue and for the rough treatment they received at the hands of the police.

By mid-August, there had been several confrontations between the marchers and mobs of thousands of angry, jeering, violent onlookers. Mayor Daley was desperate to end the disruption on the streets of his city, so as a strategic step, he agreed to negotiate with the Chicago Freedom Movement. He made it very clear that his primary purpose in meeting with movement leaders and negotiating an agreement with them was to end the marches. On August 26, 1966, the parties reached what came to be called the Summit Agreement, which included a commitment from the Chicago Commission on Human Relations to enforce the city's 1963 open-housing ordinance, an agreement from Mayor Daley to advocate for state open-occupancy legislation the following year, and a general agreement from the Chicago Real Estate Board to withdraw its opposition to open housing and to urge its members to obey the law. The agreement did not contain any timetable for the various actions specified, nor did it include any enforcement provisions. With this agreement, King announced the end of the marches—Mayor Daley's primary objective.

After the Summit Agreement was signed in August 1966, King made plans to leave Chicago. While he talked of monitoring compliance and renewing activities in the city if the parties did not meet their commitments, there was little substance to those threats. At the same time, the movement left behind the nonprofit Leadership Council for Metropolitan Open Communities, which spent the next several decades pursuing the fair-housing goals of the Summit Agreement.[5] The dramatic phase of the Chicago Freedom Movement had ended, and fair-housing legislation remained in limbo.

Meanwhile, in early 1966 President Lyndon Johnson had asked Congress to enact fair-housing legislation as part of a larger civil rights package. In April he introduced a bill to the same Congress that had passed the landmark Voting Rights Act the year before. Yet the new bill was unsuccessful in 1966 and again in 1967. In 1966 the House passed a modest fair-housing bill that covered about 40 percent of the nation's housing. In the Senate the president's proposal encountered the same southern filibuster that had greeted his initiatives the previous two years. However, unlike with the Civil Rights Act of 1964 and the Voting Rights Act of 1965, the effort to invoke cloture to end the filibuster and bring the bill to a vote of the full Senate failed. The bill died.

By 1966, public support for civil rights had waned. With passage of the Voting Rights Act, much of the country thought Congress had addressed all the major civil rights concerns and should move on to other issues. Others thought the country had already gone too far in responding to African American protests. Much of this attitude shift stemmed from white resistance to efforts to desegregate the North, as well as growing frustration with urban riots and hostility toward the growing Black Power movement.[6]

Fair-housing legislation faced particularly tough sledding because of the national scope of the bill. Previous civil rights statutes had affected primarily the South, so legislators and their constituents in much of the country were largely untouched by their passage. In the mid-1960s housing discrimination and segregation were more pervasive outside the South. If anything, fair-housing legislation would have a greater impact in the North and West than in the South, making the bill especially controversial. Worse yet, 1966 was an election year, so members of Congress were unlikely to take on any controversial matters.

Other forces almost certainly would have prevented the enactment of a fair-housing law in 1966, but the Chicago Freedom Movement inadvertently undermined efforts to pass the bill. President Johnson had used his official position, as well as his exceptional political skills, to push the 1964 Civil Rights Act and the Voting Rights Act through Congress, but he made no such effort in 1966. The Chicago Freedom Movement contributed to the president's lack of engagement, largely because of his sharply contrasting relationships with the main protagonists—Mayor Daley and Dr. King. Several other factors also played a part in the president's relatively passive approach, including his preoccupation with the war in Vietnam, his declining popularity, and, as mentioned earlier, the disruption caused by the violence in several major cities and the decreasing public support for civil rights legislation in a congressional election year.

President Johnson took few steps, either publicly or privately, to try to move the 1966 fair-housing bill through Congress. He walked a fine line by proposing progressive legislation—maintaining his image as a civil rights supporter—but not putting his political weight behind it—avoiding the impression that he was controlled by civil rights leaders. Events on the streets of Chicago contributed to Johnson's lack of aggressiveness in pursuing fair-housing legislation. He expressed no public support for the Chicago Freedom Movement, and privately, he expressed strong opposition to the marches and the violence they provoked. Johnson's response to the Chicago Freedom Movement reflected both his growing closeness to Mayor Daley and his increasing distance from Dr. King.[7]

The close political and personal relationship between President Johnson and Mayor Daley precluded the possibility of the president repeating his earlier approach and arguing for civil rights legislation. In 1965 President Johnson had made explicit reference to the police violence against marchers in Selma when he urged the country to support, and Congress to pass, the Voting Rights Act. In an address to Congress on March 15, he had condemned the violence in Selma, promised a voting rights bill, and associated himself with the southern civil rights movement when he ended his speech with the civil rights battle cry, declaring, "We shall overcome." Johnson had used similar tactics to ensure passage of the 1964 Civil Rights Act in the wake of police violence against protesters in Birmingham.[8]

Thus, in the past the president had made good use of the violence perpetrated against nonviolent demonstrators in arguing for civil rights legislation. He could have done so once again in pressing for fair-housing legislation. But the political and personal implications of Selma and Chicago were vastly different for President Johnson. Even though state and local elected officials in Alabama belonged to the president's party, he could attack the law enforcement leadership publicly, with little short-term political cost. Not so in Chicago, where the mayor was a crucial political ally and friend of the president. It was inconceivable for Johnson to point to the violence inflicted on civil rights demonstrators in Chicago, which would have embarrassed and alienated Daley. Johnson did not want, nor could he afford, to risk disrupting his relationship with Daley, who was undoubtedly the most powerful big-city mayor in the country. Johnson needed his support, and he worked hard to get it and maintain it. Daley actively supported Johnson's legislative agenda, while Johnson helped Daley get federal funding for Chicago—on Daley's terms.[9]

At the time of the Chicago Freedom Movement's marches, Johnson was contemplating a run for reelection, which would have required Daley's strong support. Johnson recognized, according to James Ralph, "that it would be politically insane for a Democratic President with aspirations for another term to meddle in a crisis in a city governed by the most powerful Democratic mayor in the country."[10] He certainly did not want the mayor to turn on him and oppose his reelection.

Instead, Johnson privately supported Daley's handling of the threats posed by the Chicago Freedom Movement. As suggested earlier, the Chicago Freedom Movement's strategy and tactics raised the ire of Mayor Daley, and he shared with the president his anger and frustration. During the course of the open-housing marches in the summer of 1966, Daley and Johnson had a number of private telephone conversations about events in the city.[11] Daley consistently criticized the movement, and Johnson repeatedly expressed his sympathy and support for Daley in the face of what the mayor described as highly disruptive and costly demonstrations.[12]

In addition to his conversations with the mayor, Johnson received reports from his staff about events in Chicago that summer.[13] He also sent a team of high-level administration officials to observe what was happening on the ground and report back to him.[14] In short, President Johnson kept himself extremely well informed about the Chicago Freedom Movement.

At the same time, the growing political and personal divide between President Johnson and Dr. King adversely affected Johnson's views about the Chicago Freedom Movement and his willingness to aggressively pursue fair-housing legislation. Johnson and King had worked together on both the Civil Rights Act of 1964 and the Voting Rights Act; there was, however, always a tension between them, in part because of their very different personalities. Johnson was brash and outspoken, while King was soft-spoken and modest. Notwithstanding their differences, they maintained a mutually respectful and constructive—if somewhat distant—relationship during Johnson's early years in the White House.[15]

By the time of the Chicago Freedom Movement, Johnson had become increasingly disenchanted with King. Daley knew about the tension between them and exploited it in seeking the president's support in the summer of 1966. The growing distance between Johnson and King arose from both strategic and political differences. Most important, King had begun to speak out publicly against the Vietnam War. In August 1965, less than a week after the president signed the Voting Rights Act, King felt that he could no longer keep silent about his opposition to the war. Johnson considered King's public antiwar statements a betrayal that ruptured an already tenuous and tense relationship. The president was especially outraged because he had worked so hard to get the landmark civil rights legislation through Congress.[16] Although King later softened his criticism of the war, much of the damage to his relationship with the president had already been done.[17] As a result, the Chicago Freedom Movement helped ensure a passive President Johnson in 1966.

While the House of Representatives passed a limited fair-housing bill in the summer of 1966, Senate opponents filibustered the bill to death. The events in Chicago had multiple effects. For supporters of fair housing, what happened on the streets of Chicago reinforced their belief in the need for federal legislation. The demonstrations also strengthened the concerns of those seeking to preserve the racial status quo. Many moderates who had supported change in the South had a much different view when the movement moved north. Although the Chicago Freedom Movement did not receive nearly as much media and public attention as Selma did, the movement contributed to the opposition among legislators. According to Justice Department official Roger Wilkins, "The most significant and best publicized opposition to the fair housing bill was . . . based on the opposition to 'conduct,' i.e., the marches of the Chicago Freedom Movement through white neighborhoods in Chicago."[18]

Much of the civil rights legislation of the 1960s had the support of a majority of the Senate; however, a coalition of segregationist southern Democrats and conservative Republicans repeatedly used the filibuster to block a full Senate vote. Thus, the filibuster was a potent weapon and a major obstacle to enacting civil rights legislation. The two-thirds vote required for cloture could be achieved only if Republicans joined with nonsouthern Democrats in sufficient numbers, paving the way for the majority of the senators in favor of civil rights legislation to vote for it.

As a result, Senate minority leader Everett Dirksen, a Republican from Illinois, played a critical role in all the civil rights legislation of the 1960s. He was a powerful minority leader who had great influence with Senate Republicans, and he was the only person capable of securing enough Republican votes for cloture to avoid a legislation-killing filibuster. Dirksen had established a pattern of withholding his support until late in the process, negotiating changes in bills that were favorable to his interests— especially mitigating their impact on the North—and then securing the Republican votes required for cloture. He also had a close political and personal relationship with President Johnson, which made his role in civil rights legislation even more crucial. The Johnson administration turned to Dirksen for support in 1966, just as it had in previous years.[19]

Early on, Senator Dirksen had expressed his strong opposition to the fair-housing bill. He argued that it was an unconstitutional intrusion on property rights and exceeded the power of Congress under the Fourteenth Amendment and the Commerce Clause. The Chicago Freedom Movement's marches into white neighborhoods hardened Dirksen's opposition to fair-housing legislation, and he blamed the marchers for the violence they encountered.[20]

The 1966 civil rights bill died in September, and it failed again in 1967. Despite its expected defeat in 1968, the bill finally made it through Congress. Explanations abound for this surprising turnaround, including President Johnson's greater resolve to get it passed, the election of several moderate Republican senators, Dirksen's last-minute switch to support cloture, and the demand for some kind of legislative action in the aftermath of Martin Luther King's assassination. There is, however, substantial evidence that the Chicago movement was one of a constellation of factors that contributed to the surprise passage of the Fair Housing Act in April 1968. In spite of its mixed short-term effects on efforts to pass fair-housing legislation, the Chicago movement's lingering positive impact came to the fore in 1968.

By 1968, the situation had changed. The Chicago Freedom Movement itself had long since disbanded, and the key players had left Chicago. In February 1967 the president's staff reported to him that Dr. King had departed the city, and the demonstrations there had ended.[21] This meant that Johnson could pursue fair-housing legislation without the risk of embarrassing and alienating Mayor Daley. Finally, King's assassination provided an opportunity for the president to call for prompt passage of the fair-housing act as a step toward fulfilling King's dream of racial equality.

In early 1968 President Johnson pressed for fair-housing legislation with an aggressiveness he had not shown previously. With his in-depth knowledge of the Chicago Freedom Movement of 1966, it is safe to assume that events in Chicago were in the back of his mind as he used his extraordinary political skills to sway both the Senate and the House of Representatives. He negotiated with senators who could provide the votes to end the filibuster and bring the bill to a vote. In the House, he urged acceptance of the Senate bill in response to King's assassination. As King had argued even before going to Chicago, and as the Chicago Freedom Movement had demonstrated, fair-housing legislation was a critical piece missing from President Johnson's commitment to racial equality.

As they had previously, opponents in the Senate used the filibuster to try to prevent a full Senate vote on what became the Civil Rights Act of 1968. As discussed earlier, fair-housing opponents had engineered a successful filibuster in 1966, even using the Chicago Freedom Movement as fodder for their opposition. Virtually all observers expected the same result in 1968.[22]

Early in 1968 Senator Dirksen still seemed unalterably opposed to federal fair-housing legislation. His continued opposition probably would have doomed the bill, but at the last minute, Dirksen changed his mind. He saw that the Fair Housing Act could be a vehicle for reducing urban violence—a critical task for Congress to undertake. In announcing his new position, he also expressed concern that African American Vietnam veterans could face housing discrimination upon their return, which he wished to prevent through federal legislation. As a senator from Illinois, Dirksen was well aware of the Chicago Freedom Movement, and notwithstanding his objection to its methods, the violent reaction to peaceful marches had made him more conscious of the depth and breadth of housing discrimination throughout the country.[23]

Whether because of Dirksen's changed position or independently of it, several moderate Republicans joined the supporters of cloture. One of them was Illinois's other senator, the recently elected Charles Percy. Percy had defeated incumbent Paul Douglas in a race in which the Chicago Freedom Movement had been a central issue. Like Dirksen, Percy had become aware of the problem of housing discrimination through events in Chicago. With these last-minute shifts, there were just enough votes to end the filibuster on the final try. Once the bill got to the Senate floor, it passed easily. Thus, when King was assassinated on April 4, 1968, the fair-housing bill had already passed in the Senate and had been debated in the House. It was passed by the House six days later and signed into law by President Johnson on April 11, 1968.

The assassination of Martin Luther King demanded prompt action by the federal government for both symbolic and practical reasons. The nation was in mourning, and congressional action represented a unifying statement about the collective loss the country had suffered. At the same time, African American communities in scores of cities, including the nation's capital, erupted in violence in the aftermath of the assassination. Some members of Congress believed that a legislative response would help address the frustrations that had triggered the violence and would restore calm and order in those communities.[24]

Ironically, President Johnson's call for Congress to enact the fair-housing bill in the wake of King's assassination may have been rooted implicitly in the Chicago Freedom Movement. The best evidence that enactment of a fair-housing law would help fulfill King's dream was the campaign he had waged against housing discrimination and segregation in Chicago during the summer of 1966. Moreover, when the bill had died in 1966, King had expressed the depth of his disappointment and his concern about the consequences, lamenting, "The executioners of the 1966 civil rights bill have given valuable assistance to those forces in the Negro communities who counsel violence. Although I will continue to preach with all my might the moral rightness of nonviolence, my words are now bound to fall on deaf ears."[25]

Supporters of the fair-housing bill used the tragedy of King's assassination to press the House for its passage. One civil rights expert suggests that President Johnson and the House of Representatives focused on open-housing legislation as a memorial to Dr. King.[26] It was the Chicago Freedom Movement that first associated King in the public eye with the issue of housing discrimination and the goal of federal fair-housing legislation. So there was a logic, or at least a political rationale, for using passage of the Fair Housing Act as a way to memorialize him.

Reflecting back on this period decades later, Joseph Califano, President Johnson's special assistant for domestic affairs, recalled: "By March 1968 there was still no hope of passage in the House. The morning after King was assassinated, President Johnson called me into his office and said, 'At least we're going to get our fair housing bill. I'm asking the speaker [John McCormack] and minority leader [Gerald Ford] to pass the Senate bill today.' He worked the phones, citing this as a last tribute to King."[27]

The day after the assassination, President Johnson urged prompt passage of the Civil Rights Act of 1968, including the fair-housing provisions. He suggested that this would be a way of continuing King's work. The fair-housing bill provided an opportunity for Congress to act quickly on a measure that could be linked directly to King's agenda. Before, during, and after the Chicago Freedom Movement, King had cited the importance of enacting federal fair-housing legislation. That movement was the one time in King's career that he focused primarily on the issue of fair housing, and his leadership of that movement made it credible to invoke his name and his memory in pressing for passage of the Fair Housing Act in the immediate aftermath of his death. Moreover, just a few months before his death, King had reiterated his support for fair-housing legislation in his testimony before the National Advisory Commission on Civil Disorders.[28]

However, quick passage would require House concurrence with the Senate version of the bill, rather than approval of its own version, followed by a Conference Committee to resolve the differences between the two. That would have resulted in delay, at least, and perhaps even another Senate filibuster and ultimate defeat. Proponents of the bill argued for concurrence with the Senate version, which would send the bill to the president for his signature.

It is unclear how much of an impact King's assassination had on the House decision to concur with the Senate's version of the bill. It was certainly on the minds of members of Congress as they debated the issue.[29]

It is not a large inferential step to suggest that Dr. King's work in Chicago less than two years before his death was also on their minds as they moved the Fair Housing Act toward passage. Once again, one of the key legislators was from Illinois: Republican congressman John Anderson from the Chicago-area community of Rockford. He, too, was well aware of the discrimination laid bare by the Chicago Freedom Movement when he cast the deciding committee vote to concur with the Senate bill rather than consider a House version of the bill.[30]

Just as cloture in the Senate had been achieved by the narrowest of margins, the House Rules Committee approved concurrence with the Senate version by one vote. After approval by the full House, President Johnson signed the Fair Housing Act into law just a week after the death of the leader of so many movements reverberating across the nation— including the Chicago Freedom Movement.

Many factors contributed to the failure of the fair-housing bill in 1966 and its ultimate passage two years later. As such, it is extremely difficult to isolate a single factor, such as the Chicago Freedom Movement, and assess the role it played in each case. At the same time, the evidence suggests that the movement had an impact in both 1966 and 1968. Ironically, the movement's marches in Chicago undermined efforts to secure passage in 1966, an unintended consequence that was directly contrary to the hopes of the movement's leaders. Mayor Daley's opposition to the movement hindered it nationally as well as locally, given his close relationship with President Johnson. Moreover, the violent resistance to the nonviolent marches in Chicago failed to generate the kind of strong public and congressional support that violence perpetrated against southern civil rights activists had produced in previous years.

Yet, in still another ironic twist, the Chicago Freedom Movement had the opposite effect—the originally intended one—when fair-housing legislation was ultimately passed in 1968. The movement had raised the consciousness of the major players, highlighting the depth and breadth of housing discrimination. By that time, the movement in Chicago had ended, and Mayor Daley was no longer an obstacle to President Johnson's pressing for passage. Dr. King was assassinated while the bill was under consideration, and the political situation had changed just enough to permit congressional action. With this act, yet another piece of the civil rights leader's dream had been realized.

Notes

The epigraph is from *The Chicago Freedom Movement—Activists Sound Off*, Chicago Public Radio broadcast, August 23, 2006, available at http://audio.wbez .org/848/2006/08/848_20060823c.mp3.

1. James M. Washington, ed., *A Testament of Hope: The Essential Writings and Speeches of Martin Luther King, Jr.* (New York: Harper San Francisco, 1991), 352–53.

2. Press release, Martin Luther King Jr., Southern Christian Leadership Conference, "The Chicago Plan," January 7, 1966, quoted in Ronald E. Shaw, "A Final Push for National Legislation: The Chicago Freedom Movement," *Journal of Illinois State Historical Society* 94 (Autumn 2001): 318. On July 11, at the first meeting with Mayor Daley after the kickoff of the campaign, the mayor refused to "announce his support for President . . . Johnson's civil rights bill that was pending in Congress." Roger Biles, *Richard J. Daley: Politics, Race, and the Governing of Chicago* (De Kalb: Northern Illinois University Press, 1995), 124.

3. See Alan B. Anderson and George W. Pickering, *Confronting the Color Line: The Broken Promise of the Civil Rights Movement in Chicago* (Athens: University of Georgia Press, 1986), 190; Adam Fairclough, *To Redeem the Soul of America: The Southern Christian Leadership Conference and Martin Luther King, Jr.* (Athens: University of Georgia Press, 1987), 133.

4. Quoted in James R. Ralph Jr., *Northern Protest: Martin Luther King, Jr., Chicago, and the Civil Rights Movement* (Cambridge, MA: Harvard University Press, 1993), 123.

5. See Adam Cohen and Elizabeth Taylor, *American Pharaoh: Mayor Richard J. Daley: His Battle for Chicago and the Nation* (Boston: Little, Brown, 2000), 423.

6. Ralph, *Northern Protest*, 174–75, 184, 186–88. "By 1966, [70] percent of whites [thought] that 'Negroes were trying to move too fast.'" Mara S. Sidney, "Images of Race, Class, and Markets: Rethinking the Origin of U.S. Fair Housing Policy," *Journal of Policy History* 13 (2001): 188, quoting James L. Sundquist, *Politics and Policy: The Eisenhower, Kennedy, and Johnson Years* (Washington, DC: Brookings Institution, 1968), 281. See also *Report of the National Advisory Commission on Civil Disorders* 38 (1988); Christopher Bonastia, *Knocking on the Door: The Federal Government's Attempt to Desegregate the Suburbs* (Princeton, NJ: Princeton University Press, 2006), 77.

7. Cohen and Taylor, *American Pharaoh*, 352. The relationship between Daley and Johnson had a rocky start—Daley had initially discouraged Kennedy

from choosing Johnson as his running mate. Once Johnson became president, however, he actively sought a rapport with Daley. Ibid., 267–70, 310, 323–24; Eugene Kennedy, *Himself! The Life and Times of Mayor Richard J. Daley* (New York: Viking Press, 1978), 171. Eventually, this rapport developed into a personal and political friendship. See Michael R. Beschloss, *Taking Charge: The Johnson White House Tapes, 1963–64* (New York: Simon & Schuster, 1997), 323–24.

8. David Garrow, *Protest at Selma: Martin Luther King, Jr. and the Voting Rights Act of 1965* (New Haven, CT: Yale University Press, 1978), 60–63.

9. Biles, *Richard J. Daley*, 148. According to Joseph Califano, Johnson's domestic adviser, "Daley was critical to the success of the Great Society [Johnson's major domestic initiative]. . . . A call to Daley was all that was needed to deliver the fourteen votes of the Illinois Democratic delegation. Johnson and the others of us had made many calls to the Mayor and Daley had always come through." Irving Bernstein, *Guns or Butter: The Presidency of Lyndon Johnson* (New York: Oxford University Press, 1996), 396.

10. Ralph, *Northern Protest*, 182.

11. Taylor Branch, *At Canaan's Edge: America in the King Years, 1965–68* (New York: Simon & Schuster, 2006), 506. In one of those conversations, Daley conflated King's movement with gang violence. Telephone conversation between Richard J. Daley, Mayor of Chicago, and Lyndon B. Johnson, US President, July 19, 1966, Lyndon B. Johnson Presidential Library and Museum, Austin, Texas.

12. Branch, *At Canaan's Edge*, 506. For instance, the president reassured Daley, saying, "There's nobody that loves you more than I do." In conversations with many politicians, Johnson did most of the talking. However, his reputation for arm-twisting, browbeating, and intimidation did not surface when he spoke with Mayor Daley. Instead, Johnson mostly listened as Daley relayed all his hopes and woes. Johnson said very little beyond expressing concern and support. Telephone conversation, July 19, 1966 (lasting more than twenty-two minutes).

13. Memorandum from Joseph Califano, Special Assistant for Domestic Affairs, to Lyndon Johnson, US President, July 15, 1966, Johnson Library.

14. Johnson sent both assistant attorney general John Doar and Community Relations Service director Roger Wilkins to Chicago, and they came away very impressed with King's work in the city. Nick Kotz, *Judgment Days: Lyndon Baines Johnson, Martin Luther King, Jr., and the Laws that Changed America* (New York: Houghton Mifflin Harcourt, 2005), 365–66.

15. Ibid., 278.

16. Robert Dallek, *Flawed Giant: Lyndon Johnson and His Times, 1961–1973* (New York: Oxford University Press, 1998), 467. In a telephone conversation on August 20, 1965, Johnson told King that members of Congress had "the impression that you are against me on Vietnam." Johnson warned, "You better not leave that impression . . . I want peace as much as you do. . . . Let's not let this country get divided." Kotz, *Judgment Days*, 345–46.

17. Kotz, *Judgment Days,* 371.

18. Quoted in Ralph, *Northern Protest,* 193–94.

19. Darren Miles, "The Art of the Possible: Everett Dirksen's Role in Civil Rights Legislation of the 1950s and 1960s," *Western Illinois History Review* 1 (Spring 2009): 86–87. See also Leonard Rubinowitz and Kathryn Shelton, "Non-Violent Direct Action and the Legislative Process: The Chicago Freedom Movement and the Federal Fair Housing Act," *Indiana Law Review* 41, no. 3 (2008): 702–4.

20. Ralph, *Northern Protest,* 192.

21. Memorandum from Nicholas deB. Katzenbach, US Attorney General, to Lyndon B. Johnson, US President, February 27, 1967, Johnson Library. For accounts of the ongoing struggle for fair housing after the Chicago Freedom Movement, see Patrick D. Jones, *The Selma of the North: Civil Rights Insurgency in Milwaukee* (Cambridge, MA: Harvard University Press, 2009), and Tracy E. K'Meyer, *Civil Rights in the Gateway for the South: Louisville, Kentucky, 1945–1980* (Lexington: University Press of Kentucky, 2009), 111–44.

22. Kotz, *Judgment Days,* 389; Jean Eberhart Dubofsky, "Fair Housing: A Legislative History and a Perspective," *Washburn Law Journal* 8, no. 2 (1969): 149. Unlike in 1966, the National Association of Real Estate Brokers did little lobbying before the Senate vote. Apparently, the organization was taken by surprise by the broad support this time around. Bonastia, *Knocking on the Door,* 87.

23. Rubinowitz and Shelton, "Non-Violent Direct Action and the Legislative Process," 709–10.

24. Florence Wagman Roisman, "Affirmatively Furthering Fair Housing in Regional Housing Markets: The Baltimore Public Housing Desegregation Litigation," *Wake Forest Law Review* 42, no. 2 (2007): 362–63.

25. Quoted in Bernstein, *Guns or Butter,* 392.

26. In July 2006 participants in the CFM held a national conference called Fulfilling the Dream, commemorating the fortieth anniversary of the movement. In his remarks at the conference, Northwestern University sociology professor Aldon Morris suggested that President Johnson and Congress focused on fair-housing legislation as an appropriate tribute to King after his assassination, given King's interest in the issue in Chicago in 1966.

27. Joseph A. Califano Jr., "It Took a Partnership," *Washington Post,* January 15, 2008, A13. See also David C. Carter, *The Music Has Gone out of the Movement: Civil Rights and the Johnson Administration, 1965–1968* (Chapel Hill: University of North Carolina Press, 2009).

28. MLK statement before the National Advisory Commission on Civil Disorders, October 23, 1967, 2791–92, http://www.thekingcenter.org/archive/document/mlk-statement-national-advisory-commission-civil-disorders.

29. See, for example, statement of Representative Albert W. Watson, in *To*

Prescribe Penalties for Certain Acts of Violence or Intimidation: Hearings on H.R. 1100 before the House Committee on Rules, 90th Cong. (1968), 56, 59–60.

30. James C. Harvey, *Black Civil Rights during the Johnson Administration* (Jackson: University of Mississippi College Press, 1973), 53.

5

The Leadership Council for Metropolitan Open Communities

Chicago and Fair Housing

Brian White

The Leadership Council for Metropolitan Open Communities (LCMOC) was a nonprofit fair-housing organization established as a direct result of the Chicago Freedom Movement. For nearly forty years it conducted fair-housing education, outreach, and legal action in the Chicago metropolitan region. It developed programs and techniques that were shared with other organizations across the city, region, and country. It leveraged its national profile, corporate board, and moral authority on issues of race to become recognized as the nation's preeminent fair-housing organization.

The Leadership Council ceased to exist in 2006 due to a lack of funding and a failure to adapt to changing times. To date, there has been no full-length analysis of the council's work, its impact, or the reasons for its success and its eventual decline and fall. Given the rich, diverse, and intertwined history of Chicago and LCMOC over the last half century, such an analysis would require a book-length treatment, not a single chapter. There are, however, a number of critical lessons to be learned from the Leadership Council that can inform our understanding of the impact of the Chicago Freedom Movement and fair housing, both historically and today. Those lessons are what I hope to convey.

In this chapter, I provide a brief look at Chicago prior to the Chicago Freedom Movement to illustrate the nature of housing, politics, and race in the city and region. I then summarize the history of LCMOC and its programs, highlighting a number of critical contributions it made. I also share my experiences as a senior staff member and explore the reasons for the organization's decline and fall, drawing on my firsthand perspective of its last few years of operation. My view is that the Chicago Freedom Movement was a success in part because it gave birth to the Leadership Council. I also firmly believe that despite its closure in 2006, the council was a success in terms of both the number of people it directly affected and the legacy of programs and practices it left behind. There is no doubt that fair housing would not be a mature part of the civil rights agenda without the Leadership Council, nor would Chicago have made as much progress in adopting an opportunity-based lens for addressing housing, land use, and many other policy issues.

History and Context: Pre-1966

Race has been a central feature in Chicago since at least the 1920s, when African Americans began to relocate there from southern cities and towns seeking jobs, political freedom, and safety. Race remains manifest in politics, economics, land-use decision making, education, and much more. It is the proverbial elephant in the room, and it has been there for so long that no one really pretends it isn't there.[1]

Whites responded to the first wave of African American migration in the 1910s and 1920s with violence, ordained bigotry, and segregation imposed by policy and force. Racial segregation was established during this period, as were political and economic institutions and policies based on and designed to perpetuate racial segregation in all aspects of Chicago daily life.[2] The second wave, which occurred during World War II and stretched into the 1960s, contributed to whites' exit from Chicago and into newly formed suburban communities. The Chicago suburbs grew by nearly 1.3 million people during the 1950s, mostly at the expense of Chicago's urban population.[3]

Whites could purchase new suburban homes and use brand-new expressways to easily connect to their jobs in the city. Segregation by restrictive covenant, exclusionary real estate practices, racial steering, lack of access to mortgage credit, and outright refusal by developers and builders to sell to blacks limited the ability of black families to live outside of black or changing neighborhoods. Unscrupulous real estate professionals pressured whites to sell, often at a loss, or risk a further loss in property value as the neighborhood changed. The agents then turned around and sold the homes to blacks at a sharp premium. In this way, neighborhoods transformed from white to black in the span of only a few years. These mostly rural, poor, and disadvantaged blacks of the second wave streamed into neighborhoods where civic institutions, non-black middle-income families, and businesses had exited or declined due to white flight. Second-wave migrants struggled to assimilate, with access to fewer resources compared with earlier generations.[4]

Politics during this period evolved in response to racial tensions. Historically, the two major political parties had competed in Chicago elections, but during the 1950s the Democratic machine methodically eliminated the Republican Party as a meaningful force in Chicago politics. White machine leaders, under the direction of Mayor Richard J. Daley, controlled access to patronage jobs, business capital, and government services. Daley was also the chairman of the Cook County Democratic machine, which allowed him to control the slating of judicial candidates and county officials, who in turn were responsible for administering the courts, setting land-use policy, and running elections. Blacks traded party loyalty and votes to secure patronage jobs, obtain political rank in Washington, and operate businesses and institutions serving the black community.[5]

In this, African Americans followed the practice of every other ethnic group in Chicago. Yet unlike previous ethnic blocs, blacks were unable to integrate into the social, cultural, and residential fabric of Chicago and were largely shut out of suburban communities. As tensions in white ethnic communities grew, white political candidates were pushed to support segregationist policies, even when their personal views favored integration or at least less segregation. The result was a polarization of the electorate and the political leadership into pronounced factions. The white ethnic machine was made up of Irish, Polish, and a mixture of Slavic groups and was based on the South, Southwest, and Northwest Sides of Chicago. The black machine had South and West Side factions, reflecting the two main black communities. White progressive nonmachine leaders were in the lakefront communities, which tended to be more affluent and located near universities. Last were the Republicans, which included business leaders, white conservatives, and traditional Illinois Republicans, who tended to be more socially progressive. Republicans were a superminority and became largely irrelevant in city electoral politics. From 1955 through the 1967 municipal elections, Mayor Daley enjoyed 70 percent support within the black community, despite his continued refusal to endorse meaningful policy changes favoring blacks. Black political elites sided with Daley when it came to addressing overcrowding in black neighborhood schools and the lack of affordable housing outside the black ghettos.[6]

The period leading up to the Chicago Freedom Movement was a time of remarkable economic growth for Chicago and the region. Mayor Daley had long desired to make Chicago into a world-class city and shed its identity as primarily a blue-collar, industrial city. This meant creating new roads and highways into the suburbs, building and growing O'Hare and Midway airports, and reshaping the city's central business district from a manufacturing and retail center into a hub for business, financial services, and civic institutions. These years saw the construction of many of the city's iconic skyscrapers.

Daley's efforts to increase the power of the Democratic machine and to reshape the city with public works and improvements had two significant consequences. First, the northwestern and western suburbs became much more attractive to Chicago firms. Suburban areas promised lower taxes, new infrastructure and housing, and less political graft. As firms and jobs moved out of the city (and out of the region, in some cases), the tax base contracted, just as Daley's growing budgets could least afford such a reduction. Firms also left behind large buildings and facilities, many of them in black neighborhoods or neighborhoods undergoing racial change. Filling these buildings and sites was a major challenge, especially given the political and social turmoil in many of these communities. Second, Daley's efforts reshaped the physical geography, pulling resources into the central city and reducing resources for the neighborhoods. Subsequent and enduring battles over resources cleaved along a "neighborhoods versus central business district" fissure.

These battle lines formed prominently over the public schools. The Chicago civil rights movement was initiated as a fight for better schools, including allocating more resources to black neighborhood schools or allowing blacks to attend schools in white neighborhoods that were better equipped and less crowded. Daley and his school superintendent responded by building temporary classrooms in black neighborhoods (converted trailers dubbed "Willis wagons," after Superintendent Benjamin Willis). Such substandard responses did not satisfy black leaders and parents or the Coordinating Council of Community Organizations (CCCO), which had become the hub for civil rights activism in the city.[7]

On the issue of housing, Daley and his allies in City Council, black and white alike, refused to advocate for substantive open housing in Chicago or housing options for poor and lower-income black families. This would have required constructing public housing outside of black communities, which white politicians refused to support. Black political leaders were also generally opposed to that idea, in part because it would have reduced the concentration of captive black votes, but also because it would have required breaking with the Daley machine. The CCCO, led by schoolteacher Al Raby, was frustrated by its failure to move the education agenda, so it invited the Southern Christian Leadership Conference (SCLC) and Martin Luther King Jr. to come to Chicago. The result was the Chicago Freedom Movement.[8]

The Chicago Freedom Movement Revisited

The Chicago Freedom Movement was a campaign lasting from late 1965 to early 1967 to improve conditions in the black ghettos of Chicago. The movement attempted to draw Mayor Daley into the kind of open confrontation that characterized southern civil rights campaigns. Daley refused to play along, using his tremendous power over the press and his black allies in politics, business, and the religious community to shape his position. Ultimately, movement organizers turned to an open-housing campaign in the summer of 1966 to highlight racial inequality in the city. Local whites reacted sharply to the demonstrations, and Mayor Daley and his allies quickly realized that these marches could escalate beyond their control. Daley, however, was not willing to engage in violent confrontations with King and the marchers, hoping to avoid what had happened in the South.

For King and the other leaders, the marches were powerful and media-friendly events, but it was not clear how they would result in any real change. The marches attacked racism, which, though widely practiced, was already outlawed by federal and local laws. The campaign organizers lacked the means to enforce existing laws, however, because they had no political power and no means to hold those in power accountable. As neither side could force the action to favor its position, a stalemate loomed.

Both sides came together in mid-August 1966 at a series of meetings, ostensibly to negotiate an end to the marches and develop a framework for achieving the marchers' goals in the areas of housing, education, and employment. Along with civil rights leaders and political officials, the meetings involved leaders from the real estate industry and business, religious leaders, and other civic notables. Ultimately, an agreement—known as the Summit Agreement—was hammered out. Among other things, it called for the creation of a new organization with the power to enforce the agreement. That organization eventually became the Leadership Council for Metropolitan Open Communities. Its early board members included many of the original participants from the summit negotiations or their organizational representatives.

For many black leaders, the Summit Agreement provided a hollow victory. Following its announcement, a faction of more militant civil rights leaders organized a march to Cicero, a suburb just west of the mostly black neighborhood of Lawndale. Cicero had a well-earned reputation for organized and violent opposition to integration of any kind. Hundreds of police and National Guardsmen ensured that the demonstrators were protected, and the march to Cicero had little impact. The national media largely packed up and left Chicago to follow King.[9]

The Chicago Freedom Movement is widely considered a failure, or at best a draw. I disagree and believe there is ample evidence that the accomplishments of the Chicago campaign were substantial and as lasting as any achieved during the civil rights movement. I believe most analyses of the Chicago Freedom Movement have failed to account for the impact of the Leadership Council.

Leadership Council for Metropolitan Open Communities: 1966–2000

Immediately following the Summit Agreement, the Chicago Freedom Movement experienced a drop-off in enthusiasm, which is typical of an evolving movement.[10] There was a sharp reduction in the energy and engagement of various groups upon the conclusion of the initial campaign. People drawn to the drama of marches, confrontation, and demands went on to other campaigns or moved on with their lives.

There were also challenges over who would be in charge of the Leadership Council, how the different groups would work together, and what the rules for action would be. The original LCMOC board comprised people who had been adversaries only the year before. So it is understandable that it would take time to establish mutual trust and to develop effective and efficient modes of operation.

The Leadership Council also struggled with the typical growing pains of any new organization. There was disagreement about what its immediate goals should be, how to achieve them, and what kind of support it could expect from inside and outside the black community. Many within the black community turned against the Leadership Council, perceiving that it had "sold out" more militant and immediate black interests for the sake of "victory." The real estate industry, a grudging participant in the organization from the start, was necessary for any success it hoped to achieve. The council struggled to figure out how to attack discriminatory practices within the industry without alienating Realtors who were on the board. The Chicago Association of Realtors was the most powerful, but several suburban Realtors' associations presented challenges as well.[11]

Not surprisingly, LCMOC's first few years produced a great deal of frustration for many of those who had been involved in the Chicago Freedom Movement. In hindsight, given the challenges it faced, it is amazing the council survived at all. With strong leadership and by building on early successes, however, the Leadership Council soon established a set of interconnected programs and strategies that it pursued relatively consistently during its four decades of existence. These included the following:

- Research on housing and related conditions affecting blacks and other minorities and underserved groups, often conducted by local universities, think tanks, and other LCMOC partners. Research helped establish the council's credibility and provided empirical evidence of ongoing racial discrimination and inequality. Research also helped model what a less segregated region would look like and what was required to achieve it.[12]

- Awareness-raising through the direct confrontation of racist practices and racist firms, along with media outreach and exposure. Direct action provided fodder for Chicago's several competing newspapers and fueled fund-raising from sympathetic donors and foundations. Much of this activism was generated by the council's testing program, which was designed to confirm individual acts of discrimination, as well as to measure the incidence of housing discrimination more generally. Testing involved matched pairs of testers, usually one white and one black, who otherwise presented identical economic attributes (income, employment, and so forth). Each tester applied for the same housing service, and their experiences were compared to see whether they were treated differently based on race or some other attribute. The Leadership Council conducted thousands of such tests to combat discrimination based on gender, religion, disability, source of income, national origin, and just about every protected class established in federal, state, and local statutes. In doing so, the council helped establish the protocols used by testing programs around the country.

- Counseling services and escorting to assist minority families make "opportunity moves," backed up by legal action to address overt discrimination. The Leadership Council counseled black families on what to expect when moving to nonblack communities, collected information on housing opportunities and community services in targeted communities, provided access to legal services, and conducted follow-up counseling after successful moves to troubleshoot any problems. LCMOC helped 7,500 low-income families move from segregated public housing developments into higher-opportunity areas through the Gautreaux Program. It also counseled thousands of black home buyers, who were often the first black homeowners in their respective communities.[13]

- Monitoring of and engagement with various housing practices, including advertising and marketing, real estate industry practices, access to mortgage credit, tenants' rights, and affordable housing policy. As noted earlier, the real estate industry was represented on the council's board, which helped foster dialogue and constructive engagement. LCMOC lawsuits often led to changes in industry practice, fair-housing training, and monitoring as a condition for settling individual cases. Real estate firms and landlords were often required to undergo Leadership Council training and to have their practices audited for years as part of that monitoring. During its tenure, the council trained more than 30,000 housing professionals in the Chicago region.[14] It also helped create opportunities for blacks with local Realtor boards, changed how firms could advertise, and produced training materials adopted across the country.

- Legal action, whereby staff attorneys and lawyers recruited from Chicago law firms filed cases in federal court and with administrative agencies tasked with enforcing fair-housing standards. The Leadership Council coordinated its efforts with other fair-housing and public-interest law firms, tenant advocacy organizations, civil rights groups, and private fair-housing organizations. Over its thirty-nine years, the council was involved in dozens of landmark fair-housing cases and demonstrated how to effectively use the Civil Rights Act of 1964 and the Fair Housing Act of 1968 to dismantle discrimination in all aspects of housing, including zoning, land development, and code enforcement. It also used local ordinances, such as Chicago's human relations ordinance, which included additional protections not found in federal law. When the Fair Housing Act was amended in 1988, LCMOC attorneys seized on the opportunity to bring new cases and to push for stronger forms of relief for their clients. The council's Legal Action Program filed more than 1,500 lawsuits on behalf of clients, most of them in federal court, and had a success rate of more than 90 percent. This aggressive Legal Action Program was essential to LCMOC's success.[15]

- Participation in political campaigns on issues such as education, human relations, employment, civil and political rights, and land-use planning, which affected social and economic opportunities for African Americans in Chicago. The Leadership Council was involved in formulating the Community Reinvestment Act (CRA) to combat redlining in mortgage lending and financial services. It was an early proponent of regionalism and consistently documented the negative consequences of the region's jobs-housing mismatch.[16]

The Leadership Council adopted a multifaceted strategy that was appropriate for the time and remains the preferred approach for similar organizations today. Whether it is done through one organization or a coalition, housing discrimination and segregation must be attacked at multiple levels. Housing opportunity must also be part of related efforts to address black-white gaps in education, employment, and political rights, among other things. This is because where one lives has a lot to do with what resources are available—or not—to oneself and one's family.

The Leadership Council's achievements highlight the importance of an engaged and focused board and strong executive management. During its early years, the LCMOC board was dominated by the business, religious, and civic leaders who had been involved in negotiating the Summit Agreement. Because those first boards included parties from both sides of the debate, they were to some extent like marriages of convenience. It took time to develop strong relationships among the board members, weed out those who were less committed to the mission, and develop functioning committees and structures. It is worth noting that many board members, including a number of founding members, retained leadership roles in the council for its entire existence, and others remained involved for decades or more.

The Leadership Council's success also depended on its executive leadership. Two of its long-serving executive directors were pivotal to its success. Kale Williams, a leader of the Chicago Freedom Movement and founder of the Leadership Council, served as executive director from 1972 to 1991. Though white, soft-spoken, and of modest build, Williams was widely respected for his commitment to social justice and minority rights, as well as his tenacity. He was widely accepted as the legitimate leader of an organization committed to advancing black housing opportunities. Williams was succeeded by Aurie Pennick, the council's first African American female chief executive. A lawyer and an accomplished administrator, Pennick led the council from 1991 to 2002, during which time it became increasingly involved in national dialogues about race, inclusion, and housing opportunity. It also gained recognition for its expertise on mobility counseling, which was promoted in the Clinton administration's housing programs.

By the start of the 2000s, LCMOC had successfully challenged many of the overt housing barriers facing blacks, establishing legal precedents that could be used across the country. The organization had solidified its role as the region's moral voice on race and housing. At the same time, the Chicago area continued to be quite segregated. A decade earlier, blacks had integrated many Chicago communities and suburbs, but in very small numbers. For the most part, the region's black population remained segregated in a small number of communities. In the western suburbs, three communities were more than half black by 1990, while most of the others remained nearly all white. In the southern suburbs, there were a number of predominantly black communities, many of which had very high rates of poverty and few economic opportunities, especially during the deindustrialization of that period. These patterns remained consistent through the 1990s.[17]

As the Leadership Council approached its thirty-fifth anniversary, it prepared a report that illustrated how far the Chicago region had to go to overcome the legacy of segregation. By 2001, 94 percent of blacks still lived in low-opportunity areas in the region. Predominantly black and Hispanic communities generally had lower levels of employment, less access to public transportation, lower community health, and weaker tax bases relative to mostly white or all-white areas. A 2005 report, *The Segregation of Opportunities*, called for a new opportunity-based framework for evaluating policies and the ongoing segregation of minorities in the Chicago region.[18]

Leadership Council for Metropolitan Open Communities: 2000–2006

The Leadership Council I joined in 2000 was a mature, healthy organization with a staff of more than thirty persons and offices in Chicago and three suburban locations. Senior staff were exceptionally experienced and incredibly smart about fair housing. They included the following individuals:

- Dave Schucker, the council's primary liaison to the housing industry, had been with the LCMOC since its creation, serving as a tester, community relations specialist, and information director. His wry humor and cluttered office belied a sharp, tough mind.
- The Reverend Jim Shannon had heard Dr. King preach as a child in Alabama and had been an LCMOC client in the early 1980s. He ran the three suburban housing centers, drawing on his personal experiences and moral convictions to inspire the confidence of minority clients who were considering moves to nonsegregated communities.
- Mary Davis, raised in public housing, had risen through the LCMOC ranks to become a nationally recognized expert on mobility programs. She ran the Gautreaux Assisted Housing Program and was fiercely devoted to the families it served, as well as its staff.
- John Lukehart, who started as a union organizer on Chicago's Southeast Side, was in charge of community relations and policy. An Iowa farm boy, John's quiet temperament and pragmatism defused many tense discussions and earned the trust of otherwise opposed groups. His mild demeanor masked a fierce commitment to racial justice and inclusion.
- Stephen Stern ran the Legal Action Program judiciously, aware of both its historical legacy and the tough opposition to civil rights during the Bush years. He filed cases he thought he could win, which he did often.

I joined the Leadership Council to administer a federally funded grant designed to combat racial prejudice and hate crimes known as CommUNITY 2000. Like many council undertakings, it was a national demonstration project, with LCMOC serving as an elder statesman relative to other organizations involved in the project. The council's work through that grant encompassed all the main strategies it used to open up housing opportunities. Programs included the following:

- Congregations Building CommUNITY. This program generated interreligious dialogue, highlighted barriers to housing choice in the region, and recruited congregations to devote services to fair housing and participate in policy advocacy campaigns. The steering committee included senior leaders from the Archdiocese of Chicago, the Jewish Council on Urban Affairs, the Council of Islamic Organizations of Greater Chicago, the National Conference of Christians and Jews, and many individual denominations representing all faiths in the region. By fostering and strengthening relationships through regular interactions, this coalition of religious groups stood together in the days after 9/11 and responded to acts of religious and ethnic discrimination and violence. The project also recruited dozens of religious institutions to the council's policy advocacy work, resulting in state policy reforms.

- Immigrants Fair Housing Roundtable (IFHR). The Leadership Council had previously recognized that the region's large and growing Hispanic population suffered significant discrimination. Other immigrants, including those displaced from ethnic conflicts in eastern Europe, Africa, and the Middle East, had come to the United States ignorant of their housing rights and often lacking the basic skills needed to assimilate, making them vulnerable to all manner of discrimination. The Leadership Council formed IFHR as a coalition of fair-housing groups and immigrant advocacy and service organizations and, through it, developed programs, training, and educational materials in multiple languages. IFHR members also attacked the discriminatory use of municipal building codes to harass Hispanics. This work led to code enforcement reforms in Berwyn, Illinois; heightened awareness of the needs of immigrants in general; and generated a unique fair-housing training program that graduated more than 200 individuals in nineteen communities as fair-housing advocates.
- Lake County Anti–Hate Crimes Task Force. Lake County is one of the seven counties making up the Chicago metropolitan region. Though smaller in population than DuPage or Cook County, Lake County had a significant number of black and Hispanic residents, located largely in small towns along the lakefront near the Wisconsin border and in the City of Waukegan. Other parts of the county included affluent suburbs, farming communities, and semirural areas. In the early 2000s Lake County was also home

to a number of avowed white-supremacist organizations. Working with fair-housing and civil rights groups, the state's attorney's office, and community leaders, the task force developed a rapid-response protocol for responding to hate crimes and convened the first countywide Summit on Human Relations, attended by hundreds of leaders and residents.

In addition to these initiatives, the Leadership Council staffed a coalition of municipal, housing industry, and civic leaders in the western suburbs (West Cook Leaders) and provided leadership to others focused on fair lending (Chicago CRA Coalition) and affordable housing (Regional Housing Collaborative). Council staff also worked with local and regional organizing efforts, such as the Interfaith Leadership Project in Berwyn and Cicero and United Power, an Alinsky-style organizing group that operated across the region to advance statewide policy reforms.

Notable accomplishments included negotiated CRA agreements with Chase Bank and Charter One to increase lending to minorities, low- and moderate-income families, and small businesses in low- and moderate-income areas. The council's staff helped pass strong antipredatory lending legislation and succeeded in incorporating inclusionary zoning into a rewrite of the Chicago zoning code. The council also secured passage of a new state law requiring all municipalities to create affordable housing plans or risk losing state funding for infrastructure and other local needs.

The Leadership Council continued to operate its own programs as well, including the nationally recognized Gautreaux Program, which resulted from a successful lawsuit requiring the Chicago Housing Authority (CHA) to desegregate public housing. An analysis of Gautreaux's impact demonstrated convincingly that, absent the council's mobility counseling, few low-income black families would have moved to nonsegregated opportunity areas in the region. Moreover, research showed that the economic, educational, and emotional benefits of relocation were especially profound for children. The second generation was far more likely to achieve higher education, gain employment, and avoid interactions with the law compared with those who did not relocate into opportunity areas or did not relocate at all.[19]

The Leadership Council also continued to engage in industry outreach and education. Through a partnership with the Community Investment Corporation, a nonprofit multifamily lender in low- and moderate-income communities, the council conducted monthly training sessions for property managers and landlords, who were required to attend this training program as a condition for receiving loans. Through this and other partnerships, the council collectively trained more than 800 industry professionals each year.

Leadership Council for Metropolitan Open Communities: Postmortem

By the early 2000s, the Leadership Council recognized that it needed to better articulate its relevance to a world that had changed—in part due to its own work.[20] The council continued to cast itself in terms of the legacy of the Chicago Freedom Movement and Dr. King, even as blacks in Chicago enjoyed ever-increasing opportunities and overt discrimination became the exception rather than the rule. The Community Reinvestment Act had expanded the products and services available to low- and moderate-income communities, and there was now an entire profession dedicated to developing affordable housing. The 1986 reforms to the federal tax code included the federal low-income housing tax credit financing program, which the state and city used to fund thousands of new units of affordable housing. The Section 8 voucher program offered support for low-income housing within the private market, while the 1988 amendments to the Fair Housing Act extended protections to persons with disabilities and families with children. The City of Chicago had established an affordable housing trust fund to help house low-income people in nonsegregated settings, and by 2001, the CHA was well into its Plan for Transformation, which called for the demolition of the infamous high-rise ghettos and the creation of entirely new mixed-income communities. *Diversity* and *inclusion* were the buzzwords used to market communities of choice. Other organizations advocated on behalf of ethnic communities and the disabled, which drew attention and funding away from African American–oriented groups such as the Leadership Council.

As for black Chicagoans, there had been a significant expansion of the black middle class by the early 2000s. After nearly two decades of affirmative action policies in education and employment, there was an explosion of black wealth and power. Michael Jordan and Oprah Winfrey were hugely successful, of course, but there were also more black CEOs of major corporations and black political elites who advised presidents and sat on the boards of major corporations. The Leadership Council and its allies found it increasingly difficult to focus on black mobility, even as it appeared that such mobility was less of a challenge. Moreover, the blacks who enjoyed the greatest mobility were those with the economic means to make choices. For the very poor and the less sophisticated, decent housing in areas of high opportunity remained out of reach.[21]

By the early 2000s, Chicago had already elected a black mayor, a black Cook County Board president, and two black US senators. One, Senator Barack Obama, would serve as the keynote speaker at the Leadership Council's final annual fund-raising reception. Chicago had black police commissioners and black leaders within the Chicago public schools and the Chicago teachers' union. The days of plantation politics seemed to be over, although many knew that white power brokers still controlled many black wards and districts. In such a world, race and discrimination and the strategies to address these issues required a much more nuanced approach.

Confronted by these developments, the Leadership Council also faced a financial crisis brought on by two main factors—an overreliance on government contracts to fund its programs, and a decline in revenue from successful legal actions. The council received funding from government contracts, but it required matching funds to cover total program costs. As its donor base diminished, the council drew on scarce general operating expenses to pay for its programs. It also dipped into reserves to cover shortfalls. Regarding the Legal Action Program, the council had historically been able to secure a portion of its funding through the settlement of lawsuits. But during the 2000s, the Leadership Council found it harder to bring fair-housing cases to federal court, in part due to the Bush administration's hostility to fair-housing enforcement.[22] To sustain the Legal Action Program in the face of reduced funding, the council pulled money from other sources, including grants and general operating funds. In hindsight, there are many, myself included, who wish the Leadership Council had fought harder against the Department of Justice and the Bush administration. It was the confrontational nature of the council's legal action that had secured victories during the 1970s and 1980s, and many of us felt that returning to that fighting spirit would have energized our base and brought us more support.

After CEO Aurie Pennick stepped down in 2002, the Leadership Council embarked on an effort to update its strategic vision, even as it addressed its mounting financial crisis. Pennick's successor had no history with the council and was viewed as an organizational technocrat who had helped turn around municipal governments. He had also worked with politically connected real estate developers and was expected to improve the relationship between the council and the CHA, its largest contract provider. He was faced with the task of trying to win over staff and funders to a new plan for the LCMOC, one that focused heavily on research, advocacy, and coalitions. At the same time, he tried to rally staff and funders to help save the organization as a provider of direct services and fair-housing education.

Despite these challenges, the Leadership Council made headway with its strategic repurposing. During this period, it invested in new research to better understand the state of segregation in the Chicago region.[23] It hired consultants to help it rethink its mission and its organizational structure. It produced seminal reports that demonstrated just how much work remained to be done to create an open community, and it provided detailed policy prescriptions for making that progress. Yet because of the financial turmoil surrounding the council, it was tough for the opportunity-based analysis to gain traction.

The organization's leadership also considered breaking it up into separate units, with services and counseling making up one unit and advocacy, research, and technical assistance another. This proposal created confusion for the LCMOC staff, its board, and its funding community. In many ways, this suggestion was a practical response to the problem with the existing funding model, but too little time was devoted to shaping consensus. In the meantime, the council was hemorrhaging funds and losing key staff. Mary Davis resigned in 2004, and Dave Schucker passed away. The Legal Action Program found itself without a staff attorney for the first time in more than thirty years when Stephen Stern stepped down in 2004. Late in 2004, the CEO resigned and was replaced by John Lukehart as acting executive director. Despite dramatic efforts to downsize the organization and an infusion of large grants from several key funders, the council would not make it to its fortieth anniversary in June 2006.

It was the end of an era, though not the end of the fight for open housing in Chicago. Staff from the organization continued their work. The Reverend Jim Shannon reconstituted the housing centers into the Regional Fair Housing Center, which operated out of a former LCMOC satellite office in southwest suburban Evergreen Park. Rob Breymaier, the community relations director, went on to head the Oak Park Regional Housing Center and served in executive roles on the board of the Chicago Area Fair Housing Alliance. I left the council to found a nonprofit community development corporation that addressed the impact of gentrification on black and Hispanic families on Chicago's Far North Side.

As for the council's many partners, most continued to work on issues of regional opportunity and affordable housing, but it was clear that the region had lost a powerful voice with the closing of the Leadership Council for Metropolitan Open Communities. That loss is still felt to this day.

Lessons Learned

There are a number of lessons to be learned from the history of the Leadership Council. Its fundamental strategy—coordinated service, advocacy, and legal action programs—can be effective. The provision of services results in real-life experiences, which can inform advocacy and help justify the need for continuing action and services. Legal action backs up these services by providing a means of challenging discriminatory treatment. Advocacy is used to reform policies and challenge the structure of inequality.

The main obstacle to this tripartite strategy is how to fund it. Increasingly, services are funded by public contracts, charities, and foundations, which tend to avoid groups that also engage in litigation. Securing funding for advocacy generally requires a reliance on key foundations and a strong base of individual donors. As for legal action, it can be effective, but only if cases are won and the monetary judgments are sufficient to cover the significant associated costs. To follow the Leadership Council's path, the formation of coalitions will likely be required, comprising different groups equipped to perform activities suitable to their funding models and missions.

Civil rights and fair housing continue to be major issues for blacks, but the framing needs to be refreshed. All blacks suffer from a dual market, but the heaviest price is paid by those who have the least financial means. Dr. King attempted to reframe civil rights as a battle against poverty. Similarly, the fight for fair housing could benefit by framing issues more directly in terms of the housing rights of the poor. This means highlighting and collaborating with groups serving seniors on fixed incomes, the disabled, and families that rely on subsidies. It also means taking up the needs of immigrants who are not documented and therefore exceptionally vulnerable to discrimination. To frame fair housing more broadly, without overlooking the ongoing struggles of black Americans, the fair-housing movement has to intentionally build interracial and intergenerational coalitions. Building such coalitions based on mutual self-interest is challenging, given funding limitations, turf issues, and intergroup power dynamics. Regular gatherings, such as the West Cook Leaders or the steering committee of Congregations Building CommUNITY, are vital to create durable relationships. In addition, the religious community, unions, student groups, and others who have roles to play in the fair-housing movement must be reengaged.

The fair-housing movement must be willing to be confrontational. In recent years, fair-housing groups have demonstrated the effectiveness of lawsuits by going after national banks, municipal governments, and others that perpetuate the dual housing market.[24] Confrontation occurs not only through lawsuits but also through direct action. The recent Occupy movement and the resurgence of organizing for social justice among young people are causes for optimism among veterans of the movement. Fair-housing groups must engage and connect with other grassroots organizing efforts and reenergize direct, nonviolent social protest for fair housing.

The fair-housing community also needs to continue to do research, update data, and connect current research to past scholarly work. The Leadership Council created many useful analyses and methods; updating these would provide continuity to measure progress. A recent example is the Fair Housing and Equity Assessment completed by the Chicago

Metropolitan Agency for Planning and the Chicago Fair Housing Alliance. Using sophisticated statistical analysis and drawing on a wide range of demographic and economic data, the report provides a framework for improving access to areas of opportunity in the metropolitan Chicago region for all people, but most notably for minorities.[25]

If anything is learned from the Leadership Council, it should be that diversity and inclusion do not happen by chance or by predestiny. Stable and diverse communities are created through intentional actions and policies that have diversity as a stated goal, and the evaluation of their success considers whether such diversity is being achieved. Dissimilarity indices continue to show that the Chicago region is hypersegregated because most groups talk about the importance of diversity but do not incorporate diversity—or the means to achieve it—into specific and measurable programs, policies, and goals backed by adequate and durable funding.

The Leadership Council had a long and largely successful tenure as the primary champion for change in Chicago-area housing options, policies, and practices. Its efforts had a readily visible and substantive impact on government, the private sector, and Chicagoland residents. Work on the myriad issues associated with slum housing and real estate had already begun when Dr. King and SCLC arrived, but it was the catalytic effect of the Chicago Freedom Movement that gave rise to the Leadership Council. There was, to be sure, disgruntlement about the results of the Summit Agreement, a feeling in some quarters that the community did not get enough out of it. But, given who was present at the negotiating table, it is reasonable to ask how much more change could possibly have come out of the summit talks.

We can never know whether demanding more change at a faster pace would have accomplished anything. We do know that there was nothing on the horizon comparable to the Leadership Council before Dr. King's arrival and the unfolding of the Chicago Freedom Movement. We must remember that the arc of history bends slowly, but it bends toward justice. The work of the Leadership Council is testament to that. It remains for current and future generations to advance us all toward the beloved community, and thanks to the Leadership Council, we know how to do that.

Notes

1. See Ben Joravsky and Eduardo Camacho, *Race and Politics in Chicago* (Chicago: Community Renewal Society, 1987); Douglas S. Massey and Nancy A. Denton, *American Apartheid: Segregation and the Making of the Underclass* (Cambridge, MA: Harvard University Press, 1993); Gregory Squires, Larry Bennett, Kathleen McCourt, and Philip Nyden, *Chicago: Race, Class and the Response to Urban Decline* (Philadelphia: Temple University Press, 1987); James R. Ralph Jr., *Northern Protest: Martin Luther King, Jr., Chicago, and the Civil Rights Movement* (Cambridge, MA: Harvard University Press, 1993). For a general history of US housing segregation, see Stephen Grant Meyer, *As Long as They Don't Move Next Door: Segregation and Racial Conflict in American Neighborhoods* (Lanham, MD: Lexington Books, 2000).

2. Allan H. Spear, *Black Chicago: The Making of a Negro Ghetto, 1890–1920* (Chicago: University of Chicago Press, 1967); James R. Grossman, *Land of Hope: Chicago, Black Southerners, and the Great Migration* (Chicago: University of Chicago Press, 1989).

3. Brian J. L. Berry, *The Open Housing Question: Race and Housing in Chicago, 1966–1976* (Cambridge, MA: Ballinger Publishing, 1979), 3–17; Squires et al., *Chicago*, 23–126. Chicago's overall population peaked in the 1950s, and most of the major loss occurred during the 1950s and 1960s.

4. Arnold R. Hirsch, *Making of the Second Ghetto: Race and Housing in Chicago, 1940–1960* (Cambridge: Cambridge University Press, 1983).

5. Richard J. Daley's role in Chicago politics has been covered extensively in a number of excellent works, including Mike Royko, *Boss: Richard J. Daley of Chicago* (New York: E. P. Dutton, 1971); Adam Cohen and Elizabeth Taylor, *American Pharaoh: Mayor Richard J. Daley: His Battle for Chicago and the Nation* (Boston: Little, Brown, 2000); and Roger Biles, *Richard J. Daley: Politics, Race, and the Governing of Chicago* (De Kalb: Northern Illinois University Press, 1995). On blacks and politics in Chicago, see William J. Grimshaw, *Bitter Fruit: Black Politics and the Chicago Machine, 1931–1991* (Chicago: University of Chicago Press, 1992).

6. Grimshaw, *Bitter Fruit*, 91–114; Paul Kleppner, *Chicago Divided: The Making of a Black Mayor* (De Kalb: Northern Illinois University Press, 1985), 66–74.

7. Fights over the quality of schools in Chicago's black and white communities and the appropriate responses to gross inequality have been ongoing for decades, including currently. See Ralph, *Northern Protest*, 13–28, and Alan B. Anderson and George W. Pickering, *Confronting the Color Line: The Broken Promise of the Civil Rights Movement in Chicago* (Athens: University of Georgia Press, 1986), 69–167.

8. For more on the Chicago Freedom Movement, see Ralph, *Northern Protest*, and Anderson and Pickering, *Confronting the Color Line*, 168–340.

9. Ralph, *Northern Protest,* 197–200.

10. Much of the early history of the Leadership Council covered here draws on Berry's *Open Housing Question,* which was commissioned by the Department of Housing and Urban Development as an evaluation of the agency and the impact of HUD funding.

11. Berry, *Open Housing Question,* 19–118.

12. The Leadership Council conducted research both independently and with others during its history. Many of its research reports can be found in the council's papers at the Chicago Historical Society and in the collections of the Center for Urban Research and Learning at Loyola University, with which the Leadership Council frequently collaborated.

13. Leonard S. Rubinowitz and James Rosenbaum, *Crossing the Class and Color Lines: From Public Housing to White Suburbia* (Chicago: University of Chicago Press, 2000).

14. This figure is based on an internal staff memo prepared in advance of the fortieth-anniversary celebration of the Leadership Council.

15. Internal memo provided by former Legal Action Program director F. William Caruso, following closure of the Leadership Council in 2006.

16. The Leadership Council focused heavily on regional solutions to inequality. This was both pragmatic and, by default, necessary. The Chicago region is heavily fragmented in terms of political geography, with more than 270 separate communities making up the seven-county region. Approximately 70 percent of the region's population is in Cook County, divided nearly equally between the City of Chicago and 126 individual municipalities. Each municipality has roughly equivalent powers to self-govern in matters related to land use, housing policy, and so forth. In the absence of overarching federal or state laws, overcoming housing discrimination often meant fighting unique battles in each of these communities. Regionalism allowed a more efficient use of resources and mitigated the need for local battles. The Leadership Council intentionally partnered with other fair-housing organizations in the region, directly and through the Chicago Fair Housing Alliance, and with organizations devoted to regional planning, such as the Metropolitan Planning Organization, the Northeastern Illinois Planning Council (now the Chicago Metropolitan Agency for Planning), and the various regional councils of government.

17. See Gary Orfield, ed., *Fair Housing in Metropolitan Chicago: Perspectives after Two Decades* (Chicago Area Fair Housing Alliance, 1987).

18. john a. powell, *Envisioning Racially Just and Opportunity Based Housing in the Chicago Region* (Leadership Council for Metropolitan Open Communities, 2001); John Lukehart, Tom Luce, and Jason Reece, *The Segregation of Opportunities: The Structure of Advantage and Disadvantage in the Chicago Region* (Leadership Council for Metropolitan Open Communities, 2005).

19. Rubinowitz and Rosenbaum, *Crossing Class and Color Lines,* 187–90.

On the lawsuit, see Alexander Polikoff, *Waiting for Gautreaux: A Story of Housing, Segregation, and the Black Ghetto* (Evanston, IL: Northwestern University Press, 2006).

20. powell, *Envisioning Racially Just and Opportunity Based Housing*. This report synthesized the thinking of the council's senior staff and became a primary directive for its subsequent work.

21. Sheryll Cashin, *The Failures of Integration: How Race and Class Are Undermining the American Dream* (New York: Public Affairs, 2004).

22. *The Bush Administration Takes Aim: Civil Rights under Attack* (Leadership Conference on Civil Rights Education Fund, 2003); Goodwin Liu, "The Bush Administration and Civil Rights: Lessons Learned," *Duke Journal of Constitutional Law & Public Policy* 4 (2009): 77–106.

23. Lukehart, Luce, and Reece, *Segregation of Opportunities*.

24. The National Fair Housing Alliance and its local member organizations have, for example, pursued large settlements against bank servicers for disparate servicing of homes in minority and nonminority communities.

25. See Chicago Metropolitan Agency for Planning, *Fair Housing and Equity Assessment: Metropolitan Chicago*, November 2013.

6

The North Shore Summer Project

"We're Gonna Open up the Whole North Shore"

Gail Schechter

> America owes much to those residents of the North Shore who have
> successfully confronted an evil system at some personal cost; who, rec-
> ognizing that human rights must take precedence over property rights,
> will not allow "things" to ride mankind. For, in the words of John
> Kennedy, "those who do nothing are inviting shame as well as vio-
> lence. Those who act boldly are recognizing right as well as reality."
> —North Shore Summer Project Steering Committee

Ask even a ten-year-old from the Chicago area what she thinks upon
hearing the term "North Shore" and the answer is likely to be "white,"
"rich," and "snobby." Chicago's North Shore is both a region and a
brand, a reality and a perception.[1]

Today, the North Shore is a patchwork of ethnic, racial, and economic diversity, with more than one in four residents a person of color
(compared with one in ten in 1980). Even so, African Americans living
in Chicago do not consider the North Shore outside of Evanston and
Skokie to be a "comfort zone" for raising their children "because of the
way they look at you, the way they treat you."[2] Less than 1 percent of
the north suburban population outside of these two Chicago suburbs is
black.

Yet there was a brief moment in time when a major surge of North
Shore residents chose to make the area a comfort zone, when thousands
of mostly white North Shore residents shifted the local culture, riding
the tide of the civil rights movement. They did this by boldly challeng-

154

ing the discriminatory behavior of their own real estate institutions, literally bringing African American families into all-white suburbs, breaking bread together, and suffusing all this activity with a faith-tinged culture of love over fear. "I may be wildly unrealistic," wrote columnist and former Glenview Village president Jack Mabley in May 1965, "but I believe that in a community like the North Shore 90 percent of the people are decent, moralistic, patriotic human beings who will do the right thing when given some direction."[3]

The story of the North Shore Summer Project (NSSP) and its aftermath is about a brave attempt to transform not only a de jure racist suburban housing market but also a de facto culture of exclusion. I argue that the NSSP's most significant legacy was not the most obvious, the changing of housing laws and real estate practices, but rather its ability to galvanize hundreds of people—white and black, particularly women—in an extremely organized fashion around an ethic of racial justice. Over the decades that followed, many of these women accomplished significant achievements, spawning affordable housing developments, local fair-housing ordinances, and human relations commissions. This language of justice, laden with religious and patriotic underpinnings and an ethic of care that made others' struggles one's own, was especially appealing to those affluent, white North Shore residents who wanted to contribute to the electrifying energy of the civil rights movement.

The North Shore Summer Project began taking root when when disparate groups of white housewives—Dora Williams and Henrietta Boal Moore in Winnetka, and a group of eight friends in Wilmette—banded together in 1961 to make sure that housing listings would be open to all.[4] Rayna Miller, future director of the North Shore Interfaith Housing Council (the successor to NSSP), recalled that when she moved into Wilmette in 1956, "The Realtors, the gatekeepers, told us our place was in west Wilmette. They decided where we could or couldn't go. East Wilmette was off-limits for Jews."[5]

One of the Wilmette leaders was "Mrs. Robert Cleland." She, like many of the other women, later became known by her own name and was a leader in her own right. Jean R. Cleland and her husband were active in the North Shore Summer Project through the First Congregational Church, UCC, in Wilmette, whose dynamic young minister,

Buckner Coe, was a leader of the movement. Cleland described their first open-housing efforts as weekly gatherings of "a handful of women" who perused the *Wilmette Life* real estate section for "for sale by owner" listings and called to see whether they would be open to black buyers.[6] According to Miller, as paraphrased by Robert McClory of the *Chicago Reader*, they were "hung up on, called communists, and informed that only Caucasians need apply. Undeterred, the ladies turned the little Thursday pastime into a crusade."[7] As Jean Cleland recalls:

> We made a little splash that way and we escorted people to open houses on Sunday afternoon when open houses occurred, even when the Realtor sponsored the showing because there was nothing to keep people from looking at a house. So we managed to recruit a few minority people, mostly from the South Side, to look at a house and then we'd gather at the end of the afternoon and have a meal together, a potluck at somebody's house. We managed to make possible two or three different purchases. At the same time, I recall escorting a couple of candidates to banks in Wilmette to see if they could get a loan and that didn't work.

Neither a "pastime" nor a "crusade," this work was intertwined with these suburbanites' spiritual and political being. This work was powered by a pervasive, national energy that urgently sought to end all forms of prejudice against African Americans. As Cleland described it, "More and more society was *alive* with a sense [that] something big is happening, something exciting, important, valuable is happening all over the country."

African American women, of course, were more than ready for change. "When was I *not* aware of what was happening?" mused Karen Chavers, who was a teenager in the 1960s. She had been raised in New Orleans, the South Side of Chicago, and Evanston. Her life converged with that of Jean and Bob Cleland when the couple literally extended their hands in welcome to Karen and her parents, greeting the Holy Cross parishioners from Woodlawn as they walked through the doors of the Wilmette church one Sunday. Chavers's parents were civil rights activists who believed "if you couldn't live in a community, you couldn't build community."[8] At that time, city and suburban congregations visited one another in solidarity, focusing on race relations, African American–Jewish dialogue, and fighting discrimination.

Holding a mirror to the white North Shore in this way, a home-grown movement was born. "The American Friends Service Committee (AFSC) has recognized the paradox of North Shore residents going to Selma to preach tolerance, so the Friends instituted the North Shore Summer Project," Mabley wrote in May 1965.[9] In fact, there would have been no North Shore Summer Project without the Mississippi Summer Project (later known as Freedom Summer). The North Shore was the most affluent, most expensive, and most politically powerful subregion of Chicago—and it was also a source of financial support for the civil rights movement in the South. According to NSSP's 1965 "prospectus," written by "participating north shore residents and students" and William Moyer of AFSC, "young people, both high school and college students, have served on the front lines of this movement with increasing moral, financial and, in some cases, physical support from concerned white suburban adults. *Nowhere has come more support for COFO, SNCC and CORE than [from] Chicago's north shore.*"[10]

Lerone Bennett Jr., the senior editor of *Ebony* magazine and a prominent African American leader, said to NSSP recruits in a Winnetka backyard during their training week: "The real missionary area in America is not Harlem but White Plains; not the South Side but the North Side and the North Shore." Pungent words like these—"white liberals cannot convert anyone in America until they convert themselves"—inspired thousands.[11] One of those young converts was Susan Gregory, a Wilmette resident and student at Winnetka's New Trier High School, where her father was an English teacher. In 1970, at the age of twenty, she wrote a memoir, *Hey, White Girl,* about what it was like to spend her senior year at an all-black high school in Chicago. She also recalled going with her parents to Knoxville, Tennessee, in 1964 for an interracial study-skills program, which heightened her awareness of racial struggles. She returned to predominantly white New Trier with a keen interest in the civil rights movement, which "became the central force in my life." She and her father joined the Chicago-based Ecumenical Institute as it organized a bus to the Selma-to-Montgomery march. And in the summer of 1965 she joined the North Shore Summer Project. New Trier had a summer seminar in "community relations" in which half the students were black, and a boy from Hyde Park High School on the South Side became her "closest friend."[12]

Susan Gregory and Karen Chavers were of the same generation, and they both had parents whose activism was grounded in religious faith. The Chavers family had lived the South–North journey. They would get in the family car and drive to see new neighborhoods and new people, experiencing racism differently on each side of the Mason-Dixon Line, as Chavers put it. In the North, Bennett told the NSSP recruits, "racism [is] grounded on a whole sick complex surrounding real estate, status, greed, and human pettiness."[13]

Bill Moyer of AFSC, a Quaker organization founded in 1917 to give conscientious objectors a way to promote peace and justice, is credited with making housing discrimination the focus of the civil rights movement in Chicago.[14] Moyer was the director of AFSC's open-housing program in Chicago, Home Opportunities Made Equal Inc. (HOME). Carol Kleiman, an active member of the program, dubbed Moyer the "Quiet Man who is quietly seeking the integration of Chicago's notoriously lily-white suburbs." According to Kleiman, Moyer organized more than 200 volunteers, whom she described generally as "that much-maligned person—most often a woman—also known as the 'white liberal' and 'do-gooder' who seeks to do something about the prevalent system of segregation in her community, to change the sameness of the complexion of her neighborhood instead of just talking about it."[15] Indeed, 15,000 suburban real estate professionals refused to serve Negroes in white areas, and Moyer repeatedly pointed out that the northern suburbs were just as much a "closed society" as the South.

Moyer, at age thirty-one, had a master's degree in social work, and his mild manner made him even more effective, according to Kleiman, in "opening the eyes of volunteers for the first time to their community's inhumanity to man."[16] Moyer had walked out of his Philadelphia-based Presbyterian church, where he was a deacon, when it excluded Negroes. After becoming a Quaker, he worked as a community organizer in Philadelphia while in graduate school, shifting away from his prior career as an engineer. In 1964 he went to Washington with Fannie Lou Hamer to support the Mississippi Freedom Democratic Party, an attempt by African Americans and their white allies to wrest control of the Democratic Party from the conservative southern faction.

For all its activity—galvanizing hundreds of residents, students, clergy, and business leaders; opening multiple "Freedom Centers"; and holding numerous rallies—the North Shore Summer Project was short-lived by design, spanning the months of February through November 1965. The purpose of the project was quite simply to open the North Shore to blacks. In February 1965 NSSP volunteers interviewed seventy-five Realtors,[17] who argued that they followed the restrictive, discriminatory practice of showing homes to potential buyers based on their race, religion, and national origin. They claimed they could not go against the wishes of the seller and that "the community was not ready" for integration.[18] NSSP leader Mrs. Sanford Blum objected, stating, "When Realtors initiate a description of a community based on its ethnic makeup, they are assuming the responsibility of social engineering for which they are neither qualified nor morally justified."[19]

Consequently, the activists decided to put these assertions to the test and set out to speak to as many as possible of the 2,000 homeowners who had listed their homes for sale that summer, as well as their neighbors. According to the NSSP's prospectus, its goals were: "(1) Raise the fact that there is a 'Negro' problem on the north shore, that the north shore (like most every other white area in the country) is closed to Negro home seekers, (2) Encourage individual residents and organizations to publicly demand that the real estate system adopt nondiscriminatory policies, (3) Work with *bona fide* Negro home seekers as they seek the services of north shore Realtors."[20]

The project aimed to build on the various North Shore fair-housing committees that had emerged in North Evanston, Wilmette, Winnetka, Highland Park, Deerfield, Northbrook, Glenview, and Skokie. Fifty student volunteers, both white and black, would be recruited to survey homeowners and ask them to list their homes only with nondiscriminatory Realtors (eventually, more than seventy students participated). At the time, the only "concession" Realtors would make was to offer to designate some units as "open occupancy," which still perpetuated a dual and therefore unfair real estate market. A secondary purpose of the project was to embolden these homeowners to stand up to Realtors by using their sheer numbers to create a mandate in favor of fair housing.

The North Shore Summer Project was intended, as reflected in its recruitment brochure, to appeal to students who saw right through not only the hypocrisy in the real estate industry but also the workings of the civil rights movement itself. It is instructive to read the pitch: "During the past two years, college students have become increasingly aware that freedom does not exist in the North. In 1965 students realize that their home towns are 'closed communities' because Negro families are denied the right to choose where they may live. This summer, many students feel they cannot in good conscience leave a closed community in the North to work on a closed society in the South. The North Shore Summer Project is for those students."

The students gathered at the outset of the project to receive formal training in topics ranging from nonviolence to housing discrimination to interviewing techniques. Tellingly, they also attended a performance of a new Benjamin Britten opera, *Noye's Fludde,* at Sacred Heart Catholic Church in Winnetka. It told the story of Noah's ark, perhaps in order to show the students the ultimate triumph of good in building a just community. Jane Erb observes, "Britten frequently based his work on the conflict between a simple man and corrupt society and this theme is dramatically present in *Noye's Fludde,* where the innocent children and animals present a strong contrast to the wickedness of the society God destroys in the flood."[21] Moyer's lecture to the students on housing discrimination followed this performance.

Meanwhile, the NSSP opened its main Freedom Center in a Winnetka storefront at 730 Elm Street. The Reverend Emory Davis, pastor of Bethel AME Church in Evanston, chaired the project's Steering Committee and was one of four religious leaders who dedicated the center on Sunday, June 20. Moyer was essentially his sole staff member, serving as the center's executive director.

While the students were pounding the pavement, adults were approaching Realtors, business leaders, and municipal officials. "We developed the perfect [equal housing] button. We thought it was pretty stunning," recalls Cleland. "So we set up little meeting places in different communities, we printed some materials, and we recruited churches to lend their support. My memory is that every Saturday in the late afternoon, we'd go to a different church for singing and rabble-rousing and reporting. There was enthusiasm."

Deployed by the Freedom Centers in ten suburbs, volunteers stood at train stations, in front of shops, and at churches and synagogues and asked people to sign the following statement:

> We the undersigned North Shore residents, believe that all
> peoples should have equal access to housing in all communities
> without regard to race, color, creed or national origin.
>   This is the American ideal. We believe in the American ideal.
>   Therefore, we ask that real estate brokers serve all customers
> alike, and that all listings, including multiple listings, be shown
> and sold without regard to race, color, creed or national origin.

By August, they had obtained a staggering total of 12,059 signatures, including from "993 professional persons."[22]

As the NSSP's survey of homeowners had revealed, real estate professionals served as the largely self-appointed gatekeepers of racial and religious exclusion. This became evident at a meeting between NSSP leaders and the North Suburban Real Estate Board, brokered by the Skokie Human Relations Commission in June 1965. One member of the Real Estate Board admonished, "You clergy and the Summer Project may go too far and the riff-raff might come in here." In response to the Realtors' offer to throw the bone of "open occupancy listings" to fair-housing advocates, Reverend Davis retorted that this "merely gives official sanction to segregated housing." Louis Pfaff, president of the Real Estate Board, argued that there were "only three or four interested colored buyers." But the Reverend Gerald Roseberry of NSSP immediately responded that there were, in fact, seventy-five.[23]

Hostility against African Americans is woven into the history of the North Shore. Only a few Evanston neighborhoods had welcomed African Americans when they fled from the South to escape lynchings in the early twentieth century. Surrounding neighborhoods and suburbs had "restrictive covenants" against African Americans, as well as Jews and Catholics. Although the Supreme Court had invalidated these covenants in 1948 (*Shelley v. Kraemer*), enforcement was lax. Racism was more subtle in the North than in the South, but African Americans knew where they could and could not go, according to Karen Chavers. Blacks were relegated to living by the "stinky sanitary canal" in west Evanston, where Chavers's aunt, who was a seamstress, lived for a time. Glencoe's black community dated back to the 1880s, when former slaves had settled in the suburb and worked the railroads. But this population had dwindled, with St. Paul AME Church, the only black church between Evanston and Waukegan, as the sole reminder of its presence. Glencoe and Evanston also had a history of segregated beaches, hospitals, hotels, and schools.

In 1959, when developer Morris Milgram decided to build "integrated housing" on a piece of land in Deerfield that no one wanted, the people of Deerfield suddenly took interest in the land and hastily passed a referendum to turn it into a park instead. Even Eleanor Roosevelt's visit in support of the development and the grassroots organization Deerfield Citizens for Human Rights failed to sway the populace. At the time, the press decried the Deerfield majority as "northern segregationists."[24]

In 1961, when a black family bought a home in Skokie, they were greeted by bricks. In 1964, when a white widow wanted to sell her home to a black family in "tiny, WASPish, all-white" Kenilworth, she received anonymous threats. She did indeed sell her home to Harold and Lillian Calhoun, a well-to-do couple (he was a former assistant attorney general), but on the occasion of their one-year anniversary, neighbors burned a cross on their lawn.[25]

What began to change, however, was the attitude that it was all right to discriminate. Bob Lemon, general manager of Channel 5 television and a resident of Winnetka, even aired a promotional piece in June 1964, "Winnetka Outsider on the Doorstep," to simultaneously promote the suburb as racially open and remind white residents that they "must live with the times" and learn from their children, whose only prejudices "center around the food they have to eat, the homework they have to do, and the TV shows they can't watch."[26] New Trier High School students created human relations clubs and held exchanges with their African American counterparts in Chicago.

"Churches and synagogues that once remained piously aloof" began to speak out, according to Robert McClory. Buckner Coe, Emory Davis, Rabbi Arnold Wolff, Monsignor Reynold Hillenbrand, and other ministers, priests, rabbis, and Baha'i leaders from throughout the North Shore used their pulpits to inspire their congregants to join the open-housing cause. "It becomes our duty as Jews, through the mandate of our own sorrowful history, and the imperatives of our faith," asserted Rabbi Philip Lipis of Synagogue Beth El in Highland Park, "to be on the side of the Negro in his search for equality." He exhorted his congregants to join the North Shore Summer Project and to make sure that the "2,000 homes listed for sale" were available to African Americans. This was no small task, considering that only five homes had been sold to African Americans in 1964.[27]

Housing advocacy was not easy for these clergy, as most of them were challenged by members of their congregations. Coe was constantly threatened with dismissal because of his civil rights stance (he dared to march in Mississippi on his own time, without asking his congregation's permission), and after the North Shore Summer Project, he, Davis, and others left, either voluntarily or by fiat. But for many years the liberal and progressive clergy held sway and influenced the activism of their lay leadership. According to Cleland, Coe "kept our spirits up like nobody else could. He influenced all of us more than any one person [through his] very strong principles."

And so these clergymen, the dozens of student participants, Bill Moyer, and the women of the Freedom Centers, most notably Henrietta Boal Moore, a Winnetka widow and mother of five, laid the groundwork for the appearance of Dr. Martin Luther King Jr. at the Winnetka Village Green on July 25, 1965. "Civil rights has come to the North Shore," proclaimed Reverend Davis when he introduced the most prominent leader of the civil rights movement to a crowd of 10,000.[28]

Dr. King had been to the North Shore before and had spoken at two Jewish congregations (Beth Emet in Evanston and Congregation Solel in Highland Park), but this was his first public speech on the North Shore—indeed, his first in any all-white suburb. African Americans were concerned about their safety if they joined the rally on the North Shore, according to Chavers, who was thirteen at the time. But her parents, who had traveled to protests as far as 800 miles away, piled her and her brothers into the station wagon and headed to Winnetka. Other parents went but did not bring their children.

During that festive day, the climax of the North Shore Summer Project, "there were guitars, folk singers, lost children, multitudes of mosquitoes, and even a group of American Nazi Party members, who came to picket the civil rights movement."[29] Headliners included writer Studs Terkel, folksingers Win Stracke and George and Gerry Armstrong, actor Oscar Brown Jr., and organizers C. T. Vivian and Al Raby (head of the Coordinating Council of Community Organizations, the hub of civil rights activism in Chicago).

David James, an NSSP member who became the first African American to buy a home in Winnetka in 1967, said, "It was a very stirring moment for me."[30] Chavers added, "It was a communal gathering. It was intense—lots of people—but there was no fear at all. I saw people that I knew going back and forth from the city and suburbs playing the welfare game together in church [an educational exercise intended to teach people what it meant to live on a poverty-level income], and we made signs together. There was no fear, no hate, no rocks that I could see. This was clearly a friendly crowd on a common mission. But it was faith-based so I wouldn't have expected anything other."

The speech Dr. King gave in Winnetka that day was one of several, and he was preparing for a major march in Chicago the following day. He was hoarse at the beginning of the speech, but he clearly recovered.[31] Before heading north from his last speech on the South Side, recalls Cleland, "Dr. King went to a private home for rest and relaxation. Some of us were invited to go there, file past him as he sat in a lounge chair, shake his hand, and move on. As we greeted him, Dr. King commented on my equal-housing button, whereupon I removed it and pinned it on his lapel."[32]

Susan Gregory described how she felt as a teenager on the Village Green: "King's voice rolled over the green into the cool summer night, and I stood behind his podium counting money collected for the movement. There so close to my own home, as in distant Montgomery, I experienced the thrill of his oratory, his beautiful phrasing, his power of conviction."[33] "What is profitable to a Realtor," he said, "is not always profitable to a city."[34]

This stirring rally was only the prelude to the rest of the summer. In mid-August the North Shore Summer Project completed its two months of research, interviewing 673 of the 2,000 homeowners whose homes were listed for sale with Realtors. Of the 462 sellers whose interviews

were completed, 72.7 percent said they would show their home to prospective buyers regardless of race, religion, or national origin. Less than 8
percent had requested restrictive listings. These findings directly rebutted
Realtors' claims that they were only following the preferences of homeowners. Contradicted just as soundly was the Real Estate Board's contention that "their job is one of 'social engineering,' that it didn't matter so
much what the seller wanted, since he was usually leaving the neighborhood, [but] how the community would feel." On the contrary, 82 percent of the 1,560 North Shore interviewees who were not moving said
they "would accept Negroes as neighbors."[35]

The North Shore Summer Project buttressed these findings with specific tales of discrimination based on testing and bona fide African American home seekers working with NSSP. For instance, David James and his
wife had been shown "the same five homes in Evanston," despite their
comfortable income and their desire to live farther north.[36] Mac Robinet, a
physics instructor at the University of Illinois College of Pharmacy, and his
wife Harriette, a former bacteriologist, had asked to see homes in Winnetka
but were refused by all three Realtors they contacted. The Realtors told the
Robinets they were "too busy" or that none of the homeowners "wanted
to sell to Negroes," even though TV cameras were rolling in one instance.[37]

The North Shore Summer Project concluded that the actions of the
Evanston–North Shore Board of Realtors violated the code of ethics of its
own national association (to engage in "fair dealing and high integrity")
and in fact upheld segregation. It used forceful language in the report of
its findings, decrying the Realtors as "arbitrary agents of a system both
evil and medieval—and alien to the religious, patriotic and moral beliefs
held dear in our society."[38] The North Shore Summer Project decided to
publicly demand that the Realtors change their policies, so it organized
what it called "the first civil rights march through North Shore villages."
On the afternoon of Sunday, August 29, the Reverend Emory Davis led
the marchers from the NSSP Freedom Center in Winnetka. They wended
their way south through Kenilworth and Wilmette, ending up six miles
later at the Evanston office of the Evanston–North Shore Board of Realtors at 3009 Central Street. At that point, Davis was set to present the
NSSP's findings personally to Louis A. Pfaff, president of the board. "We
are marching to the Realtors' office," said Moyer, "to ask them again to

take positive steps to end segregation on the North Shore."[39] Afterward, they planned to conduct an all-night vigil at Bent Park.

More than 500 people marched to the North Shore Summer Project's song:

People get ready, there's a project coming;
We're gonna open up the whole North Shore.
People get ready for the Summer Project,
you know hypocrisy will do no more. (CHORUS)

The North Shore's been blessed with such a Board of Realtors.
They don't discriminate, you'll hear them say;
They reassure us that they're fond of Negroes,
especially if you keep them far away.

Responsible people send their checks in monthly,
to help us fight the War on Poverty;
But these good neighbors know the rights of people,
Can't come before the rights of property.

You sent your food and books to Mississippi,
you even traveled to Montgomery;
Which one of you will be the first on your block,
to integrate your own community?[40]

The North Shore Summer Project wound down its activities as summer turned to fall. Some of the group's student volunteers organized local offshoots, such as For Real Estate Equality in Evanston. They also held a retreat at the Ecumenical Institute in Chicago to plan for an October conference on housing discrimination on the North Shore and to devise ways to keep the NSSP's work going. Moyer wrote a long reflection in the last *NSSP Newsletter*, released on September 14, 1965, to say that this was not an "ending" but a "rededication":

The concerned citizens here . . . will be watching and waiting and hoping that you, the Realtors, will use the month ahead to implement the finding in this report and to establish a new policy of equality opportunity in housing for all.

This next month will see no vigils, no marches, no realty-focused demonstrations. It will see, we hope, a new dawn for the North Shore, when our Realtors here will no longer be the only remaining businessmen to ask the race and religion of potential customers before serving them.[41]

The story was not over.

Most of the clergy leaders, white and black, were pushed out by their less liberal congregants or had resigned by 1970. The Reverend Buckner Coe was able to survive being spat upon by motorists while protesting in front of Wilmette real estate offices, but he could not survive the repeated attempts by some of his own congregants to oust him because of his vocal stance in favor of open housing and against the war in Vietnam.

Since the 1970s, the uncompromising leadership of the clergy on civil rights has declined precipitously. Gone are the days when Karen Chavers's Woodlawn priest would simply say, "We have a bus out front and we're going to downtown Chicago and demonstrate with placards and yell 'Jimmy Crow must go,'" and everyone would follow. The attitude changed from one of setting the standard based on the dictates of one's faith to following the wishes of one's congregation. Coe's philosophy was evident in his comments to the *Yale Daily News* upon taking a one-year residency at the university in 1970: "I chose to show that it is possible for the church to be 'the Church' in the fullest sense. . . . The function of the church is to galvanize—to recognize the needs that are not being met and meet them on a social as well as a personal level."[42]

Similarly, Emory Davis left Bethel AME Church in 1966 because of "an increasing conviction that the institutional church is not meeting the basic needs of society," including housing rights. He said his 400-member congregation "reflects the general apathy of middle class, and would-be middle class people in Evanston, regardless of race. They are comparatively well-off and satisfied to be where they are. They're afraid of rocking the status quo which finds them where they are." The secretary of the church, Charles Underwood, responded that although the congregation supported civil rights, "We don't believe demonstrations accomplish very much. Civil rights will be advanced when people's hearts are changed, and demonstrations won't do that."[43]

In the days following Dr. King's assassination on April 4, 1968, clergy like Buckner Coe felt that every white person needed to bear responsibility, "just as Christ died for our sins." It is hard to imagine a congregation today reading a litany like the one composed and read by Coe and repeated, uncomfortably for some, by those in the pews at First Congregational Church, UCC, in Wilmette on April 7. Here is an excerpt:

> Minister: O God, whose son Martin Luther King, the best friend the white man ever had, died because of a white man and because of the white racism of us all.
> People: Save us and help us, we beseech Thee.
> Minister: For the violence of white society, the violence of our institutions, the violence of our wars, the violence of indifference and neglect that destroys the poor.
> People: Forgive us, O Lord.
> Minister: For going about business as usual, thinking that problems will go away if we don't face them.
> People: Forgive us, O Lord.
> Minister: For saying "I agree with your goals but not your methods" and doing nothing.
> People: Forgive us, O Lord.
> Minister: For saying "progress must be made slowly" and doing nothing.
> People: Forgive us, O Lord.
> Minister: For pretending our nation "never had it so good" and being self-satisfied.
> People: Forgive us, O Lord.[44]

On April 11, 1968, President Lyndon Johnson signed into law the Civil Rights Act of 1968, including the Fair Housing Act (Title VIII). At last, nondiscrimination in housing was the law of the land. All the work of the North Shore Summer Project was validated with the stroke of a pen. It no longer mattered what any Realtor, homeowner, or landlord thought, now that equal housing opportunity was a legal right. Moreover, jurisdictions had to "affirmatively further fair housing"—that is, they had to promote integration.

In 1972 John McDermott, a leader in the Chicago Freedom Movement and later an officer of the Community Renewal Society affiliated with the United Church of Christ, approached his friend, the Reverend Paul Allen of the Winnetka Congregational Church, to organize North Shore congregations around housing. As Allen recalled, "John said to me, 'We have in principle won the battle for open housing among the races because of the [Fair Housing Act of 1968] . . . but we haven't tackled the problem of division by income. And this is something the religious community should be concerned about.'"[45] In 1994 McDermott told me that his dream was to see a "clergy manifesto" on open housing.[46]

In 1972 the North Shore Summer Project's founders created the North Shore Interfaith Housing Council as a "vehicle for religious concern" to support housing for low-income people and seniors, as well as to enforce fair-housing laws. Momentum for the creation of a permanent organization came from a major conference under the leadership of Allen, McDermott, and a dozen other clergy. Organizers of "The Inclusive Community: Challenge to Church and Synagogue," which took place on October 15, 1972, also commissioned a report from Loyola University titled *Housing Patterns in Six North Shore Communities*. The study measured the high level of affluence of these communities and the almost totally white nature of that affluence. The study also remarked on the persistence of poverty and the fact that nearly half of local public- and private-sector workers were priced out of the housing market.[47] More than 300 people attended this conference.

Rayna Miller, one of the most active NSSP volunteers and a former president of the Wilmette League of Women Voters, became executive director of the North Shore Interfaith Housing Council in 1975. A charismatic woman, Miller utilized her community connections to build a formidable coalition of more than sixty congregations and civic organizations and more than 500 individual donors. The Housing Council was initially housed in a Wilmette church. The interracial board included Karen Chavers, David James, and Jean Cleland.

The Housing Council's first task was to advocate for housing for low- and moderate-income seniors and families. Its first major victory was the

1977 development of Gates Manor, a fifty-one-unit low-income rental building for seniors, financed with federal funds and built on land owned by the First Congregational Church.

Miller worked closely with Kale Williams, director of the Chicago-based Leadership Council for Metropolitan Open Communities (LCMOC), and Alexander Polikoff of what is now called BPI, Business and Professional People for the Public Interest, to implement the 1969 *Gautreaux* court decision, designed to desegregate Chicago public housing by allowing African Americans to move to predominantly white city and suburban neighborhoods. In 1977 the Housing Council founded the North Suburban Housing Center, also run by Miller, as a service organization to do the painstaking work of combing apartment listings for eligible families, in conjunction with the Fair Housing Network of Chicago-area groups. Through this work, the Housing Center could not help noticing the persistence of discrimination in the rental market. It even had difficulty finding units for local workers. Mary Sample, a Wilmette resident who worked for the center, recalled, "Rayna didn't find a single business on the North Shore interested in finding housing for their workers. I was really disappointed about that."[48]

In 1983 the Housing Council and the Housing Center jointly created the Interfaith Housing Development Corporation, thus taking the development of affordable housing into their own hands. Housing policy had already undergone a major shift. Starting with the Nixon administration, the direct development of public housing by HUD came to an end. Instead, in 1974 the federal government created the Section 8 portable voucher program for the poor, allowing them to move into rent-subsidized, fair-market-rate units of their choice, although participation by landlords was voluntary. Bricks-and-mortar development became a new game of public-private partnerships and "lasagna financing," using the tax code, subsidized mortgage interest, and modest grants from the federal and other levels of government to create what became known as "affordable" housing—a market for those above the level of destitute.

But most significantly, the Housing Council's advocacy work contributed to the creation of new affordable housing in Deerfield, Evanston, Highland Park, Morton Grove, Northbrook, Northfield, Skokie, and Wilmette. Although most of this housing was for seniors, it was nevertheless an uphill political battle against neighbors, who assumed the new inhabitants would come from Chicago—in other words, poor African Americans from public housing. Miller recalls that, at one particularly contentious meeting about what became Shore Line Place, a low-income senior rental building in Wilmette, she asked a minister to "bring the collar" to lend moral authority. The council's most spectacular failure was advocating for the conversion of the empty Howard School in Wilmette into affordable housing in the 1980s. The building was ultimately torn down, and its cupola was inexplicably saved and planted in the ground of the park where the building once stood, serving as a nauseating reminder of the antipathy toward affordable housing to this day.

In the late 1980s the group's most significant grassroots accomplishment was gaining zoning rights for group homes for people with disabilities in Wilmette. It was a controversial campaign; some citizens groups were against "urbanization," while other residents championed inclusion. Some of the same language of the 1960s housing movement for racial justice was employed. Clarice Stetter, a friend of Rayna Miller and cochair of what was then called the Wilmette Coalition for Group Homes, said, "I can remember when there was religious intolerance in Wilmette, when Jews and Catholics couldn't live in certain neighborhoods. That isn't true anymore. We have a diverse community. I remember all the resistance to senior-citizen housing. A lot of the same arguments were raised. People said we don't need it. It will bring in outsiders. It will lower property values. None of this was true." Residents packed meetings about the zoning changes, and opponents tried to block them through a referendum. Ultimately, advocates of zoning reform prevailed by a margin of two to one.[49]

In the early 1990s HUD created the Fair Housing Initiatives Program, which provided funding to private nonprofit agencies to investigate housing discrimination through testing and to file complaints or lawsuits with the federal government. By then, Miller had retired, and the North Shore Interfaith Housing Council and the North Suburban Housing Center had merged to become the Interfaith Housing Center of the Northern Suburbs. The new entity took advantage of this funding to expand its fair-housing testing and to provide education to local commissions. Interfaith collaborated with the LCMOC and the City of Evanston to uncover steering and racial discrimination. Several real estate companies went out of business as a result, and one company, Baird & Warner, established a detailed system to monitor the race of all clients who saw units on the market and created a fair-housing staff position to oversee it. In 1990 Century 21 Shoreline paid a settlement of more than $200,000 to the City of Evanston.

As the 1990s unfolded, many suburbs circumvented fair-housing laws by using zoning regulations to exclude the poor, people of color, or the disabled, even while low-wage jobs were moving into the area. But the transportation system was not geared to handle the workday "reverse commute," and there was no minimum-wage housing for minimum-wage job holders, to use a common phrase. Barbara Ehrenreich's popular book on the topic, *Nickel and Dimed*, revealed what was happening at places like the Admiral Oasis Motel in the northern suburb of Morton Grove: people who were struggling to make ends meet on multiple low-paying service jobs with no benefits were living in motels because they required no security deposits, allowed weekly payments, and were close to work. The Admiral, for example, was only two doors away from Avon Corporation and was situated in a major commercial shopping strip.[50]

Morton Grove had declared a strip of Waukegan Road to be a tax increment finance (TIF) district, a state-permitted designation for a supposedly "blighted" area that, without property tax breaks, would not enjoy economic investment. At the time, the US Department of Justice had sued several suburbs for using TIFs to displace Latinos. Chicago had created more than eighty TIFs. Interfaith worked closely with Housing Action Illinois (then called the Statewide Housing Action Coalition) on statewide TIF reform and to organize the Admiral Oasis residents. Jean Cleland rose to the occasion, brokering a meeting between motel residents and the village's elected officials. Tenants sported buttons they had made that said, "I'm Not Blight." This publicized campaign was one of the earliest to highlight the suburban jobs-housing mismatch.

In the end, through the power of organizing and media attention, the tenants got time and money, but they still had to move. The same was true for residents of the next motel on the list, the smaller Fireside Inn. By the time Morton Grove acquired the Suburban Motel, the coalition of groups including Interfaith had succeeded in changing the state TIF law to protect low-income families facing displacement. The Morton Grove staff person tasked with relocating the Suburban Motel families under the first test of the new law, exasperated and unaware of the irony of his question, asked me, "Where's the affordable housing?"

Zoning that limits multifamily housing and the number of units per acre raises land prices. High prices are further buttressed by a statewide system that relies on property taxes to fund the public schools, so the best schools are in the wealthy districts—which in turn boosts property values and prices. Low-income housing, then, is viewed as a threat.

Since people of color generally earn less than whites, racial segregation persists. According to a fifty-year retrospective on life for African Americans since the 1963 March on Washington, in the City of Chicago the median income for African American families in 1960 was 62 percent that of whites; by 2010 it had fallen to less than 50 percent.[51] The black homeownership rate was the lowest of any racial group at 41 percent, compared with 76 percent for non-Hispanic whites.[52] Modest gains made by African American homeowners in the suburbs were set back by the weakened economy and the foreclosure crisis precipitated by the predatory lending practices of the late 1990s, whereby unscrupulous, unregulated subprime mortgage brokers disproportionately targeted African Americans who were cash poor but asset rich.

Housing-rights groups have had some success over the decades in framing the suburban rejection of affordable housing as a means of excluding African Americans, and they have been successful in using the court system to order remedies, such as in Arlington Heights, Illinois, in 1977 and Westchester County, New York, in 2009. Racial intent can be very difficult to prove, however. Built-out "landlocked" communities, like most of those on the North Shore, maintain their largely white makeup by zealously protecting their predominantly single-family-home character and large minimum lot sizes, thereby hiking land prices well above the means of young families, recent immigrants, people with disabilities, and retirees, with a disparate impact on households of color. The legal potency of disparate-impact claims in fair-housing suits was upheld in 2015 by the US Supreme Court in *Texas Department of Housing and Community Affairs v. The Inclusive Communities Project, Inc.*[53]

Through their lobbying arm, the Illinois Municipal League, the suburbs were responsible for watering down legislation to redress the jobs-housing mismatch. The state's Affordable Housing Planning and Appeal Act (2004) mandates that 10 percent of the housing in every Illinois community be "affordable," but there is no deadline and few consequences for noncompliance.

Forty-five years after the North Shore Summer Project rallied thousands in Winnetka, the reactionary Winnetka Home Owners Association (WHOA) mobilized opposition to a modest affordable-housing plan designed to comply with the state's affordable-housing act (aimed at retirees and workers earning $75,000 to $105,000 per year), characterizing it as "social engineering." Ironically, NSSP had leveled this same accusation against the North Shore Real Estate Board decades earlier. In a local paper sent by WHOA to every Winnetka household in an attempt to defeat the plan, one resident is quoted as saying, "Once an Affordable Housing law passes in a community, a proverbial toe gets in the door and the problems are endless. Winnetka must stop this initiative. . . . AT OUR BORDERS." Carry Buck, the leader of WHOA, wrote, "Some would say I am mean-spirited or perhaps immoral to even think of locking my front gates to keep strangers out. I say—this is America—or it used to be anyway. Get off my porch!"[54]

Over the decades, fighting for access to housing has broadened beyond African Americans. Other populations long discriminated against and subsumed under fair-housing laws have also organized: people with disabilities, immigrants, and gays and lesbians. Four out of ten immigrants now bypass Chicago for the northern and northwestern suburbs—"the new Ellis Island."[55] The Interfaith Housing Center has devoted more organizing resources to this population, particularly Mexican immigrants fighting displacement in Highwood; the mostly Pakistani Muslim taxicab drivers in Skokie, whose loss of street parking rights threatened their ability to live in the community; and parents with limited English, who get lost in the school system. Interfaith even created a series of training sessions for immigrants to encourage them to join local boards and commissions.

At the start of the 2008 school year, the Reverend James Meeks, an African American state senator, prepared to lead a protest of Chicago children at New Trier High School against inequitable public school funding.

Parents, frustrated in their attempts to engage school officials in a plan to welcome instead of shun the Chicagoans, approached Interfaith to get involved. One woman asked me, "If not Interfaith, who?" Interfaith then convened two dozen parents, clergy, and teachers in a Winnetka home and formed United We Learn (UWL), based on the recognition that access to quality education should not depend on one's zip code. UWL became a campaign of more than 200 people of diverse backgrounds and released a documentary in 2010 titled *The Education They Deserve*. The film presents student and teacher voices from the city and the suburbs, portraying the stark reality of "two worlds" firmly entrenched by a tax system that shores up racism.[56]

With the founding of UWL and Interfaith's expanded work with new immigrants, its board of directors recognized that the agency needed to end its rigid focus on housing in the northern suburbs. Although restrictive covenants no longer exist, skyrocketing housing prices exclude the historically disenfranchised, and with few exceptions, local governments do not consider diversity to be a priority. Religious congregations have generally lost interest in housing justice. The term "inclusiveness" has evolved to encompass more than inviting those of other races and religions into communities; it now means embracing people with disabilities, immigrants, families with children, and those with different sexual orientations.

In this new environment, Interfaith reached a critical juncture and reassessed its purpose, reflecting back on the progressive energy and fearlessness of its founders. In 2012 the Interfaith Housing Center of the Northern Suburbs broadened its mission to encompass the full spectrum of social justice concerns, while retaining as its core purpose the promotion of a more welcoming northern suburban region. It therefore changed its name to the simple and declarative Open Communities.

The North Shore Summer Project ushered in local fair-housing laws and human relations commissions and built a foundation based on the acceptance of nondiscrimination in housing. The most significant legacy of the work of the Clelands, the Reverends Emory Davis and Buckner Coe, David James, Bill Moyer, and the thousands of men, women, and students who participated in the North Shore Summer Project was, however, the evolution of new social justice leaders, especially among women. Its direct descendant, Open Communities, continues to act as the local conscience for fair housing and inclusiveness.

These individuals collectively challenged the North Shore "brand" of exclusivity and whiteness and opened the door to African Americans. From the perspective of those who lived through the North Shore Summer Project and its aftermath, it is difficult not to feel the exhilaration of progress: racial diversity has grown, and they no longer know all the black residents of a community, as they had in the days when they were personally finding housing for black families.[57]

"People [of all races] come and go," Marvin Miller said at a gathering of NSSP founders that I organized in 2002, "and nobody knows. Very few people care."

"My only regret is that there are not more of my people here and I think the barrier is income," responded Bill Thomas, the first African American to buy a home in Wilmette. "I don't know how much longer we'll be here if they keep knocking down $600,000 houses and putting up $1.2 million ones."[58]

The irony of the North Shore Summer Project (and something its founders did not see) is that as a fundamentally faith-based movement encompassing the quintessentially American value of being able to live wherever we choose, it unwittingly provided fodder for the dark side of liberalism: allowing continuing discrimination against poor or even middle-class people. The movement's atmosphere of welcome was all too brief, and its adherents' inner passion, rooted in a firm grasp of religious obligation and sense of justice, has dissipated to some extent in today's libertarian culture of gated communities and even gated homes.

Justice-minded residents, working against the tide of moral apathy and the loss of a sense of community, are forced to constantly react as suburban political leaders find new ways to exclude people of color, especially those who are poor. If they cannot do it through the outright denial of housing, they do it by pricing them out. To adapt a phrase from the Supreme Court, racism, like water, will always find an outlet.[59] The right to housing, regardless of income, is the last and most intransigent fair-housing frontier.

"Without intentionality, things stay the same," says Karen Chavers.

"The need for community organizing is more so now than ever," and that includes building community. Reflecting on changes over time, she concludes that there is less opportunity for personal interaction between whites and African Americans than in the 1960s. The proliferation of well-meaning nonprofit social services agencies effectively allows "good" white people who might have taken to the streets or hosted black families at their homes to separate themselves from civic life and remain strangers by writing checks.

Cleland and Chavers separately contemplate the same biblical principle: "to those whom much is given, much is expected." To both of them, this means that we are on earth to *share*. "That's why we're here, that's the human plight," Chavers says with a laugh. "You too could have bedbugs, even in Winnetka." Cleland thinks, optimistically, that "we're moving along as a society, and we're a privileged layer of society in those suburbs."

In the absence of an intentional culture of sharing, the North Shore's normal is atomization, a tendency Open Communities continues to fight through grassroots mobilization. When the social system requires ever more income to stay afloat, one's four walls become less a home or a source of nurturance and community than an economic investment. To challenge that culture requires a sense that the rights of people come before the rights of property, as the NSSP volunteers sang, and a belief that neighbors' responsibility to one another comes before all.

Notes

The epigraph is from "NSSP Sponsors: North Shore Summer Project Summary Report," *NSSP Newsletter*, September 14, 1965.

1. The North Shore consists of the following communities: Deerfield, Evanston, Glencoe, Glenview, Highland Park, Highwood, Kenilworth, Lincolnwood, Morton Grove, Niles, Northbrook, Northfield, Park Ridge, Skokie, Wilmette, and Winnetka.

2. Interfaith Housing Center of the Northern Suburbs press release, "Census 2010: While More Racially Diverse, African Americans Still Largely Absent in Chicago's Northern Suburbs," February 9, 2012; Interfaith Housing Center of the Northern Suburbs, "Outsider Perspectives on Chicago's Northern Suburbs: Based on a Focus Group Study Conducted by the University of Illinois at Chicago's Nathalie P. Voorhees Center for Neighborhood and Community Improve-

ment," October 2012, 6. The press releases, fair and affordable housing studies, and other historical documents cited in this chapter, such as the "North Shore Summer Project: Summary Report," are available on the Open Communities website: www.open-communities.org.

3. Jack Mabley, "Can Love Win over Fear on the North Shore?" *Chicago's American*, May 14, 1965.

4. "North Shore Activists Remember King," WBEZ radio, January 12, 2007, http://www.wbez.org/episode-segments/north-shore-activists-remember-king. See also "Pioneering Winnetka Rights Activist: Henrietta Boal Moore," *Chicago Sun-Times*, March 24, 2009: "She had Dr. Martin Luther King come out and speak in the Winnetka village green."

5. Quoted in Robert McClory, "Subsidized Housing on the North Shore: Guess Who's Coming to Kenilworth?" *Chicago Reader*, November 19, 1982, 3.

6. Jean Cleland, interview by Gail Schechter, April 12, 2013. Unless otherwise indicated, subsequent quotations are also from this interview.

7. McClory, "Subsidized Housing."

8. Karen Chavers, interview by Gail Schechter, September 6, 2013. Subsequent quotations are also from this interview.

9. Mabley, "Can Love Win over Fear?"

10. "Prospectus of the North Shore Summer Project," undated (most likely early 1965), NSSP Collection, University of Illinois at Chicago (UIC), emphasis added.

11. Speech by Lerone Bennett Jr., *NSSP Newsletter*, June 25, 1965, NSSP Collection, UIC.

12. Susan Gregory, *Hey, White Girl* (New York: Norton, 1970), 18–19.

13. Speech by Bennett.

14. James R. Ralph Jr., *Northern Protest: Martin Luther King, Jr., Chicago, and the Civil Rights Movement* (Cambridge, MA: Harvard University Press, 1993), 99. See also William Moyer with Elbert Ransom Jr., "End Slums and Discrimination: Open Communities: A Prospectus for a Non-violent Project to Achieve Open Occupancy throughout the Chicago Area" (HOME Inc., March 1966), Chicago Freedom Movement online archives, Middlebury College, Middlebury, VT, http://sites.middlebury.edu/chicagofreedommovement/archive/primary-sources/. This report was shared with Martin Luther King Jr. and the SCLC for their consideration as they sought a focus for the Chicago direct action campaign.

15. Carol Kleiman, "Mission in Suburbia," *Renewal*, April 1965, 14.

16. Ibid.

17. The term "Realtor" is trademarked by the National Association of Realtors.

18. "North Shore Summer Project: Summary Report," August 29, 1965, http://www.open-communities.org/files/2327/File/NSSP_1965Study_ICNS.pdf.

19. NSSP news release, June 17, 1965, NSSP Collection, UIC.

20. "Prospectus of the North Shore Summer Project."

21. Jane Erb, "Noye's Fludde," 1996, http://www.classical.net/music/comp.lst/works/britten/noyesfludde.php.

22. NSSP news release, August 19, 1965, NSSP Collection, UIC; "North Shore Summer Project: Summary Report," 5.

23. *NSSP Newsletter,* June 25, 1965, NSSP Collection, UIC.

24. Rich Samuels, "Civil Rights on the North Shore: Bringing the Movement Home," WTTW-Channel 11, aired on MLK Day, January 2002; Thomas J. Sugrue, *Sweet Land of Liberty: The Forgotten Struggle for Civil Rights in the North* (New York: Random House, 2008), 237–43. For an excellent video depicting the Deerfield controversy, see Chicago Video Project, "No Place to Live: Chicago's Affordable Housing Crisis," 2002, https://www.youtube.com/watch?v=3rMjs-R094c.

25. McClory, "Subsidized Housing," 3.

26. Samuels, "Civil Rights on the North Shore."

27. McClory, "Subsidized Housing," 3; Rabbi Lipis courtesy of Sharon Feigon, from a tape she donated to me and the Interfaith Housing Center (now Open Communities), April 30, 1965.

28. "8,000 Jam Park to Hear Dr. King," *Wilmette Life,* July 29, 1965, 1. Estimates of the turnout vary. The *Chicago Tribune* put the number at 10,000, and NSSP estimated 15,000.

29. Thomas Fitzpatrick, "Winnetka Crowd Hears King," *Chicago Tribune,* July 26, 1965.

30. WBEZ interview, January 12, 2007.

31. "8,000 Jam Park to Hear Dr. King," 1. The full text of King's speech was reprinted in an issue of the *NSSP Newsletter,* August 1965, NSSP Collection, UIC.

32. Jean Cleland, written statement read by her son, Carter Cleland, at a commemoration of Dr. King's visit at the Winnetka Woman's Club, January 15, 2007, cosponsored by the Interfaith Housing Center and the Winnetka Historical Society.

33. Gregory, *Hey, White Girl,* 19–20.

34. "8,000 Jam Park to Hear Dr. King," 1.

35. Full-page ad from the Evanston–North Shore Board of Realtors entitled "Sign a Petition! Let the People Decide the Question of Forced Housing by Referendum," *Winnetka Talk,* undated. See also "North Shore Summer Project: Summary Report."

36. Dino Robinson, "David F. James, Sr.: Influencing Social Change," *Shorefront* 6 (Fall 2004): 13.

37. "Negro Home Seekers Visit 3 Realtors, but Are Shown No Houses," *Winnetka Talk,* May 20, 1965, 4A.

38. "North Shore Summer Project: Summary Report," 7.

39. NSSP press release, August 13, 1965, NSSP Collection, UIC.

40. NSSP song, NSSP Collection, UIC. Adapted from "People Get Ready" by Curtis Mayfield. Copyright by Warner Tamerlane Publishing Group, 1965. Copyright assigned to Alfred Music Publishing. Used with permission.

41. *NSSP Newsletter,* September 14, 1965; see also "North Shore Summer Project: Summary Report."

42. "Former Reverend Coe Named Divinity Master," *Yale Daily News,* January 28, 1970, 1.

43. "Negro Cleric Quits Church," *Fond Du Lac Commonwealth Reporter,* August 10, 1966, 37.

44. From the private archives of the Reverend Donald Farley, co-pastor with Coe at Wilmette's First Congregational Church, UCC, accessed by the author May 16, 2013.

45. Quoted in Katherine Seigenthaler, "30th Anniversary," *Just Housing Newsletter,* Fall 2002, 5–6 (a publication of the Interfaith Housing Center of the Northern Suburbs).

46. John McDermott, personal communication, ca. 1994.

47. Michael E. Schlitz, *Housing Patterns in Six North Shore Communities: Wilmette, Kenilworth, Winnetka, Northfield, Glencoe, Highland Park* (North Shore Interfaith Conference on Suburban Housing Patterns, October 15, 1972).

48. Quoted in Seigenthaler, "30th Anniversary," 6.

49. Ben Joravsky, "A Zoning Controversy: Who Should Get to Live in Wilmette?" *Chicago Reader,* November 24, 1988, http://www.chicagoreader.com/chicago/a-zoning-controversy-who-should-get-to-live-in-wilmette/Content?oid=873080.

50. Barbara Ehrenreich, *Nickel and Dimed: On (Not) Getting by in America* (New York: Metropolitan Books, 2001), 27.

51. *Chicago Reader,* August 21, 2013.

52. For black demographics, see http://blackdemographics.com/cities-2/chicago/; Harvard University diversity data, http://diversitydata.sph.harvard.edu/Data/Profiles/Show.aspx?loc=308.

53. "Disparate impact can fill the void and root out the discriminatory origins undergirding current social conditions and structures," wrote the NAACP Legal Defense and Education Fund in its amicus brief in *Texas Department of Housing and Community Affairs v. The Inclusive Communities Project, Inc.* It added, "The ability to bring claims against housing practices with highly racial effects is one of the few effective means to investigate and address the legacy of *de jure* practices." http://www.americanbar.org/content/dam/aba/publications/supreme_court_preview/BriefsV4/13–1371_amicus_resp_NAACP.authcheckdam.pdf.

54. See the Open Communities archives for the Winnetka affordable-housing controversy, 2010–2012. See also my appearance on "Affordable Housing in

the Northern Suburbs," *Chicago Tonight* hosted by Phil Ponce, WTTW, April 6, 2011.

55. Hebrew Immigrant Aid Society, http://hiaschicago.org/immigrant-integration.

56. The Interfaith Housing Center was the fiscal agent for the production of *The Education They Deserve*, funded by the Sally Mead Hands Foundation. Ms. Hands was one of the founders of Interfaith.

57. Seigenthaler, "30th Anniversary," 7.

58. Ibid., 6.

59. "Money, like water, will always find an outlet." Comment by Supreme Court justices John Paul Stevens and Sandra Day O'Connor, writing for the majority in their 2003 opinion upholding campaign finance laws.

7

Tenant Unions during the Chicago Freedom Movement

Innovation and Impact

Herman Jenkins

The Chicago Freedom Movement (CFM) may be best remembered as a series of mass demonstrations demanding open access to housing for blacks and other minorities. But it also marked an important shift in the civil rights movement's focus away from the de jure rights characteristic of the Jim Crow South and toward the de facto social and economic justice that Dr. King called "genuine equality."[1] This transition was driven in part by the deep-rootedness of poverty, on the one hand, and the structural and institutional nature of the racism encountered in Chicago, on the other.[2] Although there were no Jim Crow laws in Chicago, and racial discrimination was already illegal by the mid-1960s, unequal access to opportunity and racial disparities in distributive outcomes persisted, and in some ways, these inequities were even greater in the North than in the South. The response by the CFM included two experimental efforts designed to address specific power imbalances in the structure of racial and economic relations: Operation Breadbasket, a promising selective-buying program brilliantly led by Jesse Jackson, and tenant unions, an effort to model associations of very-low-income renters on industrial labor unions.[3] This chapter describes the CFM tenant organizing effort, especially its innovative aspects and its impact in Chicago and beyond.

Telling the story of tenant unions from today's vantage point comes with a fifty-year perspective and the clarity of hindsight. Yet many things seemed clearer back then than they do now. In fact, our response to

182

increasing complexity may be the main insight to be gleaned. We quickly learned, for example, that not all landlords who owned or managed buildings in disrepair were vicious slumlords. Some were only marginally better off than their renters. Likewise, housing issues for tenants in different situations required different approaches. Tenants' issues varied, for example, by social class and income, and the problems of public-housing tenants differed from those of renters living in private-sector housing. The situations also differed for tenants in large tenement buildings versus smaller structures, as well as geographically in different cities around the country. For example, New York City was unique, given the large proportion of its housing stock that was rental. Unlike other cities, New York never developed large-scale working-class homeownership. In addition, developers were able to introduce forms of collective homeownership in New York City, such as cooperatives and condos.[4]

We also became increasingly aware of the interconnectedness between tenant housing problems and employment (or unemployment) problems, public transportation, affordable housing supply, and government policies. Tenant housing problems could not be solved in isolation; they required comprehensive, communitywide efforts that were both specialized and highly coordinated. So we aimed for greater differentiation and specialization in our tenant and community organizing efforts. Key people moved into new positions or undertook new responsibilities that reflected the changing imperatives of community organizing. Minnie Dunlap became a leader of Fifth City, a first-generation community development corporation (CDC), while Vernedia White succeeded her as president of the East Garfield Park tenant union. Shortly thereafter, Anthony (Tony) Henry, the lead organizer of the East Garfield Park group, moved to establish a nationwide tenant organization that would become the collective bargaining voice of the 4 million tenants in HUD public housing. Meanwhile, the Reverend William Briggs, pastor of the Warren Avenue Congregational Church, continued to provide professional leadership for the East Garfield Park tenant union. It soon became clear that the CDC, with its emphasis on combining community efforts with private enterprise, government policy, and support from nonprofits, would become the main type of organization for comprehensive community action. Prototypes of CDCs began to appear in Chicago, New

York City, and Newark, New Jersey, in 1966 and 1967. In New York, the Central Brooklyn Coordinating Council, an umbrella group of ninety churches and neighborhood groups, became the infrastructure for the Senator Robert Kennedy–inspired Bedford Stuyvesant Restoration Corporation, which was created on December 9, 1966, and is regarded by many as the first true CDC. On Chicago's West Side, the Ecumenical Institute, a Christian experiment in community living, began developing Fifth City. Meanwhile, in Newark, New Jersey, Father (now Monsignor) William Linder founded the New Community Corporation in 1967; it would become the largest CDC in the country.[5]

These kinds of comprehensive, grassroots-controlled community organizations require supporting networks of people and institutions to provide access to money, skills, expert knowledge, and political influence. We call the community organization and its support network a "consociation," based on a form of power sharing to achieve organizational stability and maintain democratic practices. Such consociations highlight the practicality of nonviolence as a secular basis for building trust among stakeholders. Seen through a nonviolent prism, the underlying motivations for conflict become transformed, such that zero-sum, winner-take-all outcomes change into potential win-win propositions based on cooperation, reconciliation, redemption, and enlightened self-interest. The goal of converting competitors into partners, or of building coalitions, can be strictly pragmatic and doesn't require the philosophical superstructure of nonviolence (which still strikes some as passive and mystical).

Initially, the tenant movement in Chicago attracted external stakeholders from the clergy, religious organizations, progressive lawyers, university teachers and students, unions, and civic organizations, among others. But as different aspects of the movement became more narrowly focused, the stakeholders and their resources and skills also became more specialized and grew to include banks, private real estate developers, investors, and nonprofits. True power sharing among external stakeholders and neighborhood residents meant that, for the most part, the former would have to provide substantial leadership and technical training for the latter. This was difficult to achieve in practice for a number of reasons, but I believe the ideological rubric of nonviolence helped create a space and a method for working toward it.

Finally, by way of introduction, I should mention that I was not a civil rights leader, activist, or professional; I was just an ordinary resident of the East Garfield Park neighborhood on the West Side of Chicago. To be sure, the neighborhood had its share of crime, slum housing, bad schools, and unemployment, but for me, it was home (in the sense of sanctuary), with many blocks of neat graystones and sunny, pleasant apartments as well as wide, tree-lined boulevards of old mansions, all focused around the emerald-like Garfield Park itself. I tell you this because it is important to understand that this neighborhood was much more complex and diverse than the word *slum* usually conveys (more on that later). I was a young family man working the midnight shift at the Chicago post office. I also had several side jobs ("hustles," we called them), including painting signs for local stores, doing freelance commercial art, and running a small trucking business. Life in East Garfield Park in those days had variety, texture, and intellectual vitality. On weekends I often joined aspiring writers, musicians, painters, poets, teachers, civil servants, and others at local restaurants for late-night conversations on topics ranging from philosophy and history to politics, religion, and the state of black Chicago. So, although I understood and agreed with the necessity of securing open housing and other citizenship rights for African Americans, I was particularly keen on ideas and actions to improve the local community, to make it more livable both materially and spiritually.

At those gatherings we also discussed and debated (and generally admired) Martin Luther King Jr. and his goals and methods to achieve equality in a socially integrated country.[6] I had watched Dr. King on television when he delivered his famous "I Have a Dream" speech at the 1963 March on Washington. I was intrigued by the idea of nonviolence as a method of political struggle. About that time, I stumbled onto a book about Gandhi and his use of nonviolence during the Indian struggle for independence. *Lead Kindly Light*, written by journalist Vincent Sheean, who traveled with Gandhi, gave a powerful account of the Mahatma's belief in nonviolence as a kind of *force* set in motion by truth.[7] Sheean's work inspired me to explore Hinduism more broadly as the religious and philosophical context of nonviolence.[8] I wondered whether Christianity could serve a similar purpose. Gandhi himself noted in his autobiography some significant Christian parallels to the Hindu faith experience. And I also began to see—or thought I did—how the application of nonviolence could potentially transform relations of power (in the rough capitalism of the United States) into a "nonzero-sum game."⁹ So when Bernard LaFayette, one of the leaders of the Nashville student movement, cofounder of the Student Nonviolent Coordinating Committee (SNCC), and prominent protégé of Dr. King, knocked on my door one day in the fall of 1964 to talk about nonviolent direct action and organizing East Garfield Park residents, I was ready.

The Back Story

Historically, the laws governing the relationship between landlords and tenants in the United States derive largely from feudal England and the open-field systems of northern Europe. However, the concept of "landlord" reaches back to the latifundia of ancient Rome and the *Hispania Baetica* in the south of Spain and generally refers to a system in which a peasant paid rent to the lord of the manor for the right to farm the land. In English common law such a rental agreement was known as a *lease*. The problem for tenants was that under common law, the lease was considered a conveyance of an interest in real estate, rather than a contract. Among other things, this meant that the lease agreement carried no implied warranty by the landlord that the premises were adequate for the purposes for which they were being rented, safe, or otherwise suitable for human occupancy. Renting was strictly caveat emptor. In practice, this meant that landlords had no legal responsibility (and tenants no legal recourse) for the condition of rental property. This, of course, resulted in a radical asymmetry in the relative bargaining power of landlords and tenants—the main characteristic of the landlord-tenant relationship brought to the United States by English settlers. Thus, the long history of landlord-tenant conflict has been, in essence, a struggle for tenant rights: the right to demand that the property being rented is reasonably safe and fit for human habitation and use.

Housing tenure, whether one owns or rents a home, is an important aspect of US society. Homeownership is widely regarded as a key indicator of middle-class status and unqualified citizenship and has been privileged in our political culture since the nation's beginning.[10] Historically, the landlord was considered to have fully satisfied his obligations when the renter took possession of the property. Historian Thomas J. Humphrey has documented the continuous struggle between landlords and tenants in Virginia and in New York's Hudson Valley from the 1750s through the 1790s and beyond. Organized actions by tenants, according to Humphrey, included rent strikes and armed tax revolts.[11] After the Civil War, the Industrial Revolution and immigration brought millions of new residents into urban centers, precipitating a series of acute housing shortages. Beginning in the 1890s, tenants in New York City, for example, staged rent strikes and other collective action in response to overcrowding, fires, unsafe or dilapidated conditions, and disease outbreaks. Acute housing shortages and their accompanying upsurges in tenant action tend to be periodic and are often associated with specific events and periods, such as the post–World War I housing shortage, the Great Depression of the 1930s, World War II, and Jesse Gray's Harlem rent strikes of 1963–1964.[12]

The main idea underlying tenant organizing is straightforward: the landlord has the power, but tenants have the numbers. Thus, by acting collectively as a unit, tenants can exert the "latent power of refusing to cooperate" and disrupt the usual actions assigned to the roles of landlord and tenant. Of course, organizing tenants to act collectively is easier said than done, and it can be exceedingly difficult to hold such groups together over time, especially when they comprise the poor, the working classes, and segregated minorities. Landlords have myriad maneuvers at their disposal to undermine, offset, or frustrate tenant efforts, not the least of which is housing law. This is one reason why, prior to the CFM, tenant activism in the United States was largely limited to sporadic (though sometimes successful) rent strikes, antieviction blockades, and other one-shot remedies.[13]

The Chicago Freedom Movement and Innovation

The goal of tenant activism in the Chicago Freedom Movement was notably different. It emphasized tenant participation in *partnership* with the landlord on an ongoing basis. Cold-eyed economic analysis of slum-housing income and expenses suggested that organized and motivated tenants could have a significant effect on the landlord's bottom line, so tenants would not come empty-handed to the bargaining table.[14] The goal of tenant unions in the Chicago Freedom Movement was to find common ground with landlords based on enlightened self-interest. In this sense, the CFM may be regarded as an inflection point from which the modern tenant movement emerged.[15]

The collective bargaining tenant union developed by the Chicago Freedom Movement was a specific type of voluntary consociation (i.e., with power sharing among the stakeholders), and this model has been used and adapted for various issues and contexts since the 1960s. For example, the collective bargaining tenant union modeled in important ways the consociations of nonprofits, CDCs, religious institutions, and financial intermediaries facilitating the work of community-based organizations and community rebuilding over the last half century. This speaks directly to the continuing significance of the Chicago Freedom Movement. In addition, tenant organizing in the CFM launched the national movement for tenant rights that led to paradigm-shifting changes in landlord-tenant law in the 1970s and 1980s, as well as a national network of skilled organizers and housing professionals.

The Chicago Cauldron and Catalyst

Beginning in the fall of 1965, Martin Luther King's Chicago staff began to organize tenants, most intensively on Chicago's West Side. Minnie Dunlap had moved to the West Side's East Garfield Park neighborhood five years earlier from Yazoo, Mississippi. This was a critical time for East Garfield Park, which was in the process of being "turned" from a neighborhood for white residents into a neighborhood for African Americans. As the buildings were converted from white tenants to black tenants, Dunlap saw services disappear. When she asked her landlord to fix her doorbell, he "knocked a hole into the wall and left the doorbell hanging down the wall. And the hole was big enough for my two-year-old son to get in, and I was afraid of him getting electrocuted. So I stopped paying my rent."[16] Shortly thereafter, she welcomed two tenant organizers who came to her door:

We had two organizers come from Dr. King's movement, and they had been pushing literature under the door continuously, but being the kind of person that I am, a working person, I just stepped over it and put the paper in the garbage. . . . And then when he [the landlord] came to collect the rent I still would not pay him. . . . They came . . . and said, "Could we talk to you about your landlord?"And that got my interest. So I said, OK . . . we sit down and started to talk . . . he said this man got 45 buildings; do you want to do anything about your hole in the wall? I said sure. They said, well if you come to a rally tonight and tell your story over there, we'll get your wall fixed. . . .

So I sort of made myself an organizer, and started talking with the tenants that were in the building about holding their rent . . . and maybe we could get something done 'cause Dr. King was going to come over to our building. . . . Right after that, the following week, the landlord sent someone in there and fixed my apartment and painted the whole apartment, so by the time the ralliers got there I didn't have the hole in the wall.[17]

Minnie Dunlap took up organizing in a serious way in buildings belonging to other landlords as well as her own. "I felt very enthusiastic that something could be done," she said. She soon became the president of the East Garfield Park Union to End Slums. When asked later how she felt about Dr. King coming to Chicago, she said: "When I heard that Dr. King was coming to Chicago I felt very good about that,'cause my first reaction was, 'Gee, thank you Jesus, you've sent someone to save us from the depression and the oppression that we have been getting.' . . . He was like a Christ to me that come in to lead us out of . . . the wilderness . . . I felt like we were being led to the promised land . . . out of the oppression of the way we were being treated, especially as tenants."[18] Looked at from another vantage point, we might say that it was Minnie Dunlap—and those who worked with her—who were leading their community "out of the wilderness."

In his book *Northern Protest*, James Ralph describes a rally with community residents "testifying" about their experiences, with "Martin Luther King looking on as if 'in final judgment.' The landlords John Condor and Louis Costalis also spoke, calling attention to the big bankers and mortgage lenders who were shaping real estate options in the neighborhood, and saying, 'We're with you, believe it or not.' They pointed out that they were the middlemen, and that it was the power structure that controlled the situation. We knew that banks would not lend in these neighborhoods, and we saw that could put the landlords in a bind." As Ralph described it, "King closed the session, reminding everyone that the larger system of slum exploitation and not two men, Condor and Costalis, had been on trial. Only by working together, King told his listeners, could they build a better world."[19] However, the matter was not easily settled. There were more protests, rent strikes, and a failed injunction, but finally there was an agreement.

On July 13, 1966, the East Garfield Park Union to End Slums, a federation of community organizations modeled after an industrial labor union, entered into a collective bargaining agreement with the Condor and Costalis Real Estate Company, which owned forty-five buildings in the community. The agreement specified the rights and responsibilities of both landlord and tenants, as well as a set of procedures for dispute resolution. Attorney Gil Cornfield and his colleagues at Cornfield and Feldman drew up the agreement, which represented a monumental shift because it included the obligations of both landlords and tenants. The introduction to the document states: "Unique among its features is its recognition of the tenants' right to withhold their rent if the landlord violates the contract. There have been other written agreements between landlords and tenants . . . but these agreements did not provide for direct and immediate tenant recourse through rent strikes if the agreement were violated."[20]

It is my sense that Condor and Costalis were willing to talk with us because the opponent was Martin Luther King and the civil rights movement, and there was a level of trust. Nonviolence created the context for that trust, for in nonviolence we seek to treat our opponents not as enemies but as potential partners, and we search for common ground. Nonviolence can serve as a kind of glue in negotiations. It is this willingness to trust the other participants that is the foundation of consociation: a form of organization that involves the sharing of power.

Although the Condor and Costalis agreement was pathbreaking

because of its inclusion of the right to withhold rent, it was not the first collective bargaining agreement for the Chicago Freedom Movement. In May 1966 tenants in three buildings in the Uptown neighborhood signed a collective bargaining agreement with their landlord, the result of work by the JOIN Community Union, a project of Students for a Democratic Society (SDS). Uptown was primarily a poor Appalachian white community, with small populations of Native American, Japanese, Latino, and African American residents. JOIN staffers Rennie Davis and Richard Rothstein had been working with the Chicago Freedom Movement since the Southern Christian Leadership Conference (SCLC) staff had arrived in September and had been regular attendees at the Wider Community Staff meetings held during the fall and winter, where tenant union organizing was frequently on the agenda. This agreement in a predominantly white community was also a part of the Chicago Freedom Movement, an illustration of its wide reach across the city.[21]

There were limits to the Chicago movement's success, however. Other large landlords—such as Gilbert Balin, who often articulated the slumlords' position—were not even willing to talk to tenant union organizers. We protested and picketed Balin's offices and his house, but to no avail. In an interview with the *Chicago Sun-Times*, his spokesman even accused us of extortion for demanding a dues checkoff to come out of the rent.[22]

Out of this organizing in Chicago, then, came two parallel strands: first, a broader effort to rehabilitate buildings and revitalize neighborhoods, chiefly through the vehicle of the newly emerging CDCs; and second, a mushrooming national tenants' rights movement and, eventually, a revolution in landlord-tenant law.

The Tenant Movement and the Emergence of Community Development Corporations

Creating tenant unions was never the end point; the goal was to organize the community. We initially started with tenant unions for renters and block clubs for homeowners, and we used a number of strategies as entry points to mobilize the community. As the tenant movement grew and changed, more of the energy shifted to CDCs. New approaches to housing ownership and rehabilitation were called for, and many issues needed to be dealt with at the community level, not just with individual landlords and buildings. CDCs provided a more holistic model for change, but this was an evolving effort that involved early experimentation.

SCLC, along with its Chicago partners, sought to play an active role in rehabilitating housing, beginning soon after the Condor and Costalis agreement. Ralph describes one such effort: "In December, 1966 SCLC received a four million dollar HUD grant to rehabilitate housing in conjunction with the Community Renewal Foundation, a branch of the Chicago City Missionary Society." The plan was that once the buildings were renovated, they would be jointly owned by the tenants as a cooperative. Later, the Kate Maremont Foundation, in conjunction with the Lawndale Union to End Slums, took control of some buildings in Lawndale. In the end, these were disappointing efforts. The buildings were so "fatally blighted," according to one writer, that even committed community partners could not make them work financially. Clearly, more substantial efforts were called for.[23]

As noted above, the first CDC prototypes began to emerge in the mid-1960s, around the same time as the tenant movement. The project in Bedford-Stuyvesant in Brooklyn is credited as being the first CDC, and it was the first to get national recognition. It was also the first to be funded by the new US Department of Housing and Urban Development (HUD) and major foundations.[24]

In Chicago's East Garfield Park the Ecumenical Institute, a vital community-living experiment committed to social gospel Christianity, shifted its focus to community rehabilitation. Members interviewed several hundred residents to discover their concerns and then developed a plan in response. By early 1969, Illinois governor Otto Kerner worked with the Illinois Housing Authority to give this group, now called Fifth City, a grant to rehabilitate housing units within a sixteen-block area in East Garfield Park. It was to be a mixture of renters and homeowners—a multiclass community. No one wanted to create a neighborhood with a high concentration of poor people, so there was both subsidized rental housing and housing for homeowners. This completed the Ecumenical Institute's transition into a CDC.[25]

Fifth City had a number of connections with participants in the Chicago Freedom Movement who lived and worked in the East Garfield Park neighborhood, but one was particularly important: Minnie Dunlap. A few years after serving as president of the East Garfield Park Union to End Slums, Dunlap began to work with Fifth City as it was evolving into a CDC, and she brought with her the experiences of organizing tenants and participating in the development of the collective bargaining agreements with landlords.

Fifth City began rehabilitating and rebuilding the homes in the community, eventually covering a sixteen-block area with approximately 4,300 residents. It built a community center and drew new businesses to the community. Among these were the new Bethany Hospital and a Chicago Transit Authority bus garage, which together employed about 1,000 people—a great boon to the community.[26]

These institutions, built on the consociation model of collaboration and power sharing among a variety of stakeholders, brought change to the community.

A National Network of Tenant Organizing and Advocacy

Within a few months after the Condor-Costalis agreement, forty-five tenant unions with up to 2,000 members had sprung up across Chicago, and the Chicago Federation of Tenant Unions was organized. These efforts in Chicago in 1966, combined with the success of Jesse Gray's rent strikes in New York in 1963–1964, fueled the rapid growth of tenant organizations in major cities across the nation. Within the next two years, SCLC started tenant organizations in Cleveland, and new tenant organizations emerged in thirty other cities, including San Francisco, Detroit, Boston, and Philadelphia. Many of these tenant unions developed collective bargaining agreements with landlords, following the Chicago Freedom Movement model.[27]

In January 1969 the Chicago Federation of Tenant Unions called a national organizing meeting, which was cosponsored by Gray's New York tenant organizations and supported by other groups, such as the American Friends Service Committee (AFSC). Out of this gathering, the National Tenants Organization was formed, with East Garfield Park's Tony Henry as its director (with the support of AFSC) and Jesse Gray as its chairman of the board. By the time of its first convention in October 1969, the new organization already had sixty affiliates.[28]

When the National Tenants Organization settled into Washington, DC, in 1970, organizing tenants in public housing was high on its agenda. Scattered groups were already working to enhance the tenants' voice at the local level—sometimes inspired by the War on Poverty's requirement for "maximum feasible participation of the poor," and sometimes by local civil rights activities. Dorothy Gautreaux, who was active in the Chicago Freedom Movement, was an early organizer and voice for public-housing residents in Chicago. The National Tenants Organization was able to bring these groups together into a national coalition, and during negotiations that lasted for nine months, it succeeded in forging an agreement for a new kind of lease for public-housing tenants, one that protected tenants as well as landlords.[29]

The tenant unions in public housing were more enduring than those in multifamily private housing, as the tenant population in the former was more stable. Rents were based on a percentage of income, so even when tenants' economic situations declined, they could remain in their apartments. In many public-housing projects, most of the families were receiving public assistance, which was, for the most part, a stable—if limited—source of income.

Although tenant unions were created in privately owned buildings, they proved hard to maintain for more than a year or so. Tenant unions could improve housing conditions, but families still tended to move often. The leaders, in particular, seemed to move frequently, perhaps because the leadership skills they developed gave them the confidence to leave, or perhaps because the most stable and resilient individuals took on leadership roles in the first place, and they continued to search for better opportunities. Also, the economics of drastically deteriorating buildings made it difficult for sufficient rehabilitation to be financed, even by landlords who tried to do so. Efforts to protect tenants began to shift toward legal changes that would enshrine such protections in law and toward programs to increase the availability of affordable housing. The tenant unions were successful in public housing, but in private housing, they proved to be a transitional strategy to protect tenants until landlord-tenant laws could be changed.

By the mid-1970s, national networks emerged that linked tenant organizers across the country. The National Low Income Housing Coalition emerged in 1974, and the National Housing Institute and its *Shelter-force* journal, which provided a vehicle for organizers to collaborate, share tactics and strategies, and celebrate victories, came the following year. These national coalitions were key to both winning local victories and mobilizing for change in landlord-tenant law. New groups continued to emerge through the late 1970s, 1980s, and 1990s. The National Committee for Rent Control appeared in 1979. In 1980 the National Tenant Organizing Conference was held and the National Tenants Union was formed, following what Peter Dreier called "a three-year upsurge of tenant consciousness in every major area of the nation."[30] The Coalition for Tenants Rights was formed in 1984. As legal changes occurred in various localities, often at the prompting of these groups, organizations identifying themselves as tenant unions began to organize as educational and advocacy resources for tenants, disseminating information about newly emerging tenant protections in landlord-tenant laws.[31]

The Revolution in Landlord-Tenant Law

The law firm of Cornfield and Feldman continued to do pro bono work in support of low-income tenants for nearly a decade, long after the Chicago Freedom Movement ended as an organizational alliance in 1967. They took landlords to housing court in Chicago, and when they brought in evidence of falling plaster, peeling paint, and other indicators of dilapidation, they frequently won necessary building improvements for the tenants they represented. They also protected renters from eviction, making the legal system work for low-income tenants—a rarity. The spirit of the movement lived on in this work, and in it were the seeds of legal changes to come.

This plethora of community activism prompted the legal community to take notice. In the fall of 1966, just months after the collective bargaining agreement with Condor and Costalis, the University of Chicago Law School hosted a conference on landlord-tenant law to explore problems with the current law and develop proposals for change. This effort had been prompted by Bernadine Dohrn and others from the University of Chicago Law Students Committee for Civil Rights, which had been working with the Chicago Freedom Movement for many months under the tutelage of attorney Gil Cornfield and his associates.

Two years later, a *Yale Law Journal* article discussed the legal issues involved in tenant unions. The article's author had interviewed Chicago Freedom Movement activists Tony Henry, Charlie Love, Richard Rothstein, and Meredith Gilbert, as well as Cornfield, all of whom provided information about the legal challenges facing the tenant unions—from defending the legality of picketing to the logistics of withholding rent and dealing with needed repairs.[32]

By 1969, the National Conference of Commissioners on Uniform State Laws had called together 250 attorneys and housing experts to recommend changes in landlord-tenant law. In 1972 that group released the provisions for a Uniform Residential Landlord-Tenant Act (URLTA), intended to establish a new framework for state and local landlord-tenant law. Interestingly, the goals they set mirrored many of those of the tenant movement and, in particular, the collective bargaining approach: "Equalize the bargaining positions of landlords and tenants; force landlords to meet minimum standards for providing safe and habitable housing; spell out the responsibilities of tenants for maintaining the quality of their housing units; insure tenants the right to occupy a dwelling as long as they fulfill their responsibilities." The conference explicitly stated that this act is "designed to improve the bargaining position of tenants."[33] The key components of this legal framework were: (1) the implied warranty of habitability, requiring landlords to provide habitable housing; (2) the ability to withhold rent if the landlord fails to meet his responsibilities; (3) the doctrine of strict liability, making both landlord and tenant legally responsible for damage caused; (4) a repair and deduct provision, allowing tenants to make minor repairs or provide for essential services, such as water, heat, and electricity, and deduct the cost from rent; and (5) protection from retaliatory eviction.

State and local governments began to adopt the provisions soon after they were released. A 2009 report indicated broad acceptance of these principles: twenty-five states adopted laws identical or very similar to the URLTA principles; five states already had similar laws but adopted the language of "implied habitability"; seven states added other specifics; and thirteen states had local laws covering these issues. Only North Dakota has no landlord-tenant law.[34]

In Chicago these changes came more slowly than elsewhere. In the mid-1980s the Metropolitan Tenants Organization, a coalition of many tenant groups in the city, lobbied heavily for change. During the administration of progressive mayor Harold Washington, the Chicago City Council approved a tenants' bill of rights in 1986, which offered Chicago tenants many of the rights outlined by the National Conference of Commissioners years before.[35]

Peter Dreier cites a new wave of tenant activism in the 1970s that mobilized middle-class activists concerned about rent control, condominium conversions, and the rise of absentee owners. He notes that these activists were protected by the provisions won in the late 1960s and early 1970s, particularly the protection against retaliatory eviction, which made tenant activism less risky.[36]

During the 1980s and 1990s advances in addressing low-income housing, homelessness, and tenants' rights at the national level continued to emerge, prompted by ongoing activism among professional housing activists, attorneys, and other supporters. Several new programs provided resources for communities dealing with poor housing conditions and insufficient low-income housing. Despite steep declines in federal housing assistance, these programs helped further the development of new low-income or affordable housing and provide resources for the homeless: the low-income housing tax credit (1986) provided support for the construction of low-income housing, the Stewart B. McKinney Act (1987) provided funding for emergency housing for the homeless, and the Cranston-Gonzalez National Affordable Housing Act (1990) provided a range of programs for both renters and homeowners.

In 1995 Dreier proposed a national tenant-landlord act "to provide tenants in public housing, HUD assisted developments, and private housing with a vehicle similar to the National Labor Relations Act." He suggested that tenant groups would need to win an election to become "recognized as the legitimate voice" of tenants with the authority to "bargain over rents, building conditions, evictions and other standards." While this did not come to pass, it is worth noting that Dreier's proposal parallels on a much larger scale the tenant unions developed by the Chicago Freedom Movement.[37]

The Merging of the Tenant Movement and the Housing Movement

The tenant movement has remained strong in HUD-supported housing. The National Alliance of HUD Tenants for renters in privately owned, multifamily HUD-assisted housing represents thousands across the nation and has recently mobilized to protect subsidized housing programs. However, the tenant movement in general was less active in the 1990s, and in a 2005 *Shelterforce* article, Phil Star (then on the board of the Cleveland Tenants Organization) suggests that "the tenants and housing movements were significantly different at first, with the tenants focused on improving living conditions and self-empowerment and the housers on increasing the supply of affordable housing." Activist and attorney Mike Rawson adds, "The tenants movement became the housing movement as it evolved to focus on long-term solutions in addition to fighting day-to-day displacement battles."[38]

Conclusions and Future Challenges

In some ways, it may not be much of an overstatement to say that the twentieth century was the century of tenants' rights in the United States. Driven by modernization (the Industrial Revolution, urbanization, and the impact of science and technology on society), emerging social forces placed relentless pressure on, and eventually swept aside, traditional landlord-tenant relations and the laws on which they were based. Traditionally, there had been great inequalities in the bargaining power of landlords versus tenants, a sign of dysfunction and failure in modern market economies. Usually, it takes governmental authority to correct large-scale market inefficiencies, and that was the case here, but it is important to note that *governments generally take action only when subjected to political pressure from organized tenants and their supporters.*[39] In this regard, it may be convenient to divide the tenants' rights century into two halves: the first, up to 1950, with organized pressure centered in New York City; and the second centered in Chicago, with the civil rights movement driving organized tenant pressure. The pivot point may well be the Housing Act of 1949, which declared that it was federal policy to oversee the realization "of a decent home and a suitable living environment for every American family, thus contributing to the development and redevelopment of communities and to the growth, wealth and security of the nation."[40]

During the century of tenants' rights, the government played an important role in the functioning of the housing sector of the economy, sometimes to the point of state regulation of rents (rent control or rent stabilization). In the second half of the twentieth century, the federal government's role in rental housing was largely carried out by HUD, created in 1965. In addition to HUD, significant milestones included the Fair Housing Act of 1968, the Uniform Law Commission's landlord-tenant law recommendations (1972), the Home Mortgage Disclosure Act (1975), the Community Reinvestment Act (1977), the election of Ronald Reagan (1980), the low-income housing tax credit (1986), the Cranston-Gonzalez Housing Affordability Act (1990), and President Bush's "ownership society" (2000), among others.[41]

The revolution in tenants' rights is now codified in state and local laws governing landlord-tenant relations throughout the nation. But this revolution is dynamic and has not arrived at its final conclusion. Tenants' rights victories were part of the agenda of a winning political coalition variously known as the New Deal Coalition, the Civil Rights Coalition, and, more recently, the Progressive Coalition or the Obama Coalition. But victory is not written in stone. The Civil Rights Coalition is challenged at every turn by a resurgent conservative movement that gained national power with the election of Ronald Reagan in 1980.[42] There was a 78 percent reduction in federal housing assistance in Reagan's first term. And the landlord lobby was emboldened to try to overturn rent-control laws in California and Massachusetts (they eventually succeeded). Government regulations can be (and have been) undone. And effective community-based organizations (e.g., ACORN) can be killed off. Our coalition must continue to struggle and take advantage of favorable demographic trends, such as increased diversity, and offset our weaknesses among certain segments of the population: working-class, less educated whites, especially men, and senior citizens. It is imperative that we continue to win. Fortunately, the tenant movement that exploded out of Chicago fifty years ago led to an infrastructure for organizing around housing and community development. These achievements include the following:

- The development of a highly effective (Internet-based) national communications network of skilled tenant and community organizers and community-based housing professionals, organizations, and institutions.
- Specialization in housing markets, and the emergence of an effective coalition of policy advocates on behalf of tenants in public and subsidized housing, as well as advocates for rent-control policies in certain areas.
- Adaptation of the collective bargaining contract approach, with its intrinsic principles of nonviolence, to different situations and contexts.

There is also an International Union of Tenants, with forty-four member nations, based in Sweden. It serves as a clearinghouse and forum for tenant organizers and activists around the world. Its quarterly magazine, *Global Tenant*, is published in six languages.

There were also remarkable achievements by CDCs, which got their housing focus from the Chicago Freedom Movement. Beginning with fewer than 100 first-generation CDCs in 1966 and 1967, these neighborhood-based organizations numbered more than 3,000 in 2005. The CDC model, which successfully brought together developers, bankers, and governmental and nonprofit resources to aid community organizations, became the clearest illustration of consocial power sharing among stakeholders.[43] Here, too, the government played an important role by making funding available to CDCs through a special impact amendment to the Economic Opportunity Act.[44]

Finally, we come to events in the first decade of the twenty-first century: the "ownership society," the Great Recession, the collapse of the housing bubble, and the disastrous wave of foreclosures in low-income neighborhoods that followed. Here is a situation in which both markets and the government failed. There are some disturbing echoes reverberating through the last five decades: land contracts, redlining, the savings and loan crisis of the 1980s, subprime mortgages, economic "bubbles," government bailouts, and unpunished corporate crime. This century began with George W. Bush touting the "ownership society," which had a goal of 5.5 million new minority homeowners by 2010. This was a laudable goal, but the financial markets had been deregulated, so Wall Street had no constraints and no incentives to create good mortgage products, which, as noted by Joseph Stiglitz, would have had low transaction costs, low interest rates, predictable payments, and no hidden costs.[45] A good mortgage product would have helped borrowers manage the risk of their houses losing value or the consequences of losing their jobs. What we got was greed, criminality, and millions of foreclosures.[46]

The foreclosure crisis did not affect only homeowners; it has been estimated that 40 percent of the households facing eviction as a result of foreclosure are renters.[47] The improving economy, especially some "hot markets," are experiencing sharp rises in rents due to severe shortages in rental housing.[48] Again, it has fallen to the government to correct market dysfunction. In 2009 Congress passed the Protection of Tenants at Foreclosure Act, which established rules for existing leases and required sufficient notice of lease termination (the act was amended in 2010). Now, however, we must ask, as Dr. King once did, "Where do we go from here?"[49]

Our conclusion is that the federal government must continue to intervene in the housing sector. The question is, what should be the scope and depth of its involvement? Some current measures, notably the Dodd-Frank Wall Street Reform and Consumer Protection Act of 2010, hold out some hope for imposing new regulations on Wall Street and implementing consumer protections, but they will likely be significantly weakened without a more focused effort by the Civil Rights Coalition. A form of collective ownership that has been prevalent in New York City for a century is the co-op apartment. The members of a co-op hold shares in a corporation that owns the building. The members elect a board of directors, which in turn hires professional managers, accountants, maintenance staff, and so forth. The board of directors also screens new applicants for membership and may reject an applicant without stating a reason. Except for the ownership component, this structure is similar to the collective bargaining tenant union. Tenants and stakeholders, including landlord representatives, could compose a body similar to a board of directors. This may be the logical end to which tenant participation points.

Notes

Publication of the following was made possible by the kind permission of the publisher: selections from the interview of Minnie Dunlap conducted for *Eyes on the Prize II, Two Societies: 1965–1968,* for the PBS series *The American Experience,* produced by Henry Hampton, Blackside. Reprinted by permission of Washington University Libraries, Visual Media Research Lab, Film, and Media Archive, from the Eyes on the Prize II Collection.

1. Martin Luther King Jr., "All Labor Has Dignity: AFSCME Mass Meeting, Memphis TN, March 18, 1968," in *All Labor Has Dignity,* ed. Michael Honey (Boston: Beacon Press, 1986), 175.

2. The Aspen Institute's Roundtable on Community Change defined structural racism as "the ways in which history, ideology, public policies, institutional practices and culture interact to maintain a racial hierarchy." *Poverty and Race* 15 (November–December 2006). Structural racism does not necessarily require individual agency or intentionality, and it may be driven by factors other than race.

3. In Chicago in the mid-1960s, a "tenant union" referred to a tenant group seeking a collective bargaining contract with a landlord that specified tenant and landlord duties and methods of dispute resolution. Later, tenant unions were defined more broadly; today's tenant unions are usually communitywide groups that support tenants in understanding and exercising their rights. Since the 1960s, community organizing has become a separate field with its own terminology. As used here, "community organizing" means initiating action among residents to address common problems; "community development" means rehabilitating the physical infrastructure of a neighborhood, such as housing; and "service delivery" refers to the provision of social services on a neighborhood basis. Taken together, these three are methods of "community empowerment." See Peter Dreier, "Community Empowerment Strategies: The Limits and Potential of Community Organizing in Urban Neighborhoods," *Cityscape: A Journal of Policy Development and Research* 2, no. 2 (May 1996).

4. See Ronald Lawson, ed., *The Tenant Movement in New York City, 1904–1984* (New Brunswick, NJ: Rutgers University Press, 1986).

5. Anthony Henry was a paid staffer of the American Friends Service Committee, but along with Bernard LaFayette and the Reverend William Briggs, he provided professional-level leadership and technical advice for the East Garfield Park Union to End Slums, a tenant union led by Minnie Dunlap and Vernedia White. In addition to founding the New Community Corporation, Father Linder

gave critical assistance to the Reverend Al Sampson and this writer in organizing the Newark, New Jersey, leg of the Poor People's Campaign.

6. Ideologies of racial separatism and Black Nationalism were strong in Chicago, particularly among lower-class African American males. There was also great admiration for figures such as Malcolm X and Muhammad Ali, both of whom were protégés of Elijah Muhammad and members of his Nation of Islam. Nevertheless, even the nationalists expressed admiration for King. See Harold Cruse, *The Crisis of the Negro Intellectual* (New York: William Morrow, 1967). For a discussion of the role of nationalism in black identity, see E. U. Essien-Udom, *Black Nationalism: A Search for an Identity in America* (Chicago: University of Chicago Press, 1962).

7. Vincent Sheean, *Lead Kindly Light: Gandhi and the Way to Peace* (New York: Random House, 1949). I also read an earlier printing of *Gandhi, an Autobiography: My Experiments with Truth* (New York: Beacon Press, 1993).

8. My readings included sacred texts of India: the Bhagavad Gita and a few other parts of the Mahabharata, as well as several sections of the Upanishads. I also grappled with Sri Aurobindo's *The Future Evolution of Man: The Divine Life on Earth* (Twin Lakes, WI: Lotus Press, 1963).

9. In the mathematics of game theory, a nonzero-sum game is one in which a win-win outcome is possible. For a conception of how nonzero outcomes can drive evolutionary biology, see Robert Wright, *Nonzero: The Logic of Human Destiny* (New York: Vintage, 2001). For a discussion of how they impact violence, see Steven Pinker, *The Better Angels of Our Nature: Why Violence Has Declined* (New York: Penguin Books, 2012).

10. Peter Dreier, "The Status of Tenants in the United States," *Social Problems* 30 (December 1982): 179–98.

11. Thomas J. Humphrey, "Conflicting Independence: Land Tenancy and the American Revolution," *Journal of the Early Republic* 28 (Summer 2008): 159–82; Thomas J. Humphrey, *Land and Liberty: Hudson Valley Riots in the Age of Revolution* (De Kalb: Northern Illinois University Press, 2004).

12. See Thomas Sugrue, *Sweet Land of Liberty: The Forgotten Struggle for Civil Rights in the North* (New York: Random House, 2008), 400–408.

13. Some scholars and activists argued that attempts to organize poor and working-class tenants into political interest groups were bound to fail, and that only by disrupting the normal operations of the slum system by withholding rent could progress be made. See Frances Fox Piven and Richard A. Cloward, "Rent Strike: Disrupting the Slum System," *New Republic,* December 2, 1967, 11–13.

14. See "The Economics of Slum Housing," in Richard Cotton, "Tenant Unions: Collective Bargaining and the Low-Income Tenant," *Yale Law Journal* 77 (June 1968): 1368–1400; "Apartment Building Income Expense Analysis," *Institute of Real Estate Management* 4, no. 11 (1967). Ghetto tenements tend to be old, nearly dilapidated structures that require increasingly greater expendi-

tures for maintenance and repairs, and keeping buildings clean and in good repair is usually one of the main goals of tenant collective action. The problem is that there are only a few potential sources for the additional revenue required: higher rents, a third party (e.g., government), less landlord profit, lower operating costs, or tenant sweat equity. Acting collectively, tenants can clearly make significant contributions to the last two, thereby helping the landlord protect a *fair* profit in exchange for improved housing conditions. This was the reciprocity offered by collective bargaining agreements.

15. Rent strikes began to appear in urban centers such as New York City during the 1890s, but landlord-tenant conflict had been present since the pre-Revolution period. See Sung Bok Kim, *Landlord and Tenant in Colonial New York* (Chapel Hill: University of North Carolina Press, 1978).

16. Interview with Minnie Dunlap, *Eyes on the Prize II Interviews,* June 13, 1989, Washington University Libraries, Visual Media Research Lab, Film, and Media Archive, Eyes on the Prize II Collection, http://digital.wustl.edu/e/eii/eiiweb/dun5427.0734.042marc_record_interviewee_process.html.

17. Ibid.

18. Ibid.

19. James R. Ralph Jr., *Northern Protest: Martin Luther King, Jr., Chicago, and the Civil Rights Movement* (Cambridge, MA: Harvard University Press, 1993), 63.

20. "Agreement between Condor-Costalis," in Cornfield files, cited in Ralph, *Northern Protest,* 262, n. 63; see chapter 19 for details.

21. *Chicago Sun-Times,* May 26, 1966, 4, cited in Ralph, *Northern Protest,* 262. In his speech at the July 10 Soldier Field rally, Al Raby mentioned the JOIN collective bargaining agreement as an accomplishment of the Chicago Freedom Movement (see chapter 1). On Uptown, see Todd Gitlin and Nanci Hollander, *Uptown: Poor Whites in Chicago* (New York: Harper & Row, 1970).

22. For a description of the picketing of Balin Real Estate, see "E. Garfield Plans Uncertain," *Chicago Tribune,* December 4, 1966, F1. For other stories about the challenges of tenant union organizing in Chicago at this time, see Martin Baker, Gilbert Feldman, and Mary Robinson, "Tenant Unions," in *The People vs. the System: A Dialogue in Urban Conflict,* ed. Sol Tax (Chicago: Acme Press, 1968), 273–83.

23. Ralph, *Northern Protest,* 225; Beryl Satter, *Family Properties: Race, Real Estate, and the Exploitation of Black Urban America* (New York: Metropolitan Books, 2009), 229; Alan B. Anderson and George W. Pickering, *Confronting the Color Line: The Broken Promise of the Civil Rights Movement in Chicago* (Athens: University of Georgia Press, 1986), 305–6; Cotton, "Tenant Unions."

24. Alexander von Hoffman, "The Past, Present and Future of Community Development," *NHI Shelterforce Online* (Winter 2012–2013).

25. Governor Otto Kerner led the team that prepared the *Report of the*

National Advisory Commission on Civil Disorders (New York: Bantam Books, 1968), commonly known as the Kerner Commission Report, in response to the riots in the summer of 1967.

26. See https://luigimorelli.wordpress.com/2011/02/15/a-story-of-organizational-change-from-ecumenical-institute-to-fifth-city/. Fifth City later became the Institute for Cultural Affairs, known for its community development work in the United States and abroad.

27. Peter Marcuse, "The Rise of Tenant Organizations," in *Housing Urban America,* 2nd ed., ed. Jon Pynoos, Robert Schafer, and Chester Hartman (Piscataway, NJ: Aldine Publishing, 1980), 52; Cotton, "Tenant Unions," 1369. See also Sugrue, *Sweet Land of Liberty,* 400–408.

28. Marcuse, "Rise of Tenant Organizations," 52. On the rapid rise of tenant organizations, see also Thea Flaum and Elizabeth C. Salzman, *The Tenants' Rights Movement* (Chicago: Urban Research Corporation Report, 1969), cited in Roberta Gold, *When Tenants Claimed the City: The Struggle for Citizenship in New York City Housing* (Champaign: University of Illinois Press, 2014), 310, n. 157.

29. Marcuse, "Rise of Tenant Organizations," 54. See also Peter Dreier and Woody Widrow, *Shelterforce,* October 1980, quoted in Karen Ceraso, "Whatever Happened to the Tenant Movement?" *NHI Shelterforce Online* 105 (May–June 1999).

30. Dreier and Widrow, quoted in Ceraso, "Whatever Happened to the Tenant Movement?"

31. Ceraso, "Whatever Happened to the Tenant Movement?" The Tenants Union of Washington State is one example of a group focusing on advocacy and education for tenants. See http://www.tenantsunion.org/en (accessed February 27, 2015).

32. Mary Lou Finley, personal communication, February 2015; Cotton, "Tenant Unions," 1368–1400.

33. National Conference of Commissioners on Uniform State Laws, "Residential Landlord and Tenant Act Summary," http://www.uniformlaws.org/ActSummary.aspx?title=Residential%20Landlord%20and%20Tenant%20Act (accessed January 14, 2015).

34. Tom Neltner, Doug Farquhar, and Scott Hendrick, "Analysis of Standard Requirements in State Residential Landlord-Tenant Laws," National Center for Healthy Housing, 2009, www.nchh.org (accessed January 14, 2015).

35. Residential Landlord and Tenants Ordinance, 1986. This ordinance passed after Mayor Washington's allies gained a majority on the City Council late in his administration, a political shift described in chapter 12. See Gregory Squires, Larry Bennett, Kathleen McCourt, and Philip Nyden, *Chicago: Race, Class, and the Response to Urban Decline* (Philadelphia: Temple University Press, 1987), 112.

36. Dreier, "Status of Tenants in the United States," 190–91.

37. Peter Dreier, "Organizing the New Tenants Movement," *NHI Shelterforce Online* 84 (November–December 1995).

38. Woody Widrow, "The Tenants Movement and Housers: How the Tenants Movement of the 1970s and 1980s Evolved into the Housing and Community Development Movement of Today," *NHI Shelterforce Online* 144 (November–December 2005).

39. In many cases involving racial segregation, government policies perpetuated market inefficiencies.

40. Alex Schwartz, *Housing Policy in the United States*, 2nd ed. (New York: Routledge, 2010), 1.

41. Ibid., 280–85.

42. Republican president Richard Nixon was not considered a movement conservative by many observers.

43. See David Holtzman, "The Emergence of the CDC Network," *NHI Shelterforce Online* 144 (November–December 2005).

44. Robert Kennedy influenced this amendment. See also Rachel Bratt, *Rebuilding a Low-Income Housing Policy* (Philadelphia: Temple University Press, 1989).

45. In 1999 President Bill Clinton, a Democrat, signed the repeal of Glass-Steagall, which was part of the US Banking Act of 1933. It created a regulatory separation of traditional commercial banking from investment banking in an effort to prevent banks from using customer deposits in risky investment ventures. The Great Recession, Glass-Steagall, Dodd-Frank, and the Troubled Asset Relief Program (TARP) financial bailout are ongoing political issues. My interpretation of these events is based in part on the writings of Joseph E. Stiglitz, *Free Fall: America, Free Markets and the Sinking of the World Economy* (New York: W. W. Norton, 2010); Paul Krugman, *End This Depression Now* (New York: W. W. Norton, 2012); and Josh Bivens, *Failure by Design: The Story behind America's Broken Economy* (Ithaca, NY: Cornell University Press, 2012).

46. See, for instance, Neil Barofsky, *Bailout: An Inside Account of How Washington Abandoned Main Street while Rescuing Wall Street* (New York: Free Press, 2012). Barofsky was the special inspector general in charge of overseeing the federal government's TARP, known popularly as the bank bailout program, from December 2008 until March 2011.

47. National Low Income Housing Coalition press release, "New Report Finds Foreclosure Crisis Continues to Hurt Renters," September 25, 2012, nlihc.org/press/releases/1906 (accessed April 5, 2015).

48. See, for example, "Evictions Soar in Hot Market: Renters Suffer," *New York Times*, August 28, 2014.

49. Martin Luther King Jr., *Where Do We Go from Here: Chaos or Community?* (Boston: Beacon Press, 1967).

Bayard Rustin, Dr. Martin Luther King Jr., the Reverend Bernard Lee, and the Reverend John R. Porter at a rally in the Englewood neighborhood, 1964. (Courtesy of John R. Porter)

Superintendent Benjamin Willis and racial segregation in the Chicago public schools were the focus of the Chicago civil rights movement during the first half of the 1960s. (Courtesy of Bernard Kleina)

Left to right: Al Raby, James Bevel, and Jesse Jackson, three leaders of the Chicago Freedom Movement. Raby, of Chicago's Coordinating Council of Community Organizations, cochaired the movement with King. Bevel was one of the Southern Christian Leadership Conference's most creative strategists and director of its Chicago Project. Jackson emerged as a civil rights leader through his work in the Chicago Freedom Movement. (Courtesy of Bernard Kleina)

SCLC staff organizers Jimmy Wilson and James Orange talking with West Side residents, winter 1966. (Courtesy of Johnson Publishing Company, LLC. All rights reserved.)

SCLC staff at the Warren Avenue Congregational Church in East Garfield Park: Carolyn Black, Suzi Hill, Wende Smith Kindberg, Earless Ross, Sherie Land, Diana Smith. (Courtesy of Johnson Publishing Company, LLC. All rights reserved.)

Music was important to the Chicago Freedom Movement. Jimmy Collier (with the guitar) often led the singing of freedom songs in groups large and small. He composed two songs for the Chicago movement—"Lead Poison on the Wall" and "Rent Strike Blues"—and adapted many others to conditions in Chicago. In the background is SCLC staffer Sherie Land. (Courtesy of Bob Fitch Photo Archive. © Stanford University Libraries.)

The July 10, 1966, rally at Soldier Field kicked off the summer direct action campaign of the Chicago Freedom Movement and attracted a diverse crowd of roughly 30,000 persons. (Courtesy of Bernard Kleina)

Famed gospel singer Mahalia Jackson inspired the crowd at Soldier Field and appeared at many other events supporting the civil rights movement. (Courtesy of Bernard Kleina)

King posted the demands of the Chicago Freedom Movement on the doors of City Hall. (Courtesy of Bernard Kleina)

After the Soldier Field rally, Martin Luther King Jr. and Al Raby led a march into downtown Chicago, where the "End the Slums" emblem of the Chicago Freedom Movement was prominently featured. (Courtesy of Bernard Kleina)

Andrew Young, then SCLC's executive director, joined in singing freedom songs on the march to City Hall. He played a key role in the Chicago Freedom Movement. (Courtesy of Bernard Kleina)

Vigils at real estate offices were a regular part of the open-housing campaign in July and August 1966. (Courtesy of Bernard Kleina)

The open-housing marches on the Southwest Side encountered fierce resistance. Civil rights demonstrators were harangued and attacked, and their cars were vandalized and burned. (Courtesy of Bernard Kleina)

During the open-housing marches, some local residents threw rocks and other objects at demonstrators. (Courtesy of Bernard Kleina)

On August 5, 1966, Martin Luther King Jr. led an open-housing demonstration on Chicago's Southwest Side. He was hit by a rock in Marquette Park. (Courtesy of Bernard Kleina)

The open-housing marches revealed the depth of racism in the North and showed that support for George Wallace, the segregationist governor of Alabama, was not restricted to white southerners. (Courtesy of Bernard Kleina)

Bernard LaFayette and others take a quiet moment during the open-housing march to Bogan on Chicago's Southwest Side, August 1966. (Courtesy of Chicago History Museum. Photograph by Declan Haun, ICHi-36882)

A JOHNSON PUBLICATION

EBONY

INTEGRATION: The Great
Dilemma Of The Church

WOMAN LAWYER
IN MISSISSIPPI

ELIGIBLE
BACHELORS
FOR 1966

THE
NATURAL
LOOK

New mode
for Negro
women

JUNE 1966 50c   ANNUAL BASEBALL ROUNDUP: YEAR OF THE HOLDOUT

The June 1966 issue of *Ebony* magazine features "The Natural Look," with Diana Smith, one of Dr. King's Chicago staff, on the cover. (Courtesy of Johnson Publishing Company, LLC. All rights reserved.)

Martin Luther King Jr. and Bernard LaFayette Jr. confer in Boston in 1967 as Dr. King invited LaFayette to become the national coordinator for the Poor People's Campaign. (Courtesy of Bernard LaFayette Jr.)

8

The Chicago Freedom Movement and the Fight for Fair Lending

Mary Lou Finley

On a brisk fall morning in 1965, John McKnight, Midwest director of the US Commission on Civil Rights, made a presentation in the basement of the Warren Avenue Congregational Church on Chicago's West Side on the systematic discrimination in lending that prevented African American home buyers from getting mortgages. He was speaking to a group of about eighty people, most of them young, and many of them new to Chicago. They were members of the Wider Community Staff, which included Martin Luther King Jr.'s Chicago staff and various collaborating Chicago organizations: the American Friends Service Committee, West Side Christian Parish, West Side Organization, West Side Federation, and JOIN Community Union from the Uptown neighborhood, among others.

I was there, having arrived in Chicago a few months earlier after graduating from Stanford University. I had become passionately interested in the civil rights movement while in college. Many of my fellow students had gone to Mississippi to participate in the 1964 Freedom Summer, and I had listened as theology professor Robert McAfee Brown described his participation in the Freedom Rides and lectured on social gospel Christianity. Determined to join this work, I had gone to Chicago as a West Side Christian Parish volunteer, at the urging of another volunteer I knew through the Methodist Church. The parish assigned me to be the secretary for James Bevel, who had just arrived from the South. I had grown up in Port Angeles, Washington, a small town near Seattle, and I knew I had much to learn.

John McKnight launched into a discussion of mortgage lending discrimination and its dire consequences, a practice affecting all of Chicago's black neighborhoods. He clarified for us how this complex process worked: Chicago financial institutions designated some neighborhoods as unworthy of loans based on their racial composition—that is, they were "redlined," or excluded from the regular mortgage lending process, by the banks and the Federal Housing Administration (FHA).[1] Furthermore, neighborhoods adjacent to black communities were designated "gray areas," where loans would not be made to either black or white prospective homeowners. This left the area ripe for blockbusters, or panic peddlers, as they were also called. Blockbusters—real estate agents and their erstwhile investors (sometimes the agents themselves)—would show up when they were ready to "turn the neighborhood" from white to black by selling one house to a black family and then convincing frightened white homeowners to sell to the blockbusters at rock-bottom prices, warning them that property values were about to fall dramatically. The panic peddlers then sold these houses to black families at an exorbitant profit— sometimes double the price they had paid the white families. Black home buyers obtained financing through contracts with the panic peddlers, an arrangement that offered them few protections. Under this arrangement, a buyer had no equity in the house until the contract was at least half paid off, which might take fifteen years.[2] African American families agreed to these ruthless practices because it was the only way they could purchase homes; they could not obtain regular mortgages through traditional lending institutions. Even after the neighborhood had been "turned" into an African American community, no regular mortgages were available.

If financially strapped African American families missed a payment or made a late payment, then their homes would immediately be repossessed and resold, resulting in more profit for the panic peddlers. Alternatively, the contract owners (sometimes the panic peddlers themselves, and sometimes others to whom they had sold the contracts) would tack large fees onto the mortgage payments—perhaps $1,500 for some unforeseen purpose—declare the fees due immediately, and then repossess the home when the homeowner could not pay. The house would then be sold again, and the whole process would be repeated. This exploitative system frustrated families' efforts to own homes in these West Side neighborhoods full of tree-lined streets and many old graystone two-flat and three-flat buildings that could easily accommodate a family and a renter or two.

This was a story I never forgot. It was a rude awakening for me. I began to see that this was a systemic process involving not just a few greedy slumlords or real estate agents but the major financial institutions in the city, conspiring to deprive African Americans of the dream of owning a home and building a more secure financial future.

Later, we learned that the FHA played a key role in this process of denying African Americans homeownership. FHA underwriting manuals from the late 1930s specified that "if a neighborhood is to retain stability it is necessary that properties shall continue to be occupied by the same social and racial classes." Lending institutions and appraisers adopted these guidelines and made their decisions accordingly.[3]

Initially, Dr. King's West Side staff had settled in to organize tenant unions. Within weeks, this effort evolved into the Union to End Slums, as we began to see the interconnection between poverty and poor housing, poor-quality food in the stores, lack of employment, and more. We sought a bigger frame that would address the systemic nature of these problems. John McKnight had helped outline that system for us, and we continued to develop it as we learned more and more. We called this system a form of internal colonialism, paralleling the European colonization of much of Africa, for example.[4]

In the late 1950s, while working for the Chicago Commission on Human Relations, McKnight had heard West Side attorney Mark Satter describe the contract buying system. "I was really stunned by what he was talking about," McKnight said in a 2012 interview. "I thought of this contract buying issue as a civil rights issue as it manifested at the neighborhood level." For a long time McKnight was unable to get anyone interested in taking up the issue: "The average civil rights person didn't know much about mortgages, land transfer, contracts, articles of agreement . . . it was pretty complex," he said. When McKnight returned to Chicago in the mid-1960s, he again tried to interest community activists in the contract buying issue: "I specifically remember talking with Jim Bevel. I had a little game I developed, cards and things to show people in my office how it worked. Bevel was very taken by the whole thing. He really understood it, and said he was going to present it to Dr. King."[5]

In the end, Dr. King and his executive staff decided to focus on tenant unions instead. Bevel told McKnight that they wanted to prioritize their organizing efforts on the poorest: renters, not homeowners. However, Bevel and the other movement leaders did not forget about the exploitative system of contract buying. Months later, as the Chicago Freedom Movement was preparing for a summer direct action campaign, leaders of the coalition began to concentrate on the myriad problems that created slums. They gathered at the Catholic Interracial Council in downtown Chicago to develop a list of demands for the summer campaign. The centerpiece was to be their declaration that Chicago would be an "open city," with open housing, open employment opportunities, changes in the welfare system, and an end to many other forms of discrimination. McKnight was at that meeting and recalls: "Everybody had been invited to come up with demands. I can still picture it: they were sort of pasted up all over the walls." He made sure that ending discrimination in mortgage lending was on that list, and there was wide agreement.[6]

On July 10, 1966, immediately after the rally of more than 30,000 Chicagoans at Soldier Field, Martin Luther King Jr. led thousands of marchers to City Hall, where he posted those demands on the door. The demands related to banks and savings institutions called for the following:

- Public statements of a nondiscriminatory mortgage policy so that loans will be available to any qualified borrower without regard to the racial composition of the area, or the age of the area, a policy that takes into account years of discrimination against Negro borrowers.
- Creation of special loan funds for the conversion of contract housing purchases to standard mortgages.[7]

The direct action campaign that began shortly after the July 10 rally targeted discriminatory practices in real estate offices. But we understood that lending institutions played a key role as well. On August 16 we picketed one of the major financial institutions in downtown Chicago: First Federal Savings and Loan—for us, a symbol of the industry. We demanded that it halt discriminatory mortgage lending practices. (The same day we also picketed the Board of Realtors, the Department of Public Aid, City Hall, and the Chicago Housing Authority, again to illustrate the widespread responsibility for housing discrimination.)[8]

The summit negotiations began the following day, and on August 26, when the Summit Agreement was announced, it included the following commitments related to nondiscriminatory lending:

- The Cook County Council of Insured Savings Associations, by letter, and the Chicago Mortgage Bankers Association, at the Committee meeting of August 17, 1966, have affirmed their policy is to provide equal service to and to lend mortgage money to all qualified families, without regard to race, for the purchase of housing anywhere in the metropolitan area.
- Assistant Attorney General Roger Wilkins, head of the Community Relations Service of the United States Department of Justice, has advised the chairman of the subcommittee that the Service will inquire into the questions raised, under existing law, with respect to service by the Federal Deposit Insurance Corporation and the Federal Savings and Loan Insurance Corporation to financial institutions found guilty of practicing racial discrimination in the provision of financial service to the public. While the matter is a complex one, it will be diligently pursued.[9]

The Summit Agreement put this issue on the public agenda and called to account financial institutions responsible for discrimination. Institutional practices did not change overnight, as I might have expected back then, when I was in my twenties. But changes did come—very slowly.

First, in July 1967 the FHA issued directives to the effect that buildings in "riot or riot-torn areas" were "acceptable risks" for lenders. Although the FHA linked this change to ghetto riots, it occurred less than a year after the open-housing marches and the Summit Agreement had put fair-housing issues on the national agenda. The Chicago Freedom Movement's work may well have played a significant role in generating public concern for these housing issues. Riots were often provoked by incidents of police brutality or other confrontations with the authorities, and it seems unlikely that lack of mortgage availability would have been high on the list of provocations. A law professor later reported, "In the midst of the mid-1960s urban riots, the newly-created HUD forced the FHA to relax its insurance underwriting standards in order to insure mortgages in high-risk inner city neighborhoods."[10]

Finally, in April 1968, Congress passed the Fair Housing Act, Title VIII of the Civil Rights Act of 1968. One of its provisions prohibited "discrimination in the financing of housing," setting the first legal framework against discrimination in lending. Gregory Squires notes that "subsequent court decisions have added discriminatory appraisal practices (*United States v. American Institute of Real Estate Appraisers*), discriminatory land use and zoning practices (*United States v. City of Parma*) and refusal to make home loans available or to make them available on terms less favorable than in other areas due to the racial composition of the neighborhood (*Laufman v. Oakley Building and Loan Company*) to the list of prohibited acts."[11]

In the months and years following the August 1966 Summit Agreement, nationally significant campaigns against lending discrimination emerged from West Side Chicago neighborhoods. In 1968 the Contract Buyers League (CBL) was founded in North Lawndale (the neighborhood where King had lived in a slum apartment), seeking relief for black homeowners caught in the infamous contract schemes. Also in 1968, Gale Cincotta and her neighbors launched the anti-redlining movement, fighting financial institutions' discrimination against their community from their homes in Austin, just west of the Garfield Park neighborhoods where King's staff had been organizing. In 1972 Cincotta realized that a national anti-redlining movement was necessary, so she founded National People's Action, which grew into a vigorous force during the late 1970s and the 1980s.[12]

Later, I found myself intrigued by the fact that both the Contract Buyers League and the anti-redlining movement had emerged in close proximity to where Dr. King had been living and his staff had been organizing just a year or two earlier. Could there be a connection? Others didn't seem to see a link, but I wondered. As I began this research, I looked for some connection, unwilling to believe that it was only a coincidence.

The Contract Buyers League

In January 1966, the same month Martin Luther King moved into his slum apartment in Lawndale, Monsignor John J. Egan was appointed priest of Presentation Parish in that community. As head of the Catholic Diocese's Office of Urban Affairs, Monsignor Egan had been training community organizers to work in church communities across the city. After being exiled from his downtown post by a new archbishop and sent to the West Side, he settled into the community and brought in Jesuit seminarians to do neighborhood organizing with his parishioners and their neighbors. One day in July 1967, one of those seminarians, Jack Macnamara, learned from a recently widowed woman in the parish that she had bought her house on contract at a drastically inflated price. He reported his discovery to Monsignor Egan. As McKnight explained: "Monsignor Egan knew that I knew about this. So he put together in his mind what Jack [Macnamara] was talking about and what I had been talking about. He sent Jack down to talk with me, and I spent a lot of time with Jack. He was the first person that I had run into who was on the ground floor and who said, 'This is something I need to pursue.'"[13]

This was the beginning. Macnamara, along with some fellow seminarians and students he had recruited, learned to research property records: to track down how the homes had changed hands, how much the white families had sold them for, how much the black families had paid, and who was involved as the middleman in these transactions. It was an arduous task, given the obscurity of the records. But the results were stunning. They were able to document what many people already knew: both white and black families had been seriously cheated, with black families sometimes paying twice what the white families had received. It was a lucrative business. The panic peddlers made large sums on these transactions, and they sometimes sold the contracts to other investors protected by blind trusts set up in local banks, giving many Chicago investors a stake in this system of exploitation. Some believed that many powerful people in the Democratic machine also benefited.

Ruth Wells was one of the first to confront her contract seller, Moe Forman at the F&F Investment Company. In December 1967 Macnamara, Monsignor Egan, and two others accompanied her to the downtown office of the investment company. Macnamara tells the story: "Ruth had to do all the talking. She went to challenge him and she was just ruthless. He was an idiot himself. She tells this story: When she was leaving home in the morning she prayed to God that she would have a sign that she was doing the right thing. During the course of the meeting, his hand was shaking. So, she took that as a sign from God. When he wouldn't renegotiate according to the formula, we started picketing his office."[14] Shortly thereafter, in January 1968, the first community meeting of contract buyers was held in Lawndale. At the second community meeting, Ruth Wells told her story and then asked whether anyone else was in the same situation. Beryl Satter describes the response this way: "The effect was electric. Practically every hand in the room shot up. Wells encouraged the people gathered there to 'tell your family and your friends, your neighbors and the people you work with, if they bought on contract, they should come out.' At the next meeting approximately two dozen contract buyers decided to form an organization, the Contract Buyers of Lawndale. Within months attendance at the CBL's Wednesday night meetings had snowballed. . . . The group expanded so quickly in part because it had a perfect target for its anger—Moe Forman."[15]

The goal was to get the blockbusters to renegotiate the contracts down to more reasonable prices. The rest of 1968 was devoted to picketing contract sellers at their offices and at their homes when they refused to negotiate. Picketers confronted Ames, Sureway, Best, and F&F Investments, among others. By the summer of 1968, word of the Contract Buyers of Lawndale had spread to the South Side, where another group was formed to focus on homes bought from the housing developer Universal Builders.[16]

But Jack Macnamara realized that another strategy was needed:

I remember coming back from a CBL meeting one night, and things weren't going as well. I walked into the apartment and said to a couple of the college students, 'I think we need a payment strike. . . . These guys know how to handle picketing and bad publicity. What they won't know how to handle is something that hits their pocketbook.' We brought it up to the leaders and they thought it was a good idea. They said, 'We have nothing to lose.' I knew I'd succeeded when one woman one night said, 'Well I know Mr. Macnamara doesn't want us to do this payment strike, but I think we should do it anyway.'"[17]

The families put their payments in escrow, for future payment to the sellers after the contracts had been renegotiated. The payment strike went on for many months, sometimes years, between 1968 and the early 1970s, with about 500 families participating. For their own reasons, the contract sellers did not move quickly to evict the nonpaying families, but eventually, when the evictions began, crowds of CBL members and their allies gathered at the homes to move the evicted families back in. For many months, the sheriff and his deputies backed off when confronted with hundreds of neighborhood residents determined to halt the evictions. These dramatic confrontations brought a lot of public attention to the whole issue of contract buying.

As the public became more aware of how the contract sales process drastically exploited both black and white homeowners, support came from unexpected places. Volunteers, mostly women, came into Lawndale from the northern suburbs to attend meetings and work in the CBL office. Rabbi Robert Marx from the Jewish Council for Urban Affairs was an important ally; his presence and the additional support he mobilized were critical to broadening the group's base.

At one point, the Contract Buyers League was raising money for a bond fund to appeal evictions; each appeal cost $3,000 to $5,000, far beyond the means of most families. The Chicago Province of the Jesuits agreed to put up $100,000 for the bond fund, and other Jesuit provinces collectively came up with another $150,000. "I thought I'd died and gone to heaven," Jack Macnamara said upon hearing this news. Macnamara also raised funds from allies on the wealthy North Shore and from supporters such as Tom Foran, a US attorney, and Gordon Sherman, founder of Midas Muffler.[18]

Thirty attorneys from prominent Chicago law firms offered pro bono legal services to the families facing eviction due to the payment strike. Chief among these firms was the well-known Jenner and Block. Other Chicago attorneys, including Marshall Patner, Tom Sullivan, and Bob Ming, also provided critical support.

Paralleling the payment strikes were class-action lawsuits seeking legal redress for the exploitative contracts. The battle through the courts was long and arduous. The West Side case first went to court in November 1975, and the South Side case began in 1979. In the end, both cases were lost, and the last appeal was rejected in 1983.[19] Despite these losses, a second set of lawsuits challenging the Forcible Detainer and Entry Act—the Illinois law governing evictions—went to the Illinois Supreme Court. In *Rosewood v. Fisher,* the court ruled in 1970 that the nature of the contracts—whether fraudulent or usurious or otherwise irregular—could be raised as a defense in an eviction case, giving contract buyers a chance to tell their stories. In a second case, the Durhams, a family from the South Side, argued that the eviction law discriminated against the poor because it required the posting of a large bond—several thousand dollars—to file an appeal to an eviction order. In 1972 the Illinois Supreme Court ruled in their favor, declaring invalid the part of the law requiring large bonds before filing an appeal.[20]

By July 1971, 155 contracts had been renegotiated, with an average saving of $14,000 (about half the purchase price for a house). Other families were finally able to obtain regular mortgages; the FHA had changed its policies and was beginning to make mortgage insurance—and thus mortgages—available in black communities on a limited basis.[21] Moved by the sight of families being evicted in January's cold, powerhouse black real estate developer Dempsey Travis found mortgage funds through black-owned insurers for one group of buyers.

Eventually, the sheriff and the Chicago police devised a method to conduct evictions without interference: by having the city police cordon off the street so that supporters could not reach the house. Approximately seventy families permanently lost their homes. By the time these evictions happened, however, at least some families had saved sufficient funds in the escrow accounts to buy other homes.[22]

Some of the contract buyers described another, more personal, kind of victory. Macnamara explains: "It's the individual victories that people had. One of the stories I like to tell is about Mrs. Johnson, whose Realtor would not renegotiate her contract. . . . She got up at a meeting and said, 'He won't renegotiate my contract, but that's fine with me because I'm a leader. I've got this much out of it. No man's gonna get his hand in my pocket again.' So you know, she didn't feel like she was a loser, and she wasn't."[23]

Growing publicity and public support suggest that the Contract Buyers League had a substantial effect on attitudes in the larger community. James Bevel had often explained that in nonviolent direct action campaigns, the goal is to bring the oppression out into the open; when many people see the injustice, and see it as a violation of their own values, they will support the movement's goals and call for change. Satter describes this shift in public opinion as one of the consequences of this movement.[24]

At a January 2013 event at the Hull House Museum in Chicago honoring the CBL's work, I asked Clyde Ross, vice president of the Contract Buyers League and now in his nineties, if he saw a link between the Contract Buyers League and Dr. King's work in the North Lawndale neighborhood two years earlier. "We were definitely inspired by Dr. King," he said. "He gave us courage."[25]

The Anti-Redlining Movement

In Austin, a neighborhood just west and slightly north of Lawndale, the issue of fair lending—not yet identified by that name—was approached from a different direction. At the time, Austin was a largely white neighborhood. But the residents found that if they wanted to sell their houses or wanted to obtain home improvement loans, lenders would not loan money either to them or to any potential buyer. The Austin neighborhood was part of what lenders called the "gray zone": it was adjacent to the African American community and would soon be "turned." But not yet. It was 1968.[26]

Saul Alinsky–trained community organizer Tom Gaudette, who had previously worked with the Contract Buyers League, had formed the Organization for a Better Austin to address local housing issues.[27] But it was Gale Cincotta, a superb organizer, speaker, and negotiator, who became the feisty leader and shrewd strategist for this movement. As Gale and her neighbors began to organize against the blockbusting system in Austin, they needed documentation of the discrimination in lending, so they turned to John McKnight, who by this time was director of the Center for Urban Affairs at Northwestern University in Evanston. McKnight and his Northwestern University colleagues had acted as consultants to the Contract Buyers League and had, in fact, gathered a massive amount of data about property transactions on the West Side for the class-action lawsuits, showing a clear pattern of discrimination. Although the judge in the court cases seeking renegotiated contracts had not allowed these data to be presented, the Center for Urban Affairs had formed the Urban-Suburban Investment Study Group, which continued to explore these questions. That group provided just what Gale Cincotta needed to make the case for discriminatory lending in Austin.[28]

By 1972, Cincotta had launched the national movement to take on mortgage redlining with the founding of National People's Action. Although the FHA had amended its policies by this time, local practices remained unchanged, for the most part. Cincotta became the director of National People's Action, but she always stayed in Austin and continued to press forward with the work in Chicago. Meanwhile, the anti-redlining movement spread across the country.

From another direction came the Equal Credit Opportunity Act, passed by Congress in 1974 and forbidding discrimination in credit on the basis of race, color, religion, national origin, sex, or marital status. The results of this act are visible today in those "Equal Housing Lender" signs required to be displayed in every bank. This legislation was the result of hearings concerning how difficult it was for women to get credit, and the other protected classes were added during the legislative process. This was helpful in some respects, but it did not deal with discrimination by neighborhood, the heart of the old system under which even white buyers with good credit could not get mortgages in redlined neighborhoods.[29]

Although the research provided by McKnight's team showed that the financial institutions had racially discriminatory policies and discriminated against certain neighborhoods, still missing was what Beryl Satter called "a smoking gun." It was Cincotta who came up with the idea of disclosure—requiring banks to disclose where they made mortgages. The protests continued, and in 1974 the Federal Home Loan Bank of Chicago agreed to require banks to disclose the locations of their loans. The result was the first written agreement in the nation between a community and a bank, developed by the Organization for the Northeast and the Bank of Chicago and signed in September 1974.[30]

Senator William Proxmire, chair of the Senate Banking Committee, took an interest in this Chicago success after reading an article by Darel

Grothaus, a staff member of McKnight's Northwestern University group. Proxmire saw the need for more legislation to make these remedies more widely available. He reached out to the National People's Action group and met with Cincotta and others to discuss the problems of redlining and community reinvestment. They worked together to develop and pass the Home Mortgage Disclosure Act in 1975 and then the Community Reinvestment Act in 1977. The 1977 act required banks to invest in the local communities where they operated, opening the possibility of home mortgages in previously redlined communities. These were major victories.[31]

These legal changes also launched many local groups across the nation, and they eventually came together as the National Community Reinvestment Coalition. This coalition, now more than 600 groups strong, has monitored the behavior of banks and negotiated numerous agreements between communities and banks, bringing massive new investment into previously underserved areas.[32]

Chicago has continued to play a leadership role in the development of fair-housing and fair-lending practices with the emergence of new pioneering institutions. Particularly important to fair lending has been Chicago's Woodstock Institute, founded in 1973 by Arnold and Sylvia Seinfeld to "explore and pursue the most effective strategies for dealing with discriminatory housing and investment policies in the Chicago metropolitan area." Founding board members included John McKnight, Alexander Polikoff (the attorney who took the *Gautreaux* case to the Supreme Court, charging the Chicago Housing Authority with discrimination), Al Raby (former convener of the Coordinating Council of Community Organizations and coleader of the Chicago Freedom Movement with Martin Luther King), urban planner Stan Hallett (associated with McKnight's Northwestern University group), and Ron Gryzwinski (founder of South Shore Bank, established to bring community-based banking to the African American community). The founding executive director, Larry Rosser, had links to McKnight from his work as founder of Seminarians for Racial Justice. The Woodstock Institute played a key role in negotiating the first major community reinvestment agreement in Chicago with the First National Bank in 1984. It has also provided research, legal, and advocacy support for community groups developing reinvestment agreements in the years since then. In recent years, Woodstock's focus has expanded to include other forms of predatory lending practices.[33]

In another Chicago innovation, the John Marshall Law School in Chicago developed a Fair Housing Legal Support Center and Clinic, established in 1985 in partnership with the Leadership Council for Metropolitan Open Communities. This in-house program trains law students in the practice of fair-housing law and offers free legal services to those who experience housing discrimination, whether based on race, gender, or disability. Although the center specializes in fair housing, it also provides resources on fair lending to the public and to agencies, attorneys, and other professionals; in addition, faculty members affiliated with the center teach fair-housing and fair-lending law to students at John Marshall Law School.[34]

Reflections on Social Movements and the Fight for Fair Lending

To understand the long-term impact of the Chicago Freedom Movement and its place in the long struggle for fair lending, it is necessary to describe the long-term and multifaceted effort required to accomplish a movement's goals. As suggested by Bill Moyer's model, the Eight Stages of Successful Social Movements, movement work shifts over time as the movement and its issues proceed through the eight stages, often transitioning from nonviolent direct action campaigns to lobbying for legislation, followed by setting up mechanisms and institutions to implement change. The goals of the movement often expand or become more specific as activists deepen their understanding of the issue. This definitely happened in the struggle for fair lending, as the activists discovered that, first, disclosure was needed so the public could document the exclusion of certain neighborhoods from mortgage lending; then, with that information, it was possible to require community reinvestment.[35]

We might envision a social movement as a kind of relay race, with each group, each era, each project carrying the baton for a time, moving the issue forward, and then passing the baton to the next group for the next phase of the struggle. There may be setbacks as backlash sets in or as new complications arise, but if commitments are strong, then the struggle continues. If we were to identify the runners in the Chicago movement's fair-lending relay race, we might start this way: It began in the 1950s with Mark Satter, an attorney from Lawndale who took the cases of black families who had been overcharged for their homes and forced to buy on contract because they were unable to get regular mortgages. Satter took their cases to court in Chicago, and he lost every one. But in the process, he connected with John McKnight, who carried the baton by himself for a while, until he was able to pass it on to the Chicago Freedom Movement, which made lending discrimination a public issue and gained public commitments from relevant actors in the Summit Agreement. The Chicago Freedom Movement inspired the residents of Lawndale and passed the baton to a group of residents there, who formed the Contract Buyers League. Paralleling this was a separate strand, with McKnight educating Jack Macnamara, who became the organizer for the Contract Buyers League. The baton was then passed to Gale Cincotta and the anti-redlining movement, which used research generated for the Contract Buyers League to provide solid evidence of discriminatory practices on Chicago's West Side, drawing again on the resources of McKnight and his widening circle of colleagues for additional research and advocacy support. It was the anti-redlining movement that, twenty years after Mark Satter's original work, generated enough political momentum to get national legislation passed: the Home Mortgage Disclosure Act and the Community Reinvestment Act. It took another round of activism—the next baton passing—for the National Community Reinvestment Coalition to learn how to use the newly available legal tools to develop community investment agreements, this time in close collaboration with financial institutions. Paralleling that work, another baton passed to groups such as the Woodstock Institute, as community groups and financial institutions began to work collaboratively to develop plans for community reinvestment, and to the John Marshall Law School Fair Housing Legal Support Center and Clinic, which provides education and services related to fair lending.

If we think of social movements in this larger sense, we can see all these players as part of the same process—moving toward a more just financial system that serves the needs of all citizens equitably. The Chicago Freedom Movement had a role in that process.

The Twenty-First-Century Loan Crisis

Although much progress has been made, a new lending crisis crystalized in the early twenty-first century: predatory lending practices and subprime loans and the economic meltdown that resulted. Space does not allow a detailed analysis of these events, but it is important to note that during this era, financial institutions found new ways to discriminate: a disproportionate number of African Americans and Latinos were offered these "toxic" subprime loans, even when they could have qualified for regular thirty-year mortgages—a process that became known as "reverse redlining." These subprime loans put the borrowers at greater risk of foreclosure, as the loans had onerous provisions such as balloon payments after a few years. African American and Latino communities experienced a massive loss of wealth that was far greater than that of whites. A Pew Research Center study reported that "between 2005 and 2009 Latino families and African American families lost 66% and 53% of their household wealth, respectively . . . compare[d] to a 16% drop in wealth for white households. The bulk of this decline in net worth is attributed to the loss of home equity." When home equity is gone, the effects can be devastating.[36]

Where did that wealth go? Mostly, it went to the banks, highlighting parallels with the old contract buying system. Homeowners lost their equity to the banks in the current crisis, whereas under the old system, they lost what would have been their equity to the speculators and their financial backers.

Communities of color suffered disproportionately from this recent scandalous treatment by mortgage lenders, but they were not the only ones caught in the dragnet. Many working-class and middle-class white Americans were targeted for predatory loans or subjected to grossly dishonest treatment by the banks, which, it turns out, sometimes foreclosed on homes even though all the payments had been made on time.[37] This has resulted in a much larger group of Americans who are furious at the banks (particularly the big banks)—an anger that has yet to find its full-throated public voice. The Occupy movement took up this matter in 2011 with its cries of "Banks got bailed out; we got sold out." Occupy Our Homes took action and held negotiations with lending institutions, aimed at preventing foreclosures. Lawsuits intended to compel the banks to make amends for their wrongdoing have resulted in some settlements, but not much for those who lost their homes.[38]

The massive consolidation of financial services that has taken place in the last forty-plus years, including the decline of savings and loans and the numerous bank mergers, means that the beneficiaries of all that loss have shifted, in large part, from local speculators, unscrupulous real estate agents, and the local elites to whom they were tied to national elites, as big banks became even larger. Now, those looking to reform home mortgage lending to make it fairer and more just must take on the nation's largest and most powerful financial institutions.

Another mass movement is called for at this time, working at both the local and national levels. This work must coalesce with a larger movement for financial reform that holds those large financial institutions accountable, as well as the governmental entities that enabled and shielded them under the assumption that they were "too big to fail." They need to be held accountable for defrauding so many Americans, some of whom never missed a mortgage payment, and depriving them of their homes.[39]

We could ask: How has this happened again? How could such a massive fraud be perpetrated on American homeowners by the financial powers that be? As john a. powell has pointed out, "This is a spiritual and moral project as well as a political project." He quotes Amartya Sen, who said, "It is not so much a matter of having exact rules about how precisely we ought to behave, as of recognizing the relevance of our shared humanity in making the choices we face."[40]

Policy changes are crucial, and such changes have brought us a great distance. Equal lending is still the law of the land, and federal bank examiners are questioning banks to ensure that they have met the requirements of the Community Reinvestment Act. Community reinvestment agreements have contributed to the revival of communities across the country.

Yet, in the end, we are taken back to the spirit of Martin Luther King: when leading the Montgomery bus boycott, King said the boycott was about more than buses; *it was about justice.* Similarly, we must speak publicly today about the need for housing justice, to think about what a movement for housing justice might look like. I conclude with a quote from powell: "In very important ways we are not just trying to get *things* right; we are trying to get *us* right. We need to forcefully articulate our vision of social justice and how both we and our structures fit within that vision. . . . What would fair housing [and, I would add, fair lending] look like if we understood that housing is a key way in which we build relationships? . . . If we were truly living and working in Dr. King's vision of a beloved community, a fully integrated society, what would our housing look like?"[41]

Notes

I would like to thank Jack Macnamara, John McKnight, and Darel Grothaus, who agreed to speak with me for this project; Leonard Rubinowitz for his assistance; and Clyde Ross, who tells his story so eloquently.

1. The Federal Housing Administration made maps of cities and graded neighborhoods based on their "risk levels." On these maps, the neighborhoods identified in red ink presented the highest risk, and the FHA would not insure mortgages in those areas—hence the term "redlining."

2. On blockbusting, see Amanda Seligman, *Block by Block: Neighborhoods and Public Policy on Chicago's West Side* (Chicago: University of Chicago Press, 2005), 151–62.

3. FHA manual from 1938, paragraph 937, in Gregory D. Squires and Chester Hartman, "Occupy Wall Street: A New Wave of Fair Housing Activism?" in *From Foreclosure to Fair Lending: Advocacy, Organizing, Occupy, and the Pursuit of Equitable Credit*, ed. Chester Hartman and Gregory D. Squires (New York: New Village Press, 2013), 1–2.

4. Bevel frequently used the language of internal colonialism, as did other black leaders. See "Dr. King Carries Fight to Northern Slums," *Ebony*, April 1966, 96; Stokely Carmichael and Charles V. Hamilton, *Black Power: The Politics of Liberation in America* (New York: Vintage Books, 1967), 2–32.

5. John McKnight, interview by Mary Lou Finley, Evanston, Illinois, November 1, 2012. For a description of Mark Satter's work defending black families who were being exploited by speculators, see Beryl Satter, *Family Properties: Race, Real Estate, and Exploitation of Black Urban America* (New York: Metropolitan Books, 2009); I am much indebted to Beryl Satter for her thorough research. In the 1950s black real estate professionals and black financial institutions were able to provide financing for some black home buyers, but these

resources were very limited. See Preston H. Smith, *Racial Democracy and the Black Metropolis: Housing Policy in Postwar Chicago* (Minneapolis: University of Minnesota Press, 2012), 241, 255–96.

6. McKnight interview. Also see Satter, *Family Properties*, 182.

7. "The Program of the Chicago Freedom Movement," in *Chicago, 1966: Open Housing Marches, Summit Negotiations, and Operation Breadbasket*, ed. David Garrow (Brooklyn, NY: Carlson Publishing, 1989), 104–5.

8. In this era, most mortgage lending came from savings and loan institutions rather than banks. On the demonstrations, see Mary Lou Finley, "The Open Housing Marches: Chicago, Summer '66," in Garrow, *Chicago, 1966*, 23.

9. "The Summit Agreement," in Garrow, *Chicago, 1966*, 151.

10. Gamaliel Foundation, "Progress and Prospects," quoted in Satter, *Family Properties*, 253. The riots in Newark, New Jersey, began on July 12, and those in Detroit, Michigan, started on July 23, 1967. Although there were many riots during this time, those in Newark and Detroit stood out as the most dramatic and most destructive. For the FHA change, see W. Dennis Keating, "Federal Policy and Poor Urban Neighborhoods," in *Rebuilding Urban Neighborhoods: Achievements, Opportunities, and Limits*, ed. W. Dennis Keating and Norman Krumholz (Thousand Oaks, CA: Sage Publications, 1999), 25.

11. Bruce S. Gelber, Rachel Hopp, and Stacy Canan, "Recent Developments in Housing Discrimination Law," *Clearinghouse Review* 16, no. 8 (1983): 806–14, cited by Gregory D. Squires, "Community Reinvestment: An Emerging Social Movement," in *From Redlining to Reinvestment: Community Responses to Urban Disinvestment*, ed. Gregory D. Squires (Philadelphia: Temple University Press, 1992), 8–9. Darel Grothaus reported that in the early 1970s he and Calvin Bradford, colleagues of John McKnight's at Northwestern University, attended continuing education training sessions for mortgage bankers and loan officers at savings and loans, quietly seeking information about appraisal practices. There, in the textbook on appraisals being used in the class, was "the list," identifying racial and ethnic groups and the degree of risk their presence brought to neighborhoods. "It was the smoking gun," he said. Darel Grothaus, interview by Mary Lou Finley, Seattle, August 28, 2015.

12. On the Contract Buyers League, see Satter, *Family Properties*. On the anti-redlining movement, see Michael Westgate and Ann Vick-Westgate, *Gale Force: Gale Cincotta: The Battles for Disclosure and Community Reinvestment*, 2nd ed. (Cambridge, MA: Harvard Bookstore, 2011).

13. McKnight interview.

14. Jack Macnamara, interview by Mary Lou Finley and Pam Smith, Chicago, December 4, 2011.

15. Satter, *Family Properties*, 244, quoting James Alan McPherson, "In My Father's House There Are Many Mansions—and I'm Going to Get Me Some of

Them Too: The Story of the Contract Buyers League," *Atlantic Monthly*, April 1972, 58.

16. At this point, the group's name was changed to the Contract Buyers League.

17. Macnamara interview.

18. Ibid.

19. For details of these court cases, see Satter, *Family Properties*, 320–71.

20. Ibid., 307–8, 312.

21. The FHA's role in the decade that followed, however, was far from benign. See ibid., 338–50.

22. Ibid., 451, 313–14.

23. Macnamara interview.

24. Satter, *Family Properties*, 259–63.

25. "Lawndale Conversation Series: Contract Buyers League," Jane Addams Hull House Museum, Chicago, January 31, 2013. For an account of Clyde Ross's experiences, see Ta-Nehisi Coates, "The Case for Reparations," *Atlantic*, June 2014, 54–71.

26. Westgate and Vick-Westgate, *Gale Force*, 21–28.

27. Saul Alinsky's school for community organizing had been impacting Chicago neighborhoods since the 1930s, when his first organization in the Back of the Yards neighborhood was established. He trained organizers who worked in many Chicago neighborhoods, and their work was often funded by local churches. Although Alinsky's approach was more confrontational than the style of organizing from a nonviolence perspective, there was considerable overlap in terms of working with grassroots community members and building on their concerns. See Saul Alinksy, *Reveille for Radicals* (1947; reprint, New York: Vintage, 1989).

28. Westgate and Vick-Westgate, *Gale Force*, 5–27. The Urban-Suburban Investment Study Group at Northwestern University consisted of "community activists, researchers, progressive business people, journalists, bankers, attorneys, seminarians and graduate students," and it was staffed by Darel Grothaus, Calvin Bradford, Art Lyons, and Leonard Rubinowitz. The statistical work was done by Andrew Gordon, a young sociology professor at Northwestern, using old mainframe computers and large collections of punch cards. Satter, *Family Properties*, 369–70; Leonard Rubinowitz, personal communication.

29. For the history of this legislation, see Gregory E. Elliehausen and Thomas A. Durkin, "Theory and Evidence of the Impact of Equal Credit Opportunity: An Agnostic Review of the Literature," *Journal of Financial Services Research* 2 (1989): 90–91.

30. Jean Pogge, "Reinvestment in Chicago Neighborhoods: A Twenty Year Struggle," in Squires, *From Redlining to Reinvestment*, 133–36.

31. Satter, *Family Properties*, 369–70.

32. Westgate and Vick-Westgate, *Gale Force,* 262–85, 286–324.

33. See http://www.woodstockinst.org/content/woodstock-institute-timeline-1973-2013-49; Pogge, "Reinvestment in Chicago Neighborhoods," 136–48; Spencer Cowan, interview by Mary Lou Finley, Chicago, January 9, 2014; Grothaus interview.

34. Damian Ortiz, interview by Mary Lou Finley, Chicago, November 6, 2012.

35. See chapter 21 for more details on the Moyer model. See also Bill Moyer with JoAnn McAllister, Mary Lou Finley, and Steven Soifer, *Doing Democracy: The MAP Model for Organizing Social Movements* (Gabriola Island, BC: New Society Publishers, 2001).

36. On reverse redlining and its consequences, see Douglas Massey, "Undoing the Bitter Legacy of Segregation and Discrimination," in Hartman and Squires, *From Foreclosure to Fair Lending,* ix–xii. On steering African Americans toward subprime loans, see John P. Relman, "Finding a Home for the Occupy Movement: Lessons from the Memphis and Wells Fargo Litigation," ibid., 117–19. On wealth loss in communities of color, see Shanti Abedin and Shanna L. Smith, "A Tale of Two Recoveries: Discrimination in the Maintenance and Marketing of REO Properties in African American and Latino Neighborhoods across America," ibid., 133–34.

37. See Neil Barofsky, *Bailout: An Inside Account of How Washington Abandoned Main Street while Rescuing Wall Street* (New York: Free Press, 2012), 150–58.

38. Relman, "Finding a Home for the Occupy Movement," 106–9.

39. For one proposal to link local and national efforts, see Peter Dreier's discussion of federated organizations in "Building a Movement for Fair Lending, Foreclosure Relief, and Financial Reform," in Hartman and Squires, *From Foreclosure to Fair Lending,* 298–303.

40. john a. powell, "Housing, Race, and Opportunity," in Hartman and Squires, *From Foreclosure to Fair Lending,* 263.

41. Ibid., 264–65.

9

Martin Luther King's Legacy in North Lawndale

The Dr. King Legacy Apartments and Memorial District

Kimberlie Jackson

It was April 4, 1998, the thirtieth anniversary of Dr. King's assassination. For me, that's when it began. As I headed toward my office at the Lawndale Christian Development Corporation (LCDC), I noticed that one of my coworkers had the morning's *Chicago Sun-Times* on his desk. On the front page was the famous picture of Dr. Martin Luther King Jr., Coretta Scott King, and several others leaning out the window of his third-floor apartment at 1550 South Hamlin Avenue in Lawndale. I realized the building was only a few blocks from our office. The newspaper article covered what King had done here in Chicago, but I found it troubling that the article claimed no progress had been made in the ensuing thirty years to deal with the problems King had come to Chicago to address. That article lit a fire under me. I wanted to make sure that Chicago and the rest of the world knew that plenty had happened in Lawndale since Dr. King lived here. I tore the picture out of the *Sun-Times* and laminated it.[1]

That picture became a visual reminder of Dr. King's sacrifice and the significance of this neighborhood—significant enough for Martin Luther King to come here and bring his family. I felt an obligation to do my part in carrying out Dr. King's work. I also felt a common bond with Coretta King. Like me, she had taken her kids and followed her husband to Chicago. If Dr. King and his family thought it was important to be present in this Chicago neighborhood, then I needed to take notice of that. The newspaper article mentioned everything the movement had tried to accomplish, and as I read it, I realized there was still much unfinished business. I made the movement's goals my goals, and I made that article my personal roadmap for driving the social justice movement forward. I treasure that newspaper article to this day.

A few years earlier, in 1994, I had come to Lawndale from Kansas City, Missouri, with my husband and our three small children. My husband had been hired as a youth pastor at Lawndale Community Church. This church manifests Christ's call to love and to serve by providing desperately needed resources to impoverished community members.

We moved into a third-floor apartment in the building on Ogden Avenue where the LCDC office is located. Conditions in that apartment were horrible (measured against my standards of decent living). I had lived in the city before, but I had never experienced anything like this. The first couple of months were bad enough, but then we discovered the water heater was on its way out. Worse yet, we learned we were being poisoned by a slow carbon monoxide leak, which explained my lightheadedness and frequent headaches. During that time I thought, "Is this the best we can provide?" This whole experience fueled my desire to see that nobody else had to live like that. Dr. King must have had this same feeling when he moved into the neighborhood. Some years later, when Martin Luther King III visited LCDC, he confirmed my suspicions. He recalled that it hadn't been easy. The hallway smelled, the apartment was not the best, and he and his siblings were not allowed to go outside and play like they normally did in Atlanta. Hearing the parallel with my own experience was really empowering.

The Lawndale Christian Development Corporation was launched in 1987 as one of the ministries of Lawndale Community Church. The executive director of LCDC at that time, Richard Townsell, thought that my background in real estate investing and sales and property management would fit well with the LCDC's work in developing housing. My role was to see that families had quality, affordable housing and to reestablish a high-profile sense of pride and ownership in the community.[2]

We at the Lawndale Christian Development Corporation have continued to do the work started by local activists and the Chicago Freedom

Movement. Since 1987, we have developed more than 800 units of housing—including the acquisition and rehabilitation of scores of abandoned buildings—and prepared them for sale or rent to community residents; we have infused $100 million in improvements into the community. Our after-school program for high school students, designed to ensure their college readiness, has served more than 1,000 children. Lawndale Community Church started a nearby health center in 1985 to address the lack of access to health care in the community; it now receives more than 200,000 patient visits a year and offers a fitness center, health education programs, and a café serving healthy foods.

Meanwhile, the building at 1550 South Hamlin, where Dr. King lived, was torn down many years ago, along with other buildings on that block. For decades, the only reminder of it was a pile of old bricks left over from the demolition. Over the years, many people had expressed a desire to develop the block and create retail space or senior housing or a youth center or something else, but nothing ever came together. We began to envision that the site could provide affordable housing, along with some kind of a memorial to Dr. King.

In 2005 LCDC director Townsell discovered that the land was going to become available again; the developer who had been planning to build senior housing there did not get approval to move forward. We talked with the alderman for our ward and expressed an interest, but he had already promised to give the Reverend Al Sampson an opportunity to do something with the property. Reverend Sampson had worked on Dr. King's staff in the 1960s, organizing in Lawndale, and he wanted to do something there to honor Dr. King.

Many of these lots in older neighborhoods had reverted to the City of Chicago for unpaid taxes after their buildings had been abandoned and torn down. In an effort to get the empty lots back on the tax rolls, the city's aldermen were tasked with deciding how to distribute the vacant lots in their wards. The land was often given away to developers or to local organizations in an effort to encourage rebuilding.

Our alderman agreed to broker a meeting between Sampson and Townsell. I went along with our director, as did one of the interns working with us. We met in the alderman's office, although the alderman himself wasn't there. I immediately felt a strong connection with Reverend

Sampson, and soon I understood what he wanted to accomplish. He wanted to be sure that Dr. King's legacy would be preserved, that something worthwhile would be built on the site, and that everybody would know that Dr. King had lived there. That is exactly what we were thinking. After that meeting, Sampson gave the alderman the okay for us to proceed with our project. We offered to involve him, if he chose to participate. Shortly thereafter, Townsell resigned, and there was a period when we weren't certain the construction project could go forward. In April 2007 I took over as executive director and began to look for ways to move ahead.

We went to the Local Initiative Support Corporation (LISC), a national institution that supports community development efforts in major cities, and shared our desire to build affordable housing and a King memorial on this site. The CEO of LISC advised us to consider this not just a building but a destination and memorial district. He suggested that our team go to Kansas City to see the Jazz and Negro Baseball League District there. Once we arrived, we immediately understood what we could do with the concept. In Kansas City, the original buildings where Charlie Parker, Billie Holiday, Ray Charles, and others had played were preserved, rehabbed, and reopened as jazz clubs, restaurants, and retail shops. Additionally, new housing and a museum devoted to the history of jazz and the Negro Baseball League had been built. We returned to Chicago and reshaped our original idea into a Martin Luther King Memorial District.

I was impressed with what we had seen in Kansas City, but I still wasn't entirely comfortable with our decision-making process. I felt we needed to reach out to the King family, let them know our plans, and get their support. One of our partners, a contractor, knew the Reverend Tyrone Crider, Martin Luther King III's college roommate at Morehouse. He contacted Crider, who was willing to set up a meeting with King III in Washington, DC. Accompanying me were the Reverend Randall Harris of the West Side Federation and Ben Kendrick. We shared our concept of the Martin Luther King Memorial District with his son and told him we envisioned that the development would include a library and a park, as well as housing. We proposed names for everything, including the apartment building, which we originally wanted to call the Dr. Martin Luther and Coretta Scott King Apartments. King III and his associate told us that name would not work, so after much consternation and the consideration of many options, I suggested we call the project the Dr. King Legacy Apartments. King III liked the idea, and I felt we finally had the green light to proceed.

Turning this idea into reality took a lot of work. I had been trying to acquire all the requisite city approvals and permits for a number of years. At one point, we found ourselves at a meeting in the neighborhood with Mayor Richard M. Daley, son of Richard J. Daley, who had been mayor back in the 1960s when King was here. We had been invited to present an overview of our work in the community. I took the opportunity to show the mayor the video we had recently produced on the proposed MLK Memorial District. He hit the roof when he found out we were getting resistance from his departments. "Why is this happening?" he asked. He said this should have been done a long time ago. Right then and there he asked his chief of staff to call the commissioner of housing and the commissioner of planning and tell them to get this done right away. That helped. Those city departments mobilized, and we got all the permits we needed in short order. It was fast-tracked because Mayor Daley had a strong personal interest in seeing the project completed. I believe to this day that he wanted to atone for the way his father had treated King so many years ago.

People in the neighborhood were excited. There was a sense of pride. Not a single person thought this was anything other than great. Some of the older people in the neighborhood had had personal experiences with Dr. King. One was Mr. Muldrow, owner of the Delkar Pharmacy at the corner of Sixteenth and Ridgeway, just one block away from the project site. His dad had run the pharmacy when Dr. King lived here, and whenever Dr. King was in town, he would buy his morning newspapers at Delkar. Mr. Muldrow's dad still told these stories. Dr. King's presence made a big impression.

Many people have such stories to tell. Bobbie Steele, the first woman president of the Cook County Board of Commissioners, now retired and close to eighty years old, was an usher at Stone Temple Church when Dr. King spoke there and famed gospel singer Mahalia Jackson sang there. There were small rallies in the neighborhoods, leading up to the big rally at Soldier Field. Mrs. Steele heard Dr. King speak at one of these rallies, and she remembers it like it was yesterday. One day, she took her five-year-old son to Dr. King's Lawndale apartment, and he looked out the window and spoke to them. That moment substantially impacted the course of her son's life. Robert Steele is now a Cook County commissioner.

In 2007–2008 we were in the midst of securing funding for the building when the economy crashed. Suddenly, no one was lending, and nothing was being built anywhere in Chicago. Things started to look pretty bleak, but I guess God was with us. Because the banks weren't lending, the federal government passed a stimulus bill to fund projects in communities across the country. These projects had to be "shovel ready," as they put it. We were definitely shovel ready! We were able to exchange our low-income housing credits for cash, which resulted in savings on construction interest. Those savings put us in a position to borrow less money and pay a lower interest rate than anticipated, ensuring that the Dr. King Legacy Apartments, the MLK Fair Housing Exhibit Center, and the Roots Café would become a reality.

The community was excited about the MLK Memorial District, and we invited as many people as possible to participate in the design and development process. We even hosted an art contest in the area elementary schools. More than 700 fourth- through sixth-graders submitted drawings depicting their dreams for the community. Many had no idea that Dr. King had once lived steps away from their school and their homes. This provided a special opportunity for a history lesson. The children were really jazzed! They shared their newfound knowledge with parents, siblings, and anyone who would listen. It even encouraged one little gentleman, Isaiah Bolden, to memorize the famous "I Have a Dream" speech and recite it to his parents and anyone else who would listen. Later, he created a drawing for permanent display in the MLK Fair Housing Exhibit Center.

For me, it had been a huge journey to get to that point. Once we had the blessing of the mayor, the King family, Reverend Sampson, and the community, we were ready to rock and roll! In 2009 we announced that the project was definitely happening. During construction, people from every walk of life, thousands of people, visited the site. They came from as far away as South Africa and Germany, from embassies in Washington,

DC, and from many other places. Community residents also came to see the project come together, amazed that it was actually happening.[3]

During this time, a local resident and member of the Lawndale Community Church shared a story with me. She had a friend at one of the cancer centers in the city, and she told us that when the center was built, they put prayers in the foundation of the building. She told us, "You should do that too." There is power in prayer, so of course we would do that! I'm sure Dr. King prayed many times here. Why not keep the practice going? So when people visited the site, we had them write prayers on slips of paper. We gathered about a thousand of them, and they are literally in the walls of the building. When the contractors heard that their assignment was to put these prayers in the walls, they were all for it. They even took pictures of the prayers and sent them to me. Dr. King was a minister, and what he did was based on faith. We had to be sure to include that in the building that carried his name.

With construction almost complete, the West Side Federation of Chicago, Holsten Management, Lawndale Christian Development Corporation, Citibank, and about forty volunteers hosted a Rental Application Day on Dr. King's birthday in January 2011. It was a very cold day in Chicago, with temperatures in the single digits. But that didn't stop hundreds of people from lining up outside beginning at 3:30 a.m. to apply for an apartment. Many had their children with them. The doors opened at 9:00 a.m., and by the end of the day, we had taken more than 400 applications for thirty-six apartments.

Eventually, the mix of families selected to move into the apartments was exactly what we wanted. Some families had been living in homeless shelters; some heads of household were schoolteachers or nurses; there were single-parent and two-parent households. Rents ranged from $289 to $989 per month, based on income. We tried our best to give everyone an opportunity.

On the eve of April 4, 2011, more than 600 people, including Martin Luther King III, Congressman Danny Davis, Cook County president Toni Preckwinkle, retired Cook County president Bobbie Steele, state representative Art Turner, Mayor Richard M. Daley, community leaders, civil rights leaders, business leaders, and community residents, all gathered to celebrate the opening of the Dr. King Legacy Apartments. The streets were blocked by a tent to house the celebration. The ribbon-cutting was an exciting moment.

Martin Luther King III was the keynote speaker. When we brought him over to see the new apartment complex, built on the site where he stayed during the summer of 1966, he shared his experiences of the neighborhood, and he shared the story of who really killed his dad. According to King III, James Earl Ray did not kill his dad. King and his family had met the person responsible, and they had forgiven him. That day, I believe we all felt we were witnessing a part of history that had never been told.[4]

During the Chicago Freedom Movement, Dr. King made a passionate statement when he moved his family into the Lawndale neighborhood. That took commitment and courage. The very least we can do is honor his efforts and his family's sacrifices. To ensure that the world understands and continues to appreciate what Dr. King did, we created the Exhibit Center as part of the MLK Memorial District. It took years of research, gathering local history to make sure we told the story in a way that young people could understand. We wanted youth in the community to appreciate the rich history of Dr. King's presence in this neighborhood and how it impacted the world. Because of the Chicago Freedom Movement and follow-on Chicago organizations, I can live anywhere. My parents can get a mortgage. I grew up with my grandparents owning their own home. I want everyone to have those same opportunities. Dr. King and the Chicago Freedom Movement helped pave the way.

Notes

1. "'Up South' in Chicago," *Chicago Sun-Times,* April 4, 1998, 1.

2. For more information about the approach of the Lawndale Christian Development Corporation, see Wayne Gordon and John M. Perkins, *Making Neighborhoods Whole: A Handbook for Christian Community Development* (Westmont, IL: InterVarsity Books, 2013). Wayne Gordon is the founding pastor of Lawndale Community Church.

3. For more details, see Antonio Olivo, "Martin Luther King, Jr.: Site of Civil Rights Leader's Chicago Home May Become Affordable Housing Complex as Part of New Historic District," *Chicago Tribune,* April 1, 2009.

4. For a critique of the official story of Dr. King's assassination, see William Pepper, *An Act of State: The Execution of Martin Luther King,* updated ed. (London: Verso, 2008).

10

The Movement Didn't Stop

Jesse L. Jackson Sr.

It has been almost fifty years since Dr. King appointed me to be the director of Operation Breadbasket in Chicago, and it is fitting for me to offer some reflections on the reverberating significance of the Chicago Freedom Movement, which set so much in motion.

Dr. King came to Chicago in 1966. That was the year after the confrontation in Selma. President Lyndon Johnson signed the Voting Rights Act that protected the right to vote on August 6, 1965. We'd been denied the right to vote except for a short, intermittent period during Reconstruction for 346 years: *346 years*. And so the movement in Chicago was building on that momentous historical decision. When Dr. King came to Chicago, there was already a great body of activism.

Dr. King was the designated home-run hitter that gave Chicago the focus and star power. By his sheer presence he challenged the national and international media to pay attention to his actions and give some focus to the urban struggle in Chicago. The waters were troubled before he got to town. Dr. King was the big rock that created the big splash. The concentric circles—the ripples—went far beyond Chicago. It was the greatest urban movement of its kind ever, and it continues to reverberate even to this day.

The movement did not stop when Dr. King left Chicago in 1967. Some people stopped, but the movement did not stop. The problem is that so often the movement in Chicago has been seen from the perspective of only one angle among many angles. It has been seen through a keyhole, and not through a door. I want to describe what I saw from my vantage point. I'm reminded of the New Testament, where the same story of Jesus and his teachings is told from different vantage points by

236

Matthew, Mark, Luke, and John. They saw the same thing, but from different angles. I want to explore with you my experience in our movement, and my understanding of it.

Free but Not Equal

The struggle in 1966 was a freedom movement. We were not free then. We were not free to move west of Ashland Avenue. We were not free to move into the southern or northern suburbs. You had a segregated city, unlike some other cities, with African Americans on this side, Irish and Polish on that side, the Jewish community living on the Near North Side, and a big-time, centralized, powerful mayor who was anti-progressive at the time—Richard J. Daley. You had this constant confrontation and friction going on. There were several restrictive covenants—we could not even live in parts of Hyde Park.[1] Usually when we did it was in the coach houses behind the big houses, even in Hyde Park, in 1966. We were not free.

We were not free for 246 years of slavery. We were not free in the nearly 100 years of Jim Crow. We were not free to move where we chose in Chicago in 1966, and there was no federal protection until the Fair Housing Act of 1968, which came out of the Chicago movement.[2] There is a fundamental shift today. Unlike 1966, today we are free. The movement for freedom was won.

Today we are free, but not equal. Today is a different stage of our struggle. The struggle today is about equity and equality. Nearly everyone supports freedom and diversity today. But if you ask questions about equity and equality in the areas of professional services, payment parity, procurement budgets, it is considered to be proprietary information. That's what I mean by free but not equal.

Take, for instance, the history of city contracts in Chicago. In 2006, under Mayor Richard M. Daley, minority contracts dropped to a low point of 9 percent in a city roughly 40 percent African American. Free, not equal. That same year, prime construction contracts in Cook County dropped from 26 to 17 percent. African Americans, Hispanics, Native Americans—free, but not getting equal access to contracts, jobs, capital.

Or look at the situation of the development of skills. Go to Twenty-Sixth and California on the West Side today. On one corner is a vast empty lot where the Washburne Trade School used to be—a school that once trained generations how to be skilled tradesmen. Today that school is closed down. Across the street is a $150 million jail. A first-class jail and a closed-down trade school. Free, but not equal access to education and skills development.

In a real sense, today is another stage of our struggle, which can be likened to a four-movement freedom symphony. The first movement was the emancipation of the slaves: a 246-year battle, rooted deeply in our Constitution. The second movement was another 100-year struggle to end legal segregation. The Voting Rights Act of 1965, the third movement, was the enabling legislation for the Fifteenth Amendment, which came ninety-five years after its ratification in 1870! And we continue to work on a constitutional amendment to ensure the right to vote for all Americans of proper age and citizenship. But you can be out of slavery, out of Jim Crow, have the right to vote, and starve to death. You're still stuck in slums unless there's access to capital, education, industry, and technology. Hard work and effort matter, but inheritance and access mean even more. The resources in Chicago were waiting to be called into action, and Dr. King was the coalescing force at the beginning of this fourth movement.

My Journey

Let me go back through my journey leading toward the Chicago campaign. July 16, 1960: I was jailed in Greenville, South Carolina, for trying to use a public library along with seven classmates. I was nineteen. Earlier that year in Nashville, Tennessee, John Lewis and James Bevel and Bernard LaFayette, under Jim Lawson's leadership, were preparing to sit in. Meanwhile, four students in Greensboro, at North Carolina A&T, staged a sit-in at the Woolworth's. We became classmates, those that sat in there. In the fall of 1960 I transferred from the University of Illinois, where I was on a football scholarship, to North Carolina A&T.

I was jailed again in 1963 in Greensboro for trying to patronize a restaurant, and I was accused of inciting a riot. I was a football player and became president of the Student Council and the second Vice Grand Basileus of the Omega Psi Phi fraternity. During that season I met Al Sampson, a student at Shaw University, as we sought to desegregate Raleigh, the state capital. At the capital, during the North Carolina State Student Legislature, the black students could not stay in the same hotels as our white counterparts. Also during that season I met the Reverend Calvin Morris. In the spring of 1962 he was a lead singer in the Lincoln University Glee Club and a fraternity brother. We actually marched in Washington together on August 28, 1963.

In 1964 I chose to enter Chicago Theological Seminary, where I met the Reverend Henry Hardy, a graduate student at the University of Chicago. And that's when—on that very first day—I met Gary Massoni, my close friend and longtime colleague. In time we met Lucille Lowman, the Reverend Clay Evans's secretary, who later became our first employee at Operation Breadbasket, and the Reverend Ed Riddick, who was our lead researcher. Then I met the Reverend Willie Barrow.

When Dr. King announced in the fall of 1965 that he was coming to Chicago, it created great excitement, and resentment. Mayor Richard J. Daley, the Reverend Joseph H. Jackson, the ministers who were on the city payroll, and the black aldermen known as the "Silent Six" did not want him in Chicago. When Dr. King's arrival became imminent, Mayor Daley sent him a telegram and asked for a meeting before he met with the community. Dr. King refused, saying he was compelled to meet with the people first.[3]

In anticipation of Dr. King's arrival, I organized ministers to meet every Wednesday. Reverend Clay Evans and Reverend John Thurston, Reverend A. P. Jackson, Reverend Frank Simms, Reverend Shelvin Hall from the West Side, and others would meet with Dr. Al Pitcher and Dr. Franklin Littell, professors at the University of Chicago Divinity School and Chicago Theological Seminary, respectively. They discussed the social gospel. The ministers from the community were steeped in practical church matters, and the professors were actually teaching them the social gospel and urging them to preach about this and not just about private salvation.

That summer I needed a job, and Governor Sanford sent me a reference letter for Mayor Richard J. Daley.[4] I went to get a job, and he offered me a job as a toll collector and sent me to the Fifth Ward. I was not impressed with the opportunity.

I was a member of John Johnson's mother's church.[5] "I want you to meet Johnny," Mrs. Johnson said, and she took me to meet with him. Mr. Johnson said to me, "You communicate much too well to be a toll collector. I want you to be on the street selling magazines."

There was a lot going on in Chicago. One summer I worked on the West Side, at the American Friends Service Committee's Project House, along with Tony Henry and Kale Williams. Bernard LaFayette and I began working together on the campaign against lead paint poisoning, using urine tests to screen neighborhood children.[6]

There was a riot in August 1965—a fire truck killed a black woman on the West Side. Larry Landry and Nahaz Rogers and Doug Andrews led the rebellion.

At the same time there was the Urban Training Center for Christian Mission. The Reverend C. T. Vivian had left SCLC and joined with Archie Hargraves and Dean Jim Morton to teach urban ministry as we transitioned out of the South. One characteristic of C. T.'s training course was "the plunge." A minister was learning urban ministry, urban action. Ministers would be given $5 and sent to the streets to feel what life was like—to find shelter, food, and work for three days on $5. It was called the plunge, trying to make them get some sensitivity away from prosperity gospel.

Also, Saul Alinsky was organizing The Woodlawn Organization (TWO) and the Back of the Yards neighborhood. Out of TWO came the Reverend Arthur Brazier, the Reverend Lynwood Stevenson, Squire Lance, and brother Leon Finney.

There's always been an independent streak of politics in Chicago, from Earl Dickerson, an African American attorney and community activist who successfully argued before the US Supreme Court against racially restrictive covenants in housing; to Ben Lewis, the first black elected alderman of the Twenty-Fourth Ward on the West Side, who was assassinated, perhaps by organized crime; to Gus Savage and Sammy Rayner, who were later elected to the legislature. My point is that there was a context in which Dr. King came into Chicago. He did not come to raise the dead; he came to inspire the living—and to give our struggle focus.

Dr. King, SCLC, and Chicago

There was a tension in the SCLC over choosing either Chicago or New York. But ultimately, because of the Coordinating Council of Community Organizations (CCCO), a strong body of community and activist organizations with credibility and resources, Dr. King chose Chicago.

With C. T. Vivian at the Urban Training Center and James Bevel joining the West Side Christian Parish to work on Chicago's West Side, there was a confluence of forces and timing in 1966. During that season, many of us were attracted to Bevel's charisma and free style.

And during that time Al Sampson, while here on assignment for Dr. King, was staying with me. Jackie was back home preparing to give birth to Jesse Jr.

After studying in the morning, I would do my street work in the Kenwood area in the afternoon. At that time there were rival organizations, Kenwood and Oakland, in the fight over building a new school in that area, led by a lady named Hannah Smith Anne Rose. I became the director of the joint organization, Kenwood-Oakland Community Organization, or KOCO. Our first office was at the corner of Forty-Third and Lake Park. And KOCO was not the only active new organization. In Englewood, there was the Reverend John Porter and Reverend Berry working closely with him. On the West Side, Chester Robinson was leading the West Side Organization (WSO), and Nancy Jefferson was director of the Midwest Community Council. So when Dr. King did come, he found the movement.

Biweekly meetings were held at Bill Berry's house in Hyde Park. People like Darryl Grisham and George Johnson and Cirilo McSween were a part of those meetings, as well as Dr. James Buckner, Dr. Andrew Thomas, Dr. Quentin Young. The Urban League had a big influence in CCCO. It was downtown connected—Bill Berry was the smartest non-politician in town.[7]

Black politicians and many black preachers went public against Dr. King. They held a press conference with Mayor Daley, and some ministers actually said, "Must Daley bear the cross alone?" How shameful. One day, the Baptist Ministers' Conference met at Reverend B. F. Paxton's church, True Light Baptist Church. The idea of Breadbasket—Dr. King's program—was to be presented, and the proposal was for me to direct it. The Reverend Clay Evans was the president of the conference, and Reverend Paxton was the host. Paxton said to Reverend Evans, "Don't bring any of those King ideas to the floor." Evans said, "Dr. King is a legitimate Baptist preacher. You may vote the ideas down, but at least you must hear Dr. King's proposition." Reverend Evans said, "You can reject it, but bring it to the floor." When he did that, Reverend Paxton went and got his pistol, and the church emptied. The meeting shifted to the Fellowship Missionary Baptist Church, where Reverend Evans was pastor.

Reverend Evans was a hot, charismatic preacher, but he was not connected to CCCO, that wing of our struggle. I was trying to figure out how to capture his attention by using Dr. King's charisma—because I knew Reverend Evans had that special body of qualities about him, if we could somehow get him connected theologically and emotionally. I had an idea of how to awaken the Reverend Evans's sense of Christian purpose. And so I took him, along with Gary Massoni, down to see a woman named Mrs. Eva Corley, who lived on Forty-Fourth Street. And there she sat in a slum-ridden house with an absentee slum landlord. She was sitting there with her feet swollen, like she had some kind of elephantiasis, and beating off rats with a stick. She could not feel her feet; she could only see them. Her son had Down syndrome, and her husband was lame, he was an invalid. And Reverend Evans looked upon her and had compassion and cried. Gary took pictures of that moment, and we rushed those pictures down to *Jet* magazine, to the editor, Bob Johnson. Bob Johnson then took those and made a story with it. "Urban Minister Reverend Clay Evans Stands with Dr. King," and it was all over America—"Reverend Evans with Dr. King." At that time, he was not a strong ally.

Then I told Dr. King that I'm going to meet with Reverend Evans on Thursday and I want you to call him on the phone in his office. And so I went to meet Reverend Evans; Lucille Lowman was his secretary. The telephone rang and Lucille said, "Reverend Evans, telephone."

And he said, "Lucille, I've told you when I'm in counseling don't interrupt me. I could be in prayer."

"Reverend Evans, telephone," she repeated. "It's Reverend Dr. Martin Luther King."

"Look," he said to me, "I think I'll pick it up."

"Well, come on Dr. and preach at my church next Sunday," Reverend Evans told King. And Dr. King had access to that pulpit. At the time, Reverend Evans was building a new church facility. After Dr. King preached at his church, Mayor Daley and the Cook County Democratic political machine shut down all access to capital. For seven years, Fellowship Missionary Baptist Church could not get money to complete the construction of its church on Forty-Fifth and Princeton. Eventually, we broke the hold of those banks; we got that church built. That happened through the ministers. We confronted the banks: First National Bank, Continental Bank, all of them.

Before Dr. King came, the ministers I had organized met at Fellowship on Fridays. Once Dr. King introduced Operation Breadbasket, the business people and others met at Chicago Theological Seminary on Saturday mornings. Our Saturday broadcasts came out of these meetings. The broadcasts became so successful that Leonard Chess, owner of WVON, dropped the show with Congressman William Dawson on Saturdays in favor of Breadbasket at ten o'clock, as it still is today. This shift in WVON programming represented a crack in the political and economic power structure in Chicago. Breadbasket's leveraging of businesses spread through Chicago to Memphis and, after Dr. King's assassination, on to Wall Street. In his last address in Memphis, Dr. King said, "Jesse Jackson says that we've come here to spread some pain, if we can't get some joy. And we want to get these garbage workers organized, but if not we're going to challenge corporate America."

Breadbasket never did stop. It gave Dr. King some short-term victories. Two black contractors built the first National Tea supermarket at Forty-Seventh and Calumet. We met Adlai Stevenson, the state treasurer, at Dr. Buckner's house. We said, "The state needs to put money in black banks." He said, "The state cannot do it because the banks are too small." We argued that if the black community can invest in the state treasury, then the state can reciprocate and put money in our banks. This led to changes in the rules and the growth of minority-owned banks. This came out of the Chicago movement.

Cirilo McSween became Dr. King's treasurer. One day I'll never forget. Dr. King came to Chicago. He had an appreciation of Breadbasket's ability to get jobs and contracts, but he always saw a bigger picture of public policy and the governmental scene. He came to borrow $35,000 from Cirilo to get money for SCLC's payroll. Black banks couldn't lend it; it was too much, and they were under scrutiny. SCLC didn't have any collateral. White banks wouldn't lend it because they were being hostile when Dr. King came in to borrow money. I said, "Doctor, would you stop by Al Boutte's house just briefly, to get a donation from him?"[8]

"I can't because I'm really busy, I need to get back to Atlanta," Dr. King said. "I need to borrow the money and fill out the papers."

I said, "Please stop by Dr. Boutte's house."

He said, "I can't."

So Chauncey Eskridge, his lawyer at the time, said, "Doc, please stop by just for a moment and let's see what Boutte will do."

Dr. King agreed, and when he walked into Boutte's house, there was Al, Cirilo McSween, John Johnson, Al Johnson, and the like, and they gave Dr. King $55,000. They were able to do that because we'd gotten their products on the shelves—got Johnson products facing in the store and got Joe Louis Milk and Parker House Sausage space in the stores. Breadbasket had gotten them construction contracts. It was a combination of that private development and that social dimension that made things happen. Dr. King wept because he had never seen black ministers and businessmen that responsive before. He developed a new appreciation for the impact our work could have on the private-sector economy.

We began to build coalitions. It wasn't just black and white. It was black and many shades of white. We built black-Latino coalitions. There were some Native Americans; there were some working-class white people, labor, there were progressive white people. It wasn't just black and white. There were people in each of those communities that could relate to us if we reached out to them—and we did. This evolved out of that sense of who we were. We were a multiracial, multicultural coalition—a coalition of conscience. Each phase built on a previous phase that came out of that.

In January 1966 Dr. King moved into an apartment on Hamlin Avenue on the West Side. And then came the open-housing marches during the summer. Whites on the Southwest and Northwest Sides of Chicago reacted violently to the peaceful marches. That we could have these mass marches with hundreds or even a thousand demonstrators was not simply spontaneous. Dr. King didn't just say come and people came. CCCO, TWO, KOCO, WSO, and other community organizations mobilized people by the thousands—and quickly. There was an infrastructure to challenge the power structure that did not exist anywhere else.

The open-housing marches rocked the power structure of the city. They upset Mayor Daley and Archbishop Cody and even caused some tension between SCLC and CCCO and the Urban League. I remember a big rally in Liberty Baptist Church on a Friday night after we'd been marching. And the place was packed. Dr. King announced that we would not march in Cicero on that Sunday. He'd had a meeting the day before with Archbishop Cody, Mayor Daley, and other notables. An agreement—the Summit Agreement—was reached, and in exchange, Dr. King said he would not march into Cicero. It would be too violent, too risky. And he agreed in that meeting not to march.

But there was so much anger about it—the Freedom Baby would not go back in the womb. And so Bob Lucas led the Cicero march on that Sunday, just marched anyhow because the Freedom Baby would not go back into the womb. But the King dynamic made even that march possible. These activities later led to the 1968 Fair Housing Act, the federal legislation that came out of Chicago. Eventually, we had four movements in town at the same time: the West Side "end the slums" movement, the open-housing movement, the schools crusade with CCCO, and Breadbasket.

In 1969 the Black Expo (Black-Minority Business and Cultural Exposition) was launched. The labor unions, led by Charlie Hayes and Addie Wyatt of the United Packinghouse Workers, as well as Jim Wright and Bill Lucy, formed the Coalition of Black Trade Unionists. These developments shifted the frame of reference for the movement and politics from Atlanta to Chicago. For the first three years the Black Expo was sponsored by SCLC, later by Operation PUSH. In 1972 PUSH Expo was a five-day event held at the International Amphitheater in Chicago, with participation from black businesses, scholars, entertainers, and politicians. Five hundred businesses exhibited their products, and about 900,000 people attended the event. We sought to give "exposure" to our businesses that could not afford advertising. Once we got the Expo moving, it began to spur urban development all across the country—in Cleveland,

Cincinnati, Atlanta, New York, and LA. How did St. Clair Blooker and Charles Billups get those National Tea jobs? Because those negotiations came from the idea that there needed to be corporate connections to the black community.

So much that was African American on the national stage came out of Chicago. The infrastructure was here, and it grew stronger with the movement. In Chicago you had the largest African American–owned media company, Johnson Publications, with *Jet* and *Ebony;* black manufacturers, a black meat company, and Parker House sausage. You had the most black advertising agencies, the most black car dealerships, and the most black-owned McDonald's. You had a combination of black businesses that Breadbasket and Operation PUSH supported and strengthened. You had George E. Johnson Sr. from Johnson Products, which created Afro-Sheen in the late 1960s, when Afros became popular; his was the first African American company to be listed on the American Stock Exchange. Johnson Products was the exclusive sponsor of *Soul Train* (the TV dance program that aired from 1971 to 2006). And *Soul Train* with Don Cornelius came out of Chicago. Soft Sheen came out of here, as did Luster Projects, led by Joy Luster.

So while Breadbasket in Atlanta consisted of ministers fighting for jobs and rights, here it became an economic development plan, with what we called the spokes of a wheel. Construction guys had never had a chance to build, the product guys didn't have a chance to put their products on the market; there was also the issue of putting more money in the black banks. Each area became a spoke, and together there was a whole wheel of economic development. This whole new range of black economic organizations came out of the Chicago movement.

This gave Dr. King some immediate victories to announce, such as Sealtest Milk, a company that had discriminated against blacks. That's why in his last speech in Memphis on April 3, 1968, Dr. King mentioned our work with Sealtest Milk. By that time, people in Memphis and Ohio were developing their own plans for selective buying campaigns and were targeting Sealtest Milk—and other milk companies—just as we had in Chicago. We also had victories with Jewel stores and the A&P supermarkets.

We really can say that Harlem was the cultural capital, but the movement capital became Chicago because Chicago became a permanent force for defining urban policy and an urban agenda for building coalitions.

Impact on Politics

This movement generated creative power to advance independent politics. It did not start the impulse for independent politics in Chicago, but the movement propelled it forward. Breadbasket set up a political education class, out of which emerged Leon Davis and people like Alice Tregay, Janice Bell, Frank Watkins, Anna Langford, Lou Jones, and Peggy Smith Martin. Bill Cousins, Dick Newhouse, Charlie Chew, and Fred Hubbard won elections as independents. Congressman Ralph Metcalfe ultimately rebelled against the Daley political machine, and Harold Washington rebelled and eventually became mayor in 1983.[9]

And during that season of struggle, 1968, Dr. King was killed. Robert Kennedy was killed. The Democratic Convention in Chicago followed, and Daley exploded against Grant Park demonstrators. Out of that convention, Julian Bond went to another level of his leadership and visibility by being nominated a Democratic vice presidential candidate, but he had to decline because he was too young.

There was the Con-Con convention (Sixth Illinois Constitutional Convention) in 1969, with voices like Al Raby and Cliff Kelly.

Then came 1972. We were discussing a black political challenge in Chicago for the presidency. Shirley Chisholm and Bella Abzug led a revolt in New York, and Chisholm ran for the presidential nomination of the Democratic Party—the first African American to run for president. We kept fighting for progressive politics, for inclusion; the Democratic Party had new rules for 1972 that we had worked for (known as the McGovern rules, because he had chaired the committee establishing them). These rules mandated that state delegations have a certain percentage of women and members of minority groups. But Mayor Daley would not accept the McGovern formula for inclusion, and his delegation did not meet the requirements. In Miami, at the Democratic National Convention, a progressive delegation from Chicago, cochaired by alderman William Singer and myself, unseated Mayor Daley and his people at about 9:00 p.m. that Friday. The next morning we had our first Saturday Operation PUSH meeting in our new (and current) national headquarters in Chicago, but at about 4:00 a.m. it was firebombed. It has been firebombed a total of three times. George McGovern rose as the Democratic nominee for president at that 1972 convention.

The seed that Dr. King planted grew into a tree of activism. And that tree has been watered by almost fifty years of Saturday morning meetings. There are branches of Breadbasket, then Operation PUSH, beyond Chicago; PUSH is in twenty-five cities. The Reverend Al Sharpton, twelve years old in 1972, joined the tree in New York City, and Reverend Bill Jones and Reverend H. H. Brookins in Los Angeles and Reverend Brown in Indianapolis also joined.

Fast-forward to 1983, the boycott of Chicago Fest. Chicago Fest was supposed to be Mayor Jane Byrne's coronation. We had gotten her elected as mayor by breaking the back of the machine, but she was a big disappointment. We began to break away from fear, being locked into the machine. So we thought, how are we going to do this boycott? Because of Black Expo in '69, '70, '71, we could say to Stevie Wonder and other musicians, "Don't cross our picket line," because we had a relationship. The success of that boycott was an extension of '66. It was the Saturday morning crowd—people like Nancy Jefferson from the Midwest Community Council on the West Side and Renault Robinson and Leon Finney—who were a part of that protest.

Congressman Harold Washington came around one day and said, "I'm not going to run for mayor. I like my job in Congress and I can't do it." But then he came back on a different day as the successful boycott was ending. We had turned it into a massive voter registration campaign. It was the same movement, now sixteen years old. We did *not* leave. Harold said, "I'll run if you all register 50,000 new voters and put $250,000 on the table: 50,000 new voters shows that you guys are serious, and $250,000 shows you've got some money to do polling and all of that." We registered 250,000 new voters and put half a million dollars on the table!

So then Barack ran in 2008. With the old rules, under "winner take all," Hillary would have been the winner because she won California, Texas, Ohio, Pennsylvania, Florida. Under the new rules for proportional distribution of delegates, Obama won. With proportional distribution, all candidates that achieve a threshold vote, a certain minimum percentage, receive the share of the representatives from that district corresponding to the proportion of votes they received. We had worked to change those rules in the Democratic Party in 1988, when I ran for president the second time. Even Obama's winning is connected to the '66 movement. There's a direct link between his running and my running and his winning and our new rules. The '66 movement never stopped. Obama's original funders were the same group that helped Dr. King and Harold Washington. Barack came to PUSH on many Saturday mornings early on, when he was running in the primary for US Senate and nobody took him seriously; Chicago became fertile ground for the first African American president. Some of the same people who worked on his campaigns worked on Harold Washington's campaign for mayor and for the city during the Washington administration, and worked on my campaigns. It's all connected.

When President Obama was elected, people started to say we are postracial. He got white votes, just as Carl Stokes got white votes. Really, we are not so much postracial as post-Selma—in that before Selma, blacks could not vote. White women couldn't serve on juries in many places. There was the fight for the ERA—the Equal Rights Amendment granting equal rights to women. Eighteen-year-olds couldn't vote, even though they could serve in Vietnam. People on college campuses couldn't vote in their college towns. You couldn't vote bilingually. You couldn't vote proportionately until 1988, meaning that a vote for a candidate from a minority party would not be a wasted vote. So what's called postracial—which is hype, really—is really post-Selma. Out of the Selma voting rights campaign came not only voting for blacks but also the vote for eighteen-year-olds, voting for students on campuses, bilingual voters, and proportionality. It was post-Selma, not postracial. And this group is bigger than that group. This group is now a rainbow coalition.[10]

The old group that used to be southern Democrats are now southern Republican conservatives. They shifted after the 1965 Voting Rights Act. It was this coalition that created the New South.

The civil rights movement even benefited the Super Bowl. What does the Super Bowl have to do with civil rights? You couldn't have the Carolina Panthers, Atlanta Falcons, New Orleans Saints, Jacksonville Jaguars, Miami Marlins, Houston Astros, San Antonio Spurs, and others playing behind the Cotton Curtain. You couldn't have had the Dallas Cowboys and the Houston Texans behind the Cotton Curtain, black and white together, sitting together behind the Cotton Curtain. So we pulled down those walls and made possible not only the New South, in terms of breaking down walls, but all that automotive industry and high-tech, tourism and government investment that has come to the South. More than that, Jimmy Carter, Bill Clinton, and George W. Bush couldn't have been nominated or won. No southerner could become national president because of the stigma of being racist. We freed them up, too!

Keep Swinging

What happened? What are some of the fruits? I hear people say, "We lost." Well, did we lose? We got the Fair Housing Act in 1968. That came out of Chicago. The Chicago experience in 1966 nurtured an independent political movement nationally. People like Richard Hatcher, the first black mayor of Gary, Indiana, elected in 1967; Carl Stokes, the first black mayor of Cleveland, Ohio, also elected in 1967; and Ken Gibson, elected mayor of Newark, New Jersey, in 1970, came here to gain strength about how to do a dynamic, urban movement. That energy came out of Chicago.

The Chicago Freedom Movement was unfolding only one year after Selma, I'll remind you. It shook up blacks inside the machine. Harold Washington, who was inside the machine, set up right across the street. Willie Port took us to meet him one day; Harold wanted to meet with me. I knew *of* him, but I didn't know him. We talked all day and Harold said, "I'm in this machine. I don't like this—this is an uncomfortable position." Harold began to describe how this thing worked and how he resented the machine, how it chewed up people and how it violated people. That's why one of Harold's first acts as mayor was to kill the patronage system. He was in it, but he resented it, and when he was elected, he helped break it up.

What came out of this movement? The Breadbasket negotiations with A&P supermarkets, Jewel Tea, automakers and dealers nationally, Budweiser, 7 Up, Coca Cola—these are urban negotiations. And as I said, other cities used the model.

Cirilo McSween came out of this movement and became Dr. King's treasurer and Harold Washington's treasurer. Al Johnson was also Harold's campaign treasurer for a time. You cannot separate Harold Washington's campaign from the movement. Al Johnson took a year off to work for Harold for $1 a year. Al was the first black person to be granted a General Motors dealership in 1967. Later he was granted a Cadillac dealership. He was in that meeting that gave Dr. King money. And Al contributed and raised a total of $50,000 for Obama's campaign for the Senate, organizing Obama's first large contribution. Other black urban executives helped Obama as well.

When the Reverend James Meeks was about ten years old, he was not into playing ball, so he would come up and watch the broadcast every Saturday. He was inspired by Reverend Willie Barrow and Reverend Ed Riddick and Reverend Calvin Morris and me. And so the ministry of Reverend Meeks comes out of the Chicago movement. And Reverend Clay Evans embraced enlightened theology.

We also sought to build a national movement in the 1984 and 1988 campaigns, a Rainbow Coalition. This was a multiracial, multicultural political movement built around shared values. At these conventions there were more people outside than inside: black people supporting civil rights, immigrants supporting immigration reform, Native Americans supporting sovereignty. That effort was one of the outgrowths of the Chicago movement. So too were the historic successes of Carol Moseley Braun, the first black female US senator in American history, and, of course, Barack Obama.

The movement's success in Chicago was substantial, and it's still unfolding. Out of the movement in Chicago came five black congressmen, three US senators, and a president. And I didn't leave and go back to a little town in the South. We stayed here. We're still here. My leadership came out of the Chicago movement.

In closing, this is a new Chicago today. And it's a new urban America. But there was always this thing, this God factor that I cannot forget. After Al Sampson and I talked to C. T. Vivian in Selma on the telephone from Chicago Theological Seminary, after he had been beaten on the Edmund Pettus Bridge on Bloody Sunday during the Selma campaign, a group of students from Chicago Theological Seminary went to Selma. Sheriff Jim

Clark had hit C. T. on the mouth the week before. C. T. and I were coming out of the side of the Brown's Chapel AME Church in Selma, and we saw the sheriffs coming up the street. We said we're going to make a right turn and go up to the public housing projects to avoid the police. I jumped out of the car and went into a woman's house—the door was wide open. And she said, "Who is there?" I said, "We're with Dr. King." She said, "Are you sure?" and I said, "Yes ma'am." She came down, and C. T. walked into the house. She said, "Are you really with Dr. King?" And we said, "Yes ma'am." And she said, "Can I trust you?" And we said, "Yes ma'am, we're with Dr. King." She said, "I wash rice at the local café. The owner, when he said that they don't know who killed that Reverend (James Reeb), he's lying. We know who killed that man. These guys drank beer in our place all the time and these guys on that occasion followed that man, and there was blood on their stick."

C. T. and I went back to Mrs. Amelia Boynton's house, where Dr. King was staying, and told him, and he called the FBI. At that time, attorney general Bobby Kennedy was trying to convince King not to march into Montgomery, but he did not agree. There was always that God factor. How did we know to go in that woman's house? Some of this can't be planned—except that you can't hit the ball unless you're swinging. That's why it's a movement, because you plan, and then there are plans beyond your plan. SCLC didn't come to Chicago to do open-housing marching; we came here to support CCCO's efforts. The marches were the God factor. We didn't come here to make Breadbasket the national phenomenon it became, but when you're moving and keep swinging, either the bat's going to hit the ball or the ball's going to hit the bat. We never could have won a battle if we didn't fight. And we never lost one.

We were victorious. This is a new Chicago and a new urban America. What's different today is how the ground has shifted. Today we have first-class jails and second-class schools. Today we are free but not fully equal. We did not fail to move—the fence moved back.

My point is that today as we march on, we must now fight to maintain our gains. We have shifted from a General Motors–based economy to a Walmart-based economy. We left the South to come up north to get jobs with retirement programs and benefits packages and union jobs. Now we're fighting for what's left of a service-based economy. We're trapped now with globalizing capital, but not globalizing human rights, workers' rights, women's rights, children's rights, and the environment.

Through all these changes, I urge you, don't let them break your spirit. You should say, "How proud I am, how beautiful I am, how much esteem I have," *and* understand you still have limited access to industry and power and politics. Our future is not looking in the mirror at how glad I am, how good I look, how good I feel. We need to look out the window. It's out there in the objective world, with the pain, where the real world is.

Dr. King saw the bigger picture. He was not fooled by Mayor Daley; this movement did not stop because of that summit meeting. The immediate gratification was economic development and jobs, but Dr. King's long-range idea was for the government to have a massive reconstruction plan.

No matter how great the odds are, don't let the weight of our problems crush your spirit. That's why love still conquers all. Love is stronger than racism, hatred, and fear. Love can conquer racism, anti-Semitism, homophobia. Love still conquers all. Saint Paul said it's not flesh and blood but powers and principalities. Let's not argue about people's sexuality and all that, but rather about the right to a house, health care, jobs, and education, about evening the playing field.

There's something about that thing called faith. The Bible says, "If my people, who are called by my name shall humble themselves and pray, and seek my face, and turn from their wicked ways," then God will forgive our sins.[11] And then God will heal our land and keep our hope alive. God bless you, and keep on marching.

Notes

This chapter is adapted from the closing address at "Fulfilling the Dream: The Chicago Freedom Movement Fortieth Anniversary Commemoration and Action Conference," Harold Washington Cultural Center, Chicago, July 23–26, 2006. Other material is from interviews with Reverend Jackson conducted by Mary Lou Finley and Pam Smith on July 26, 2011, and May 21, 2014.

1. Hyde Park is the home of the University of Chicago, and at that time it was Chicago's only integrated neighborhood.

2. The Civil Rights Act of 1968, also known as the Fair Housing Act of

1968, expanded on prior civil rights acts, especially the Civil Rights Acts of 1866 and 1964. The 1968 act was passed one week after the assassination of Dr. Martin Luther King. See also US Department of Justice, Civil Rights Division, www.usdoj.gov/crt/crt-home.html, and Leonard Rubinowitz's chapter 4 in this book.

3. Telegram from Mayor Richard J. Daley to Martin Luther King Jr., June 1966, City Council Proceedings and Correspondence, Illinois Regional Archive Depository, Chicago.

4. Jackson had been an intern in the office of Governor Terry Sanford of North Carolina.

5. John H. Johnson, founder of Johnson Publishing, publisher of *Ebony* and *Jet* magazines.

6. See chapter 13 for a discussion of this youth project addressing the high rate of lead poisoning in the city's housing, especially in poor neighborhoods.

7. Bill Berry was executive director of the Chicago Urban League. The others were prominent African American business leaders: Darryl Grisham, president of Parker House Sausage; George Johnson, founder of Johnson Hair Products and the first African American to have his company listed on the New York Stock Exchange; Cirilo McSween, a highly successful agent for New York Life Insurance and later the owner of eleven McDonald's franchises in Chicago; dentist Dr. James L. Buckner, a founder of African American–owned Seaway Bank; Dr. Andrew Thomas, a physician who served the poor from his office at the Robert Taylor Homes housing project; and Dr. Quentin Young, a founder of the Medical Committee for Human Rights. All were lifelong activists and civic leaders.

8. Al Boutte was one of the founders, with George Johnson, of Independence Bank, the largest black-owned bank; he served as its president.

9. Peggy Smith Martin was elected to the Illinois General Assembly in 1972 and 1977, the second African American woman to serve. Lovana "Lou" Jones served twenty years in the Illinois House of Representatives beginning in 1986. Attorney Anna Langford was elected as an alderman to the Chicago City Council. Alice Tregay and Janice Bell organized the political education division of Breadbasket/PUSH and, with Frank Watkins, served as key strategists and organizers for many political campaigns. Leon Davis was another key figure in organizing political campaigns; he also served on the Chicago Board of Education and as chairman of the Board of Governors for State Colleges and Universities of Illinois.

10. In 1970 Congress, while extending the Voting Rights Act, added a provision to lower the voting age to eighteen. After the Supreme Court ruled that this provision applied only to federal elections, Congress passed the Twenty-Sixth Amendment to the Constitution in 1971, lowering the voting age to eighteen; it was ratified by the required number of state legislatures in just two months.

11. Second Chronicles 7:14.

11

Perspectives on the Legacy of Jesse L. Jackson Sr.

Al Sharpton

In 1968, the year Martin Luther King Jr. was assassinated, I was thirteen. I was going to be fourteen that October. Dr. King was killed in April. There was a great amount of social activism in the country at that time. It was the end of the 1960s. The African American community was dominated where I grew up in Brooklyn, New York, by Black Power advocates and various Black Nationalist groups. Because I was in the church, I was in an organization called Operation Breadbasket, which was the economic arm of Dr. King's organization.

Now, you must understand in the climate of that time, to be in Breadbasket or to be in a church-based nonviolent movement was considered conservative. All my peers were bang-bang, shoot-'em-up revolutionaries or back-to-Africa Nationalists. So they considered what we were doing moderate, when what we were doing was just really getting things done. As you can see, forty years later I am still in the middle of that argument. But we were boycotting stores and we were making corporations adjust their exploitative ways much like Occupy (Wall Street) is talking about now, and we were registering voters.

What a lot of commentators miss and historians ought to get is that Reverend Jackson brought the King movement national. Had Jesse Jackson not succeeded with Breadbasket in Chicago, and eventually expanded it around the country, Dr. King's base would have been a regional southern base. Dr. King was a southern hero with a global reputation, but he had a southern organization. When he was killed and Dr. Abernathy took over, Dr. Abernathy could not in many ways deal with a national base

255

because that national base did not understand the southern rural minister prototype; we didn't relate to that autocratic "old preacher" style, because we were dealing in a contemporary urban context. I come from Brooklyn. I never sat in the back of the bus. I don't know anything about not drinking out of a water fountain. We dealt with a different level of racism. And the folks we were going to school with were Panthers, Nationalists, and white kids fighting against the war in Vietnam.

I grew up across the bridge from Greenwich Village, and we were dealing with smoking reefer and free love and Nationalists or Panthers. In the midst of this, the Abernathy mode didn't appeal to us—because again, I'm thirteen years old. Reverend Jackson, who at that time was about twenty-six or twenty-seven, would come to New York. He was much more urban—even though he was born in the South—much more identified with what was going on. I never saw Reverend Jackson wear a necktie until 1972—literally. He might have had some, but he didn't wear them. He would wear a dashiki and a Martin Luther King medallion. He would wear a buckskin vest, but he would preach the King tradition and economic rearrangements; he had a theory called the "King-dom" theory, about how we would rearrange the economic order. This was forty-five years before you ever heard of Occupy Wall Street.

I became youth director of New York's Breadbasket under his national leadership in 1969. Out of that came a generation of younger activists on his model, like Andy Young and Hosea Williams and others were on the King model. One way you judge the strength of a tree is by the fruit that it bears. Strong trees bear strong fruit. If you've got a tree with no fruit on it, it is a barren tree. It may be an attractive tree, but it's barren. It may look good, but you can't get any fruit off of it so it can't feed anybody. Out of Dr. King came Ambassador and Mayor Andrew Young. Out of Dr. King came Hosea Williams, who did great civil rights organizing in the South. Out of Dr. King came people like Bernard LaFayette and James Bevel and Jesse Jackson. And out of Jesse Jackson came me in civil rights, (attorney) Lezli Baskerville, who is the queen of black colleges when she is on her throne, and so many others. So out of his ministry—many of us were twelve or thirteen years younger than him, as he was to Dr. King— he developed a generation of activists who had to negotiate between the extremes and the moderates.

The reason I can tell this is because I lived it.

I remember in 1970 Kenneth Gibson was running for mayor of Newark, New Jersey, and Reverend Jackson came to New York and told us to go over and help Ken Gibson run. There was a very famous activist poet by the name of Amiri Baraka (formerly Leroi Jones), and Reverend Jackson sent us over to Broad Street to Baraka's Nationalist headquarters, named Spirit House. We'd go to Spirit House to get our orders about what to do to get the vote out for Ken Gibson. So I grew up in church and Operation Breadbasket, and I went and knocked on doors with my folks. All of us were maybe fourteen years old then: that's how Jackson fashioned a generation.

Now, it comes to 1972, another place people like to omit from history. We try and go from 1968 to 2008, like we just leapfrog from Dr. King to Barack Obama becoming the president of the United States.

Like I said, I grew up in Brooklyn, in the 'hood; we didn't have a whole lot of outlets in the house, so we had to get what they called an extension cord. The way we would watch the little TV in the back is we would have an extension cord go down the hall; if you don't have a good extension cord, you will not have electricity. And the reason a lot of people have lost their power now is they are not connected to 1968 and the work after. They're trying to go from 1968 to 2008, like we were just asleep for forty years and woke up and everything was good. That is not what happened.

It is not only untrue but it is unfair, and if you do not understand all of what came in between, you will lose where you are because you don't know how you got there.

One of the critical points to look at is 1972. There was a meeting in Gary, Indiana, called the National Black Political Convention. The conveners of the convention included Congressman Charles Diggs, one of the founders of the Congressional Black Caucus; Amiri Baraka; and Mayor Richard Hatcher, who had just been elected mayor of Gary, Indiana, largely by the mobilization of Reverend Jackson, who was right up the road in Chicago. Dr. King's work was critical in Cleveland; he helped get Richard Hatcher elected mayor there in 1967. The battle in Gary was between the Nationalists and the moderates, who wanted to argue about how we deal with voting.

That year, Shirley Chisholm ran for president. I was youth director of her campaign; this was the first year I was going to be able to vote. I couldn't vote in the primary; I couldn't vote until that November. I'll never forget when Reverend Jackson got up to speak; the Nationalists didn't want him to speak, and the moderates didn't want them to speak. He was able to pull that convention together, mobilize it into a political force, and it was so acute that Daley, who had been invincible, was prevented from seating his delegates at the Democratic Convention in Miami because Reverend Jackson formed a coalition with a progressive Chicago alderman named William Singer. It was the first time we believed that we could penetrate power, because to unseat Richard Daley in 1972 was unthinkable.

All of these were steps toward empowerment.

So just like you can't go from 1968 to 2008, you can't start at 1984 with Reverend Jackson. You have to deal with how he changed the economic arrangements with Operation Breadbasket and Operation PUSH and then how he dealt with the political arrangement by chipping away at these mayors and congressional offices and taking the myth off these people like Daley—all of this led to our moving forward. It culminated with the 1984 and 1988 races, but the groundwork had already been done; the Bible says, "So as a man thinketh, is he." Our minds have to get it right. Most of black America and most of white America were still on the balcony in Memphis where Dr. King was killed, until Jackson moved us forward economically and politically. Now, there were other players—and there were other players when Dr. King was out there. But Reverend Jackson set the tone going into the eighties, just like Dr. King set the tone in the sixties.

Part of the work of the after-King generation that Jackson led was to maintain the victories won in the 1960s. So when people talk about this being the Joshua generation, no, the Joshua generation was coming right out of Moses, and there was a thirty-year battle to keep the right wing from revoking or reversing the Civil Rights Act, the Voting Rights Act, the Fair Housing Act, the things that the King-led sixties did. There was a rear move all the way from Nixon to Reagan to revoke the Voting Rights Act, which expired every five years. That did not happen because there was a sustained national movement that stopped that. It wasn't that

Reagan woke up one morning and said, "You know, I'm wrong, let's not revoke the Civil Rights Act and Voting Rights Act." They were backed down. That was just as hard and, in many ways, more complex because you're dealing more institutionally now, more so than the achieving of it in the first place. You needed more than drama—you needed the ability to have drama and you had to have strategy; you had to play the Beltway and the march route to keep the Civil Rights Act and the Voting Rights Act.

Later, in the 1990s and the beginning of the twenty-first century, when we're dealing with things like racial profiling and police brutality—all of that was protected under the Civil Rights Act—we couldn't even have fought them if the Civil Rights Act had been undone in the 1980s and 1990s; we take all that for granted now. So with the results of that movement came people that your generation looks up to.

In the political arena, 1984, Reverend Jackson convened people from all over the country and said, "Let's run somebody for president." But colleagues of his in the movement were in elective office and couldn't run. I'm talking about Andrew Young, who had been mayor of Atlanta, had run for governor of Georgia, and had been ambassador at the United Nations under Jimmy Carter; Coleman Young, who was the mayor of Detroit. They wouldn't run. All the elected leaders wouldn't run. There was this great fervor for running somebody. No one had really run since Shirley Chisholm, and her campaign was not based in our community.

In that process, Reverend Jackson said they were once again trying to undermine the Voting Rights Act, and we needed to put numbers (of voters) on the books, so he started a southern voter registration crusade. He got on a bus and went through the South, all through the South, including Mississippi and other places. He got William Bradford Reynolds, head of the Justice Department's Civil Rights Division under Ronald Reagan (even though it was an oxymoron to have a Civil Rights Division under Ronald Reagan, we did), to come down to Mississippi. And the next thing I know, Reynolds is standing up in the middle of Mississippi, holding hands and singing "We Shall Overcome." Imagine how that played back at the White House under Reagan! That's why you have never heard of Reynolds; I think that was the last thing he did.

During that voter registration drive, people started saying, Why are we waiting on one of the elected officials? Why don't you run Reverend Jackson? That is where the slogan "Run Jesse Run" started. He did not enter it with the idea of running. It emanated from the people.

Also, out of his run in 1984 he made issues public that had not been public before. One was apartheid in South Africa. Nelson Mandela was considered by much of the American public to be a terrorist. Ronald Reagan and his administration considered him a terrorist. For Jesse Jackson to come into the mainstream presidential debates talking about representing and recognizing the African National Congress, which was at that time considered terrorist, was unthinkable. The mainstreaming of the antiapartheid movement in this country came from Reverend Jackson. Now, there were others involved in the antiapartheid movement, but they could not mainstream it because they were not in the mainstream. The mainstreaming of that issue came from Reverend Jackson, because then it became an issue of "majority rules," and it became something that the other candidates who were going to be the nominees in the two central parties in this country had to respond to. They never had to respond to that before.

The other part of this that is significant, that you cannot underestimate, is that Reverend Jackson broke the barriers in the progressive side of the body politic with the concept of a "rainbow coalition." He said the only way we can win for the average American is we cannot have a black movement or a brown movement or a white progressive movement or a Latino movement or an Asian movement. We must have a rainbow where everybody can keep their identity but flow together. I'm not asking for you not to be black, I'm not asking for you not to be Latino, I'm not asking you not to be who you are—gay or lesbian—we all should be part of one rainbow. Now that sounds easy in 2011. In 1984 and 1988 it was different: it was heresy to black preachers that we're going to have a coalition with gays and lesbians, because they were preaching that was a sin. It was heresy. It was unthinkable to white progressives that blacks would sit at the table and actually decide what the leftist strategies were going to be, because we had as many people biased on the Left as we did on the Right and because the Left wanted to call all the shots.

The idea of a rainbow was new in 1984; by 1988, it got more votes than any runner-up in the history of this country in a primary setting. It caught fire, and it is what maintained a progressive movement going forward. The roots of starting an American progressive movement revival started with the Rainbow Coalition in 1988. And it has grown to whatever, but it started there because we were never all in the room together until then.[1]

So in many ways, I would say that from the economic fights we're dealing with today—that Jesse started in the 1970s—developed political empowerment that has resulted in the first black attorney general and first black president. And he established the whole concept of coalition building. He defined the last part of the twentieth and the first part of the twenty-first century, and he brought about a new wave of leadership, which is now seeing a new generation of leaders come behind them.

Let me leave you with this. If you want to understand the relevance and the historical significance and the immovable legacy of Jesse Louis Jackson, look at where we are today and know that it was rooted in his continuing Dr. King's work and innovating on his own. Because let's remember: Dr. King did not bring Jesse Jackson into the movement; he brought him into SCLC. Jesse had already led movements in Greensboro as a student, and he had integrated the library in his hometown. Jesse was already an activist. He just joined and combined with Dr. King, but he was already in motion.

Look at a rainbow. When does a rainbow come? A rainbow comes after the storm, before the sunshine. We could not get to the sunshine of Obama without the rainbow of Jackson after the storm of the King era: the jailings, the house bombings, the shootings. The storm was over. Jackson led us out of the storm, and look out: there's a rainbow! If we do this together, we can stay out of the storm. Out of the rainbow belief we saw sunshine. We went from the outhouse to the White House in 2008, but we had to see the rainbow first, because the rainbow showed us that the storm was over and sunshine was possible. If you pass the rainbow and go straight to the sunshine, you're going to get scorched. If you go through the rainbow, you'll get a suntan and be ready for a new season.

Thank you and God bless you.

Notes

This chapter is adapted from the transcript of a speech given by Al Sharpton in November 2011 at Georgetown University on the occasion of "A Celebration of Life Legacy," honoring the Reverend Jesse Jackson and broadcast on C-SPAN. Reprinted with permission of the author.

1. When Jesse Jackson ran for president in 1984, he surprised many when he took third place in a field of seven candidates, behind senator Gary Hart and former vice president Walter Mondale. Jackson garnered 3,282,431 primary votes, or 18.2 percent of the total, and he won primaries or caucuses in Louisiana, the District of Columbia, South Carolina, and one of two separate contests in Mississippi. More Virginia caucus-goers supported Jackson than any other candidate, but Mondale won more Virginia delegates. Jackson's platform included the following: reversing Reaganomics and Reagan tax cuts for the wealthy, rebuilding the nation's infrastructure, cutting the defense budget and redirecting those funds, reducing mandatory minimum sentences for drug-related crimes, ratifying the Equal Rights Amendment, establishing a single-payer health care system, supporting family farmers, providing reparations for descendants of black slaves, and increasing support for public education and community colleges. For more information, see Frank Clemente and Frank Watkins, eds., *Keep Hope Alive: Jesse Jackson's 1988 Presidential Campaign* (Boston: South End Press, 1989), and Jesse L. Jackson, *Straight from the Heart,* ed. Robert D. Hatch and Frank E. Watkins (Philadelphia: Fortress Press, 1987).

12

The Rise of Independent
Black Political Power in Chicago

Don Rose

Chicago has a long history of electing a few black politicians to public office. But in the 1960s the city was still in the thrall of Mayor Richard J. Daley's political machine, which routinely traded favors for votes. Loyalty to the machine was paramount. Precinct captains rounded up the votes for machine candidates, offering patronage jobs, Christmas turkeys, and other favors in exchange (and sometimes threatening serious penalties for noncooperation). In this context, the six black aldermen serving on the Chicago City Council in the mid-1960s were known as the "Silent Six," due to their unwillingness to challenge Mayor Daley, even during the heat of the civil rights movement in Chicago. Congressman William Dawson, an African American who served in Congress from 1943 until his death in 1970, was a key figure in the Chicago machine, and when he died, Daley passed Dawson's congressional seat on to Ralph Metcalfe.[1]

The movement for independent black political power was a movement to elect politicians—generally Democrats—who would be willing to challenge the mayor and the rest of the Democratic Party machine in the city, and it grew enormously beginning in the 1960s. So, although the independent black political movement began before Dr. King came to Chicago, it was certainly stimulated by him and the Chicago Freedom Movement, as well as by the other civil rights activities that came before.

Chicago's independent black political movement really began in 1963, in the heat of the civil rights battle over schools, when a group of eight independent black candidates ran for City Council. A number of them were movement people, including Timuel Black, who ran in the Fourth Ward, and Charlie Chew, the only black candidate who won, replacing a white alderman. In 1966, while Dr. King was in Chicago, two independents, Richard Newhouse and Charlie Chew, ran for the state senate. Dr. King had meetings with both of them. Both won and served in the Illinois senate for decades—Chew until he died in 1986, and Newhouse until he retired in 1991. Dr. King was certainly conscious of these political campaigns, but he was trying to be "nonpartisan" or nonpolitical, because I think he felt being political would circumscribe him.

Also while Dr. King was in Chicago, Fred Hubbard ran for Congress in the First Congressional District, the seat Harold Washington eventually won. During the campaign, Hubbard was shot, and Dr. King paid a very public visit to him in the hospital, which was his way of endorsing him without actually endorsing him.

I would say that from the late 1960s onward, the movement itself— such as it was—became more politically focused. In 1967, during the waning days of the movement, two more black aldermen were elected— Sammy Rayner (Sixth Ward) and attorney Bill Cousins (Eighth Ward), both of them active in the movement. Cousins later became a judge—an accomplishment that was certainly abetted by the movement. Cousins was a delegate to the Coordinating Council of Community Organizations (CCCO) from the Chatham-Avalon Community Council. Rayner was a funeral director and offered his place of business, A. A. Rayner and Sons, to the civil rights campaigns.

In 1969 Al Raby, a key civil rights leader and former convener of CCCO, was elected to the Illinois State Constitutional Convention, the only black independent delegate. Former Black Panther Bobby Rush began to run for office after the murder of Black Panther leaders Fred Hampton and Mark Clark in December 1969.[2] Rush ran for the state legislature twice and for alderman twice. He won his alderman race in 1983, the year Harold Washington was elected mayor. In 1992 Rush was elected to the US House of Representatives, where he still serves.

In 1971 attorney Anna Langford, a longtime civil rights activist, was elected to the City Council. For the first time, the City Council included two women. The other, Mary Lou Hedlund from the north lakefront, always gets credit for being the first woman elected, because Langford wasn't officially elected until a few weeks later in a runoff. Langford served one term in the 1970s but later returned to serve two additional terms beginning in 1983, the year she retired from practicing law; she retired from the City Council in 1991. Hedlund was a "machine alderman," as many pointed out, proving that a woman could be just as big a machine hack as any man. But Langford clearly came out of the independent black political movement.

The next big victory, also in 1971, came when we filed the first Voting Rights Act lawsuit based on the racial gerrymandering of the boundaries for the City Council wards. It didn't go too far because the judge didn't quite get it. He gave us one ward for a new election but failed to fully understand the pattern of discrimination. Two attorneys and I put this case together, and Bill Cousins, as a City Council member, was the plaintiff in *Cousins v. City Council*. Subsequent remaps kept this issue alive.

More independent state legislators were elected in the latter 1970s, but then the system changed. The multimember system, with two seats in each legislative district, was changed in the 1990s to a single-member system, with only one seat in each district. Under the old system, with two seats per district, it was easier to elect an independent. We were able to get some black independents into the Illinois house of representatives; Carol Moseley Braun was one of the first, in 1978. Single-member districts were promoted as a "reform" by Pat Quinn (the recent governor), who was a big supporter of referendums. One of the few things we can do by referendum in Illinois is change the structure of government, which is what Quinn wanted to do. Governor Quinn was somewhat of a movement person himself, but on this issue, he was on his own. Cutting back on the size of the legislature was supposed to be an economizing measure, but it had some deleterious effects; it was not racially motivated, but the change to single-member districts made it more difficult to elect independents.

During the 1970s, an increasing number of independent black officials were elected, some of them replacing white aldermen. As Daley's operation saw this happening, they started putting up their own blacks for election—another effect of the movement. In 1971 Daley nominated—which was tantamount to electing—the first African American as city treasurer: Joe Bertrand. There are only three citywide offices—mayor, treasurer, and clerk—and Bertrand was the first African American to hold a citywide office. Traditionally, the city treasurer had been Jewish. Putting Joe Bertrand in that position represented a recognition of the growing influence of the African American community in Chicago politics.

Congressman Ralph Metcalfe running as an independent was another milestone. After redistricting in 1971, Metcalfe's congressional district included Hyde Park for the first time—a neighborhood with an independent base. He began to act more like an independent—something he had long wanted to do—prodded by his son, Ralph Jr., who was a very strong movement man. In particular, Metcalfe took on what William Grimshaw describes as "the one issue that united the black community across the class spectrum: police brutality."[3] In 1976 Daley dumped Metcalfe, and the Democratic Party nominated someone else for his seat. Metcalfe ran as an independent in the Democratic primary against Irwin France, a Daley functionary (a black one) who had held a number of different positions. Metcalfe won overwhelmingly in one of the biggest African American victories—getting 72 percent of the vote in the primary. This was a huge step forward, defeating the machine and winning such wide support.

In 1972 Edward Hanrahan, the state's attorney who had ordered the raid that resulted in the murder of Hampton and Clark, was up for reelection. We ran an independent liberal Democrat against him in the Democratic primary and lost. We then switched to a liberal Republican, Bernard Carey, and the black vote was overwhelmingly against Hanrahan and for the Republican—a real sign that the black community was breaking away from the Democratic machine. Carey was white, but his politics was liberal. I ran both these campaigns. It was one thing to vote for an independent Democrat, but to achieve a huge vote—and victory—for a Republican was another significant breakthrough.

Then came 1979. Jane Byrne (who had not yet been discredited) ran for mayor and won with an overwhelming black vote.

Danny Davis, an independent, began his political career in 1979 as alderman of the Twenty-Ninth Ward, and he served as commissioner of the Cook County Board from 1990 to 1996. He won his congressional seat in 1997 and has been representing the West Side in Congress since then.

In 1980 we elected two independent African American congress-men—Gus Savage and Harold Washington—both of whom were running against "machine blacks." Savage, a journalist, had been a supporter of CCCO and part of the open-housing campaign, as well as a long-time supporter of the movement for independent black politicians. He was around from the earliest days, before people even knew there was a movement!

The biggest victory came when Harold Washington was elected mayor in 1983. He had run for mayor in 1977 in a special election to replace Richard J. Daley, who had died in office. At that time, Washington didn't get a huge black vote, but he did carry some of the black wards. This was typical of what was happening in cities throughout the country. There was usually a trial run, with the black mayoral candidate losing, but the next time out, a black would win, as occurred in Newark and Detroit. It was a conscious strategy to run even though the chances of winning were not good, but knowing that it was building for the future.

In 1983 there were three candidates in the Democratic primary: incumbent mayor Jane Byrne; Richard M. Daley, son of former mayor Richard J. Daley; and Harold Washington. Many people were aware that with two whites and one black running, splitting the vote was a possibility. It was a very narrow split. In the Democratic primary, Washington got 36 percent of the vote to Byrne's 34 percent, and Daley's 30 percent.[4] It was a close contest in the general election as well, with Bernard Epton coming closer to winning the Chicago mayoral race than any Republican in decades. (The last Republican mayor of Chicago was defeated by Democrat Anton Cermak in 1931.[5])

The real increase in black voter registration came just prior to the Washington campaign. In the fall of 1982 more than 200 community organizations and more than 100 ministers joined together to register voters in churches, in welfare offices, and at events such as the "Voter Fever Family Registration Day" in Washington Park, which featured rock music, gospel singers, and on-site voter registration. Between 1979 and the election in 1982, there was a "net gain of over 127,000 black voters, with 87% of eligible blacks registered (compared to 78% of whites). In the fall 1982 election, turnout jumped to 56%, from 34% three years earlier."[6] One of the things that became very clear was that the African

American community would vote independently, but the candidate had to have some credibility, some real chance of victory.

Washington's first two years as mayor were difficult. This was the era of the "Council Wars." He had an opposition block—the Vrdolyak 29 against the Washington 21—which made it virtually impossible for him to accomplish anything. Around the third year of his first term, a case filed earlier in federal court on the racial gerrymandering issue, alleging that ward boundaries had been established in a manner that discriminated against black and Latino voters, came to a head. A US appellate court judge ruled that an earlier effort to redraw the boundaries did not go far enough, and new elections had to be held in several wards. In 1986 Washington's supporters (black and Latino) won four of seven seats, enough to give him control of the City Council and end the Council Wars.[7]

In 1983 Charlie Hayes, a union leader with the United Food and Commercial Workers, was elected to Congress, filling the vacancy created when Washington was elected mayor. During the years of the Chicago Freedom Movement, he had been a leader of the United Packinghouse Workers, a union with very strong ties to the civil rights movement; in fact, he had served on the Agenda Committee during the open-housing marches.[8]

Dorothy (Wright) Tillman, a member of the Southern Christian Leadership Conference staff during the era of the Chicago Freedom Movement, was elected alderman from the South Side's Third Ward during the Washington era. She served from 1985 until 2007, when she lost to Pat Dowell. Tillman was known for her vociferous defense of the black community and for her arguments in favor of reparations.

After the Chicago Freedom Movement, Al Raby of the CCCO shifted his energy toward building an independent black political movement. He was well connected to the unions and served for a while as an organizer for the National Education Association. He became involved with Project Vote, a national group conducting massive voter registration campaigns, and at one point served as its chairman. When Harold Washington was elected mayor in 1983, Raby served as his campaign manager. During the Washington administration, he was appointed head of the Chicago Commission on Human Relations—the city department responsible for enforcing antidiscrimination laws. After he left the Washington administration, Raby worked for the Haymarket Group, a political consulting group, alongside others who had been involved in Washington's campaign. Raby remained active in politics until the day he died.[9]

In 1992 Carol Moseley Braun became the first African American woman elected to the US Senate. Illinois voters chose another African American to represent them in the US Senate when they elected Barack Obama in 2004.

The growth of black political power in Chicago also had an important impact on the nation. Back in 1967, after the end of the major civil rights campaigns in Chicago, the National Conference for New Politics met at the Palmer House over Labor Day weekend, with about 3,000 in attendance. Planners hoped to coalesce the civil rights movement, the peace movement, and the student movement and run Martin Luther King for president, with Dr. Benjamin Spock, the well-known pediatrician and antiwar activist, for vice president. However, this effort fell apart over the Black Caucus, which demanded half the vote at the conference, even though it represented only 20 to 25 percent of the group. Some were convinced that this demand had been instigated by agent provocateurs, possibly from the FBI. This was the era of the FBI's COINTELPRO, which was actively trying to disrupt civil rights and peace groups, so this would not have been surprising.[10] This kind of disruption had also occurred in Chicago. Some people thought Martin Luther King should run in the Democratic primary rather than as an independent, but he really didn't want to run for office at all. Of course, he was killed in April 1968, just seven months later. By that time, plans for protests at the 1968 Democratic Convention in Chicago were already under way.

The movement for black political power kept growing, both in Chicago and elsewhere in America. Carl Stokes was elected mayor of Cleveland in 1967, and Richard Hatcher was elected mayor of Gary, Indiana, that same year. SCLC staffers took breaks from their civil rights organizing to work in these campaigns. Chicago lagged behind in this regard, as a black mayor was not elected there until 1983. There were a lot of national parallels, and things changed. People began to realize—I don't know how aware they were, but realization was seeping into Chicago and into the national consciousness—that gaining civil rights victories depended on winning political office. In 1964 the Mississippi Freedom

Democratic Party—an integrated group—had tried, unsuccessfully, to unseat the all-white Mississippi delegation to the Democratic National Convention in Atlantic City. After the 1968 Democratic National Convention in Chicago, changes in Democratic Party rules were developed by a committee headed by Senator George McGovern. The McGovern rules specified that convention delegations had to include a requisite number of women and minorities. By 1972 the new rules were in place, and at the Democratic Convention in Miami, there were many African American delegates, including many civil rights activists, as well as more women and other minorities. It was at this convention that Jesse Jackson and Bill Singer, a progressive white alderman from Chicago, assembled a delegation that met the requirements of the McGovern rules, challenged Mayor Daley's delegation at the convention, and actually unseated Daley's delegates and replaced them.

Shirley Chisholm was the first African American to run for president in the modern era. She ran in 1972 but didn't complete the campaign, dropping out after several primaries. After Chisholm's run, it was not startling to see an African American run for president. Two African Americans—Carol Moseley Braun and Al Sharpton—were candidates for president in 2004.

And, of course, Jesse Jackson ran for president in 1984 and 1988. By the time Jackson ran in 1984, he was already a well-known figure. In 1966, while Dr. King was still in Chicago, he had chosen Jackson to lead the Chicago chapter of Operation Breadbasket, the SCLC's economic justice project. In 1971 Jackson formed his own organization, Operation PUSH (now the Rainbow PUSH Coalition). By the time of the 1984 presidential campaign, Jackson had been running voter registration drives for some time, and he had a following. (For more information on Jesse Jackson and the Rainbow PUSH Coalition, see chapter 11.)

In both 1984 and 1988, the fact that Jesse Jackson persevered through the entire campaign added to his credibility and to the credibility of the process. In 1988, with his Rainbow Coalition, Jackson captured 6.9 million votes and won eleven contests—seven primaries (Alabama, the District of Columbia, Georgia, Louisiana, Mississippi, Puerto Rico, and Virginia) and four caucuses (Delaware, Michigan, South Carolina, and Vermont). He also scored March victories in Alaska's caucuses and

Texas's local conventions, despite losing the Texas primary. Briefly, after he won 55 percent of the vote in the Michigan Democratic caucuses, he was considered the front-runner for the nomination, having surpassed all the other candidates in total number of pledged delegates.[11]

When Barack Obama won the Iowa primary in 2008, proving that a black man could win Iowa, that was an inspiration everywhere. He "made his bones" in Iowa. When I think about all this, I see it as a continuum. What would have been possible for Obama without the movement? The state senate seat he won in 1996 was the seat that Richard Newhouse, an African American, first won in 1966. Newhouse was replaced by Alice Palmer, another movement person; her husband, Edward "Buzz" Palmer, was a founder and executive director of the African American Police League, an organization of black policemen committed to protecting members of the black community and further integrating the police force. These tendencies—civil rights issues and black politics— came together concurrently, and some people were involved in both, like myself and Gus Savage and Bennett Johnson and many others.

It is difficult to quantify the impact of the Chicago Freedom Movement. How do you quantify the impact of events in Birmingham? Dr. King expanded the movement and the consciousness, even though civil rights activity began to decline after 1967 and political activity took its place. There is no question that King's presence multiplied the interest within black communities. Some people worked purely in politics, and some worked mostly in other areas, such as efforts to get rid of Chicago school superintendent Ben Willis. The people who were active and interested in the movement, whether they participated in political work or not, were certainly involved in the black community and voted independently. Mayor Daley was seen as an enemy of both.

Political scientist William Grimshaw describes the long-term impact of the black community's alienation from Mayor Daley and the Daley machine in this way: "Beginning with Daley's first election in 1955, the poor black wards emerged as the machine's electoral stronghold. . . . [But] its seemingly solid black support actually rested on a shaky foundation. When the civil rights movement swept into the city in the 1960s the foundation collapsed. Voters in the poor black wards grew disillusioned with the machine and withdrew from politics. The middle class black wards broke into open revolt with nearly all of them electing anti-machine aldermen during the latter half of Daley's mayorality."[12]

As we have seen here, it was not just antimachine aldermen who won elections but also state legislators, congressmen, and eventually senators, laying the groundwork for the success of Barack Obama.

Notes

1. The City Council elects aldermen from each of Chicago's fifty wards. The ward committeemen, chosen by the Democratic Party, are highly influential in determining what happens in the wards, including who runs for public office. In the 1960s they oversaw the precinct captains responsible for turning out the vote for the Democratic machine. For more information on the operation of the Chicago machine, see William Grimshaw, *Bitter Fruit: Black Politics and the Chicago Machine, 1931–1991* (Chicago: University of Chicago Press, 1992).

2. Black Panther leaders Fred Hampton and Mark Clark were murdered in a nighttime police raid ordered by Cook County state's attorney Edward Hanrahan. The police claimed there had been a shoot-out, but a federal grand jury determined that the police fired between eighty-two and ninety-nine shots, while only one bullet came from inside the apartment. That single round was later determined to be caused by a reflexive death convulsion after the raiding team shot Clark. Hampton was murdered while still in bed. This attack sent shock waves through black Chicago. Hampton was twenty-one years old, deputy chairman of the Illinois Black Panthers, and an eloquent speaker. Eighteen-year-old Mark Clark was the organizer of the Peoria, Illinois, Black Panther Party. See Jeffrey Haas, *The Assassination of Fred Hampton: How the FBI and the Chicago Police Murdered a Black Panther* (Chicago: Lawrence Hill Books, 2010), 89–93.

3. Grimshaw, *Bitter Fruit*, 137.

4. Gary Rivlin, *Fire on the Prairie: Harold Washington, Chicago Politics, and the Roots of the Obama Presidency*, rev. ed. (Philadelphia: Temple University Press, 2013), 102.

5. For information on the election of Anton Cermak in 1931, see Rivlin, *Fire on the Prairie*, 28.

6. Paul Kleppner, *Chicago Divided: The Making of a Black Mayor* (De Kalb: Northern Illinois University Press, 1985), 146–49.

7. For more information on the "Council Wars" and the court case that ended them, see Rivlin, *Fire on the Prairie*, 162–71, 223–26.

8. The United Packinghouse Workers later combined with other unions to form the United Food and Commercial Workers. For more information on the civil rights activities of the United Packinghouse Workers, see Cyril Robinson,

Marching with Dr. King: Ralph Helstein and the United Packinghouse Workers (New York: Praeger, 2011).

9. Al Raby died of a heart attack on November 23, 1988, at the age of fifty-five.

10. COINTELPRO was a counterintelligence program operated by the FBI in the 1950s and 1960s; in the 1960s this campaign aimed to discredit the civil rights movement and other social movements by various forms of subterfuge, such as offering nonexistent housing and transportation to volunteers, funding media campaigns to make black activists look angry and disturbed, sowing dissension between different civil rights groups, and frightening the family members of activists. For more information on COINTELPRO and the civil rights movement, see Taylor Branch, *At Canaan's Edge: America in the King Years, 1965–68* (New York: Simon & Schuster, 2006), 708–9, 735. COINTELPRO was made public when antiwar activists broke into the FBI office in Media, Pennsylvania, in 1971 and released documents to the press describing these operations. See Betty Medsger, *The Burglary: The Discovery of J. Edgar Hoover's Secret FBI* (New York: Vintage, 2014), 329–41.

11. Frank Clemente and Frank Watkins, eds., *Keep Hope Alive: Jesse Jackson's 1988 Presidential Campaign* (Boston: South End Press, 1999).

12. Grimshaw, *Bitter Fruit*, 20.

13

Roots of the Environmental Justice Movement

A Community Mobilizes to End Childhood Lead Poisoning

Sherrilynn J. Bevel

> I've always been amazed at these white men who would come around and give your boy a toy for Christmas, while his son is learning how to make tools. . . . When does he set the school up to make sure that the school teaches every boy science? When does he set the school up so that all boys have the opportunity—and girls—to be engaged in research and development, production and marketing in industrial processing? When does he do *that*?
>
> —James Luther Bevel

On a sunny spring day in 2006, I had the good fortune to tag along with Bernard LaFayette, who was on his way to Chicago's East Garfield Park neighborhood to speak to a group of students at Al Raby High School. Their principal, Janice Jackson, had invited Bernard and Chicago Freedom Movement veterans Mary Lou Finley and David Jehnsen to help the students better understand the roots of the movement in their city. As one of many volunteer organizers of that year's conference on the Chicago Freedom Movement, I wondered whether the students were aware of the struggles for equality that had taken place in their community. Did they know that their school's namesake had played a critical role in bringing the national civil rights movement to Chicago? There was a formal, expectant quiet as we sat down at a large rectangular table under the fluorescent lights, where a score of talented young people were waiting for us to join them.

"Not far from where we're sitting," LaFayette told them, "a group of high school students just like yourselves created a project that helped keep a lot of the younger children in the neighborhood from getting very sick and dying." I had known Bernard LaFayette my entire life and had heard many stories told by him and about him. This tale, however, was entirely new to me. I looked around. The students were as intrigued as I was to hear Bernard tell the story of how Marshall High School students had gone door-to-door collecting urine samples to screen the neighborhood children for lead poisoning.

"Battle in a Death House"

In the summer of 1964, LaFayette, a seasoned veteran of many civil rights campaigns in the South, including Selma, had come north as director of the Urban Affairs Program of the American Friends Service Committee (AFSC), joining Anthony "Tony" Henry, director of AFSC's Project House on the West Side. Henry, a community organizer, had been one of four African Americans to integrate the University of Texas at Austin. Project House offered community residents access to meeting space and office facilities, along with the expertise of other experienced organizers.[1]

Lucki Melander Wilder, a college student at the time, had started as a Project House volunteer in 1964. She later joined the staff. In the late summer of 1965 the problem of childhood lead poisoning came squarely into the field of view of the movement's staff and volunteers. Wilder and LaFayette both recall the distress of a young mother who had been participating in community meetings when two of her children started exhibiting serious symptoms. One child had paralysis in one arm, and the other had a swollen abdomen. Both children had just been diagnosed with lead poisoning. The children's mother and other neighborhood residents had many questions about the nature and cause of the sickness. The president of the block club where the poisonings first came to light approached the staff of Project House and asked for help in providing information to concerned families. Soon a larger emergency forum was planned, and local parent groups, churches, and community organizations sent representatives. A pediatrician from the Medical Committee for Human Rights attended to answer the parents' questions. During the ensuing discussion, it became very apparent that slum conditions were at the heart of these poisonings, which had resulted in twelve deaths in 1965 of which the community members were aware. At that first meeting, the East Garfield Park residents decided to form the Citizens Committee to End Lead Poisoning (CCELP) to work together on addressing the problem.[2]

It has been well known for centuries that ingesting lead damages the human brain and nervous system, causing fever, seizures, permanent cognitive deficiencies, coma, paralysis, and even death. The developing brains of small children are particularly vulnerable. Despite this danger, the useful properties of lead have made it very attractive to industrial manufacturers. Over the last century, its use in paints and ceramic glazes, as an additive in gasoline, and in many other applications has contributed to human exposure to hazardous levels of environmental lead. Scientist Clair Patterson demonstrated that lead does not occur naturally in any significant amount as an element in the human body; however, the amount of lead in the bodies of poor, disproportionately black children living in slum housing often rose to levels high enough to cause apparent neurological damage. Cracking and peeling paint in slum housing left a spray of deadly chips and fragments that infants and toddlers put in their mouths, ingesting the lead.[3]

Project House could not afford to pay staff to conduct door-to-door testing, so it decided to recruit high school volunteers. Nurtured by community activists Lucki Wilder and Tony Henry, students from Marshall High School became CCELP's foot soldiers. One of these volunteers was Robert Gore, now a media consultant and documentarian living in New York City. Gore told me, "As in the Birmingham movement," when activists had been threatened with firing, having loans called in, and other forms of economic retribution, "had adults volunteered [in Chicago], they would have been subject to reprisals, such as the loss of city jobs." The students, who called themselves Students Organized for Urban Leadership (SOUL), had already been active in Project House programs. Said Gore, "[We] were organized to deal with the conflicts among young people in the community. We were training them in nonviolence." Once the SOUL members learned about lead poisoning and began creating their own informational materials, they canvassed the neighborhood to warn residents of the danger. Their outreach included manning booths at community health fairs and participating in other community events. Lucki Wilder and another youth working with her created a twelve-panel comic book called *Capt. CCELP v. Lethal Ed in "Battle in a Death House."* The comic, which depicts a family battling for the lives and health of its three children, provided a medium to explain prevention and treatment to community residents.[4]

Initially, CCELP's primary focus was alerting people to the dangers of lead poisoning and how to prevent it. Gore and others collected data on lead hazards in the neighborhood's apartment buildings. "There was a formula which we used to find problem areas in buildings and to educate parents on what generally created the hazard. Leaky pipes = falling plaster = chipping paint," he remembers. The goal of collecting such data was to become better informed themselves, as background for demanding safe housing from Condor and Costalis and the other large management companies in their West Side neighborhood. Safe housing was ultimately the most effective form of prevention. Gore saw these lead screenings as an integral part of the overall movement to end the slums. These early efforts would gradually build the political will to address the issue.[5]

Long before neighborhood residents and Project House staff began organizing around the issue of lead poisoning, a few committed advocates for children had been active among journalists, medical professionals, and scientists. The *Chicago Daily Defender,* the city's African American newspaper, sounded the alarm in earnest after an incident in late 1959. Residents had discovered that spent battery casings being dumped in their neighborhood could be used as a long-burning source of heat for their apartments. Unfortunately, the lead in the casings caused the deaths of two children and forty other cases of lead poisoning. The Chicago business owner who had dumped the casings was later arrested.[6]

Citing the 108 cases of lead poisoning that had been reported so far that year, the Chicago Board of Health's Dr. Samuel Andelman warned in a *Chicago Daily Defender* article on September 7, 1960, that the disease was "of epidemic proportions." Quickly, it became clear that these deaths and injuries were being caused by substandard housing. On March 27, 1961, the *Defender* carried a story about a report presented by Dr. Joseph Greengard to a City Club of Chicago committee on lead poisoning in children. He explained that Cook County Hospital had admitted 180 (mostly black) children with lead poisoning in 1960. Andelman, Greengard, and a handful of other dedicated physicians, including Drs. Joseph Christian and Bohdan Celewycz of Chicago's Poison Control Program, continued to sound the alarm. With Greengard's support, the other three physicians developed an inexpensive, noninvasive method of detecting lead poisoning in asymptomatic children using urinary coproporphyrin as a screening test. In spite of all this, and in spite of children continuing to become ill and die from ingesting lead-based paint, Chicago's City Council was unwilling to allocate resources to screen poor black children. The Medical Committee for Human Rights, a progressive coalition of physicians, had tried and failed to muster the political will and resources in the City Council.[7]

Cook County Hospital and many private hospitals treated children with lead poisoning symptoms, but there was no outreach to find cases before they became critical or fatal. Scientists from Argonne Labs, in Chicago's western suburbs, trained Lucki Wilder, who mentored and supported the students of SOUL, on the proper way to collect, store, and test urine samples. Clarence James, who went on to attend Morehouse and Harvard, was one of the high school students who went door-to-door collecting urine samples. James devoted his adult life to a social justice ministry, particularly addressing the needs of underserved youth.

During the anti–lead poisoning campaign, the basement of Project House became a makeshift laboratory, where students in white lab coats conducted the urine tests. Students also helped organize a large community rally, and Jimmy Collier wrote a song about lead poisoning. The Board of Health, Dr. Quentin Young, and other doctors from the Medical Committee for Human Rights helped with the testing.

From September through November 1965, the high school students collected close to 600 samples, resulting in the discovery and treatment of four definite cases of lead poisoning. The new testing method, which measured coproporphyrin in urine and analyzed it using atomic spectroscopy, had made testing less expensive and less invasive, and the students of SOUL had proved its efficacy in the field. These students contributed time, discipline, and loving concern to help the youngest and most vulnerable members of their families and communities.

CCELP's screening program attracted the attention of the City of

Chicago Board of Health. Bernard LaFayette spoke to a Board of Health official and reported that the Project House students were finding many children with lead poisoning on the West Side. He asked why the city was not screening children for lead poisoning, to which the official replied, "If we did that, the hospitals would be full." An astounded LaFayette responded, "Would you rather the funeral homes be full of children?"[8]

Soon the Board of Health moved to create and fund a comprehensive screening program.[9] In December 1965 it announced plans to use War on Poverty–funded workers to implement a program similar to the one CCELP had initiated. Wilder and LaFayette had hoped the city would hire the young people of SOUL, but none of the students was given the opportunity to work with the Board of Health. Wilder was very disappointed. Instead, CCELP's student members continued to canvass and test through May 1966, "to serve as a reminder to the city of the seriousness of community concern about lead poisoning," according to Wilder.

Out of the ferment generated by CCELP came the Chicago Board of Health's screening program, the first mass screening program in the nation and the first time a community-based effort spurred such a wide-scale response to the issue. The students of SOUL and their mentors had generated enough awareness and outrage so that the City of Chicago had to respond. Resources were allocated for massive screening in a case-finding program for the prevention and treatment of lead poisoning.[10]

In a two-year period beginning in 1966, 68,744 Chicago children were screened for lead poisoning by the city's Board of Health. Six percent were found to have lead levels of 50 micrograms per deciliter or higher in the blood, a level now considered to be dramatically high. (It is now known that children can be negatively affected at levels below 10 micrograms per deciliter, so preventive measures are instituted in those with levels exceeding 5 micrograms.) As a result of the screening process, there was a significant rise in reported cases, and fatality rates plummeted. By 1968, there had been a 70 percent reduction in lead poisoning fatalities, and the city had treated more than 700 children found to have high lead levels.[11]

As outrage spread that young children were losing their lives or being permanently damaged by something preventable, so did the idea of community-initiated testing. Organizations and activists in other parts of

Chicago joined the fight for safer housing and began canvassing their neighborhoods to screen young children for lead poisoning.[12] It was the mid-1960s, and Chicago was a hotbed of organizing activity around multiple issues. Childhood lead poisoning became a focal point for action.

One important grassroots initiative was led by Vivian Rothstein in the Uptown neighborhood on Chicago's North Side. Rothstein had earlier been involved with the Congress of Racial Equality (CORE) in Berkeley, California, and was one of the Berkeley students recruited to participate in the 1964 Freedom Summer in Mississippi, where the question of how to build an interracial movement had been under serious consideration by the Student Nonviolent Coordinating Committee (SNCC) and other organizers. Rothstein joined the Economic Research and Action Project of Students for a Democratic Society (SDS), which had seriously taken up the challenge to organize poor whites in northern cities to build an interracial movement. In early 1965 Rothstein moved to Uptown in Chicago to become a full-time organizer with SDS. Uptown was home to many Appalachian whites, along with a few Native Americans, Hispanics, and blacks. For income, she worked as a program aide at Hull House, a social services agency with a venerable history as a settlement house for immigrants.[13]

The War on Poverty was just getting started, and Rothstein had been hired by Hull House to work with a program called Girls Streets. Most of the girls who participated were high school dropouts, and it was Rothstein's job to teach them child-care skills or help them acquire expertise in beauty culture. There was tension between Rothstein and the Hull House administration because the latter interpreted the program's mandate as "having the girls learn to be babysitters. That was supposed to be their professional development," Rothstein told me wryly. Rothstein's ideas of child-care skills were very different, so she and a coworker decided to start a lead poisoning prevention program after hearing about the work CCELP had done. Rothstein helped the girls develop informational materials and a screening program, and she supported and encouraged those girls who took part in demonstrations against hazardous housing. As an active community organizer, she knew a lot of people in the neighborhood. Although the girls' families and the community supported her efforts, Hull House eventually fired Rothstein.

Rothstein does not recall exactly when she first heard about the lead testing initiative. She told me, "We had an organizers' union in 1966. So movement activists were meeting quite regularly and that's how we stayed aware of what was going on." (Amid a growing climate of disillusionment with liberal, interracial politics, the organizers' union later fractured along racial lines.) In addition, other SDS organizers working in the Uptown neighborhood had been collaborating with the Chicago Freedom Movement staff since the fall of 1965, so news may have traveled through that route as well. Soon, lead poisoning awareness campaigns spread to Woodlawn and other parts of the city.

Dr. Quentin Young was another connection. He had been an active supporter of the CCELP project in East Garfield Park, and he was also one of the founders of the Medical Committee for Human Rights, known to Rothstein and other Mississippi Freedom Summer volunteers as their health care providers. Naturally, as Young and others returned to Chicago, they remained part of the larger network of movement folks to which Rothstein was connected.[14]

The Citizens Committee to End Lead Poisoning, growing out of organizing efforts in East Garfield Park, sparked both the Board of Health's mass screening program—the first in the nation—and myriad other grassroots efforts in Chicago, bringing public awareness of the dangers of lead poisoning to families across the city.

National Lead Policy and Environmental Justice

The events in Chicago were occuring within the context of research on the effects of environmental lead and national policy on lead-based products such as tetra-ethyl lead gasoline additives, which had been introduced in the United States in the 1920s. Over time, research on lead had come under the influence of the lead industry. Dr. Robert Kehoe, the industry's most prominent and vocal spokesperson for the "safety" of lead, was the medical director of Ethyl Corporation as well as director of a research lab funded by lead and automotive interests. Kehoe influenced ideas about what were thought to be "safe" levels of lead in the body, dismissing concentrations that are now almost universally acknowledged to have toxic effects. These effects—such as distractability, reduced IQ, and the like—

do not constitute frank clinical symptoms and are below the threshold of what was initially considered symptomatic lead poisoning—meaning levels high enough to induce death, paralysis, blindness, and other easily observable impairments. With multiple contributing sources of lead, poor children in substandard housing were subjected to toxic loads.[15]

Dr. Kehoe, hired by the gasoline industry to tout the safety of lead, maintained that some lead in the human body was natural and that the body "threw off" excess lead. However, in the mid-1950s Kehoe's work was challenged by Clair Patterson, who used mummified remains to test for lead and found that, contrary to Kehoe's assertions, there was very little lead in the human body from natural sources. Concern was rising, and some cities took action.

Medical officials in Baltimore had confronted the problem of lead in the city's predominantly older housing stock and attempted to control it through the regulation of lead paint. The law proved ineffective, as it was rarely enforced. So in 1957 Baltimore mounted the first urban screening program to detect lead paint in dwellings. It was discovered that 70 percent of the tested homes had paint that contained significant amounts of lead. Secondarily, there was some testing of children. The Baltimore Health Department's recommendation of extensive paint removal was opposed by landlords and abandoned as not cost-effective. New York City had instituted a successful case-finding program in the 1950s that was ongoing. New York's program relied heavily on blood testing and on determining whether there was any history of pica—the eating of unnatural substances. Urine testing provided an affordable, painless screening method that was available to many more children.[16]

The CCELP screening program, which was copied by the City of Chicago, was eventually adopted by other major cities as well, thanks to organizing efforts by Scientists in the Public Interest, CCELP, and other groups. David Elwyn, a biochemist, had been instrumental in providing training and support to Project House staff and volunteers. In the spring of 1967 he made a presentation on Chicago's lead poisoning coalition of scientist- and citizen-activists at a symposium sponsored by Scientists in the Public Interest. As a direct result, the Rochester Committee for Scientific Information became interested in the issue and approached Rochester's Urban League about forming a similar partnership.

New York City's Scientists' Committee for Public Information also directly acknowledged the Chicago and Rochester projects when it announced its decision to disseminate information about lead poisoning to the public and to partner with community groups. By 1970, vocal civic organizations had convinced New York City officials to undertake the nation's second mass screening program using the new mass spectroscopy technology, which allowed large numbers of samples to be processed efficiently and relatively inexpensively.[17]

Environmentalist Robert Gottlieb notes: "By 1970, dozens of inner-city based community organizations and coalitions were organizing to address lead paint issues, primarily in East Coast and Midwestern cities such as Rochester, Washington, New York, and Baltimore."[18] In Boston and Oakland the Black Panther Party took the lead in addressing childhood lead poisoning. The Harlem Park Neighborhood Council was key in investigating and addressing the disease in West Baltimore. In New York it was the Young Lords, a Puerto Rican community action group—or what Johanna Fernandez calls "a politicized gang"—that had first emerged in Chicago almost a decade before. Like the Black Panther Party, the Young Lords engaged in community service work and agitated for social justice. In response to the massive brain damage and near death of eighteen-month-old Gregory Franklin, they led a lead testing program in conjunction with medical school residents from New York Medical College. Joined by a few local politicians, the Young Lords were able to get their message to a broad audience. Congressman Ed Koch from the Bronx wrote to Mayor John Lindsay: "Even the conservative Mayor Richard J. Daley of Chicago had a more advanced lead poisoning prevention program than New York."[19]

Although there were conflicts over the use of resources—funding for President Lyndon Johnson's War on Poverty created urban contexts in which even the best possible uses of such monies might be contested—at least there were resources available.[20] At the federal level, the Children's Bureau in the Department of Health, Education, and Welfare, along with other public and private organizations, began to highlight the issue, and the US surgeon general issued a statement on lead poisoning.[21] In 1971 Congress passed the Lead Paint Poisoning Prevention Act, making federal funds available to support widespread screening.[22] From 1972 to 1981 federally funded projects screened 4 million children.[23]

Although clear lines have been drawn from the civil rights movement to the second wave of the women's movement, to national liberation movements around the world, and to the fight for accessibility for the disabled, among others, the story of CCELP illustrates how citizens living in substandard housing were able to partner with scientists, doctors, and committed public health officials all over the nation to reduce mortality and morbidity among poor black children. Further, the strategic, racially integrated alliance between Scientists in the Public Interest—whose motto was "Scientists inform, citizens act"— and community groups composed primarily of neighborhood residents was effective in building a coalition that helped change local and federal policy on lead-based paint.

Along with the work of Cesar Chavez and other Chicano community leaders opposing the use of toxic pesticides, the fight against lead poisoning can be seen as an outgrowth of the publication of Rachel Carson's *Silent Spring* in 1962 and the budding environmental movement that ensued, as well as the older tradition of industrial hygiene (now called occupational medicine), which had deep roots in Chicago. Additionally, people of color continued to develop an expanded consciousness of their human rights. Several years of civil rights activity around the country had piqued the national consciousness. Passage of the Civil Rights Act of 1964 created a framework for discussion and legal action that is a fundamental part of today's environmental justice movement.[24]

CCELP is credited with igniting the media attention and the political will that resulted in local government officials allocating resources for a mass screening program for lead poisoning. In addition to identifying cases and providing medical care to affected children, an integral part of CCELP's focus was the availability of safe, affordable housing. As we have seen, CCELP's campaign spread first to other activists and youth groups in Chicago. Ultimately, CCELP served as an inspiration and a model for similar organizations in many major cities across the United States, and it is credited with helping to catalyze the federal Lead Poisoning Prevention Act of 1971, in addition to many changes in local housing codes related to lead exposure.

Impact on Youth

After sharing his story that morning in 2006, Bernard LaFayette engaged the students in a dialogue about their interests and concerns. I was still marveling at the dynamic approach and uniqueness of the CCELP's student project under the broader umbrella of the Chicago Freedom Movement and the movement to end slums. Here was a "nonviolent movement pedagogy" that honored and released the power in black young people. The nation had already witnessed it burst forth in sit-ins and Freedom Rides: college students turning themselves into a self-governing, active force for social justice. In Birmingham, high school and middle school children had faced dogs and fire hoses to demonstrate to the world the force of the racism and hatred that confronted them in their daily lives. The Birmingham movement had prompted President John F. Kennedy's call for what would become the Civil Rights Act of 1964.

Beginning in the late summer of 1965, a group of Chicago teens, community activists of all ages, and movement organizers (most of whom were still in their twenties) were reaffirming the movement's power to upend the existing leadership paradigm.[25] Here again, in mid-1960s Chicago, was a story of high school youth and movement activists offering different answers to the questions: Who leads? Who teaches? Whose analysis? Who has access to science and industry?

By the time they began screening children for lead poisoning with their colleagues in SOUL, Clarence James and Bob Gore were already eloquent spokespersons about the inferior education they and other black students were receiving in the Chicago public schools. The January 21, 1966, issue of *Muhammad Speaks*, a weekly newspaper published by the Nation of Islam, included an article highlighting youth participation in the Chicago Freedom Movement. It featured a photograph of seven youths from Marshall High School who were active with AFSC's Project House. At seventeen, Clarence James had already been arrested for participating in a nonviolent protest against "Willis wagons"—the mobile classrooms, named after superintendent Benjamin Willis, that were Chicago's inadequate answer to overcrowded schools. The article also quoted a presentation James had made before the Chicago Board of Education: "I think one of the best ways to solve the dropout problem is to provide students with sure goals. If students knew they could get into trade unions or get other good-paying jobs, many wouldn't drop out of school."[26]

"This is a model of how you approach a problem: first, the awareness, then education for the community—we trained the students and educated the community—then, direct action," Bernard LaFayette explained. With a studied understanding of nonviolence, he and other organizers had implemented what Gandhi would have called a "constructive program."[27] LaFayette continued: "You have to first understand cause and effect. You have to narrow it to the affected population, in this case, the young kids. The next thing is to identify a program that can prevent or cure the problem, identify community resources and then collaborate with them. Then you need to design a strategy to implement the program, in this case, by informing parents, testing urine, and helping students know where to go. This is the holistic approach to addressing the problem. We didn't just march and protest. We did something about the problem by intervening and preventing further victimization." One of the results of this approach, according to LaFayette, was that "the students started seeing themselves as being significant persons in the community, in that they were helping to save the lives of the children. They were also learning how to put the knowledge they were learning to practical use, rather than just studying to pass a test. Practicing chemistry motivated them to learn more about chemistry, so that their grades began to reflect this new interest in chemistry, and this caught the attention of their teachers. This prompted a visit from a couple of the science teachers to Project House. They wanted to see what had prompted this new interest in science classes."[28]

One of the striking similarities between CCELP's comic book and the drawings and handbills produced by the participants in Uptown's Girls Streets program is the sense of purpose and efficacy they convey. The informative and inspiring writings, along with the drawings and lettering done by hand in pencil (and in one case a typewriter), show that these young people felt empowered to inform parents and other residents of the dangers threatening the most vulnerable members of their community.[29]

CCELP's roots and philosophical linkages drew directly on community-centered methods and practices of teaching and learning as exemplified by Ella Baker, Myles Horton, and James Lawson through the Highlander Folk School, Citizenship Schools, and the participatory organizational structure of SNCC. In his earlier work in the South, Bernard LaFayette had been steeped in these practices through Horton's workshops at Highlander and Lawson's nonviolence workshops in the Nashville student movement, and as a SNCC staff member. The lessons from previous campaigns were transmitted to students in Chicago via frequent contact with LaFayette and Henry, as well as with James Bevel, SCLC's director of direct action and project director for the Chicago movement. Both Clarence James and Robert Gore remembered the latter being directly involved with them. Many other seasoned civil rights activists, including Martin Luther King, became part of this extended community.[30]

As urban environmental historian Sylvia Hood Washington argues, it would be a mistake to assume that the civil rights movement singlehandedly gave birth to the modern environmental justice movement.[31] She reminds us that concern over living environments has existed in black communities for well over 100 years. At the same time, long-standing strands of protest and organizing activity can be traced *through* the civil rights movement. For example, one of the early watershed moments of the environmental justice movement was the protest against a proposed toxic waste dump in Warren County, North Carolina, in 1982. Congressman Walter Fauntroy, the Reverend Benjamin Chavis, and Dr. Joseph Lowery—all of them active leaders of the civil rights movement—were arrested that day. Lowery was a founding member and third president of the Southern Christian Leadership Conference (SCLC). "A native of Oxford, North Carolina, Dr. Benjamin F. Chavis, Jr. began his career in 1963, as a statewide youth coordinator in North Carolina for the Reverend Dr. Martin Luther King, Jr., and the Southern Christian Leadership Conference," states Chavis's website. And Fauntroy was the director of SCLC's Washington, DC, office for many years before being elected to Congress.[32]

The goals and pedagogy of the Citizens Committee to End Lead Poisoning should be considered in light of the continuing fight for the recognition of a constitutional and a human right to education, as well as an end to policies promoting the disproportionate mass incarceration of young people of color. Clarence James clearly understood what was needed in 1966, when he was just seventeen years old: "Talking and preaching does little good. The only way to keep students interested in school is by providing better academic stimulation, better facilities and better jobs for the students to look forward to."[33] He knew that poor youths in urban areas need to be exposed to methods of learning and being in the world that empower them. Our challenge is to make educational processes relevant to all young people by connecting education to future participation as citizens in the polity who are able to contribute goods and services in a market economy.

Notes

I would like to thank Mary Lou Finley and Pam Smith for generously sharing transcripts of two interviews they conducted. Their notes, ideas, and feedback, along with Jim Ralph's, were invaluable. I am also grateful for the wisdom and foresight of Lucki Wilder and Vivian Rothstein, who saved materials created by the youth volunteers and generously shared them with me.

The epigraph is from a speech my father gave at Demopolis, Alabama, in 1992. See https://www.youtube.com/watch?v=KayUqVPMPzw (accessed February, 23, 2015). He was SCLC's project director during the Chicago movement.

1. Obituary for Anthony Ray Henry, *Houston Chronicle,* January 11, 2008; Joseph Gerson interviewed by Erik Owens, *Boisi Center Interviews (Newsletter)* 83 (January 30, 2014): 3, http://www.bc.edu/content/dam/files/centers/boisi/pdf/s14/Gerson%20transcript%20-%20final.pdf (accessed December 5, 2014); Bernard LaFayette, interviews by Sherrilynn Bevel, Chicago, October 2011 and March 19, 2014; Bernard LaFayette, interview by Mary Lou Finley, Seattle, January 21, 2014.

2. Lucki Wilder, interview by Sherrilynn Bevel, Chicago, October 27, 2011; Lucki Wilder, interview by Pam Smith, April 2009; Ann Koppelman Simon, "Citizens vs. Lead in Three Communities: Chicago," *Scientist and Citizen,* April 1968, 58–59.

3. Jane S. Lin-Fu, "Historical Perspective on Health Effects of Lead," in *Dietary and Environmental Lead: Human Health Effects,* ed. Kathryn R. Mahaffey (Amsterdam: Elsevier, 1985), 43–64; Clair C. Patterson, "Contaminated and Natural Lead Environments of Man," *Archives of Environmental Health* 11 (1955): 344. See also Jerome Nriagu, "Historical Perspectives on the Contamination of Foods and Drinks with Lead," in Mahaffey, *Dietary and Environmental Lead,* 1–41. The deleterious effects of lead in the human body have been known for centuries. With the exception of some occupational exposure,

lead poisoning is almost always a result of children eating "lead-bearing, non-food objects." David Elwyn, "Childhood Lead Poisoning," *Scientist and Citizen,* April 1968, 53. According to Elwyn, between 1954 and 1964, 138 Chicago children died of lead poisoning; during the same period, 128 children died in New York City. By the early 1970s, it was learned that the ingestion of paint chips was not the only cause of lead poisoning; fine dust in the air that settled on everything in the household contained sufficient lead to cause poisoning in children. See Peter English, *Old Paint: A Medical History of Childhood Lead-Paint Poisoning in the United States to 1980* (New Brunswick, NJ: Rutgers University Press, 2001), 174–75.

4. Wilder interviews; Robert Gore, telephone interview by Sherrilynn Bevel, April 22, 2014; Lucki Wilder, *Capt. CCELP v. Lethal Ed in "Battle in a Death House"* (Chicago: Citizens Committee to End Lead Poisoning, 1965), Lucki Wilder personal archives.

5. Gore interview. For additional background on conflicts over Chicago housing, see Beryl Satter, *Family Properties: Race, Real Estate, and the Exploitation of Black Urban America* (New York: Metropolitan Books, 2009).

6. Alvin C. Adams, "Two Tots Die from Fumes of Free Fuel; 40 Injured," *Chicago Daily Defender,* December 22, 1959.

7. "Lead Poisoning Claims Child," *Chicago Daily Defender,* September 7, 1960; "Lead Poisons Slum Tots," *Chicago Daily Defender,* March 27, 1961; Barbara Berney, "Round and Round It Goes: The Epidemiology of Childhood Lead Poisoning, 1950–1990," *Milbank Quarterly* 71 (1993): 12; Joseph R. Christian, Bohdan S. Celewycz, and Samuel L. Andelman, "A Three-Year Study of Lead Poisoning in Chicago," *American Journal of Public Health* 54 (August 1964): 1241–51. Chicago physician Quentin Young, one of the founders of the Medical Committee for Human Rights, continued to serve as a resource to community members as they formed the Citizens Committee to End Lead Poisoning and moved forward with their plans. See Quentin Young, *Everybody in, Nobody Out: Memoirs of a Rebel without a Pause* (Friday Harbor, WA: Copernicus Healthcare, 2013).

8. LaFayette interview, January 2014.

9. Simon, "Citizens vs. Lead," 59; English, *Old Paint,* 152.

10. Berney, "Round and Round It Goes," 12. See also English, *Old Paint,* and Christian Warren, "Childhood Lead Poisoning," in *Emerging Illnesses and Society: Negotiating the Public Health,* ed. Randall M. Packard, Peter J. Brown, Ruth L. Berkelman, and Howard Frumkin (Baltimore: Johns Hopkins Press, 2004), 234–35. Warren concludes that there are not enough feature stories on lead poisoning to provide evidence that local protest and educational activity influenced federal policy in 1971. He cites Lin-Fu's ongoing efforts to inform federal officials and the public prior to passage of the Lead Poisoning Prevention Act of 1971. However, the twelve feature stories he mentions are signifi-

cant, considering that lead poisoning primarily affected a group whose interests were not proportionally represented in the mainstream media. The reciprocal nature of the interaction between scientists and citizens produced useful data and funding at the local level for abatement, which naturally increased municipal governments' requests for federal assistance. We do not know the extent of Lin-Fu's involvement with Scientists in the Public Interest, the Medical Committee for Human Rights, or similar organizations; however, we do know that Lin-Fu herself wrote, "With the social turmoil of the 1960s, lead poisoning was recognized as an important pediatric health problem," and "Chicago began the nation's first mass screening program for the disease." Lin-Fu, "Historical Perspective on Health Effects of Lead." In a climate where urban riots devastated the inner cities in 1968 after the assassination of Martin Luther King, it could be argued that federal officials were particularly sensitive to urban community action groups, regardless of whether major mainstream media outlets carried feature stories about childhood lead poisoning.

11. Elwyn, "Childhood Lead Poisoning," 56–57; Simon, "Citizens vs. Lead," 59.

12. Simon, "Citizens vs. Lead," 59; LaFayette interview, January 2014; Wilder interviews.

13. Jennifer Frost, *An Interracial Movement of the Poor: Community Organizing and the New Left in the 1960s* (New York: NYU Press, 2005); Vivian Rothstein, interview by Sherrilynn Bevel, Chicago, June 16, 2014 (subsequent quotations are from this interview). See also Jane Addams, *Twenty Years at Hull House* (1910; reprint, New York: Signet Classics, 1999), and Todd Gitlin and Nanci Hollander, *Uptown: Poor Whites in Chicago* (New York: Harper & Row, 1970).

14. Wilder interviews.

15. Ibid.; English, *Old Paint*, 152; Berney, "Round and Round It Goes," 20; Herbert L. Needleman, *Human Lead Exposure* (Boca Raton, FL: CRC Press, 1991).

16. Christian et al., "Three-Year Study of Lead Poisoning in Chicago"; Elwyn, "Childhood Lead Poisoning," 56–57. See also Lin-Fu, "Historical Perspective on Health Effects of Lead," 53.

17. David J. Wilson, "Childhood Lead Poisoning," *Scientist and Citizen*, April 1968, 60; Glenn L. Paulson, Edmund O. Rothschild, and Joel Buxbaum, "Childhood Lead Poisoning," *Scientist and Citizen*, April 1968. In the introduction to this issue of *Scientist and Citizen*, Rene Dubos, president of Scientists in the Public Interest, cited Chicago and Rochester and announced that plans were under way in two additional cities to start similar programs. See also "Implementation of the Lead Contamination Control Act of 1988," Center for Disease Control, *MMWR Weekly* (May 1, 1992), 288–90, in which the CDC notes that Chicago had the first mass screening program for lead poisoning.

18. Robert Gottlieb, *Forcing the Spring: The Transformation of the American Environmental Movement*, rev. ed. (Washington, DC: Island Press, 2005), 247.

19. Gerald Markowitz and David Rosner, *Lead Wars: The Politics of Science and the Fate of America's Children* (Berkeley: University of California Press, 2013), 47; Johanna Fernandez, "Between Social Service Reform and Revolutionary Politics: The Young Lords, Late Sixties Radicalism, and Community Organizing in New York City," in *Freedom North: Black Freedom Struggles Outside the South, 1940–1980*, ed. Jeanne F. Theoharis and Komozi Woodard (New York: Palgrave Macmillan, 2003), 270–72.

20. Says Rothstein, "The War on Poverty was just getting started. There was a lot of exclusion of the poor from the War on Poverty."

21. Lin-Fu, "Historical Perspective on Health Effects of Lead," 53, 63–64.

22. Berney, "Round and Round It Goes," 10.

23. Lin-Fu, "Historical Perspective on Health Effects of Lead," 54.

24. Rachel Carson, *Silent Spring* (1962; reprint, New York: Houghton Mifflin, 2002). Early industrial hygiene pioneer and physician Alice Hamilton lived at Hull House in Chicago for a decade while she investigated industrial lead poisoning and other toxins in the workplace; by 1915, she was known as "the foremost American authority on lead poisoning." Barbara Sicherman, *Alice Hamilton: A Life in Letters* (Urbana: University of Illinois Press, 2003), 180. See also Robert Bullard, *Dumping in Dixie: Race, Class, and Environmental Equality* (Boulder, CO: Westview Press, 2000).

25. Barbara Ransby, *Ella Baker and the Black Freedom Movement: A Radical Democratic Vision* (Chapel Hill: University of North Carolina Press, 2003).

26. "Negro Teen-Agers Ripen in Throes of Unrest?" *Muhammad Speaks*, January 21, 1966.

27. See Joan V. Bondurant, *Conquest of Violence: The Gandhian Philosophy of Conflict* (Princeton, NJ: Princeton University Press, 1988).

28. LaFayette interview, January 2014.

29. Rothstein, personal archives.

30. Clarence James, interview by Sherrilynn Bevel, Skokie, Illinois, November 2012.

31. Sylvia Hood Washington, *Packing Them In: An Archaeology of Environmental Racism in Chicago, 1865–1954* (Lanham, MD: Lexington Books, 2005).

32. Website of Benjamin Chavis, http://drbenjaminfchavisjr.wix.com/drbfc (accessed February 24, 2015).

33. "Negro Teen-Agers Ripen in Throes of Unrest?"

14

Youth and Nonviolence

Then and Now

Pam Smith

Youth played a critical role in the civil rights movement in the South. In 1960 college students launched the lunch counter sit-in movement in Greensboro, North Carolina, that spread across the South. The Children's March in Birmingham, Alabama, in 1963 played a crucial role in passage of the Civil Rights Act of 1964, as the nation watched the peacefully protesting students, some as young as elementary school age, being brutally attacked by police dogs and fire hoses. With the formation of the Student Nonviolent Coordinating Committee (SNCC), students took time away from their classes to bring voter registration drives to small towns and rural areas all across the South.[1]

Less is known about youth organizing for civil rights in the North, including that which occurred during the Chicago Freedom Movement. In this chapter I examine the movement's work with young people, especially its engagement of youth gangs, and then discuss efforts in the past decade to bring the tenets of nonviolence and organizing to another generation of Chicago's young people.

Youth and Nonviolence in the Chicago Freedom Movement

Youth organizing in the Chicago Freedom Movement had two purposes: it offered opportunities for youth to experience the power of nonviolence, and it provided "troops" for the movement itself. Martin Luther King's decision to come to Chicago was motivated at least in part by the Watts riot in Los Angeles in the summer of 1965 and the desire to show young African Americans that nonviolence offered a better way to improve conditions in their communities. Project director James Bevel often spoke to youths about the movement's need for their presence and commitment.

SCLC civil rights organizers had worked with gangs before, for example, in Rochester, New York, where they had been invited to act as an intervention team after riots occurred there. But as far as we know, the Chicago work represented the first effort to bring nonviolence training to gang members in an attempt to convince them to redirect their energies away from violence, toward reconciliation with other gangs, and toward nonviolent direct action to address community issues.[2]

Organizing youth felt like a natural approach for those who had joined the movement when they were young. Dr. King's field staff was young: the Reverend James Bevel, director of the Chicago Project, was twenty-eight years old, and the members of Bevel's staff in Chicago were in their twenties or late teens. Youthful energy was one of the strengths SCLC brought to Chicago, although black youths were already stirring in the city.

As news of the southern civil rights movement reached Chicago, there were efforts to integrate Chicago's public facilities and tackle other civil rights issues. City parks with beaches along Lake Michigan were a particular site of conflict; in 1957 a mob of 6,000 to 7,000 whites threatened a small group of black families and chased them from the beach in what became known as the Calumet riot. Youths from CORE and a group of University of Chicago students held a wade-in at nearby Rainbow Beach in 1961. In 1962, after two black students at Crane High School were attacked by Mexican and Italian students, the Crane students organized a march, 1,000 strong, down Taylor Street, the heart of the nearby Italian community, with a nonviolent discipline that mirrored actions in the South. Also in 1962 the University of Chicago's CORE chapter, led by undergraduate student and social action chair Bernie Sanders, staged a sit-in at the president's office, demanding the integration of university-owned housing in the neighborhood. Many high school students participated in the school boycotts of 1963 and 1964, in which 225,000 and 175,000 students, respectively, stayed out of school; many of them attended Freedom Schools, learning black history in local churches.[3]

In the summer of 1964, the year prior to Dr. King's arrival in Chicago, Bernard LaFayette, then a twenty-four-year-old civil rights activist from the South and already a veteran of sit-ins, Freedom Rides, and a voter registration campaign in Selma, came to Chicago to work for the American Friends Service Committee (AFSC) to experiment with nonviolence in the North. He began organizing youths on Chicago's West Side. David Jehnsen, a Brethren Service volunteer at the West Side Christian Parish; AFSC's Tony Henry; and LaFayette started Students Organized for Urban Leadership (SOUL), a group of John Marshall High School students who launched the project to detect childhood lead poisoning in the community. Robert Gore, Clarence James, and Claudette Morin, all of whom had previously done civil rights organizing, served as student leaders (see chapter 13). Jehnsen transformed the West Side Christian Parish youth group into the Parish Youth Action Committee and supported them as they organized students at Crane High School and then led a march of 500 to 600 students to a downtown Chicago rally in support of better schools.[4]

By November 1964 LaFayette had already organized a three-day workshop on nonviolence at Camp Reinberg in Palatine, Illinois. James Lawson, who had led nonviolence workshops during the 1960 Nashville student movement, joined LaFayette in facilitating the workshop. Discussion leaders included Al Raby from Chicago's Coordinating Council of Community Organizations (CCCO), Glenn Smiley from the Fellowship of Reconciliation, and Chicago community leaders Diana Blackwell and Pat Packard. Approximately 100 young people attended, a mix of both gang-affiliated and nongang-affiliated youths.[5]

To LaFayette, SCLC's involvement with the gangs was primarily about respecting their humanity; however, he also saw the practical benefits of their engagement: the groups were well organized and could be of service to the movement. "The gangs were structured with rules and procedures, goals and expectations," he explained. "They had a hierarchy of leadership, folks who were in command, and they had discipline." Attempting to break them up was never a consideration. "We wanted them to stay intact and by association with us, learn another kind of power." The task was not easy; nor was success guaranteed. An adult attendee at the Camp Reinberg conference commented, "Those street gang members who came from the West Side with their latent but vicious, angry violence made it very challenging for the Nonviolent Workshop to win proselytes to its cause."[6]

In addition to the lead poisoning detection work and the nonviolence workshops, some of these youths and young adults went to Selma to help with the voting rights campaign in early 1965. Among those traveling south were Jimmy Wilson, who grew up on the West Side, and Jimmy Collier, a college student originally from Arkansas, both of whom later became part of SCLC's Chicago staff. Lamar McCoy, a former West Side gang member who was later on the SCLC field staff, carried the American flag at the front of the march from Selma to Montgomery. This nonviolence work with West Side youths laid the groundwork for the organizing that began when James Bevel and the field staff came to Chicago in September 1965.

After Dr. King's staff arrived from Atlanta, youth-related work focused on the gangs. James Orange, originally from Birmingham, and Al Sampson, a graduate of Shaw University in Raleigh, North Carolina, were assigned gang outreach, education, and organizing responsibilities. Quite by accident, Orange had joined SCLC in Birmingham in 1962. Fresh out of high school, he had attended a mass meeting at the Sixteenth Street Baptist Church to meet a young woman who was singing in the choir. He sat in the front row, unaware that the other students sitting there had volunteered to picket a local store the following day. Orange decided to go along, he was arrested, and his long civil rights career began.[7] Al Sampson, who would be ordained by Dr. King in 1966 during the Chicago campaign, had been president of the NAACP chapter at Shaw University and was arrested during the student sit-ins of 1960. Sampson joined SCLC in 1963 and went to Chicago with Dr. King in 1965.[8]

Black street gangs in Chicago had emerged as early as 1919 as an organized response to violence by white gangs who invaded the black community. But according to Useni Perkins, it was not until the 1960s that black street gangs began to vent their frustration and perpetuate violence against the black community "due to the influence of drugs, corruptive prison experiences, and the failure of community-based programs." Perkins notes that there was a major breakdown in the governmental institutions intended to serve and protect black youth: the Chicago public schools, the Department of Children and Family Services, and the Juvenile Court. This failure produced more young people who lacked marketable skills and were relegated to the streets and prisons. In addition, there was an economic crisis in the community: between 1947 and 1958, production jobs in Chicago proper dropped 27 percent, and all jobs dropped 14.8 percent; many jobs moved to the suburbs, leaving behind those who lived in the city. These structural economic changes hit young men hard, particularly young black men, whose unemployment rates were twice those of comparably aged whites.[9]

Gang activity and membership began a slow upward spiral. Gangs turned to criminal activities, and the control of turf became a priority. "They couldn't get regular jobs, so they sold illegal things and became entrepreneurs," explains Bernard LaFayette. "That was the reason they were territorial; 'this is my market.' They didn't want competition in their territory. You had to get permission to go over there."[10] By controlling turf, the gangs were able to extort monies from businesses and intimidate community members. As drug trafficking became a lucrative source of revenue (as it did among gangs of all ethnicities across the country), violent competition for the control of territory became more and more intense.[11] Gang violence occurred both within and across racial and ethnic lines, with recruitment drives accounting for many homicides. To stem the tide of violence, the YMCA, Chicago Boys Clubs, Chicago Youth Centers, and Hull House Association began outreach programs to divert gang members' energy to more productive activities and to locate jobs for them, but these programs had limited success.[12]

This was the gang landscape the Chicago Freedom Movement outreach and organizing teams faced in 1965. Beginning in the fall of 1965, Orange, Sampson, and Bevel worked together to transform youth discontent into nonviolent action. They were seasoned civil rights activists and had no illusions that young blacks in the North would be as receptive to their appeal as young blacks in the South.[13] Orange's work with the gangs got off to a tough start:

They said they needed someone to organize the gangs and . . .
I went out and started talking with some of the kids [on the]
South Side. A couple of kids were fighting and I didn't know

it was a gang fight. I went over there, say, "Hey man, brothers ain't got no business fighting. Y'all oughta be trying to fight the system and here y'all fighting each other." And both of 'em turned on me and I guess what surprised them was I didn't fight back. I went to the doctor and just had a busted nose, busted lip. The next morning I went back to the area with Jimmy Collier, who was a guitar player, and a white fellow named Eric Kindberg who was on staff. When I got out of the car, about 25 guys started walking towards Eric. I said, "Hey, hold it man, now wait a minute. I done took that last whipping y'all gave me last night, but we're not gonna keep taking whippings. If y'all want to talk about how you get out of the slum," I said, "that's what we here for." And Jimmy took out his guitar and started singing "The Ghetto." That's how we did it in Chicago.[14]

A short time later, Sampson worked to recruit the Blackstone Rangers to join the Chicago Freedom Movement. With the help of Larry Patterson, a former basketball player and youth organizer, and Ernie Jenkins, head of the YMCA's Street Program, Sampson met with the Blackstone Rangers and convinced them to participate in nonviolence training. He also set up a time for Dr. King to play pool with members of the gang.[15]

By the time Dr. King arrived in Chicago in 1966, the Conservative Vice Lords on the West Side were already thinking differently about their role in the community. One of them put it this way:

In the three years from 1964 to 1967 we stopped gang wars and started to build a new kind of Vice Lord Nation. . . . Between 1967 and 1969 we opened several businesses and community programs. The police never thought they would see the day when we put our minds to do something like that. They always considered us gangbangers. Not even the younger fellas thought we could change. . . . The gangbanging stopped for a number of reasons. The chiefs saw that the younger cats were coming up like they had and that this was a dead end, and some guys cut the gang loose because they got shot up or locked up. Another reason was that people started to think about civil rights.[16]

In early 1966, soon after Dr. King moved into a run-down apartment at Sixteenth and Hamlin Streets on the West Side, six youngsters and two members of the Vice Lords stopped by to say hello and "meet the leader." Dr. King visited with the youths, and later that week he toured the neighborhood with them. His goal was to build a relationship that would lead to their participation in the movement. Not every encounter was so easy, however. In her book *My Life with Martin Luther King, Jr.,* Coretta Scott King wrote about her apprehension when some gang members came to the apartment one day while her husband was taking a nap. The young people complained about the social conditions in the community and about white people being involved in the movement. Andrew Young talked with the youths while Mrs. King made them sandwiches, easing the tension, and the young men spoke with Dr. King after he woke from his nap.[17]

Dr. King's apartment was not far from what was known as "bloody Sixteenth Street," in Vice Lord territory; in fact, the pool hall that served as the gang's de facto headquarters was just two blocks away.[18] One of the Vice Lord's leaders reported that they had many discussions with Dr. King in and around his apartment on Hamlin. "We were labeled a gang," he said, "but we always considered ourselves protectors of the community. . . . There were a lot of conversations on the back porch as well as in the hall. . . . We had ideological struggles—well, you could call them respectful arguments, with Dr. King about what was the best method for addressing problems in the community, was it violence or nonviolence?"[19]

Why the Vice Lords chose to change their focus to civil rights and community development is not entirely clear. The arrival of Bernard LaFayette and later the SCLC staff in Chicago, and their subsequent work in training some gang members in movement history and nonviolence, was one factor. Another possible explanation is the War on Poverty. Through this program, federal funds began to flow into the black community for job training and other social services. Street gangs sometimes benefited from these grants.[20]

Soon after moving into North Lawndale in early 1966, Dr. King met with police commander George T. Sims of the Fillmore District, Sergeant Edward McClellan of the Human Relations Division, and Robert Harness and Henry Miles of the Second and Seventh Wards, respectively, and offered to help stem the tide of youth violence. He promised that every effort would be made to prevent violence, but he warned that civil disobedience would be used and the jails might be filled.[21] Dr. King understood that the community's problem was at least partly related to educational opportunities. At a July 26, 1965, rally during the summer campaign to integrate and improve the public schools, King had declared to an estimated 20,000 to 30,000 people that Chicago's social structure was in need of "redemption and reform" and that young people—both black and white—had been crippled educationally by gerrymandering and closed classrooms. He urged Chicagoans to demand "total renovation of our educational system."[22]

At meetings held first in May 1966 in Woodlawn, then in Englewood, James Bevel, known for his dynamism and bold approaches (the Children's March in Birmingham had been his idea), used footage of the Watts riot to reach young gang members with the message of nonviolence. "The man has kept us afraid of each other, fighting each other, killing each other—and getting away with it," he said. "A man who throws rocks at a man with a machine gun is not only violent, he's a fool." Thirty people were killed in the Watts riot—only five of them white. Bevel called for 3,000 young people to "be on call by June 1st, at a moment's notice to close down Chicago." Thousands of youths were needed, he explained, to ensure that wave after wave of young people would be available to continue the protests in the face of mass jailings—a strategy used successfully in the South to force the attention of local officials. Closing down the Dan Ryan Expressway by lying across it was another potential nonviolent direct action tactic discussed at the meetings.[23]

The police showed up at the next day's meeting of thirty teenaged gang members held at Englewood Methodist Church (later moved to the Southtown YMCA), anticipating that it might turn violent with a repeat showing of the Watts riot film. Andrew Young explained to the police that the intention of the meeting was to redirect youth energies and that the meeting was private because the gang members refused to attend if police were present.[24]

SCLC's educational and training activities culminated in an all-day meeting in the East Room of the Blackstone Sheraton Hotel on Saturday, June 11, 1966. The purpose was to urge the gang members "to try out a new weapon—nonviolence—and to examine the extent to which the gang members were thinking about the larger community." At the close of the conference, the participants named the meeting the first annual "Turf-masters" convention. Black, white, Native American, and Latino gang members were in attendance, along with ministers from the Urban Training Center, attorneys from the American Civil Liberties Union (ACLU), and workers from the YMCA and Unitarian-Universalist Church—about 200 attendees in all. Eighteen gangs, representing roughly 2,000 gang members citywide, participated, including several gangs composed of young women. Al Sampson, who conducted a workshop on nonviolence, was asked by one of the young people, "Where does nonviolence come in when police [are] beating you in the head?" Such mind-sets presented a challenge SCLC had anticipated.[25]

At the meeting, testimony was taken from young people who talked of a "closed-out society" that included seemingly impenetrable police brutality and poverty. Jay Miller, executive director of the ACLU in Chicago, suggested that the participants gather information on police brutality that could be used in court. The gang members also talked about the skills and experience they possessed to better their communities. Dr. King was present at the meeting and emphasized that violence might win some temporary victories but not permanent peace. "We don't need any guns. We don't need any knives. We don't need any Molotov cocktails. We have something more powerful," he preached. "Power in Chicago means getting the largest political machine in the nation to say yes when it wants to say no."[26]

The *Chicago Defender* reported that Darris Williams, a member of the Gonzato Disciples, was inspired by the meeting and observed, "Martin Luther King is a tough stud. Maybe we'll get a better deal now." There had been similar meetings in the past to quell violence and shift the focus to community empowerment, but those efforts had resulted in little action because some gangs did not participate. A Disciple said, "A conflict might still come up. We may still get a humbug until we get the other clubs to move up, [but] I think everything is going to be different now," he predicted. The group had decided, at least for the moment, to exchange violence for nonviolence.[27]

A council consisting of two members from each gang and adult members of the organizations working in subject-specific areas was proposed. The committees were organized around housing, health, education, employment, welfare, and recreation, with an overall goal of ending the slums.[28] LaFayette reflected that the conference helped gang-affiliated youths discover what they had in common and think about how to resolve their differences. "We looked at them not as a menace to the community but a resource."[29] Orange later expressed his awe: "Those guys just sat down and started talking about working together. From that period on, we worked with these guys."[30]

On June 6, 1966, just a few days before SCLC's meeting with the gangs, James Meredith, an air force veteran and the first African American to desegregate the University of Mississippi, had been shot during his 220-mile "march against fear" from Memphis, Tennessee, to Jackson, Mississippi. Dr. King postponed for two weeks the start of direct action in Chicago, originally scheduled for June 10, and flew to Meredith's side. He and other civil rights leaders pledged to continue Meredith's march. SCLC leaders in Chicago boarded a bus with eight gang members, chosen by the chieftains who had participated in the Sheraton conference, and headed south to join the march. These gang members likely witnessed a pivotal point in the movement, as SCLC's "Freedom Now" chant competed with Stokely Carmichael's more militant "Black Power." In a poignant moment, Meredith, who had rejoined the march after being treated for his wounds, pointed his walking stick at James Orange, who was shouting "Freedom," and told him to shut up. Bewildered, Orange responded, "We can say 'Black Power' but we can't say 'Freedom'?" As intense as the Meredith march was, Dr. King never took his mind off Chicago. One historian concluded that Dr. King realized both he and nonviolence needed a victory.[31]

As schools prepared to close for the summer in June 1966, the threat of violence still loomed large. Efforts by the community to get gangs to surrender their guns had not been entirely successful. As a result, the US Department of Treasury announced plans to enforce the Federal Arms Act to combat the use of sawed-off shotguns, zip guns, and other weapons. The police warned gang members about the penalties for violating the firearms law: a five-year prison sentence and $2,000 in fines. Bevel cautioned gang members that nothing could be gained from violence.[32]

Even so, a three-day riot broke out in mid-June along Division Street in a Puerto Rican community, instigated when a police officer shot a young man. The incident quickly became "the metaphor for everything that was wrong with white society," said Chicago historian Mervin Mendez.[33]

On Sunday, July 10, Dr. King delivered a passionate speech to a crowd of at least 30,000 at Soldier Field to kick off the summer direct action campaign. Al Raby spoke in solidarity with the Puerto Rican community, which had recently experienced its first major riot:

> We saw, too, in an unfortunate but predictable kind of incident, the first revolt of our oppressed Latin American community. Out of a desperation bred by the injustices visited upon them, just as they are visited upon us, an explosion—which tragically is what it took to wake up the city's eyes about another variety of social injustice. The grievances of our Spanish speaking amigos are the same as ours, and we joined hands with them and we are here together today to say both "we shall overcome" and "nos otros [venceremos]." They, as we, are without job opportunities, without community services, without proper representation, and without the specialized educational facilities they need. We have seen this mutuality of problems from the Delta of Mississippi to the grape fields of Delano, California, and right in the hearts of our cities.[34]

The rally was well under way when hundreds of Blackstone Rangers filled the upper rafters, carrying a banner depicting a .50-caliber machine gun; they had been invited to the rally by Dr. King's staff, along with the Vice Lords and the Disciples. Their message, as described by one observer, was "count us in or cut it out," referring to their demand to be included in decisions about the black community, especially about black youth.[35] It seemed that their stance had been hardened by the new Black Power rhetoric filling the air.

Another incident at the rally involved an offhand comment allegedly made by a senior member of Dr. King's staff and overheard by one of the Blackstone Rangers. Apparently, one of King's chief lieutenants said they didn't need gangbangers because "they weren't goin' to do nothin' but disrupt the rally." Sampson responded that it wasn't his place to decide who was needed and how to get things done. The gang member who overheard this conversation said:

> I brought it back to Pep [a leader of the Vice Lords] and said if the dude feels this way and he's supposed to be King's number one man, then we don't know how King feels and I believe we're frontin' ourselves off. Pep said there wasn't no reason for us to stay there so we rapped with the other groups and when we gave our signal, all the Lords, Stones, and Ds stood up and just split. When we left the place was half empty and that left the King naked. Later, King sent somebody down to set up a meeting in his apartment, so Pep, Bobby, and a couple of them went over to find out what was happening. King said he didn't know who made the statement but he did need us. He said that he would need the troops and we knew he needed the troops.[36]

On July 12, just two days after the rally at Soldier Field, another riot broke on the West Side, this time in a black community in the vicinity of Roosevelt and Throop. It lasted for several days. The confrontation began when police turned off a fire hydrant that children had been playing in, attempting to keep cool on the fifth consecutive day of sweltering, ninety-degree-plus temperatures. The police noticed the open hydrant when they arrived on the scene to investigate a report that some youngsters had boarded an ice cream truck that was stuck in a pothole and taken some ice cream. Within a short time of the hydrant being turned off, the incident turned into a full-blown riot, with some gang participation. Police hurled their nightsticks, severely injuring at least seven people.[37]

King's staffers and their West Side associates took to the streets, trying to calm the situation. But the police treated the civil rights workers as if they were rioters. "My role was to go in with the gangs and to try and redirect them from confrontation with the policemen where we knew they would get killed," said LaFayette. "So I worked directly with them. I was small and maybe I looked like a gang member but we were able to keep them from having a confrontation directly."[38] The next day, Dr. King held a meeting at Shiloh Baptist Church that attracted 1,000 young people, many of them gang members.

Another strategy employed by SCLC and CCCO to quell the violence involved WVON, a popular black talk radio station. During this campaign, called Operation Cool, WVON broadcasted continuous messages for people to stay cool and keep off the streets—and it worked. Even so, news reports credited the police and the National Guard, called in by Governor Otto Kerner and Mayor Daley, with ending the rioting. But as King told one reporter, "If we had not been on the scene it would have been worse than Watts."[39]

King and his colleagues met with Mayor Daley at the end of the day, and he agreed to provide sprinklers that could be attached to fire hydrants, allowing the children to cool off in the stifling heat. The mayor also agreed to open more swimming pools and to appoint a civilian committee to improve police-community relations. King reported that this was a first step. Still, the atmosphere remained explosive. The toll was high: two dead, eighty injured, and $2 million in property damage, aimed primarily at white-owned businesses and the police.[40] On July 21 Dr. King issued a statement defending the Chicago Freedom Movement from Daley's charges that it had instigated the disruptions on the West Side; instead, King connected the riots with dismally poor ghetto conditions.

In the days and weeks following the gang conference at the Blackstone Sheraton and the Meredith march, the Chicago Freedom Movement was busy preparing for a summer direct action campaign focused on open housing. Orange came up with the idea to use gang members as marshals for the open-housing marches:

> We was talking about marching in Gage Park, and I said the best thing to do is get them guys to be marshals. Nobody could see them being nonviolent, but we started having workshops, freedom songs, and taught them the songs that we did in Birmingham. They started out bad, in so many words, but ended up good. And they said, "Okay, we'll be your marshals." The first day we went out there, they had shotguns and everything. So we said, "All right, anybody that's too afraid to go with no weapons, we don't want you to go because we don't want no scared people with us." That irritated [them] because we was telling them that they was chicken. We collected their weapons, weapons we didn't even know they had, four or five boxes full.[41]

Throughout July and August 1966, gang members—some of them now believers in nonviolence, some of them not quite there yet—served as marshals during the open-housing marches and played a crucial role, deflecting bricks, bottles, and other items thrown at the marchers. Orange described the strategy of arranging the youths in such a way as to encourage interaction among the different gangs: "I said, 'The worst thing that can happen is to let the gang kids get together. Why don't we separate them, put a Ranger, Vice Lord, Roman Saint, Cobra—you know, we just pair them off.' That's what we did, and they got to know each other. After the first two or three marches, after they saw who the enemy was, we didn't hear no more on radio or TV about violence with the gangs versus gangs."[42]

LaFayette commented that the gang members learned very quickly what their responsibilities were during the march through Marquette Park: "They were disciplined and they had courage, which was one of the requirements for a good marshal. So once they had the training they worked out beautifully. It was really something to see them participate— knocking down bricks and broken bottles."[43] Although the gang members performed their duties well, they could not prevent local whites from assaulting demonstrators and striking Dr. King in the head with a rock. After that incident, King remarked that the hatred he saw in Chicago was worse than anything he had seen in the South. Referring to the gang members serving as marshals, King said: "I saw their noses being broken and blood flowing from their wounds; and I saw them continue and not retaliate, not one of them, with violence."[44]

The gang members had been convinced to give nonviolence a chance, but at a meeting held later that night, they made it clear that they had not signed up for the kind of attacks they had witnessed earlier in the day from whites. According to Sampson, Jeff Fort, head of the Blackstone Rangers, organized this meeting, which took place at Dr. King's apartment and was attended by all the major Chicago gangs. The Stones argued with King about the dangers of nonviolence. After listening to them, Dr. King asked: "If a building was burning down and you had the ability to save it, what would you do?" Impatient, the Stones replied, "Everybody knows you use water to put out the [expletive] fire." Dr. King responded, "Water is [a good] option, because you don't put out fire with fire."[45]

The goal of the Chicago Freedom Movement's work with the gangs was to show them the power of nonviolence. Gang members signed on and participated in constructive civil rights work. They listened and learned the principles of nonviolence and were inspired to express new hope for the future and to perform their duties in the marches nonviolently. Not all gang members could be permanently swayed, however. The structural inequalities affecting their everyday lives—deep poverty, poor-quality schools, joblessness, substandard housing—were formidable barriers. Also, for some, violence had become an entrenched way of life, with police brutality being a contributing factor.

SCLC's work with gang members was controversial at the time. Historian James Ralph reported that "one Chicago police commander claimed that the gangs had been 'stirred up' by SCLC's activity" and that "a city youth official criticized SCLC for urging the gangs to unite against the white establishment."[46] Andrew Diamond, commenting later on SCLC's work with gangs, noted that the freedom movement helped give them a sense of their own historicity, even though they did not remain committed to nonviolence. He concluded, "The SCLC-CCCO was surely somewhat out of touch with the reality of many gang members," noting that Black Power resonated more strongly with them.[47]

Nonetheless, I suggest that this work with the gangs made it clear that, under some circumstances at least, these young men and women could mobilize their energy for positive ends on behalf of their community and could commit to nonviolence. We might ask, did this engagement with the Chicago Freedom Movement and nonviolence have a lasting impact on these gang members? Although a full answer to this question would require further research that is beyond the scope of this chapter, we can summarize a few dimensions of the story.

At least two of the gangs, the Conservative Vice Lords and the Blackstone Rangers, continued their involvement with community development efforts and civil rights–Black Power issues through 1969. These two groups, in cooperation with the Disciples (a South Side gang), continued to work collaboratively for several years, culminating in a joint campaign in 1969 to open jobs in the construction industry to African Americans.

The Conservative Vice Lords opened an ice cream shop, an Africathemed store, and an art studio in their neighborhood in 1967. Along with other organizations, such as the West Side Organization, they formed the West Side Community Development Corporation. Researcher David Dawley arrived in the community in 1967 and helped the Vice Lords get grants from the Ford Foundation and Sears and Roebuck (among others) to support their work in developing community enterprises and learning to operate them. Substantial funds were poured into the community. Although these efforts evoked pride and infused positive energy into the community, they collapsed shortly after 1969 as funding dried up, Dawley left the community, Mayor Daley declared his "war on gangs," and Chicago police took a much harsher approach to gangs.[48]

Some Vice Lords became involved with projects of the Chicago chapter of the Black Panthers, headquartered near the group's neighborhood. One report suggests that West Side youths were affected by what they perceived as the Chicago Freedom Movement's lack of success, and some joined the Panthers. The Illinois Black Panther Party, founded in 1968, focused significantly on "survival programs," such as the free breakfast program for children, often held in churches, and a free medical clinic. Party chairman Fred Hampton was an eloquent speaker and a gifted organizer with a lot of civil rights experience, including organizing at his high school and heading both the Maywood and the Illinois NAACP Youth Councils. One particularly interesting dimension of the Black Panthers' work in Illinois was the effort to build a "Rainbow Coalition" and collaborate not only with gangs in the black community but also with those from the Latino community and the poor white community on Chicago's Near Northwest Side, all of which were becoming politicized. However, the December 1969 murder of twenty-one-year-old Hampton by the Chicago police in the middle of the night while he was still in his bed devastated the group and sent shock waves through Chicago's black community and much of Chicago.[49]

The Blackstone Rangers worked with South Side community groups such as The Woodlawn Organization and the Kenwood-Oakland Community Organization, and they received a federal grant for a job training program. At the same time, they continued their street-related activities. The Blackstone Rangers were invited to join SCLC's Poor People's Campaign in Washington, DC, in the spring of 1968, and a group of them moved into Resurrection City, the tent city on the National Mall where the protest was being held. They were eventually sent home by campaign organizers after their behavior proved disturbing to the other protesters. Though the Rangers' relationship with community and civil rights groups was fraught with difficulties, it continued into the early 1970s. The Blackstone Rangers were also in conversation with the Black Panther Party on the West Side, a collaboration that had not proceeded very far, but far enough to inspire a police effort to sow dissension between the two groups. The FBI sent the leaders of each group a letter saying that the other wanted to kill him. This ruse was not successful, however, and both laughed at the effort.[50]

In June 1969 the Conservative Vice Lords, the Black P. Stone Nation, and the Black Disciples merged to form the LSDs—which stood for Lords, Stones, and Disciples. The LSDs, which had an estimated 50,000 members, were co-led by the heads of the three groups. They were also part of the Coalition for United Community Action (CUCA), led by the Reverend C. T. Vivian, former SCLC executive staff member in Atlanta before coming to Chicago in 1965, and the Reverend Jesse Jackson, head of Operation Breadbasket. This coalition of sixty community groups, including the gangs, had come together to fight oppression in the community.[51]

CUCA planned to take action against the construction trade unions for failure to comply with the affirmative action program, Title VI of the Civil Rights Act of 1964, and the president's Executive Order 11246.[52] The coalition claimed that closing down construction sites was the only way the union officials would understand the point they were trying to make. Vivian explained that the goal was not just to obtain training, jobs, and higher positions within the construction field; they wanted to change social conditions and rebuild the ghetto. He warned, however, that if any construction workers refused to cooperate with them, then they would not use force. For weeks, the LSDs—with Vivian, Jackson, and others— marched on building sites, first in the African American community and then downtown and elsewhere, calling for change. Work stopped. Finally, Mayor Daley called a meeting that involved the movement activists, the developers, and the unions, and out of that meeting came the Chicago Plan, guaranteeing 20,000 jobs in the construction trades for African

Americans and other minorities. Some works about the northern struggle for civil rights, such as Thomas J. Sugrue's *Sweet Land of Liberty*, neglect this important dimension of the Chicago story.[53]

This campaign built on the earlier work of the Chicago Freedom Movement, which had initiated collaboration among the gangs while encouraging them to think of themselves as political actors in the community. In addition, the campaign drew on the long civil rights experience of both C. T. Vivian and Jesse Jackson. It was a final, powerful demonstration, during the era of civil rights and then Black Power, of the possibilities for change. Diamond has written about this period (from the early 1960s to the early 1970s) as a time of gang politicization, when the gang leaders, in particular, saw themselves as political actors in their communities. Particularly important during this era were the interracial collaborations fostered by SCLC and cultivated by the Illinois Black Panthers a few years later. Diamond describes SCLC's involvement with the gangs as "a key turning point" in the history of the "super gangs" or "Nations," as they preferred to be called.[54]

After the Chicago Police Department created its Gang Intelligence Unit (GIU) in 1967, the police used force, surveillance, weapon turn-ins, intergang mediation, stop-and-frisk, and an array of other strategies to control gangs, according to historian Simon Balto. They also used "less savory, coercive measures." Some gang members and community activists accused the GIU of physical abuse, threats, and intentionally exacerbating intergang conflict. A favorite strategy of some GIU officers, Balto writes, was to drive a gang member around the city and drop him off deep in a rival gang's turf if he failed to provide them with the information they sought.[55] These strategies worsened the already tense relationship between the police and community members.

Police crackdowns fragmented the gangs, and their focus on community development and civil rights declined significantly or, in some cases, disappeared. By the 1980s, deindustrialization robbed Chicago of even more jobs. Crack cocaine eventually invaded these communities, providing the final coup de grace to community development and politicization efforts. (Jakobi Williams argues, however, that the Panthers' Rainbow Coalition flowed into the coalition that elected Harold Washington as Chicago's first black mayor in 1983.)[56]

Youth and Nonviolence in Chicago in the Twenty-First Century

Nonviolence work with youth in the last decade and a half has had two foci—stemming the tide of youth violence and teaching young people how to organize to address issues in their community. This work is done in Chicago through many excellent organizations, and unfortunately, they cannot all be included in this chapter. Here, I feature four efforts descended from the Chicago Freedom Movement and the civil rights movement of the 1960s: Kingian nonviolence training at North Lawndale College Prep; the Chicago Freedom School; a research and video project carried out by students at the Al Raby High School for Community and Environment, which was an integral part of the Chicago Freedom Movement's fortieth anniversary commemoration in 2006; and We Charge Genocide, named for a 1951 antilynching group.

Nonviolence Training

In the past decade, the epidemic of youth violence in Chicago has become even worse than in the mid-1960s, although the number of homicides is roughly the same. Rather than riots, which were the public face of youth violence in the 1960s, today's issues are police brutality and youth-on-youth violence. With the imprisonment of many gang leaders in the 1990s, these organizations no longer follow a top-down model, with clear direction given from a central leader. The top-down gang structure generated considerable violence, but with today's fragmented hierarchy, gang-related crime is much more random, resulting in even more senseless violence.

In 2012 the Youth Safety Council of Mikva Challenge (a civic leadership organization named for Judge Abner Mikva) released a report called *Blueprint for Peace*. The report, authored by youths, aimed to share best practices for the prevention of violence, interventions to stop existing violence, and the reintegration of violent offenders into the community after incarceration. Acknowledging that many youth workers, teachers, parole officers, counselors, and community leaders are involved in violence prevention work, the report suggested that Chicago implement a more intentional strategy to train individuals how to create peaceful environments and develop peaceful youth. It concluded that more antiviolence work needs to be done at the middle and elementary school levels and that Chicago needs to develop a comprehensive "peace" training plan for youth workers. The authors recommended that such training be expanded citywide and follow the strategies and principles of Kingian nonviolence, Dr. King's approach to conflict reconciliation. This recommendation was inspired by the work of students and staff at North Lawndale College Prep, "one of the few high schools in the city that does not have metal detectors."[57]

North Lawndale chemistry teacher Tiffany Childress discovered the Kingian nonviolence curriculum, developed by Bernard LaFayette and David Jehnsen and drawing on lessons they learned during the Chicago Freedom Movement. The methodology includes teaching the six core principles of nonviolence, the types and levels of conflict, and the six steps in conducting a nonviolent campaign (see chapter 20). Together, these elements challenge practitioners to address the root causes of violence and work to create the "beloved community." Childress became a certified Kingian nonviolence trainer and brought these ideas to North Lawndale in 2009.[58]

North Lawndale College Prep is located in gang territory on Chicago's West Side, in the same neighborhood where Dr. King lived in 1966. That community ranks among the most violent of Chicago's seventy-seven neighborhoods.[59] Yet in recent years, the rate of violence at the high school has dropped by an astounding 70 percent.[60] A core element of the Kingian program at North Lawndale is peer training. In 2010 Childress called in senior Kingian nonviolence trainers Jonathan Lewis and Kazu Haga to work with her in teaching the students to become nonviolence trainers themselves. One part of that training involved a role-playing exercise in which two boys got into a conflict over a girl in the school cafeteria. As the conflict escalated, Lewis stopped the exercise and asked:

"What are some nonviolent responses that the students could have taken that would have resulted in a different outcome?" The ideas came quickly. "What if the first boy pulls up another chair and introduces himself to the second boy?" one young man suggested. The students realized that if they took a minute, they could think of dozens of ways to handle situations that easily escalate. Lewis explained that one of the most important tenets of Kingian Nonviolence is to suspend your first judgment. "Maybe the second boy meant no harm, and maybe the two kids would end up being great friends. Yet, in our society, we are always taught to distrust people. Thinking through possible nonviolent responses to conflict helps people realize that they already understand how to de-escalate conflict. They just need to get creative and they need to practice."[61]

Later in the training, one of the students learned that a close friend was in critical condition at a local hospital, having been involved in a real-life shooting incident. Haga reported: "A conversation about the violence in Chicago followed. At one point in the discussion, Childress told the students: 'This level of violence is not normal. I've seen wealthy neighborhoods in Chicago where young people getting shot is not part of the daily reality. Even in this neighborhood, 50 years ago we did not have this level of violence.'"[62] Many of the students found this hard to believe. The violence they witnessed, and in some cases fell victim to, was so pervasive that it had become normalized. In an interview Childress explained, "You hear a lot of fatalism. Most students don't see beyond survival. You have to see beyond survival to see yourself as a social change agent. They think this is everyone's reality. We're [saying], like, no, this is a race and poverty issue." Childress believes that, fifty years after the Chicago Freedom Movement, the goal is the same—to be able to talk to people at the top (i.e., government officials) about community problems—"and that's what we're doing, helping the students to build the self-confidence and discipline to see themselves differently."[63] Childress said the six principles of nonviolence are posted around the building as a reminder to challenge status quo thinking. "It doesn't mean that it's all perfect. In a large institution there are a lot of values and ideas coming from a lot of places, but I think it's important for us to have a peace culture in this place."[64]

With the support of school principal and founder John Horan, Childress has conducted several professional development training sessions for the faculty and five-day workshops for students chosen by teachers at the school. "The kids are the most well-equipped and knowledgeable source for figuring out how to make their schools peaceful," she said. "They know their peers, they know what would make good incentives, and they know who's ready to jump off. So you have to make them an authority so they can have ownership of the process."[65] Childress added that the curriculum is not about teaching people to turn the other cheek; it is about teaching people how to confront the forces of violence and injustice in their lives and create a real, lasting peace—understood in Kingian nonviolence as positive peace.[66]

One aspect of creating a culture of peace at North Lawndale College Prep, as opposed to stopping sporadic violence, is spreading students' desire and expectation of peace throughout the school community. At an advanced training workshop in 2011, a long line of freshmen walked into the room. A senior student and popular athlete approached the line, welcomed the new students to the school, and then announced in a firm voice, "At this school we're about peace—so don't come in here bringing any foolishness from the streets." A pause ensued, followed by a question to the line: "Understood?" Some of the underclassmen nodded affirmatively, but their expressions could not hide their surprise and unease. This initiation of sorts was their introduction to the school culture at North Lawndale College Prep.

Other Chicago high schools have inquired about establishing the Kingian nonviolence program at their locations, but Childress cautions: "There are all kinds of different values out there. We've had parents tell us that they don't feel comfortable with this because we could be setting up their son or daughter to get killed. 'My son has to defend himself, and if he is labeled as what they call "scary" or if he comes across as afraid of fighting he may get attacked—so we can't.' It's hard when you start challenging family culture, especially when it's gang territory and there are moms and dads who are high-ranking gang members." She warns that Kingian nonviolence is hard work. "Teachers and administrators, we tend to want the 1, 2, 3. But this is a philosophy and you have to work it. There are no short-cuts to developing peaceful schools."[67]

During the Chicago Freedom Movement, gang members experimented with nonviolence—and some were transformed. Although gang violence persists in Chicago and around the nation, negatively affecting untold numbers of young people each year, there is an antidote in Kingian nonviolence. In Chicago, if the student leaders of Mikva Challenge have their way, Kingian nonviolence just might expand out from North Lawndale and spread a culture of peace throughout Chicagoland schools.

The Chicago Freedom School

The Chicago Freedom School (CFS) was inspired by the Freedom Schools that operated during Mississippi Freedom Summer in 1964. Established with seed money from the Girl's Best Friend Foundation, the school began in 2007. Its mission is to "create new generations of critical and independent thinking young people who use their unique experiences and power to create a just world." The school operates a year-round program with an intensive summer component focused on research and documentation, leadership strategies, social and political consciousness, movement and liberation strategy, and relationship and identity development. Toward that end, the school provides training and educational opportunities for youth and adult allies in developing leadership skills through civic action. The CFS wants young people to discover their own power to make change—"not only for themselves, but also for their communities and the world."[68]

CFS events are planned around moments of history through its "communiversity," revisiting such subjects as the sit-ins of the 1960s and the Freedom Rides. The events are typically attended by about 300 young people, with schools often bringing busloads of students. Speeches or films are followed by a debriefing during which young adults read their written reflections aloud at the front of the room, one feature of popular open-mic events highlighting spoken word and rap. "We try to find themes that connect with issues of today," said founding director Mia Henry. "And we don't pick and choose between types of oppression. We talk about all social movements and types of oppression." This approach is not always easy. One summer, Henry recalled, a mother withdrew her child from the program because gay rights was part of the curriculum. "This is not a cafeteria. You can't pick oppressions. You can't be antiracist, but then be sexist or heterosexist," Henry said.[69]

The program seeks to enfold the struggles of people of all backgrounds. For example, the PBS series *Chicano!* about the Mexican American civil rights movement—one of the least studied social movements of the 1960s—was shown to the students. Henry feels it is important to fill the gaps in the historical record. Part 3 of the series, *Taking Back Our Schools,* was especially effective for the CFS's young audience because it showed young people conducting a school walkout to protest the high dropout rate, crumbling schools, and lack of Mexican American teachers—problems that still exist today. A follow-up activity involved CFS students holding their own school walkout to protest Illinois budget cuts in education.[70]

The intensive summer program has a particular focus each week, such as youth criminalization. "We try to take young people from issue to action," said Henry. "This includes identifying their constituency to ensure the success of their cause." She believes that activism has not been discussed enough in schools. "Even the best teachers do not have time to talk about social movement history."[71]

Social media are often used at the school as a means of transmitting positive messages. Some students have made rap videos about antiviolence workshops and posted them on YouTube, publicized their projects on their personal Facebook pages, and created content for the local public radio station, Vocalo. The youths at the Chicago Freedom School are more transient than those in many other social programs, and they are socially motivated. The CFS has been able to foster strong ties through direct in-person communication and relationship building, embodying the CFS principle of in-person activism.

Commemorating the Chicago Freedom Movement

The fortieth anniversary commemoration of the Chicago Freedom Movement in 2006 benefited from the input and energy of a host of young people who both explored the history of the movement and served on a youth committee to develop ideas for conference activities. Under the guidance of their dedicated teachers Stacy Wright and Tamara Hagen, and with the enthusiastic support of principal Janice Jackson, students from the Al Raby High School for Community and Environment on Chicago's West Side met on Saturday mornings for nearly two years, conducting research, interviewing movement veterans, learning about nonviolence, and producing a video highlighting housing aspects of the Chicago movement and the poor-quality education that existed when Dr. King came to Chicago. The student oral historians were Charles Williams, Quincee Williams, Christine Herron, Zakira Tenny, Oscar Smith, Morgan Scoyners, Kevin Love, Tyion Bridgeman, and Shardae Brown. The students drew parallels between what they were learning about the mid-1960s and the ongoing social and economic challenges in their communities today. As part of the project, Charles Williams wrote a paper titled "Housing and the Chicago Freedom Movement," which won him recognition by the governor of Illinois as one of the fifteen best "Student Historians of the Year." His paper was published in the online journal *Illinois History,* making it accessible to hundreds of viewers.[72]

The Raby students screened their video at the fortieth commemoration conference and received accolades for their dedication and substantive work. During the question-and-answer session, the young people commented that although they admired the work of King and Raby, it was the actions of ordinary people they remembered most. Principal Jackson believed the project helped the students understand Al Raby the man and gave them valuable interviewing and media skills.[73] Bringing this story forward into their generation was an important form of youth activism.

We Charge Genocide

We Charge Genocide (WCG) is a grassroots, intergenerational effort to give voice to the young people targeted by police in Chicago. Led by founder and director Mariame Kaba, the group's ultimate goal is to end police violence. The name We Charge Genocide is drawn from a 1951 group protesting the lynching of African Americans. In November 2014 WCG sent a delegation of eight youths to Geneva, Switzerland, to present evidence of police violence at the fifty-third session of the United Nations Committee against Torture (UNCAT). Members of the delegation were Breanna Champion, Malcolm London, Page May, Asha Rose, Todd St. Hill, Monica Trinidad, Ethan Viets-VanLear, and Ric Wilson. The group was following up on its shadow report "Police Violence against Youth of Color," submitted to UNCAT after a period of documentation, research, and collection of testimony. They hoped, by addressing the United Nations, to increase the visibility of police violence in Chicago and expose the continued impunity of police officers who abuse, harass, and kill youths of color in Chicago every year.[74]

On the second day of the session, the delegation decided to stage a walkout during a presentation by US government representatives, initiating a historic protest inside the United Nations. From the beginning, We Charge Genocide had hoped for an official statement from the international body naming the Chicago Police Department as a source of torture in the United States. Following their return to the States in December 2014, the WCG youth delegation spoke to an audience of more than 200 in Chicago at a public "report back" on their experiences in Switzerland. Twenty-year-old Asha Rose read a powerful statement prepared by the eight members of the delegation that accused the Chicago Police Department of torture:

> We are told by our teachers, by our parents, and by the government that police are supposed to keep us safe. We are told that part of their job is to look for and stop violence. But our report shows that in Chicago, the police are a source of violence and are completely unaccountable.
> Only 10 out of every 10,000 complaints filed against highest offending officers were met with meaningful penalties. Most of the atrocities are committed against Black and Brown bodies. As a 20-year-old Black girl in the United States who has never seen the police keep anyone safe but has seen them harass people in their own neighborhoods, coerce confessions out of Black children, beat people while in handcuffs, and explicitly degrade people based on the color of their skin, it is extremely hard for me to believe that the state is keeping us safe or intends to.
> There is no legitimate mechanism for pointing to the police as source of violence and what that tells us is that violating our bodies does not count, that our safety does not matter.
> This narrative goes back to enslavement of Black people in the US, a history of Black codes—laws that rendered Black people criminal for doing anything and nothing at all, to the state—

sanctioned lynching and rape of Black bodies as spectacle and as sport.

The US legal system has since functioned to uphold hierarchies and justify criminalization, police and punishment. In Chicago, 92% of taser uses involved a Black or Latino target. A Black person is 10 times more likely than a White person to be shot by a police officer.

We have to understand statistics like these, this system of policing, as being built on that history. We are in a perpetual state of crisis that cannot be fixed from within the system. We need a rethinking of how safety can be achieved. We need power to be shifted from y'alls police to our people.

And so our delegation of eight Black and Brown young people who have traveled here are not asking for any favors, are not accepting any apologies. We are calling on you to admit to the endemic and structural violence that exists within this system of policing and criminalization.

We charge torture. We charge genocide.[75]

As a result of the WCG delegation's report and presentations, UNCAT, in its concluding remarks, referred specifically to Chicago police shootings and to the "fatal pursuit of unarmed black individuals." The committee also mentioned Chicago's lack of statistical data on police brutality and the police department's failure to show investigations addressing the issue. UNCAT referenced the death of twenty-three-year-old Dominique Franklin Jr. in the Old Town neighborhood in May 2014, when he was Tasered by a Chicago police officer following a retail theft incident: "The Committee is particularly concerned at the reported current police violence in Chicago, especially against African American and Latino young people who are allegedly being consistently profiled, harassed and subjected to excessive force by Chicago Police Department officers."[76]

Responses to killings of young African American men by police and "vigilantes"— Trayvon Martin in Florida; Michael Brown in Ferguson, Missouri; Tamir Rice in Cleveland, Ohio; Freddie Gray in Baltimore; Laquan McDonald in Chicago; and many others—have resulted in new youth activist groups, including the Dream Defenders, the Million Hoodies Movement for Justice, Black Lives Matter, Millennial Activists United, and more, focusing on police violence in African American communities.

Through programs such as Kingian nonviolence at North Lawndale College Prep, activism at the Chicago Freedom School, the public awareness campaign undertaken by students at Al Raby High School, and the international advocacy of WCG, young people are gaining the skills they need—in research, communication, organizing, advocacy, and street intervention—to support their efforts in bringing about a more just society. Learning about and reinterpreting historical events such as the Chicago Freedom Movement can help adolescents and young adults understand that social movements are almost always started by people much like themselves.[77]

Notes

Publication of selections from the following works was made possible by the kind permission of their respective publishers and representatives:

Kazu Haga, excerpts from "Chicago's Peace Warriors," *Rethinking Schools* (Winter 2011–2012). Copyright 2011 by *Rethinking Schools*. Reprinted by permission of *Rethinking Schools*.

Al Raby, excerpts from speech at the Soldier Field rally, July 10, 1966, box 4-21, Al Raby speeches, 1965–1966, CCCO Papers, King Center Library and Archives. Reprinted by permission of the King Center Library and Archives.

Sue Sturgis, excerpts from "Remembering Rev. James 'Shackdaddy' Orange," *Facing South*, March 3, 2008. Copyright 2008 by the Institute for Southern Studies. Reprinted by permission of the Institute for Southern Studies.

Statement of the We Charge Genocide Student Delegation to the United Nations Committee against Torture, November 2014. Copyright 2014 by We Charge Genocide. Reprinted by permission of We Charge Genocide.

1. On the Birmingham Children's March, see Glenn T. Eskew, *But for Birmingham: The Local and National Movements in the Civil Rights Struggle* (Chapel Hill: University of North Carolina Press, 1997), 259–98. See also David Halberstam's *The Children* (New York: Fawcett Books, 1998), which chronicles the remarkable impact of the young activists who led the nonviolent movement in Nashville, Tennessee, in the early 1960s, and Thomas Bynum's *NAACP Youth and the Fight for Black Freedom, 1936–1965* (Knoxville: University of Tennessee Press, 2013), which profiles the work of NAACP youth councils and college chapters, predating CORE and SNCC.

2. Bernard LaFayette, telephone interview by Mary Lou Finley, May 12, 2015.

3. Andrew Diamond, *Mean Streets: Chicago Youths and the Everyday Struggle for Empowerment in the Multiracial City, 1908–1969* (Berkeley: University of California Press, 2009), 221–30, 237–39; Rick Perlstein, "A Political Education," *University of Chicago Magazine,* January–February 2015, 46.

4. David Jehnsen, "Introduction to the Third Generation of Kingian Nonviolence Faculty and Certified Trainers" (unpublished manuscript, June 2013), 7.

5. Diana Blackwell, "3-Day Workshop Studies Nonviolence," *Chicago Defender,* November 28, 1964, 16.

6. Bernard LaFayette, interview by Mary Lou Finley, Atlanta, January 9, 2011; Bernard LaFayette, interview by Judy Richardson, October 21, 1988, *Eyes on the Prize II Interviews,* Washington University Digital Gateway Texts, http://digital.wustl.edu/e/eii/eiiweb/laf5427.0154.091bernardlafayett.html (accessed November 14, 2014).

7. Sue Sturgis, "Remembering Rev. James 'Shackdaddy' Orange," *Facing South,* March 3, 2008, http://www.southernstudies.org/2008/03/remembering-rev-james-shackdaddy-orange.html (originally published in Bob Hall, "With the People," *Southern Exposure,* Spring 1981).

8. See http://www.aaregistry.org/historic_events/view/rev-al-sampson-voice-action; Fred Gaboury, "Remembering the Rev. James Orange," *People's World,* February 19, 2008, http://www.peoplesworld.org/remembering-the-rev-james-orange.

9. Useni Eugene Perkins, *Explosion of Chicago's Black Street Gangs: 1900 to Present* (Chicago: Third World Press, 1987), 40–42, 33–34; John F. McDonald, *Employment Location and Industrial Land Use in Metropolitan Chicago* (Urbana: University of Illinois Press, 1984), 10–18, cited in Diamond, *Mean Streets,* 176. See also William Julius Wilson, *The Truly Disadvantaged* (Chicago: University of Chicago Press, 1990).

10. LaFayette interview, 2011.

11. Perkins, *Explosion of Chicago's Black Street Gangs,* 32.

12. Ibid., 31.

13. James R. Ralph Jr., *Northern Protest: Martin Luther King, Jr., Chicago, and the Civil Rights Movement* (Cambridge, MA: Harvard University Press, 1993), 93.

14. Sturgis, "Remembering Rev. James 'Shackdaddy' Orange."

15. Natalie Moore and Lance Williams, *The Almighty Black P Stone Nation: The Rise, Fall, and Resurgence of an American Gang* (Chicago: Lawrence Hill Books, 2011), 41.

16. David Dawley, *A Nation of Lords: The Autobiography of the Vice Lords,* 2nd ed. (Prospect Heights, IL: Waveland Press, 1992), 106–7.

17. Coretta Scott King, *My Life with Martin Luther King, Jr.,* rev. ed. (New York: Henry Holt, 1993), 261–62.

18. Betty Washington, "Dr. King Meets with Top Cops; Map Plan to Prevent Violence; Vice Lords also See SCLC Chief," *Chicago Defender,* January 29, 1966, 1; Edmund J. Rooney, "Dr. King's New Address Just off 'Bloody 16th Street,'" *Chicago Daily News,* January 25, 1966, cited in Dawley, *Nation of Lords,* 109.

19. Lawrence Johnson, telephone interview by Mary Lou Finley, February 15, 2015.

20. Diamond, *Mean Streets,* 235; "U.S. Hiring Gang Leaders," *Chicago Defender,* July 6, 1966.

21. Washington, "Dr. King Meets with Top Cops."

22. "Chicago No Promised Land, Says King," *Chicago Defender,* July 27, 1965.

23. "If Demands Aren't Met, Bevel Seeks 3,000 to Close Chicago," *Chicago Defender,* May 10, 1966, 1.

24. "SCLC Raps Cops for Handling of Teen Meeting," *Chicago Defender,* May 12, 1966.

25. LaFayette interview, 2011.

26. Betty Washington, "Youth Gangs Organize on City-Wide Basis," *Chicago Defender,* June 13, 1966.

27. Ibid.

28. Ibid.

29. LaFayette interview, 2011.

30. Sturgis, "Remembering Rev. James 'Shackdaddy' Orange."

31. Aram Goudsouzian, *Down to the Crossroads: Civil Rights, Black Power, and the Meredith March* (New York: Farrar, Straus & Giroux, 2014), 248.

32. "Schools Close Amid Threats of Teen Summer Violence: U.S. to Take Away Weapons," *Chicago Defender,* June 25, 1966.

33. Mervin Mendez, interview with UIC student Erika Rodriguez for the Chicago Gang History Project, January 27, 2002, http://www.uic.edu/orgs/kbc/latinkings/lkhistory.html (accessed September 2014). Mendez commented, "After these riots, the perception of the Puerto Rican community was very negative. But at the same time the power of the community, of the Puerto Rican community had increased ten-fold. For example we were able to change the regulations, the height and weight requirements for police officers and subsequently we eventually were able to get more police officers of Puerto Rican descent and Latino descent in the police department. We were able to get the city of Chicago to advertise its programs to the Latin American community, to really be bilingual, Spanish and English, for the first time."

34. Al Raby speech, box 4-21, CCCO Papers, King Center Library and Archives.

35. Moore and Williams, *Almighty Black P Stone Nation*, 40.

36. Dawley, *Nation of Lords*, 110.

37. Amanda I. Seligman, *Block by Block: Neighborhoods and Public Policy on Chicago's West Side* (Chicago: University of Chicago Press, 2005), 217; Ralph, *Northern Protest*, 109.

38. LaFayette interview, 2011.

39. "Riot Erupts on Westside: 300 Police Restore Order," *Chicago Defender*, July 14, 1966. See also "Leaders Voice Ideas on Riots," *Chicago Defender*, July 18, 1966.

40. Ralph, *Northern Protest*, 111–12.

41. Sturgis, "Remembering Rev. James 'Shackdaddy' Orange."

42. Ibid.

43. LaFayette interview, 2011.

44. Martin Luther King Jr., *The Trumpet of Conscience* (1967; reprint, Boston: Beacon Press, 2010), 20.

45. Moore and Williams, *Almighty Black P Stone Nation*, 42.

46. Ralph, *Northern Protest*, 95.

47. Diamond, *Mean Streets*, 271–72.

48. Dawley, *Nation of Lords*, 126–33, 191–94.

49. Jon Rice, "The World of the Illinois Panthers," in *Freedom North: Black Freedom Struggles outside the South, 1940–1930*, ed. Jeanne F. Theoharis and Komozi Woodard (New York: Palgrave Macmillan, 2003), 41–64. See also Jakobi Williams, *From the Bullet to the Ballot: The Illinois Chapter of the Black Panther Party and Racial Coalition Politics in Chicago* (Chapel Hill: University of North Carolina Press, 2013), 54–59, 87, 93–96, 125–66, and Jeffrey Haas, *The Assassination of Fred Hampton: How the FBI and the Chicago Police Murdered a Black Panther* (Chicago: Lawrence Hill Books, 2010), 89–93.

50. See Moore and Williams, *Almighty Black P Stone Nation*, on this group's evolution. On the Poor People's Campaign, see ibid., 83–84. On FBI efforts to disrupt a potential Blackstone Rangers–Black Panther Party alliance, see ibid., 98–99.

51. "Teen Gang Coalition Lending a Hand," *Chicago Defender*, October 9, 1969.

52. "Unions Facing Court Action," *Chicago Defender*, July 24, 1969.

53. Angeliki Panagopoulos, "The Role of Gangs in the Construction of UIC: Chicago's LSD Gang Coalition at the End of the 1960s," *Chicago Defender*, July 29, 1969. See also Vivian's account in chapter 1 of this book and Eric Gellman, "'The Stone Wall Behind': The Chicago Coalition for United Community Action and Labor's Overseers," in *Black Power at Work: Community Control, Affirmative Action and the Construction Industry*, ed. David Goldberg and Trevor Griffey (Ithaca, NY: Cornell University Press, 2010), 112–33. Ultimately, only hundreds of jobs resulted. The plan was significantly thwarted over time by

the withdrawal of federal support for affirmative action, budget cuts, and union resistance. Nonetheless, it inspired similar plans in other cities. For Sugrue's volume, see Thomas Sugrue, *Sweet Land of Liberty: The Forgotten Struggle for Civil Rights in the North* (New York: Random House, 2008).

54. Diamond, *Mean Streets*, 282. Gang politicization had a long history in Chicago. Irish gangs such as the Hamburg Club, once led by future mayor Richard J. Daley, metamorphosed first into clubs and then into the Democratic machine. This was well known, at least to the leaders of the Blackstone Rangers and the Conservative Vice Lords. Johnson interview; Moore and Williams, *Mighty Black P Stone Nation*, 18; Diamond, *Mean Streets*, 265.

55. Simon E. Balto, "MLK's Forgotten Plan to End Gun Violence," *History News Network*, July 8, 2013, http://historynewsnetwork.org/article/152489 (accessed December 12, 2014).

56. Diamond, *Mean Streets*, 307–12; Williams, *From Bullet to Ballot*, 125–66.

57. Mikva Challenge, *Blueprint for Peace: 2012 Chicago Peace Campaign: Everyone Can Be a Peace Worker* (Chicago, 2012).

58. Kingian nonviolence training for trainers is offered yearly at summer institutes sponsored by the Center for Nonviolence and Peace Studies at the University of Rhode Island and elsewhere by arrangement.

59. See http://crime.chicagotribune.com/chicago/community/north-lawndale.

60. Kazu Haga, "Chicago's Peace Warriors," *Rethinking Schools* (Winter 2011–2012).

61. Ibid.

62. Ibid.

63. Tiffany Childress, interview by Pam Smith and Mary Lou Finley, Chicago, September 2011.

64. Ibid.

65. Haga, "Chicago's Peace Warriors."

66. Childress interview.

67. Ibid.

68. See http://chicagofreedomschool.org/about-us/.

69. Mia Henry, interview by Pam Smith and Mary Lou Finley, November 5, 2010.

70. Ibid.

71. Ibid.

72. Governor Rob Blagojevich, press release, "Gov. Blagojevich Announces 2007 Student Historians of the Year: 15 Junior and Senior High School Students Have Best Essays Published in a Statewide History Magazine," April 25, 2007, http://www3.illinois.gov/PressReleases/ShowPressRelease.cfm?SubjectID=3&RecNum=5908 (accessed January 5, 2015).

73. Janice Jackson, interview by Pam Smith and Mary Lou Finley, Chicago, October 15, 2013.

74. "Summary of We Charge Genocide Trip to United Nations Committee against Torture," December 15, 2014, http://wechargegenocide.org/tag/united-nations/ (accessed January 6, 2015).

75. This was not the first time the Chicago Police Department had been accused of torture. Former detective and commander John Burge served four and a half years in prison for torturing more than 200 African American men between 1972 and 1991 in order to force false murder and rape confessions. See http://www.chicagotribune.com/news/chi-burge-storygallery-storygallery.html.

76. United Nations Committee against Torture, "Concluding Observations on the Third to Fifth Periodic Reports of United States of America," November 28, 2014.

77. Loyola's Center for Urban Research and Learning, working with Mikva Challenge in Chicago, developed a civic participation curriculum for middle school and high school students using the Chicago Freedom Movement as a key case history. See Loyola University Center for Urban Research and Learning and Mikva Challenge, *A Curriculum on Civic Engagement* (Chicago: Center for Urban Research and Learning, 2009).

Part 4

Stories from the Chicago Freedom Movement

15

Music and the Movement I

Music and Grassroots Organizing

Jimmy Collier with Allegra Malone

My grandfather was an accomplished musician, my grandmother as well. We played a lot of music in our family, and my grandparents taught me how to play different kinds of instruments. Early on, I was exposed to jazz, country, blues—everything. I started playing guitar and piano—performing at twelve years old at the military base near home. I grew up in Fort Smith, Arkansas, and my family lived on the edge of the black community. Our house faced the black part of town. The white kids lived across the alley from us, so I was used to hanging with whites, which was unusual for that time. I went in their houses, mainly through the back doors, but we still had fun and played together. People driving by sometimes yelled at us, especially if we were in front of the white kids' houses, but the neighbors allowed it, and we kids didn't really think about it. As a child, I cared about all people, regardless. We were Methodists (AME Church), so I was raised to see all people as having equal value. I remember taking sides when some black kids got beat up at a school football game by some whites; it was horrible, and it made me angry. After that, the blacks were looking for whites to beat up, but I didn't agree with that. I truly was an outsider, and because of that, I ran away from home a lot. I've always had a rebel streak.

I joined the air force at age fifteen. I was ready to get out of Fort Smith, and I managed to convince the recruiters—I really don't know how—that I was seventeen. Later on, after I turned seventeen, I told them what had happened, and I was able to get out of the air force at that point. But I didn't want to go back to Fort Smith. The segregation there bothered me. So I decided to go to Chicago and live with my uncle and go to junior college there.

Early Experiences in Chicago

When I got to Chicago in 1961, the civil rights movement was in full swing. The NAACP was integrating Calumet Park; that was my first involvement in civil rights in Chicago.[1]

Later, I worked with CORE, and we had demonstrations about all kinds of things. At one point during the protests about school segregation in Chicago, I was arrested with Dick Gregory and several dozen others. We went into court and refused bail, so about thirty of us stayed in jail for thirty days. We were segregated from the rest of the prisoners. They said we were political prisoners. I think they were trying to protect us. In the midst of all this, I went to the March on Washington in August 1963 with a group from Chicago.

At one point I worked with Tony Henry at the American Friends Service Committee (AFSC). One summer I was a junior counselor for his youth program out of Project House, which paired teens from Winnetka—a wealthy suburb—and teens from the West Side on a trip to Maine. During that time I lived with Tony in the dormitory of an old school. Later, I was Bernard LaFayette's secretary in AFSC's downtown office, right after he first came to Chicago. I had picked up typing skills and other office skills while I was in the air force. But I didn't keep that job very long; he fired me because I was never in the office. I wanted to be part of the action. It was the tail end of the beatnik era; there were coffeehouses with folk singers, especially in Old Town and another neighborhood on the South Side. So I sang and played in those coffeehouses in my turtleneck sweaters. Odetta was big; Terry Collyer was big. I was in awe of those people, but I played too.

To the South

After the first march across the Edmund Pettus Bridge in Selma in March 1965, on what became known as Bloody Sunday, the Selma movement put out a call for food, bedding, camping gear, and other things needed for the march to Montgomery. The religious groups on the campus of the community college I attended collected a carload of materials, and I went along with the person who was driving it to Atlanta. I stayed on in Atlanta, where I met James Orange, who was on the SCLC staff there. He was a singer too, so I hung out with him a lot. Eventually, I got on staff with SCLC and was assigned to do voter registration in Demopolis, Alabama, about fifty miles west of Selma.[2] I always carried my guitar, and I played everywhere: rallies, meetings, in the community.

We did some good work there, but it didn't pan out. Demopolis didn't happen; it was Selma that happened. SCLC tended to pick one place that was ready to go and put a lot of energy there. It paid off in Selma. Here, too, I sang at rallies and mass meetings and on marches and picket lines. I always had my guitar with me; it's in all the pictures.

When SCLC was ready to go to Chicago, it wanted people with city experience, so naturally those of us who had come from Chicago were sent north to be part of that effort; this included Suzi Hill, Sherie Land, Jimmy Wilson, and myself. Claudia King, who had spent the summer doing voter registration work in Americus, Georgia, was from Chicago too, and she joined the staff shortly after we arrived there. Others who had been working with us that summer (1965) in the South were also sent to Chicago by SCLC: James Orange, Dot Wright (Dorothy Tillman), Lynn Adler, Eric Kindberg, and Anne Gillie Kindberg.[3]

Organizing in Chicago with SCLC

After the visibility achieved by Dr. King and SCLC in the South, there was a buzz, but it wasn't enough to automatically pull people in from Chicago and elsewhere. We had to appeal to people in their own environments and circumstances, and so we did. Small community gatherings were how the movement started, in churches, in homes, and at community meetings.

I was a musician first, and that was my main contribution. You have to be aware and sensitive to what is going on around you. You have to be a good listener as well. You have to be bold, confident, and able to think outside the box. Who can talk? Who has facilities, or a big house that you can use as a meeting place? That's what we tried to find out. We went to bars, clubs, beauty shops and talked to people in Chicago, since we really didn't have the church community. We contacted people already doing things in the community, and they would usually help. I went and got people involved in meetings and rallies, and I took my guitar with me. I'd sit around and play and wait to see what happened. A couple times I got arrested for sitting on the street playing, because the cops knew the power of music could draw people.

James Orange and Eric Kindberg—trained SCLC field staffers—were the ones I learned from. Cities were new territory. In the South we usually worked with older people, women and church people. In cities like Chicago we had to reach other parts of the community if we were really going to get something going. In contacting people you had to go where they were. James Orange was a big guy, a tough guy, with a gentle spirit. That helped.

We were on their streets—James, Eric, me, and my guitar. We contacted gangs like the Vice Lords and the Blackstone Rangers. We knew if we could get young people involved it would draw their parents. I would make up songs about them, which would lighten things up a little bit. I met with gang leaders on the street and asked them to leave us alone while we spoke to young people, trying not to be scared. It's always a matter of knowing the right folks to talk to. We didn't want to deal with any really dangerous people. With gangs, there's always a risk they can take things the wrong way. They liked music, though. I could make up a song on the spot about whatever, and they liked that. Dr. King liked that, too. The music had a real role.[4]

Music and the Art of Community Engagement

We tried to be positive, but truth be known, Chicago was a tougher proposition than the South. It seemed overwhelming: the complexity, the larger numbers of people involved, the various leaders and established organizations to coordinate with. In the South things were simpler and more inspired. The Windy City could be pretty cold. There wasn't the same sense of spiritual inspiration in the streets of Chicago as there was in the South. Spirituals that spoke of suffering, redemption, and the Promised Land wouldn't draw the people in. Black people in Chicago had left the South behind. It was the big-city blues that black people listened and related to. I had to change the focus and style of my playing and singing.

We played for people who were already gathered when we got there, and there was always joy, despite the circumstances. There was laughing and singing—music, drinking, dancing, babies—and people were surviving. In many of the places we visited, discussing issues and community organizing was not at the top of anybody's agenda. Like I said, I had to make my music fit the circumstances. I played R&B-style songs rather than the church songs I played in the South. I played whatever people liked, but I would change the words of popular songs to somehow be about equal rights and the freedom fight. People like songs about themselves. You can take old spirituals and add people's names in them, make them modern. In Chicago we used music from the Impressions—"I'm So Proud" and "Keep on Pushing"—and Curtis Mayfield's "People Get Ready."

The movement music had to be a young music; it had to catch people and engage them right away. Music has always sustained suffering people by giving them a voice and, in that independence, a sense of pride. The role that music has played in the fight for freedom in oppressed cultures reaches as far back in history as political oppression itself.

As the organizing progressed, I began opening up for Dr. King. We would perform while the audience was waiting for him to arrive, and his arrival time was always secret, so we never knew how long we would be playing. Those opening performances had to be done in a purposeful way; it wasn't just playing songs and entertaining people. People were kept waiting up to two hours, and it was my responsibility to entertain them until he got there. It was my job to get people in the spirit of Dr. King's message, to open them up to the possibilities of the movement. I got people inspired with the songs I played, and once King got there, they forgot about me.

One time, while we were working in Chicago, Dr. King bought me a new guitar! My guitar had gotten really battered in the South. Dr. King must have noticed and said to Ralph Abernathy, "Can we get Jimmy a better guitar?" They gave me $500 to buy a new one!

The Music

Music is powerful and gentle. I tried to use music to bridge some gaps between blacks and whites. In the North, white people seemed to like folk music, and for black folks it was more rhythm and blues. I tried to use both. Sometimes I heard music on the radio I wanted to use, or I would read about songs or take a suggestion. Back then, to learn a song you had to listen to the record over and over, figure out the chords, and write out the lyrics yourself. The book by Guy Carawan and Candie Carawan, *We Shall Overcome: Songs of the Southern Freedom Movement*, was always a great source—my song bible.[5] I would sometimes do songs that Bernard LaFayette and Jim Bevel wrote when they were in jail in the South, sometimes changing the words around to make them appropriate to situations in Chicago. One song I often sang was a Curtis Mayfield song, "Never Too Much Love."[6] The verse I wrote for organizing in East Garfield Park goes like this:

I like to drink whiskey, I like to drink wine.
I'd like to have some now but I don't have time.
I have to fight for my freedom, got to fight for it now,
Come and join with Dr. King and we'll show you how.

We had to show people we weren't wimpy and that we were just like everybody else, fighting to deal with difficult life circumstances. We worked to be truthful, and sometimes the truth was very dark.

Over time, I figured out that as a musician, it's not about you. You have to make a deal and find common ground with your audience, no matter where you are or who they are. It's not just "let us be nonviolent and do our thing—and just don't screw it up." You're in other people's territory, and you are an outsider no matter what color you are; the gangs can either talk to you or whip your ass. Thugs, criminals, and people with bad childhoods, drug dealers, and pimps—that's just how they come up. There's a certain sense of understanding of civil rights, but they use violence to deal with any kind of conflict in their world. There's that manly, macho sense of pride that prevents them from embracing nonviolence as a solution. When Martin Luther King went to Memphis, he didn't have us to work the streets and apartments to bring people in; there was nobody to do all that preliminary community work. Things got violent as a result, because it lacked that people-to-people foundation.

In Chicago there were kids living in tenements, and they were eating flakes of lead-based paint and getting brain damage from it. I used my music to tell that story to anyone and everyone, especially the families living in the tenements. I never wrote anything that didn't have a call to action. Even if I didn't say it directly, somewhere in the story was evidence that something should happen, through the song. I would sing different versions of songs like this, depending on where I was and who I was singing to.[7]

Lead Poison on the Wall[8]

Chorus:
Lead poison on the wall, kills little guys and little dolls
It kills them big and it kills them small
While we stand by and watch them fall,
And the landlord does nothing to stop it all,
That death on the wall . . . death on the wall.

There's poison in the paint, enough to make a little child faint,
Enough to blind his eyes, enough to make him die, from the . . .

There's plaster falling from the ceiling, plaster falling and plaster
    peeling
Doesn't the landlord have any feeling? Someone's responsible for all
    that killing, from that . . .

Urine samples and knocking on doors, label of paint in all of the
    stores
Rally and action and you cannot ignore, There's still children dying,
    so we've got to do more on that. . . .

Poor housing was a key issue in Chicago. In "Rent Strike Blues" we were dealing with the concept of people withholding their rent. We were in the ghetto, so a blues format was more appropriate than an old spiritual. The words of the song talked about going on a rent strike: "Rats on the ceiling, rats on the floor, landlord won't fix it, I can't take it anymore." The idea was to blame the landlord, with the solution being withholding the rent. Maybe I should have taken more time, like a jingle writer. But I wasn't working for Disney, and if the meeting was tomorrow, you had to finish. It was Chicago, and the blues was the right musical form. Later in the 1970s, as the tenants' rights movement grew around the country, "Rent Strike Blues" was on an album called *We Won't Move: Songs of the Tenants' Movement.*

Rent Strike Blues[9]

I got the rent strike, I got the rent strike blues
I got the rent strike, I got the rent strike blues,
Well if the landlord-y don't fix my building
Gonna have to try and move.

Well, I got rats on the ceiling, rats on the floor,
Rats all around, I can't stand it anymore
Going on a rent strike, got to end these blues
Well if the landlord-y don't fix my building
Gonna have to try and move.

I went next door to see a friend,
Landlord won't fix the building and the roaches let me in.
Going on a rent strike, got to end these blues
Well if the landlord-y don't fix my building,
Gonna to have to try and move.

Well, no fire escape have we got, no money has the landlord spent
If he don't fix the building ain't going to get next month's rent!
Got to go on a rent strike, got to end these blues
If the landlord-y don't fix my building,
Gonna to have to try and move.

Don't care what you do, don't care what you say
Everybody black and white 'titled to a decent place to stay

Going on a rent strike, got to end these blues
If the landlord-y don't fix my building
Gonna have to try
Gonna have to try
Landlord-y ain't about to fix my building
I ain't about to move!

I tried hard to adjust my style, to do a better job of reaching people and telling the people's story. I tried to use the music to connect the dots between the situations in those tenements, a sense of hope, and the power ordinary folks have to make things a little better.

After the Watts riot in the summer of 1965, I wrote "Burn, Baby, Burn." Sadly, that's the message everyone seemed to remember from that riot. I wanted to tell that story but also turn it into another kind of energy. I changed it in the last verse. I switched to "Learn, baby, learn." I thought it was important to end on a constructive idea. People still use this song when they want to talk about the rage at Dr. King's assassination. I am glad they do, but it puzzles me why nobody else ever sings that last verse. Just me.

There was a woman at Chicago's AFSC office who knew the famous folk singer Pete Seeger. When he came to town, this woman arranged for me to meet him, and he invited me to play in the concert that night. I was eighteen years old then. (We later became friends and used to go skiing together with our sons.) I learned from Seeger how to get people to sing along. He had figured out some things. You had to coax folks into it, be a conductor. Help people feel the energy and then start bringing them along, don't just perform. Make them a part of the performances. Pete figured out how to play with one hand and direct people with the other. You had to tune your guitar a certain way to do it. Pete would do that all the time. The opportunity to watch him and be on stage with him was incredible.

I'd try anything if I thought it would work musicwise. I tried hard to tune in to the audience. Am I following a choir? Who are the other performers? What is the mood? Are people scared? Are we likely to be going to jail? Is there a media campaign? How can the music serve a positive purpose to the audience? I felt it was important to expose myself emotionally so that the audience could do the same thing.

You are guessing as a musician, and sometimes while you are waiting to play, you figure it out—sometimes not until you are onstage. Rhythm and words—the feel and groove need to be relevant to the cause, climate, and situation. It's good to have something that is repeatable, so people can remember the message and join in. If you can bring people up from the audience, it really helps.

Commitment is the key; the instruments almost don't matter. People see the commitment and feel the songs. What you want to accomplish is plugging the people into the universal language of music. It defies limitation by race, culture, or creed. If you can get people to go beyond these ideas—the constructs within their own minds—they're ready to go somewhere. Somewhere may not be that far, but you're going in some direction. Even if you're just traveling to the next song, you're doing something.

Gender, age, nationality, race—you can trump all those things and create a sense of unity among people with music because all music has pieces of other music in it. You can bring people into feeling like we are one unit with the music. Language can't do that; few things can accomplish that. Music is so powerful for movements, and in movements that sense of unity has to be there. There is a song that talks about this. It says, "When the people are united, the victory is coming near."

Our performances were sometimes loud, in people's faces. Sometimes they were soft and introspective, like "Walk that Lonesome Highway" or "Do What the Spirit Says Do." I would start with those two a lot, as they were quieter. Because I could sing it, I would change it around—saying "clap if the spirit says clap," to get people engaged.

I got people to talk to each other. That's a little tricky. It can be distracting, but if you know what you're doing, you can bring people back, and they are more together than before. It's about creating community and connection among people with the universal language of music.

In March of 1966 the Chicago Freedom Movement held a major fund-raising event—the Freedom Festival—at the International Amphitheatre in Chicago. Dr. King gave a compelling speech, and performances by Harry Belafonte, Mahalia Jackson, and comedian Dick Gregory provided entertainment for the 12,000 people who attended.[10]

On July 10, 1966, more than 30,000 people gathered in the sweltering Chicago heat at Soldier Field to rally in support of an "open city" and especially open housing. The issue of black folks being forced to live in ghettos had come to a head. After Dr. King's speech, which detailed a twenty-four-point list of demands to landlords and government officials, he and other SCLC leaders led a march through the South Loop that ended with King posting the movement's demands on the door of City Hall.[11]

Herb Kent, legendary disc jockey at radio station WVON, was the master of ceremonies at that rally, and he started by introducing the opening musical acts. King's campaign drew an outpouring of support from the musical community, as the civil rights movement was inspiring popular artists of all genres who wanted to participate. Notable performers at the rally were Mahalia Jackson; Mavis Staples; Peter, Paul, and Mary; Dick Gregory; Oscar Brown Jr.; and the Andrew McPherson Sextet. The music was a mix of what these artists were doing in their careers at the time and included freedom songs such as "We Shall Overcome," as well as folk protest music and jazz. The performances excited and engaged the large audience, who later listened ardently to King's demands for an "open city." Public events like the rally at Soldier Field became possible because the foundation had been built, because of community action. Boots on the ground connecting with everyday people was the starting place.

Popular Music and the Movement

King's leadership, as well as that of other civil rights leaders and community activists of the 1960s, gave minorities a powerful voice in the public sphere. This voice crossed over into white culture and inspired folk music artists as well. Musicians such as Bob Dylan, Judy Collins, Joan Baez, Pete Seeger, Phil Ochs, Country Joe and the Fish, and Peter, Paul, and Mary were writing music that came to be called "protest music," referencing racial injustice and government oppression both directly and through story.

The folk artists of the 1960s were not, however, the first people to voice a desire for freedom and equality through music. Oppressed people and cultures have always used music as a way to fight for and celebrate freedom. Old spirituals, sung a cappella with clapping and foot stamping, were musical sustenance in times of slavery; they expressed the pain. These songs also held clues for those preparing to escape: "Follow the Drinking Gourd" meant to watch for the North Star as the way to freedom, and "Steal Away to Jesus" meant the coast was clear and it was time to go.

These songs were relevant and meaningful to plantation workers. Work songs, called "field hollers," used call-and-response singing, which helped synchronize tasks and ease the burden of difficult labor. Slaves made recreational music on string instruments such as the banjo, violin, and guitar. The intricacy and power of this music stirred the interest of white slave owners, who often had their workers perform for them privately and at parties. Black plantation music in all its forms was the origin of what later evolved into jazz and blues; it also influenced various folk artists and traditions. Traces of African music can be found in nearly every musical tradition and style since then.

By the early 1960s, picket lines, rallies, and churches were filled with gospel, folk, and R&B music, and commercially successful pop artists were publicly supporting King and his campaign. Well-known musicians like Harry Belafonte and Curtis Mayfield and the Impressions were writing hit songs inspired by the movement that became movement anthems. "People Get Ready" was Curtis Mayfield and the Impressions' first major hit. Mayfield, a Chicago native, wrote that song, which became the sound track to the movement; its lyrics lifted people up with the promise of change. Another Motown soul artist named Sam Cooke emerged with "A Change Is Gonna Come," a song lyrically encrypted with the tale of injustice, suffering, and triumph of the movement. This was an incredible time in popular music because there was so much happening in the world, and artists were responding to it.

The Poor People's Campaign and Singing Tours

I didn't stay in Chicago after Bevel left at the end of 1966. Eric Kindberg and I got a letter of reference from Dr. King to Vincent Hallanan, a lawyer for the longshoremen's union in San Francisco. We moved west, became longshoremen, and joined the union. At that point, it was all older guys; we were the little darlings.

While we were in San Francisco, I got a call from SCLC asking if I would go to New York City and work for the Poor People's Campaign. "You have Chicago experience, so would you go to New York?" they asked. I agreed to go. Frederick Douglass Kirkpatrick from Louisiana agreed to go too. We had played music together during the Selma campaign. When we got to New York, we played music and ended up using the music as an organizing tool all over New York City; it worked, too!

The Poor People's Campaign was so important, but it didn't get completed. Dr. King wanted to connect the poor people we brought to Washington with Wall Street and show civil rights supporters how the whole system worked. It fizzled before we got to Wall Street. After King was killed, the Poor People's Campaign almost fell apart. People were in shock and grief, and it was a miracle the campaign happened at all.

After the Poor People's Campaign, and up until 1972, I would go to demonstrations of all different kinds; oftentimes I just read about things happening in the paper, and I showed up with my guitar and played. When I talk about "playing," I'm not talking about concerts, but singing and playing music at rallies, on picket lines, that type of thing. I was also playing songs in coffee shops on my own or anywhere I could get an audience. We worked a lot doing advance work for Pete Seeger, who was taking the *Clearwater*, his 100-foot sailboat, up and down the Hudson River, doing concerts and talking about cleaning up the Hudson.

Later I had a booking agent and a band, and we traveled all over the East Coast. I was alone sometimes with my instrument, but my booking agent would set things up for my band as well. For a short while, Wende Smith—who had been on staff with us in Chicago—and I were singing in Herbie Mann's band. We traveled by bus, and when we were at colleges, I would stay in the bus, and the other guys would get put up in the dorms. It was great working for the schools because they would take care of us; we got paid on time, we got put up. I was really living a musician's life then. The role of my music at this time—a mix of movement and human rights—was to engage people, to get them to stop and listen, to ponder, to feel something. We sang pop, country, rock, R&B.[12]

Later on, there was a lot going on about rights for disabled people—access to buildings, access to transportation, and workers' rights for the disabled. Everyone wanted rights, and we felt that our support of universal human rights was as important as the fight for black civil rights.

Most of the leaders in the movement, including Dr. King, were people who had the talent and resources to be doing something else; they chose to play a part in the movement, and they sacrificed. Dr. King could have been a wealthy preacher like his father, but he chose the movement. The antiwar and civil rights movements are dots that got connected by Dr. King and the people behind him. We all learned how to connect the dots that were intelligently analyzed by really smart people; it's all economic, when you break it down. It's not just about being put in the back of the bus but also about having the money to do what you want to do: that's what freedom is. Class and racial oppression is just the means of keeping everyone from having the financial freedom to do what they want. Everyone deserves access to the same resources.

All people have a right to voice what they feel are their obstacles to happiness. I may not know what it's like to be disabled. Whites wouldn't understand what it's like for black people before we had rights. Men don't know what it's like to be a woman. In the 1960s these movements happened one after the other, and they were all inspired by the civil rights movement. You can go down the line and see that many of the same people are involved in many human rights causes. Activists put themselves in the shoes of oppressed people and fight for many different things; a victory for one is a victory for all.

Since 1972, I've lived out in the country on a ranch in California, near the mountains. For a while I took up being a cowboy and sang a lot of western songs. I still sing sometimes for labor groups and community groups and groups that want to hear the music from the civil rights movement days. If I can be of value, relevant, now, providing comfort or inspiration, that's good. But I really don't want to be in somebody's way. We have to do what unites the young people. The combination of seasoned wisdom and young people is where most social change starts. You need the young energy, that fearlessness, the belief that you can make a difference and you can make it today. Back then, we had that energy. Now, we have to make it about the current generation. But when we tell the stories of the successes, that's useful. It's important to show evidence of past success in order to inspire future generations.

Looking back at all the music from that time in Chicago, I can say I would rather be out on the picket lines singing "Rent Strike Blues" to people who want better living conditions than be a big-name performer who comes in for one performance to back the cause. Playing for them gave me spiritual strength.

Notes

This chapter is based on interviews with Jimmy Collier conducted by Pam Smith and Mary Lou Finley in Oakhurst and Fresno, California, in March 2011. Allegra Malone assisted with the writing process.

Lyrics from the following songs are used with permission:

"Lead Poison on the Wall," by Jimmy Collier. Copyright by Jimmy Collier, 1966 and 1990. Used with permission.

"Rent Strike Blues," by Jimmy Collier. Copyright by Jimmy Collier, 1966 and 1990. Used with permission.

"Never Too Much Love," by Curtis Mayfield. Copyright by Warner-Tamerlane Publishing Group, 1964. Copyright assigned to Alfred Music Publishing. Used with permission.

1. See Christopher Reed's chapter 3 for a brief discussion of the history of Calumet Park and Rainbow Beach.

2. For a memoir on the civil rights movement in Demopolis, including stories about Jimmy Collier, see Dick J. Reavis, *If White Kids Die: Memories of a Civil Rights Movement Volunteer* (Denton: University of North Texas Press, 2001).

3. SCLC's Summer Community Organization and Political Education (SCOPE) project had approximately 800 fieldworkers that summer, registering voters in six southern states in counties with large African American populations. Several who went to Chicago worked in Alabama: staff member Dot Wright (Dorothy Tillman) in Choctaw; staff member Suzi Hill in Gadsden in Etowah County; and summer volunteer Lynn Adler in Hale County, one of those who stayed on after the end of the summer. See Willie Seigel Leventhal, *The SCOPE of Freedom: The Leadership of Hosea Williams with Dr. King's Summer '65 Student Volunteers* (Montgomery, AL: Challenge Press, 2005).

4. See chapter 14 by Pam Smith for a discussion of the work with gangs.

5. Guy Carawan and Candie Carawan, *We Shall Overcome: Songs of the Southern Freedom Movement* (New York: Oak Publications, 1963). This book was later incorporated into Guy Carawan and Candie Carawan, *Sing for Freedom: The Story of the Civil Rights Movement through Its Songs* (Montgomery, AL: New South Books, 2007).

6. "Never Too Much Love," in Carawan and Carawan, *Sing for Freedom,* 238:

Too much love, too much love
Never in this world will there be too much love.
Too much love, too much love
Never in this world will there be too much love.
I like to drink whiskey . . .
I don't know but I think I'm right
Folks in heaven both black and white
I don't know but I've been told,
Folks in heaven won't tell me where to go.
Too much hate, too much hate
Always in this world there is too much hate,
Too much war, too much war,
Always in this world there is too much war.

7. See chapter 13 by Sherrilynn Bevel on the campaign against childhood lead poisoning.

8. Also available in Carawan and Carawan, *Sing for Freedom,* 230–31, and on the album *Singing for Freedom,* Jimmy Collier with Diana Smith (Bratt) and James Orange (Chicago: Parish Records, 1966). The album was produced by the West Side Christian Parish, Chicago.

9. Also available in Carawan and Carawan, *Sing for Freedom,* 232–33. See also Jimmy Collier, "Rent Strike Blues," on *We Won't Move: Songs of the Tenants' Movement* (Smithsonian Folkways Recordings, 2007).

10. James R. Ralph Jr., *Northern Protest: Martin Luther King, Jr., Chicago, and the Civil Rights Movement* (Cambridge, MA: Harvard University Press, 1993), 75.

11. Estimates of the number of people at the Soldier Field rally vary; some claim as many as 50,000 attended.

12. Jimmy Collier and Wende Smith can be seen in the documentary film *Black Roots* (1970), produced by Lionel Rogosin and recently remastered and re-released. Collier's "The Fires of Napalm," an antiwar song, has been translated into other languages and used around the world.

16

Music and the Movement II

Music for an Urban Movement

Gene Barge with Allegra Malone

In the 1960s popular music was making its own statement; all the black artists of the time were influenced by the fight for equal rights. When Dr. King came to Chicago, all the black musicians were involved in or contributing to the movement through their music and beyond. While Dr. King didn't believe in violence, he did believe in civil disobedience and protest. As far as I can tell, people all over the world have learned to put their issues and emotions into songs. Our music was part of the long history of protest music. The music of the freedom movement inspired people to get out in the streets and get ready to change the world.

I arrived in Chicago in June 1964, right before Dr. King spoke at a huge rally at Soldier Field.[1] I went to work for Chess Records. I came to Chicago from Norfolk, Virginia, where I had been playing with a lot of Norfolk musicians. I had a big success there: I did a song called "A Night with Daddy G," and this song became number one on the charts. It was after that song that I became known as Daddy G. I'm a saxophone player, arranger, writer, and producer. At Chess Records in Chicago I produced a lot of different people.

Operation Breadbasket and the Breadbasket Band

When Dr. King first got to Chicago, he declared it one of the most racist cities in the United States, and it truly was. But Chicago was a hoppin' town—it was hot to trot in Chicago! There was a lot going on here.

There was turmoil, but it was rich with creativity, and music was everywhere. Jazz and blues were big in Chicago. In those days, you would see musicians standing out on the street corner playing their instruments and singing. Maxwell Street was filled with street musicians who would just play the blues all day and night, and sometimes the crowds would gather around them.[2]

After World War II black people were coming up from the South looking for jobs and more opportunity. Unfortunately, when they got here, they didn't find much, though it was still better than the South. Discrimination in Chicago was rampant, and the job market was controlled by the Chicago Democratic machine and white unions. It was difficult to find work and decent housing, and that was part of what King was here to work on. Operation Breadbasket got started because Dr. King wanted an economic arm to the movement. He felt that black people were at the bottom. He'd say, "We don't have small businesses, we don't have jobs in corporations. We need to start from the bottom." Dr. King appointed Jesse Jackson as the director of Breadbasket in Chicago.

The group of musicians I was working with had a lot of meetings with Jesse Jackson, helping him to get Breadbasket started. Some people didn't want to follow him at first because he was so young, just twenty-four years old and a student at the seminary. Early on, we met at soul-food restaurants on the South Side; I especially remember Helen Maybell's Soul Queen and Gladys's. We kept having to move the meetings to bigger and bigger spaces, from Forty-Seventh and South Parkway to Forty-Fifth and King Drive to a theater on Seventy-Ninth Street.

There were black businesses in Chicago making their own quality goods, but getting those goods into stores, finding retail space to rent, and being approved for business loans from banks were among the obstacles that kept the playing field tilted against us. We needed black entrepreneurs, so Operation Breadbasket was formed to focus on building the economy. Operation Breadbasket's objective was also to get black people jobs besides just janitorial positions and such, so we organized massive protests and boycotts of major brand-name products like milk or soda. We insisted that the manufacturers and retail stores start to hire blacks for decent-paying jobs and also put some of the products of black businesses on their shelves. So many blacks had been regularly purchasing those brand-name products we were boycotting that the companies took a real financial hit from the boycotts. It worked.

The Breadbasket Saturday morning meetings had music from the earliest days; Ben Branch was the first director of the Breadbasket Band; I assisted him, and we started it together. We were joined by some of Chicago's more notable musicians, including drummer Charles Walton, trumpet player Burgess Gardener, trombonist John Watson, and bass player Jimmy Willis. A short time later guitarist Wayne Bennett joined the Breadbasket Band. When the band started it had seven pieces: guitar, bass, drums, keyboard, and two or three horns. I was very busy at Chess Records, so I wasn't there very often for the programs at first, but I did play with the band sometimes and continued to assist with the organizing. Later, I became the director of the band, but that was after Dr. King had been killed.[3]

We played every week for the Breadbasket Saturday morning program, broadcast on radio station WVON. The Saturday morning program was a combination of inspiration, prayer, political rally, and church. There would be guest speakers, sermons, and folks reporting on different things going on in the community. It was a great way to reach people who couldn't make it to meetings. WVON was the primary black radio station, and it kept everybody informed as to what boycotts, rallies, and events were coming up and inspired listeners to participate.

At first, all the officials in Breadbasket were ordained ministers, so they were attuned to gospel music. We were jazz musicians, so we played a lot of music that was a fusion of gospel and jazz. There really was this fusion of styles in music in general at that time, and the same thing happened in our band.

A lot of the music comes from the black church: jazz, music from New Orleans, was always drawn from gospel music and from spirituals like "Nobody Knows the Trouble I've Seen." And the great black college choirs were an influence; for instance, choir director Noel Rider wrote a lot of a cappella music for the college choirs, and it was recorded on Black Side. We were all raised on this. So the music we did was a blend of Deep South music influenced by the church and jazz. We worked together to come up with a relevant repertoire: in fact, we played everything— jazz, R&B, old spirituals, blues, and gospel. Jesse Jackson really liked the music; he liked it a lot.

We had many special songs, like "I Wish I Knew," a jazz freedom song Billy Taylor wrote, "Breaking Bread Together," and, of course, "We Shall Overcome" and other older civil rights movement songs. We played a mix of old and new in our own style, and we really drew people in.

Leonard Chess of Chess Records helped Jesse Jackson get his spot on WVON at 10:00 a.m. on Saturday mornings; at that point, Chess Records owned radio station WVON. In fact, Chess Records had a lot to do with Jesse Jackson's work. We would raise money through remote broadcasts to support Breadbasket and later PUSH, and we gave him time on the air.

Some black people were afraid to deal with Dr. King when he came to Chicago and Breadbasket was formed. The Reverend Clay Evans deserves a lot of credit because he stepped up to the leadership of Breadbasket; a lot of black people were down on Dr. King. Even many of the black ministers would not support him. Clay Evans was also a great singer, and when I was writing, producing, and arranging for Chess and later Stax Records, I was his producer, and I worked with him on all his music.

Dr. King left Chicago after a tough time; when he was marching he got hit by a rock. I think he only came back to Chicago a few times after that.

Memphis, 1968

The Breadbasket Band went to Memphis with Jesse Jackson when he traveled there to support Dr. King and the garbage workers' strike. I didn't go, though, as I was playing in Chicago that evening. The band was scheduled to play at the rally in support of the strikers on the evening of April 4, 1968. Just before dinnertime Ben Branch and Jesse Jackson were in the courtyard at the Lorraine Motel, and Dr. King came out on the motel balcony. They were talking back and forth. We all knew that "Precious Lord, Take My Hand" was one of Dr. King's favorite songs. Dr. King called down to Ben Branch, "Will you all play my song for me tonight? And play it real pretty." That was his last request.[4]

Within a few weeks of his death, we did a tribute album for him called *The Last Request*, with Ben Branch and the Breadbasket Orchestra and

Choir. They played "Precious Lord, Take My Hand," and the Reverend Clay Evans sang with them.

Chicago: Breadbasket Continues

The work continued.

In 1969, as part of entrepreneurial development efforts through Breadbasket, we began having what were called Black Expos. One of the expos that really stayed in my mind was held at the International Amphitheatre at Forty-Second and Halsted. Black merchants were able to display all their goods, and people came from all around to buy things and support black businesses. Expos were aimed at both consumers and retailers. The hope was that merchants would come, see the products, and start carrying black-made merchandise in their stores. We got great support from some major musicians. They all came to play a concert when the expo opened, and it provided quite a draw. We had Quincy Jones, the Jackson Five, Isaac Hayes, Roberta Flack, Aretha Franklin, and Boz Skaggs, and of course, the Breadbasket Band played.

Those expos were a big success. They really brought awareness, and they got black products on the shelves of some stores for the very first time. Hair products and cosmetics, such as Ultra Sheen and Soft Sheen hair care products, were huge for black business; those were some of the first products that changed things. Local businesses began to see things in terms of green rather than just black and white.

Unlike in the South, there wasn't much stopping us from voting in Chicago. At all those events the musicians and the leaders were trying to get black people fired up to get out there and use our votes. When we started to get black politicians into office, it made a huge difference. That took things to another level and helped with the economic side of things; loans, jobs, and more started to become more accessible to blacks. And all the work of the movement, of Operation Breadbasket, was showing up everywhere. It was huge when Cirilio McSween became the first African American to have a McDonald's in Chicago; McSween also served as the treasurer for SCLC. Now there are black merchants and companies and employees everywhere.[5]

There were issues with the leadership in Operation Breadbasket in

1971, and the Reverend Jesse Jackson's organization in Chicago became independent and changed its name to PUSH—People United to Serve Humanity (now the Rainbow PUSH Coalition). I used my experience in the music industry to pull together some incredible musical support for PUSH. We still had the radio show, and we still did events, but it was different without Dr. King.

Popular Music and the Spirit of the Movement

At Chess Records and later Stax Records, I worked with many gospel singers. Every artist I worked with was creatively influenced by what was going on here with the Chicago Freedom Movement. I worked with Sam Cooke's old group, the Soul Stirrers, and with Inez Andrews. I wrote a song called "I Don't Know What This World Is Coming To," which was recorded by the Violinaires from Detroit, and it became a hit song in those days. There were a lot of mainstream R&B hits that echoed the possibilities of the movement. Around that same time, Curtis Mayfield and the Impressions had cut "People Get Ready," which became the movement's soundtrack. Mayfield, a Chicago native, wrote the song, which had uplifting lyrics that promised change. Sam Cooke soon emerged with "A Change Is Gonna Come," a song about the roots of injustice and the hope for a better life; it was a song clearly inspired by his gospel roots. A lot of the jazz musicians wrote protest songs befitting the era we were in, many songs protesting the infringement of freedoms and offering hope. Chicagoan Eddie Harris's "Freedom Jazz Dance" was a notable one.

In the early 1970s, when the Reverend Marvin Yancey was the PUSH choir director, I produced another album with the PUSH choir for Gospel Truth, the Stax religious label. It was a good album.

On a different musical front, legendary jazz saxophone player John Coltrane composed the riveting ballad "Alabama," inspired by the bombing and murder of four girls at the Sixteenth Street Baptist Church in Birmingham, Alabama. On Sunday, September 15, 1963, as an act of racially motivated terrorism, the black church was firebombed, resulting in the death of four little girls. Coltrane composed the piece in the cadence of Dr. King's style of speaking, using the sound of his instrument to express the highs, lows, intonation, and power of King's words. So King's freedom campaign was inspiring musicians in all different capacities, from all different traditions. Also inspired to speak out against those acts of racist terrorism in 1964, singer-songwriter Nina Simone recorded the powerful "Mississippi Goddamn."

Of course, there was the daughter of a Detroit Baptist preacher, the Reverend C. L. Franklin, who was a friend of Dr. King's and a leader in the movement. By the early 1960s a young Aretha Franklin had already made a name for herself as a gospel singer, eventually crossing over to lend her powerful voice to blues and soul music. Her 1971 recording of Simon and Garfunkel's "Bridge over Troubled Water" became another solid contribution to the popular music of the freedom movement.

There were always musicians with Dr. King, participating in the marches, rallies, and gatherings—well-known black musicians, but also white folk musicians like Bob Dylan, Pete Seeger, and Joan Baez who traveled with him. They were great because they brought greater exposure to King's message, and they connected civil rights to other social justice and labor movements for their white audiences. Many in those audiences were moved to participate in and support the movement. The music was always a bridge, and even after Dr. King was killed, the music of protest still propelled the movement.

Music is an important instrument of soothing people's souls and also of uniting people who wouldn't necessarily be ready to work together otherwise. And music is spiritual—there's no overhead, there's no cost when someone stands and sings a song out on a street corner or at a rally. Nobody loses anything; they only gain. Music can be warm and loving, and that kind of music doesn't offend people; people listen, and it reaches them. Music has been used in every social justice movement in history, all over the world. When there are political rallies and people know that a big-name artist like a Smokey Robinson, an Aretha Franklin, or a Bob Dylan will be there, they come. Sometimes they mainly come to hear the music, but they always listen to the people who speak after the music is played. For a movement, you can get your message across much more successfully to an audience who has already been engaged by the power of the music. There were always musicians with Dr. King and the other leaders of the movement because the music moved people. It's a special way to shine a light on an issue or a feeling and open people up to the possibilities, like freedom, justice, and progress. And it always will.

Notes

This chapter is based on interviews with Gene Barge conducted by Allegra Malone in Chicago in May 2013.

1. The 1964 Soldier Field rally was organized by Chicago civil rights organizations in support of the campaign for better schools. See Robert McKersie, *A Decisive Decade: An Insider's View of the Chicago Civil Rights Movement during the 1960s* (Carbondale: Southern Illinois University Press, 2013), 69. See also chapter 1 on the schools campaign, described as a prelude to the Chicago Freedom Movement.

2. Paul Street, *Still Separate and Unequal: Race, Place, Policy and the State of Black Chicago* (Chicago: Chicago Urban League, 2005); Carolyn Eastwood, *Near West Side Stories: Struggles for Community in Chicago's Maxwell Street Neighborhood* (Chicago: Lake Claremont Press, 2002), 203. See also Ron Grossman, "Chicago's Love Affair with Maxwell Street," *Chicago Tribune,* August 30, 2014. Maxwell Street was the heart of a lively old immigrant community on Chicago's Near West Side. The Sunday Maxwell Street market had been Chicago's official open-air market since the early twentieth century and was a frequent gathering place for musicians.

3. Charles Walton was a jazz drummer and music educator; he taught at Malcolm X College in Chicago from 1970 until his retirement in 1989. In the early 1990s he authored *Bronzeville Conversations,* oral histories of the jazz and blues scene in Chicago. Burgess Gardener is a well-known jazz musician and composer who played with Count Basie and Ray Charles, among many others. Currently he plays with the Burgess Gardener Orchestra in Chicago. John Watson was a music teacher and well-known jazz trombonist who played with Count Basie and later became an actor in Chicago. Wayne Bennett, a blues and jazz guitarist, was especially well known in Chicago for his work with Bobby "Blue" Bland. He later played with the house orchestra at the Apollo Theater in New York and the Regal Theater in Chicago.

4. See Michael Eric Dyson, *April 4, 1968: Martin Luther King, Jr.'s Death and How It Changed America* (New York: Basic Civitas Books, 2008), 45.

5. See also chapter 12 on the rise of independent black politicians in Chicago.

17

Women in the Movement I

The Women of SCLC-WSCP Take Action

Molly Martindale

My first job after graduating from college was as a subsistence worker at a West Side Christian Parish (WSCP) storefront church on Roosevelt Road in Chicago. I had decided to "take care of home first" by volunteering here in the United States instead of going overseas to teach English in a program sponsored by my college. From September 1964 to September 1965 I helped with the youth group, ran a small tutoring program, sang in the choir, made home visits with the pastor, and generally did whatever was needed in the church. Then in the summer of 1965 the West Side Christian Parish hired the Reverend James Bevel, one of Dr. King's top organizers, to be its program director and to develop a nonviolent civil rights movement in the WSCP area. From then on, my job became working with that civil rights movement.

The parish's hiring of Bevel was an important consideration in Dr. King's decision to choose Chicago as SCLC's focus in the North and to make the West Side its local base. SCLC field staff who had been working in the South were sent to Chicago in September 1965, and three WSCP staff members joined them; I was one of them. We were a group of about thirty, mostly in our twenties and a few even younger—women and men, black, white, and Latino.

It was taken for granted that men and women on the field staff would do similar organizing work in the community, as they had in the South, particularly during SCLC's Summer Community Organization and Political Education (SCOPE) project in 1965, in which many of those who joined the Chicago staff had participated. However, men were in the leadership roles, and women did traditional office tasks such as running the switchboard and the mimeograph machine, taking minutes at meetings, and greeting visitors. Other women had specialized responsibilities. For example, Claudia King served as press secretary, Ann Gillie and Bennie (pronounced B'*nay*) Luchion served as the public relations committee, and Lynn Adler worked with Luis Andrades on the organizing team in the Latino community, as both spoke Spanish. One historian, commenting on gender roles in the southern civil rights movement, noted that, "in comparison to the division of roles within the rest of American society, the civil rights movement was strikingly egalitarian." The same could be said for the West Side field staff doing the organizing.[1]

Two events that occurred during my time with the Chicago Freedom Movement have always seemed especially significant to me, although neither of them made headlines. One was important mostly to those who were directly involved, and the other was important on a national level. Both events were instigated by the black women on the staff. The first was a series of meetings the SCLC-WSCP staff women held in the spring of 1966 to address disrespect and sexism (although it wasn't yet called that); the second was the "making" of the June 1966 cover of *Ebony*, the leading black-published magazine at the time.[2]

The SCLC-WSCP Women's Meetings

For the field staff, the fall and winter of 1965–1966 was a time of great learning, confusion, and sorting out of roles and overall direction. We spent the fall in meeting after meeting, learning as much as possible from Bevel about the theory and practice of nonviolence and from black Chicagoans about issues they faced, particularly the widespread slum conditions. Many other groups already active in the black community—particularly on the West Side, but some from the North Side as well—participated in these meetings. As time went on, we had more and more interactions with people in other organizations and with the numerous volunteers, mostly women, who came to help.

Over the winter, Bevel and the field staff decided to organize landlord-specific tenant unions and to develop a grassroots group, the Union to End Slums, among the residents of East Garfield Park, a process that we expected to take several years. But Dr. King wanted a major direct action campaign by the summer of 1966, and there was indecision about whether to focus on the long-term development of tenant unions or the direct action campaign. This dilemma was very wearing on the field staff.[3]

In addition to the conflicts and uncertainties over our focus, our personal and interpersonal lives and our interactions with numerous volunteers and fellow organizers were a source of anxiety. There were shifting sexual liaisons and romances, each with its own complexities, including racial issues.[4] Interracial relationships were uncommon in the mid-1960s, and as staffers became connected to one another in various ways and new relationships developed, tensions arose. For example, according to one staff member, black women "feel hostile toward both Negro men and white women because of the myth surrounding white women and because of the feeling Negro men may have that they're really into something if they go with a white woman."[5]

In early April 1966 the black women on the staff decided they needed to do something about the disrespect they felt from other staff members—both black men and white women—and, to some degree, among themselves. Their concerns were about racial disrespect from the white women and gender disrespect from the black men. They called a meeting with the black men to tell them how they felt. The details of that meeting have been forgotten, but it is clear that the women were unsatisfied with the results because they decided to call a meeting of all women on staff, both black and white, to discuss these issues; no men were allowed. This was a radical step in those days, for two reasons. First, though the late nineenth- and early twentieth-century women's movement raised many women's issues, there was very little public—or even private—discussion of the pervasiveness of sexism in the mid-1960s. It was generally assumed that men would be in charge in the workplace and in the public arena and would be "head of household" at home.[6] Second, it was highly unusual for black and white women to gather together to discuss gender issues. For black women—as well as for many white women in the movement—the devastating effects of societal racism were far more important.

We met one evening in April in an empty apartment on the West Side. Approximately fourteen women were there—half were black and half were white. We sat on the floor around the walls of the room, and one by one, each woman told the history of her own first interracial encounter. For example, one of the white women recounted that the first black person she met was a maid in her mother's house, while another recalled the African Americans who came to her church youth group to discuss discrimination in the late 1950s. One of the black women said she used to beat up little white kids on the way home from school. Racial disrespect became the theme of the meeting. This process was very serious and sometimes wrenching, and it ended up taking the whole evening. We realized we hadn't had time to discuss the recent staff issues that had led to the meeting in the first place, so we decided to spend a weekend at Pleasant Valley Farm, a Chicago City Missionary Society summer camp north of Chicago where we had previously gone on staff retreats.[7]

While the women were attending that first meeting in the city, some of the male staffers were phoning the apartment to find out what was going on; they thought we might be trading information about them. Needless to say, it made the men even more uncomfortable when we decided to go away overnight without them. If women getting together to discuss important issues was simply not done at the time, then spending a whole weekend together—without men—was even more shocking. (Of course, all-male meetings happened all the time.)

At Pleasant Valley Farm, Patti Miller, a white staff member, read some passages from Betty Friedan's *The Feminine Mystique*. This helped us think not only about our second-class roles as women in the overall society but also about our role in a movement dedicated to obtaining civil rights for everyone. One of the passages suggested that women did not listen to other women in meetings, and we realized this was true: we didn't listen to each other, just to the "important" men. Further, we did not have confidence that these "important" men would listen to our ideas. For example, Ann Gillie, who was working on public relations with her male counterpart, Bennie Luchion, said that no matter which of them came up with an idea, Bennie always presented the idea at staff meetings because they thought that Bevel—like most men—would not pay attention to a woman's idea.[8]

Another important issue raised at Pleasant Valley Farm was the tension surrounding a white woman who had recently joined the staff. She was dating a black man who was also dating a black woman on the staff at the same time. The white woman explained that when she was new to the staff, this man was the only person who really talked to her, and he was the only one who offered to help her move. Also, she didn't know he was dating the other woman. Although this wasn't the only instance of inter-racial dating, the discussion defused the tension around that particular situation, and we continued to discuss the mechanisms of racial and gender discrimination within the staff. By the time the weekend ended, all the women had a shared understanding of the issues, and we were ready to present what we had learned to the men.

During the weekend, we made notes about what we wanted to say, and Mary Lou Finley, Bevel's secretary, put together a two-page draft statement titled "Some Observations by the Women of the SCLC-WSCP Staff." All the women reviewed it together before coming up with the final version to share with the men. In retrospect, this statement shows how naïve we were in terms of identifying the manifestations of sexism. For example, we said, "The problem was not conflict between black and white—not personality clashes, but a real lack of respect for each other—and a lack of respect for people generally. It's hard to respect other people when you don't respect yourself—and that seemed to be the real problem. . . . We may be insecure about our ability to work, about our masculinity or femininity, or just about our worth as people."[9] We "victims" blamed ourselves for being treated as second-class human beings, focusing on our own insecurities rather than on the powerful sexism that permeated all our relationships. (Today, we might call this internalized oppression.)

We invited all the men on the staff to a meeting where we intended to present our statement and then have an open discussion. However, only a few men came, and only one of them seemed to understand what we were talking about. Looking back, we were foolish to think the men would be responsive; they too were recipients of the notion that men should be in charge, just as we were, but they were the beneficiaries of that scheme. There was no particular motivation for them to see things differently. Bevel accepted the logic of what we were saying, but afterward, we noticed that he didn't change his behavior.

Even though our newfound knowledge didn't have much effect on the men on the staff, the women had a new sense of sisterhood. Our commitment to civil rights had expanded to include an awareness of our shared position as women on that staff and in society as a whole. We had raised our consciousness together before it became a common practice among women, and the black women had taken us there.[10]

The SNCC Women's Position Paper

Until preparing to write this chapter, I was unaware that women in the Student Nonviolent Coordinating Committee (SNCC) had presented a somewhat similar statement at a retreat in Waveland, Mississippi, in the fall of 1964, a year and a half before our meetings in Chicago.[11] The SNCC statement was put together by a few white women just before the retreat, although they had been quietly documenting instances of sexism within their staff for a couple of months. Black women didn't participate in the statement's preparation. Lynne Olson notes in *Freedom's Daughters*, her history of women in the civil rights movement, "The handful of black women who agreed with the paper's main premise believed that it was neither the time nor the place to vent such internal grievances, with the movement's mission still unfulfilled and with SNCC coming under increased attack from outside."[12]

The statement, entitled "Position Paper: Women in the Movement," was much more socially and politically sophisticated than ours, perhaps because we had spent only one weekend contemplating sexism within our staff. The SNCC document was well thought out and included a descriptive list of eleven incidents. In it, the women pointed out the close analogy between the positions of blacks and women in society:

> The average SNCC field worker finds it difficult to discuss the woman problem [i.e., sexism] because of the assumptions of male superiority. Assumptions of male superiority are as widespread and deep-rooted and every much as crippling to the woman as the assumptions of white supremacy are to the Negro. Consider why it is in SNCC that women who are competent, qualified, and experienced are automatically assigned to "female" kinds of jobs such as typing, desk work, filing, library work, cooking and the assistant kind of administrative work but rarely the "executive" kind. . . . The woman in SNCC is often in the same position as

that token Negro hired in a corporation. The management thinks it has done its bit. Yet, every day the Negro bears an atmosphere, attitudes, and actions which are tinged with condescension and paternalism, the most telling of which are when he is not promoted as the equally or less skilled whites are.[13]

Although the language of our statement was more tentative and self-effacing that that of the SNCC women's statement, it is striking that neither group expected to be taken seriously, and both expressed concerns about the expected reception by the larger community. The SNCC women concluded their statement by saying: "Maybe the only thing that can come out of this paper is discussion—amidst the laughter—but still discussion . . . maybe sometime in the future the whole of the women in this movement will become so alert as to force the rest of the movement to stop the discrimination and start the slow process of changing values and ideas so that all of us gradually come to understand that this is no more a man's world than it is a white world."[14]

Our reticence was well founded, since most men on the SCLC-WSCP staff discounted our concerns. Generally, the SNCC women had a similar experience. Lynne Olson reports, "When the women's paper was read by SNCC staffers, many responded with jeering and mockery. . . . It was regarded as a bad joke, bringing up an issue that was felt to be trivial and beside the point at a time when the movement itself was floundering." Mary King, one of the writers of the statement, was also struck by the ridicule, but she later reported the exceptions: "Bob Moses and Charlie Cobb liked our paper and respected it."[15]

The SNCC statement is unique, in that it was the first public airing of issues related to sexism within the civil rights movement, albeit in the context of deep divisions between white and black women on staff. The SCLC-WSCP statement is unique, in that it and the meetings leading up to it were the result of black women and white women working together.

The "Natural"

A few months before the black women on the SCLC-WSCP staff took up the problem of sexism in the workplace, they had addressed another kind of issue involving *Ebony* magazine. Since its founding in 1945, *Ebony* had always been the purveyor of positive images of black life for the black community. Published in Chicago, it became a nationwide success. In the mid-1960s it was selling at least 850,000 copies a month and could be found in the homes of blacks at all levels of society. It was a large-format publication in which photographs and other images were as important as the articles that accompanied them. In an August 2005 issue of *Jet* magazine, *Ebony* was described as "a picture magazine . . . with dazzling photographs that highlighted Black achievements, role models, and positive lifestyles." Later in the same article, John H. Johnson, *Ebony*'s founding publisher, was quoted on the subject: "We believed then (in 1945)—and we believe now—that you have to change images before you can change acts and institutions."[16]

The February 1966 issue of *Ebony* featured what proved to be a controversial cover story entitled "Are Negro Girls Getting Prettier?" The photos on the cover, as well as those accompanying the article, all showed lighter-skinned black women with straight or straightened hair. The story produced a variety of responses. For example, "Letters to the Editor" in the April 1966 issue included some writers who were annoyed that the women shown were not geographically representative; others pointed out that Negro girls had "always been pretty," and some readers really liked the article. The rest agreed with the point of view expressed by the following letter writer—that the women pictured were too reflective of white culture:

> If you ever publish an article of this nature again, I think you should view the "sisters" through your own eyes and not through the eyes of a "Chuck" and his standards.
>
> The majority of us are dark brown with bold features. The girls on your cover do illustrate various types of beauty. You have, however, omitted several other beautiful types which are much more typical of our people.
>
> [The article] should be called "Are Negro Girls Getting Whiter?"[17]

The black women on the SCLC-WSCP staff were among those who reacted strongly to the article. They didn't like it—at all. They stormed across town to the offices of Johnson Publishing and demanded that all copies of the issue be removed from newsstands immediately. According to Diana Smith, publisher John H. Johnson told them: "That's not how it's done."[18]

Soon thereafter, Phyl Garland, then on *Ebony*'s editorial staff, was assigned to prepare an article on the "natural" hairstyle. Garland's article appeared in the June 1966 issue with a full-page cover photo of the same Diana Smith. (See this book's photo section.) The cover announced: "The Natural Look: New Mode for Negro Women." Accompanying the article were a few other photographs of SCLC-WSCP staff women, as well as photos of professional women in the Chicago area who wore "naturals."[19]

Even though the stated purpose of *Ebony* magazine was to present positive images of "Negro people" (in the language of the time), this was the first time in its history that an ordinary dark-skinned woman wearing a natural hairstyle had ever appeared on the cover. In the article, Garland wrote:

> Throughout the ages, American women of color have conspired to conceal the fact that their hair was not like any other. This key element in the black female's mystique was, until recently, challenged only by a few bold bohemians. . . . For the girl in the street—the coed, the career woman, the housewife, the matron and even the maid who had been born with "bad" or kinky hair, the straightening comb and chemical process seemingly offered the only true paths to social salvation. . . . Not so today, for an increasing number of Negro women are turning their backs on traditional concepts of style and beauty by wearing their hair in its naturally kinky state.[20]

Two of the SCLC-WSCP staff women were quoted in the article, discussing their reasons for protesting the February feature article. Suzi Hill said:

> We, as black women must realize that there is beauty in what we are, without having to make ourselves into something we aren't.

. . . [The natural] is practical. It rids us of those frustrations Negro women know so well, the fears that begin when you're little. So many little Negro girls feel frustrated because their hair won't grow, or because they have what is called "bad" hair. They aren't made to realize that they have nothing to be ashamed of and go through a lifetime of hiding from themselves—avoiding swimming, being uneasy at dances when they start to perspire, because their hair will "go back," running from rain. By the time they're adults, this feeling has become so much a part of them they're even afraid to answer the telephone if their hair hasn't been done. Negro women are still slaves, in a way.[21]

Diana Smith observed:

Economics is a part of it, too. . . . It's a shame, but many poor Negro housewives take money that should be grocery money and use it to get their hair done. Now that wigs have come along, I see kids whose families are on welfare wearing them to high school—wigs and raggedy coats. Society has forced the standard of straight hair on them to the extent where they feel it's something for which they should sacrifice."[22]

The "Natural Look" article also elicited a variety of responses to the hairstyle itself, from high praise to mean-tempered criticism. Of the sixteen letters to the editor printed in the August 1966 issue, seven writers appreciated it, six were opposed to it, and three were noncommittal. Among those who wrote were Ossie Davis and his family: "Ruby [Dee] and my two daughters told me I ought to write to you and tell you how much we enjoy your magazine, especially the 'Natural Look' article by Phyl Garland in the June 1966 issue. Marvelous! Keep it up." Other letters stated: "For Negroes to judge themselves by another race's beauty standard is like trying to make a poodle look like a collie." Another noted: "The Natural look is not only appealing to the eye. It gives us a much-needed sense of identification." Among those affronted by the images accompanying the article were these comments: "[The article is] attempting to set the Negro back 100 years. . . . The young ladies who are practicing this look are just plain lazy nappy-haired females." And: "If they are so anxious to reflect their African heritage, why don't they wear rings through their noses? . . . It's presumptuous to subject the public to the sight of their dry, nappy looks."[23]

Both the February "Prettier" feature and the June "Natural Look" feature have been mentioned in subsequent books and articles addressing black women's hair. To me, a 2009 article represents the coming to fruition of the SCLC-WSCP staff women's desire to present the natural option as a kind of self-affirmation. In that article, a black woman looks back at her response to "The Natural Look," published just after she graduated from Berkeley High School in 1966: "There was a young black woman on the cover wearing what we today call a short Afro. The accompanying article addressed issues of African roots, racial pride and political nationalism. I could relate. I felt reborn in light of the article's suggestions. . . . With the copy of *Ebony* in hand, I went straight to our local beauty shop and asked the hair dresser to cut my hair just like the photo on the cover." Her mother was not happy about the change, and she got negative comments from many other people too, but she persisted: "With each negative comment I grew stronger in what I believed. My roots were on the inside of my head and not just on the outside. My Natural experience taught me to stand for what I believe. After many years my Mother came to accept and even adopt a Natural hairstyle for herself. At her request she was buried wearing a Natural."[24]

In a very different context, well-known British historian Arthur Marwick wrote about *Ebony* magazine and the two 1966 feature articles in his book *A History of Human Beauty*. About the "Natural" cover, he repeats a comment from one of his earlier publications: "The cover photograph was of the most beautiful black woman I personally have ever seen, an absolutely beautifully proportioned and intensely appealing face, surmounted by close-cropped fuzzy hair." He goes on to say: "I have no doubt that the majority of readers, female as well as male would agree with me if they could see this photograph. . . . For once this was no model or blues singer, but a 20-year-old Chicago civil rights worker."[25]

In their book *Hair Story*, Ayana D. Byrd and Lori L. Tharps write about the history and culture of black hair, from Africa in the 1400s to the present day. In discussing the mid-1960s, they write: "Between 1964 and 1966, colored people and Negroes 'became' Black people. And these Black people overwhelmingly chose to adopt a new, Black-identified visual aesthetic that not only incorporated an alternative to straight hair but actually celebrated it. . . . In the mid-sixties, Black hair underwent its biggest change since Africans arrived in America. The very perception of hair shifted from one of style to statement."[26]

The African American women of the Chicago Freedom Movement staff played a part in this dramatic shift toward the natural hairstyle and, with it, a new sense of black pride.

It was the black women of the SCLC-WSCP who came up with the creative idea to get all the women on staff together to address common issues, in spite of our deep historical and personal differences. Our meetings were a direct, organic outgrowth of the civil rights movement's ideals of equal treatment and creative, nonviolent problem solving. It is hard to imagine another setting in those days where such meetings could have occurred. The same women were responsible for the first feature article in a major black magazine on the natural hairstyle and the first cover photograph of an ordinary (i.e., noncelebrity) black woman in that nationally distributed magazine.[27]

Appendix: Some Observations by the Women of the SCLC-WSCP Staff, April 1966

Why the Women Met Together

We did not meet because we wanted to keep secrets. We did not meet to plot and plan and scheme on men. We met because we wanted to feel free to express ourselves.

We live in a society which defines woman's role as housekeeper, wife and mother . . . witness the Feminine Image presented in everything from *Family Circle* and *Glamour* magazines to TV. We learn early in our lives that men are to do the interesting and important things; our job is to wash dishes, have babies, and be a support to men. Even though we violently disagree with this interpretation of womanhood, it is so ingrained in us that we find ourselves influenced by it in spite of ourselves. We find that when we are in a group where men are present, we tend to shut up and let men do most of the talking. And so we met this time by ourselves—knowing that in the presence of men we wouldn't have had enough self-confidence to talk about our real feelings.

The Problem: What Is It?

We met because we felt hostility in the air; we met because we were feeling stifled and unable to live up to the potential we knew we had. We didn't know what was wrong . . . but we met to try and find out.

After long and intense discussions we saw that the things we had felt were not the real problem, but symptoms of something deeper. The problem was not conflict between black and white—not personality clashes, but a real lack of respect for other women—and a lack of respect for people generally. It's hard to respect other people when you don't respect yourself—and that seemed to be the real problem.

The Problem: Why Is It?

We all understand from our discussions about people in the slums that everybody needs to feel like they're important—like they're somebody. At the same time everybody fears that they are just another nobody—not capable of really doing anything worthwhile. We're all insecure—unsure of ourselves, afraid we'll fail, afraid to fail. We may be insecure about our ability to work, about our masculinity or femininity, or just about our worth as people.

What does this insecurity cause us to do? Two things: First, we find ourselves responding—to people and problems—in terms of our own needs; we do things which will build up our own egos, to assure ourselves that we're somebody, that we're important. In doing this, we can't really respond to the other person and his needs, and as a result we often disrespect people—trample over their feelings, and grind them into the dust—not because we want to, but because we're so busy worrying about ourselves that we are unable to think about others' feelings. We walk by a visitor in the office as if he didn't exist—or as if he didn't have any business being there. We squash someone's new idea because we want our own to be chosen instead . . . we begin to hurt and even destroy each other—not because we want to; we desperately want to respect people because we know how important that is. But we just keep messing things up.

Insecurity does something else; it immobilizes us, making it impossible for us to work. We're afraid to fail . . . we don't think we can do anything; we become stifled and can't create.

We're just unsure about ourselves.

The Problem: How Does It Manifest Itself?

1) One-upsmanship—trying to make ourselves look good at the expense of someone else.
2) Feeling stifled—we can't fulfill our potential . . . nobody encourages us to take that first step and get ourselves out on a limb.
3) Sex—a special problem for us.
   a) Because of the immense amount of time we spend working, and spend together, we don't have any real personal life—there's so little time, and somebody's business quickly becomes everybody's business. The personalness of close communication, intimacy which we all want and need is hard to find—sometimes sex becomes the only place where we can seem to find it, where we really share with one other person.
   b) The need to feel accepted, to have someone make you feel you're worthwhile, and that you're a part of things can also be a reason for sex (think about volunteers).
   c) How can we be sure we are respecting people, not using them?
   d) Women are whole people, not just playthings. . . . They want and need to be related to as whole people.

The Problem: What to Do?

1) Insecurity causes us to hurt and destroy each other . . . we need to work consciously toward helping other people develop confidence in themselves. (If I have no confidence in myself, but you believe in me, I can begin to develop self-confidence.)

2) Think about this: I find that if I dislike somebody, it's often because they are threatening to me; they highlight my own insecurities; they are good at something I want desperately to do but can't, etc. My reaction toward them (dislike) is not based on them, but on my own problem.

Conclusion

Most of us don't mean to disrespect people—we just get caught up in something which makes it very hard for us to respond to others as human beings with feelings and problems of their own.

Afterthoughts

Another problem: Our society conditions us to tune out when women begin to speak; this denies women the chance to really develop. We have to work consciously to overcome this—just like we have to work to consciously overcome racism.

Notes

I couldn't have written this chapter without shared memories and thoughtful feedback. Many thanks to Mary Lou Finley, Lynn Adler, Diana Smith, Claudia King, Patti Miller, Charles Love, Jimmy Collier, Laura Meserole, David Jehnsen, Linda Wagner, Sandy Wagner, Ron Goodenow, and Patricia Bruno.

Passages from Phyl Garland, "The Natural Look," *Ebony*, June 1966, 142–48, are reprinted here courtesy of Johnson Publishing Company, LLC. All rights reserved.

1. Willy Siegel Leventhal, *The SCOPE of Freedom: The Leadership of Hosea Williams with Dr. King's Summer '65 Student Volunteers* (Montgomery, AL: Challenge Publishing, 2005), 512–24. Four women on the Chicago field staff had worked in SCOPE's voter registration project: Claudia King in Americus, Georgia, and in Alabama: Lynn Adler in Hale County; Dorothy Wright (Tillman) in Choctaw County; and (Anna) Suzi Hill in Etowah County. On gender roles in the civil rights movement, see Sara Evans, *Personal Politics: The Roots of Women's Liberation in the Civil Rights Movement and the New Left* (New York: Vintage, 1980), 41.

2. The word "sexism" didn't exist yet; it first appeared in print in 1968. In some circles, these matters were referred to as "the woman problem." See Casey

Hayden, "Fields of Blue," in *Deep in Our Hearts: Nine White Women in the Freedom Movement*, ed. Constance Curry, Joan C. Browning, Dorothy Dawson Burlage, Penny Patch, Theresa Del Pozzo, Sue Thrasher, Elaine DeLott Baker, Emmie Schrader Adams, and Casey Hayden (Athens: University of Georgia Press, 2000), 365. See also http://finallyfeminism101.wordpress.com/2007/10/19/feminism-friday-the-origins-of-the-word-sexism/ (accessed December 1, 2014); cover photo, *Ebony*, June 1966.

3. See James R. Ralph Jr., "Mobilizing the City," in *Northern Protest: Martin Luther King, Jr., Chicago, and the Civil Rights Movement* (Cambridge, MA: Harvard University Press, 1993), 43–91.

4. The sexual revolution, commencing around 1960 with the introduction of birth control pills and the decriminalization and wider accessibility of birth control, brought some women more personal freedom. On the sexual revolution, see Kermit Mehlinger, "The Sexual Revolution," *Ebony*, August 1966, 57–62, and Gail Collins, *When Everything Changed: The Amazing Journey of American Women from 1960 to the Present* (New York: Little, Brown, 2009), 149–77.

5. Francis Ward, "Startling Report on White Female Workers in 'White Queen Complex' Angers," *Jet*, June 9, 1966, 21.

6. Collins, *When Everything Changed*, 5–8. In 1964, only twelve women served in the US House of Representatives, and Margaret Chase Smith was the lone woman in the US Senate. Help-wanted ads were still separated into "Help Wanted: Women" and "Help Wanted: Men," but things were beginning to change. President Kennedy's Commission on the Status of Women issued its report in 1963, after which Congress passed the Equal Pay Act. The Civil Rights Act of 1964 prohibited discrimination against women. Collins, *When Everything Changed*, 71–75, 81.

7. In the spring of 1966 the SCLC-WSCP staff women included Carolyn Black, Candy Dawson, Suzi Hill (Love), Wende (Smith) Kindberg, Claudia King, Diana Smith (Bratt), Dorothy Wright (Tillman), Lynn Adler, Sherie Land, Mary Lou Finley, Ann Gillie, Anita Hill, Molly Martindale, Patti Miller (Stone), Melody Heaps, and Kris Neumann.

8. Betty Friedan, *The Feminine Mystique* (New York: W. W. Norton, 1963). Patti Miller (personal communication, December 2011) reported that she focused on chapter 2 ("Happy Housewife") and chapter 13 ("The Forfeited Self"). See also Ellen Willis, "Radical Feminism and Feminist Radicalism," in *The Sixties without Apology*, ed. Sohnya Sayres, Anders Stephanson, Stanley Aronowitz, and Fredric Jameson (Minneapolis: University of Minnesota Press, 1984), 94, for the reaction of New Left men to women who raised issues of sexism: "We were laughed at, patronized, called frigid, emotionally-disturbed man-haters—and worst insult of all on the left—apolitical."

9. See the appendix to this chapter for the full statement.

10. Consciousness-raising groups were one of the main organizing tools of the women's liberation movement of the early 1970s. See Sara Evans, *Tidal Wave: How Women Changed America at Century's End* (New York: Free Press, 2003), 10–15, and Collins, *When Everything Changed*, 186–90.

11. "SNCC Position Paper (Women in the Movement)," in Evans, *Personal Politics*, 233–35.

12. Lynne Olson, *Freedom's Daughters: The Unsung Heroines of the Civil Rights Movement from 1830 to 1970* (New York: Simon & Schuster, 2001), 336. There has been some confusion about the authorship of the SNCC position paper; the byline originally read "Name Withheld by Request." A 2013–2014 online dialogue among SNCC women clarified that the statement was written by a group of white women that included Casey Hayden, Mary King, Elaine DeLott Baker, and Emmie Schrader Adams. (Theresa del Pozzo was also identified as a member of the group in Francesca Polletta's account, cited below.) It was the result of many discussions on women's issues in the Literacy House in Tougaloo, Mississippi, where they lived and gathered during 1964. See www.crmvet.org/disc/women2.html (accessed December 4, 2014), especially comments by Chude Pam Allen and Casey Hayden. Hayden also reported elsewhere that they were familiar with Simone de Beauvoir's *The Second Sex* (New York: Bantam, 1961) and Doris Lessing's 1962 feminist novel *The Golden Notebook* (New York: Harper Perennial Modern Classics, 2008). A year earlier, SNCC women had staged a protest at the SNCC office in Atlanta over the kinds of issues noted in the position paper. See Casey Hayden, "Fields of Blue," in Curry et al., *Deep in Our Hearts*, 364–66; Elaine DeLott Baker, "They Sent Us This White Girl," ibid., 271–72; Casey Hayden, "In the Attics of My Mind," in *Hands on the Freedom Plow: Personal Accounts by Women in SNCC*, ed. Faith S. Holsaert, Martha Prescod Norman Noonan, Judy Richardson, Betty Garman Robinson, Jean Smith Young, and Dorothy Zellner (Urbana: University of Illinois Press, 2010), 382; Mary King, *Freedom Song: A Personal Story of the 1960s Civil Rights Movement* (New York: William Morrow, 1988), 450–53; and Francesca Polletta, *Freedom Is an Endless Meeting: Democracy in American Social Movements* (Chicago: University of Chicago Press, 2002), 260 n. 11.

13. Evans, *Personal Politics*, 235. In 1977, a decade later, a group of black feminists issued the Combahee River Collective statement, defining the systems of oppression that affected them: "We are actively committed to struggling against racial, sexual, heterosexual, and class oppression, and see as our particular task the development of integrated analysis and practice based on the fact that the major systems of oppression are interlocking." The Combahee River Collective, "A Black Feminist Statement," in *All the Women Are White, All the Blacks Are Men, but Some of Us Are Brave: Black Women's Studies*, ed. Gloria T. Hull, Patricia Bell Scott, and Barbara Smith (Old Westbury, NY: Feminist Press, 1982), 13–22. For an earlier discussion of black women's issues, see Frances Beale, "Double

Jeopardy: To Be Black and Female," in *The Black Woman: An Anthology*, ed. Toni Cade (New York: Signet, 1970).

14. Evans, *Personal Politics*, 235.

15. Olson, *Freedom's Daughters*, 335; King, *Freedom Song*, 450.

16. "Remembering John H. Johnson, 1918–2005," *Jet*, August 29, 2005, 16–17.

17. "Are Negro Girls Getting Prettier?" *Ebony*, February 1966, 25; "Letters to the Editor," *Ebony*, April 1966, 14, 18, 20.

18. Diana Smith, personal communication, November 2011.

19. Phyl Garland, "The Natural Look," *Ebony*, June 1966, 142–48. Garland later became the first African American and first female tenured professor in the Journalism Department at Columbia University, specializing in reporting on cultural affairs, especially music.

20. Ibid., 143.

21. Ibid.

22. Ibid.

23. "Letters to the Editor," *Ebony*, August 1966, 12–16.

24. Claudette Vernado, "Natural for Life," *Naptural Roots*, December 2009, 9.

25. Arthur Marwick, *Beauty in History: Society, Politics and Personal Appearance: 1500 to the Present* (London: Thames & Hudson, 1988), 365; Arthur Marwick, *A History of Human Beauty* (London: Marwick, Hambledon & London, 2007), 198.

26. Ayana D. Byrd and Lori L. Tharps, *Hair Story* (New York: St. Martin's Press, 2001), 51.

27. For another story of women who worked with the Chicago Freedom Movement, see Amy Schneidhorst, "The YWCA and Older Women's Activism: Women Mobilized for Change and Racial Justice in Chicago, 1965–1967," chapter 4 in *Building a Just and Secure World: Popular Front Women's Struggles for Peace and Justice in Chicago during the 1960s* (New York: Bloomsbury Academic, 2013). An interracial group of women organized by Joan P. Brown of the YWCA and Carol Kleiman and Henrietta Moore from fair-housing groups in Chicago's North Shore suburbs, with support from Coretta Scott King, participated in the open-housing marches and provided other support. At one point, 35 representatives of the group met with Mayor Richard J. Daley and called for specific changes in housing policy, while another 250 women from the group held a silent vigil on the sidewalk outside City Hall dressed in "pumps and white gloves." They believed that "if enough well-behaved, well-dressed, well-spoken 'responsible' women articulated our concerns from a feminine point of view . . . minds would change and the appropriate social change would follow." Women Mobilized for Change, "Freeing Ourselves," cited in ibid., 95.

18

Women in the Movement II

Dorothy Gautreaux

Hal Baron

Long before there was a *Gautreaux* decision, there was Dorothy Gautreaux—a builder of community, a breaker of barriers, an inspiration and organizer to her fellows, a visionary. It is fitting that the *Gautreaux* case has been carried on in her name.[1]

I can still visualize this intense yet wonderfully warm, brown-skinned woman as she participated in the planning and strategy meetings of the coordinating body of the Chicago civil rights movement during the 1960s. Dorothy always brought to the often rancorous debates a sense of hope and possibility. When discussion became stymied over abstract principles or personalities, she punctured the posturing by quietly stating what she and her small band of tenant organizers were going to do—specifically. For many of us, Dorothy's judgment was the touchstone of whether a proposal had merit and should be acted upon.

The resources of her spirit more than compensated for the modest material goods at her command. Her fellow Chicago Housing Authority (CHA) activists remembered, "When you were down, she would lift you up." She had the knack of drawing people out, encouraging them to act on their own behalf. A tireless organizer, she was demanding both of herself and of others. She produced results because her demands were tempered by patience and understanding.

Dorothy Gautreaux was of, by, and for the tenants in public housing. Her very being contradicted the perceived wisdom that CHA tenants lived under such heavy control and threat from the political machine that they could not be expected to stand up for themselves. Her view was that the tenants both could and ought to direct their own lives. She set out to prove that proposition by example.

For many years Dorothy lived in the Altgeld-Murray Homes on the furthest southern reaches of Chicago. Before the flourishing of the civil rights movement, she sought to "build community" out there—she organized Girl Scouts, Boy Scouts, and PTAs. Somehow she also managed to balance the hectic schedule of an organizer with the time-consuming demands of good parenting: she and her husband raised three daughters and two sons. In these tasks she was assisted by the bonds she forged with neighbors and friends. As one of them summed it up, "She was a community-minded person."

In Chicago the civil rights movement first took shape around de facto segregated schools. Dorothy Gautreaux took advantage of this situation to improve the quality of education in the all-black Carver Schools that served the students from Altgeld-Murray. She was instrumental in establishing a separate administration for the high school and served as president of its PTA. Her focus expanded as she organized her fellow tenants to go to demonstrations and support boycotts around the city.

Then, as the civil rights movement took greater shape and eventually joined forces with Dr. Martin Luther King Jr. to form the Chicago Freedom Movement, Dorothy became the tribune of the CHA tenants within its councils. The image of tenants that she projected was not that of victims of abuse but of people with potential to be tapped. She was constantly nurturing that potential in one housing development after another, holding workshops to help tenants gain the voice she knew was theirs, organizing carloads of neighbors and newfound friends to join the next demonstration. With great pride, she brought Dr. King to Altgeld for a rally.[2]

Dorothy Gautreaux and the thousands of black women and men like her around the country made the *Gautreaux* suit against the Chicago Housing Authority possible. Their dreams, their determination, and their challenges made it clear that the old order could not stand.

Unfortunately, she did not live to see the Court find in her favor against the Chicago Housing Authority. Regrettably, we have not had her wise counsel in implementing the decision.

Fortunately, however, Chicago has had the example of Dorothy Gau-

treaux. It is a noble one to pass on to future generations. The day Dorothy left us, she was still organizing. She had moved out of CHA housing.
In the morning before she went to the hospital for what was to be her last
treatment, she was on the phone putting together a meeting that night to
form a block club in her new neighborhood.

Little wonder that five years later, her old neighbors at Altgeld-Murray
battled the bureaucracy at City Hall to have a new facility named the Dorothy Gautreaux Child-Parent Center. They met stiff resistance. But, following Dorothy's example, they won.[3]

Notes

This chapter was adapted from a previously published paper entitled "What Is
Gautreaux?" issued in 1991 by Business and Professional People for the Public
Interest, Chicago. It is reprinted here by permission of Business and Professional
People for the Public Interest, Chicago.

1. In early August 1966, while the open-housing marches were still in progress, the American Civil Liberties Union filed a class-action lawsuit against the
Chicago Housing Authority (CHA) on behalf of tenants and those on waiting
lists, charging that the practice of locating public housing in the black community
was a violation of the Civil Rights Act and the equal protection clause of the Constitution. Dorothy Gautreaux was listed as the first plaintiff, so the suit became
known as *Gautreaux v. CHA*. The suit moved through the courts over many
decades and was won at the Supreme Court level by Alexander Polikoff and his
team of attorneys. The remedies established were known as Gautreaux Programs.
See Alexander Polikoff, *Waiting for Gautreaux: A Story of Segregation, Housing,
and the Black Ghetto* (Evanston, IL: Northwestern University Press, 2006).

2. The demands of the Chicago Freedom Movement addressed to the Chicago Housing Authority were as follows: "programs to rehabilitate present public housing, including such items as locked lobbies, restrooms in the recreation
areas, increased police protection, and child care centers on every third floor;
no more public housing construction in the ghetto, until a substantial number
of units are started outside the ghetto." Those addressed to both the Chicago
Housing Authority and the Chicago Dwelling Association included "a program
to vastly increase the supply of low cost housing on a scattered basis. The program should provide for both low and middle income families." See "Program
of the Chicago Freedom Movement, July, 1966" in *Chicago, 1966: Open Housing Marches, Summit Negotiations, and Operation Breadbasket*, ed. David Garrow
(Brooklyn, NY: Carlson Publishing, 1989), 105.

3. Many women were involved with the Chicago Freedom Movement

through the Coordinating Council of Community Organizations (CCCO), where Dorothy Gautreaux was a delegate from the Altgeld-Murray Parents Council. Jorja English Palmer and Addie Wyatt served on the Action Committee responsible for planning the open-housing marches. Palmer was a representative from the Chatham-Avalon Community Council and led the shopping expedition to Gage Park. When she passed away, the Illinois senate passed a resolution honoring her "profound influence in the lives of countless people, fighting for justice and equality." Wyatt was vice president of the packinghouse workers' union and went on to become a national labor leader and founder of the Coalition of Labor Union Women. Mattie Hopkins and Mary Perry served on the CCCO Steering Committee in 1966. Hopkins was a delegate from Teachers for Integrated Schools; she later served on the Chicago Board of Education. Perry was a delegate from the Citizens Housing Committee and was a lifelong civil rights activist. Irene Turner was a longtime delegate from the Committee to End Discrimination in Chicago Medical Institutions, where she started working with Dr. Quentin Young in the 1950s. See Mary Lou Finley, "The Open Housing Marches: Chicago Summer '66," in Garrow, *Chicago, 1966*, 42, 45; Alan B. Anderson and George W. Pickering, *Confronting the Color Line: The Broken Promise of the Civil Rights Movement in Chicago* (Athens: University of Georgia Press, 1986), 479, n. 66; Ron Grossman, "Irene Turner, 76, Social Activist," *Chicago Tribune*, April 24, 1997; Senate Resolution 0561, State of Illinois, January 12, 2006, http://www .ilga.gov/legislation/fulltext.asp?DocName=&SessionId=50&GA=94&Doc TypeId=SR&DocNum=561&GAID=8&LegID=22660&SpecSess=&Session=. For additional information on Addie Wyatt, see Marcia Walker-McWilliams, *Reverend Addie Wyatt: Faith and the Fight for Labor, Gender, and Racial Equality* (Urbana: University of Illinois Press, 2016).

19

Labor and the Chicago Freedom Movement

Gil Cornfield, Melody Heaps, and Norman Hill

After the Selma campaign and passage of the Voting Rights Act in 1965, the civil rights movement entered a new phase. It had, as Martin Luther King Jr., put it, "left the realm of constitutional rights" and entered the arena of "human rights." "The Constitution," he added, "assured the right to vote, but there is no such assurance to the right to adequate housing or the right to an adequate income." Dr. King knew that ensuring decent housing, a good education, and sufficient income for all citizens would be no easy task. It required new sets of understandings and new approaches.[1]

The Chicago Freedom Movement was Dr. King's first effort to blaze a new path. The Chicago campaign sought to end slums and, in so doing, find new vehicles to create economic security for the poor and for disadvantaged communities. Meeting the challenges of this new "human rights" campaign would require a different coalition than had been necessary in the past. Up until the launch of the Chicago Freedom Movement, labor unions had been a critical supporter of the Southern Christian Leadership Conference (SCLC). Renowned progressive labor leaders had befriended Dr. King and had long championed his cause. His close advisers included Bayard Rustin, head of the A. Philip Randolph Institute, an organization supported by the AFL-CIO and other unions that encouraged a greater black presence at all levels of the labor movement; Ralph Helstein, president of the Chicago-based United Packinghouse Workers of America (UPWA); and Norman Hill, a young civil rights leader with the Congress of Racial Equality (CORE) who had become the legisla-

373

tive and civil rights representative of the Industrial Union Department (IUD) of the AFL-CIO. SCLC's turn northward and its decision to make Chicago the center of a campaign to redress economic and social issues would require a more complex, targeted organizing campaign and a more structured coalition with labor than had been necessary in the past.[2]

As an industrial epicenter, Chicago was home to a thriving labor movement comprising the old CIO industrial unions and the old AFL craft unions. The craft unions represented white workers who felt threatened by integration, which, in their minds, would take away their good-paying jobs. They had always been more conservative and had not supported SCLC's civil rights campaigns. Both the craft unions and the industrial unions were part of the Chicago Federation of Labor. Because of the influence of the craft unions, the Chicago Federation took a cautious approach to the Chicago Freedom Movement.[3]

The industrial unions, however, quickly embraced SCLC's Chicago drive. In addition to Ralph Helstein's influence, Charlie Hayes, the UPWA's District 1 leader, was a longtime participant in and supporter of the civil rights movement. Addie Wyatt, who would become the first woman vice president of the national union, was president of UPWA Local 56 and a major contributor to SCLC.[4] The IUD, an organizing arm of the AFL-CIO, had strong leadership at the local level through Charlie Chiakulas and Carl Shier, both veteran organizers for the United Automobile Workers (UAW). These unions, plus some of the newer public employee unions and the lawyers representing them, provided strong support. In particular, Gil Cornfield, a labor lawyer and founding partner of Cornfield and Feldman, a labor law firm that represented many progressive unions in Chicago, became a central strategist in the campaign.

Early in the Chicago Freedom Movement, James Bevel, SCLC's Chicago campaign director, hired Melody Heaps, a local community organizer and daughter of Alvin E. Heaps, a prominent national labor leader from the Retail, Wholesale, Department Store Union (RWDSU). The RWDSU would go on to organize the largest hospital workers' union, Local 1199. Cornfield and Heaps were able to connect local and national labor leadership with SCLC's Chicago movement. In addition, they recruited progressive attorneys to represent the Chicago Freedom Movement's organizations and demonstrations.

No one could have anticipated the energy, resources, manpower, and focus needed to take on the institutional racism embedded in the economic institutions and policies of the North. For the movement to succeed, it would require a melding of labor's organizing experience and SCLC's nonviolent philosophy and organizing vision. As historian James Ralph observes in *Northern Protest*, King believed the civil rights and labor movements had to join forces, "for the needs of the society as a whole." They needed to "fashion a framework for civil rights–labor cooperation. The centerpiece of the program . . . would be the infusion of labor organizers into the ghettoes, an initiative the IUD had endorsed at its 1965 annual convention."[5]

One could argue that this approach—even more so than the ultimate focus on open housing—was the most creative means of bringing economic justice and power to the people in the community. The strategy was to develop a strong, on-the-ground organizing partnership among SCLC, Chicago community organizations, and organized labor. The enterprises that emerged from this newly constructed partnership were the tenant unions, which evolved into a collective bargaining campaign and resulted in the formation of the Lawndale Community Union.

Tenant Unions

In an effort to reveal the blight and inhumane living conditions of the slums, tenant organizing began on the West and North Sides of the city. With the help of SCLC and its labor leadership, a tenant union federation emerged from the work of the East Garfield Park Union to End Slums and the Lawndale Union to End Slums. Coordinating with these efforts on the West Side were the JOIN Community Union, an organizing effort by the Students for a Democratic Society (SDS) in Chicago's Uptown neighborhood, and the Tenant Action Council, an organizing drive involving the mixed-income housing complex called Old Town Gardens in the gentrifying community known as Old Town.[6]

In early 1966 tenants on the West Side had begun a rent strike. "The strike," Gil Cornfield remembers, "was over the poor conditions and services among apartment dwellers in the community and centered on a handful of absentee owners and their real estate companies which controlled many, if not most, of the large apartment buildings." Residents held mass meetings where they aired their grievances and developed their strategy. "The rent strike," Cornfield recalls, "was resulting in wholesale eviction proceedings being brought by the affected real estate companies in the Circuit Court of Cook County."[7]

With Cornfield's assistance, a strategy was developed to challenge each eviction in court, contending that if a tenant's nonpayment of rent was in response to the landlord's failure and refusal to maintain the rental premises in accordance with the requirements of the municipal code, this could be used as a defense in an eviction case. In housing court, defense attorneys presented photographs of the deplorable conditions, along with supporting testimony about unheeded complaints to the landlord. This strategy resulted in the finding that evictions were no longer pro forma, and the attendant legal costs would be borne by the landlords. At each eviction proceeding, the court was filled to overflowing with tenants and members of the community. This legal strategy, coupled with the ongoing rent strikes, prevented landlords from breaking the strikes through evictions.

Cornfield and other attorneys represented tenants in support of the organizing effort. As more tenant unions were created, more legal support was needed. Barbara Hillman, a new attorney at Cornfield's firm, and Bernadine Dohrn, a law student at the University of Chicago and leader of the progressive Law Students Committee for Civil Rights, became central figures in supporting the tenant union drive. Melody Heaps was in charge of recruiting and managing legal representation not only for tenant unions but also for civil rights workers who might be arrested because of their protest activities.

Beyond court petitions, the coalition of labor and the Chicago Freedom Movement became the platform for conceptualizing the development of a tenant union federation that would use collective bargaining to change real estate management practices. Collective bargaining would empower residents to demand decent, safe housing and result in a fundamental change in the landlord-tenant relationship.

When massive rent strikes in properties held by the Condor and Costalis real estate firm became too onerous, the firm agreed to negotiate. Because of Cornfield's labor background, the idea of a collective bargaining agreement covering all tenants in Condor and Costalis properties in East Garfield Park and parts of Lawndale was conceived. The collective bargaining approach was intended to improve housing conditions to conform to municipal codes and to strengthen community organization and leadership within a democratic framework.

In the fall of 1966, testimony before a subcommittee of the Illinois legislature's Robert Mann Commission, tasked with exploring the housing problem in Chicago, clearly reveals the vision of the new collective bargaining strategy and the melding of civil rights and community organizing with labor organizing. In the introduction to his testimony, Al Raby noted that the partnership of labor, community, and civil rights leadership would be critical to tackling this "massive problem of housing." He said: "Those organizations supporting the Federation are my own Coordinating Council of Community Organizations [CCCO]; the Southern Christian Leadership Conference, whose president is Dr. Martin Luther King, Jr.; the Industrial Union Department, AFL-CIO, whose Regional Director is Mr. Charles Chiakulas; the United Auto Workers directed by Mr. Robert Johnston; the United Packinghouse Workers of America; the American Federation of State County Municipal Employees Unions; and the American Federation of Teachers."

In addition to Raby, others who testified included Carl Shier, representing the IUD, who was on loan from the UAW for the Chicago campaign; the Reverend William Briggs, head of the East Garfield Tenants Union; Samuel Smith and Meredith Gilbert of the Lawndale Union to End Slums; David McCullough, director of the Tenant Action Council; and Gil Cornfield, attorney for tenant organizing.

In his testimony, Raby stated:

It is the tenant union movement which will provide a mechanism for—

1. Organizing slum dwellers to counter the enormous power and exploitative forces which live off a closed housing market . . . fostering the overwhelming growth of slums;
2. Organizing the slum dweller around issues of vital importance to him, i.e., housing;

3. Development of his own ego and sense of participation in the making of social and economic policy which inevitably affects his life;
4. A viable structure through which the collective bargaining agreement can be sought for the purpose of raising issues concerning the rights of tenants in respect to their landlords;
5. The development of a stewards training program to educate the tenant to his community responsibility and public services available and how to utilize them.

Additional testimony about the history of the tenant union movement clearly articulated the new strategy:

> The leadership of CCCO and SCLC conceived of the possibility of dealing with landlords as a union would deal with management, through a collective bargaining contract, giving tenants the right to bargain and arrive at enforceable agreements concerning conditions under which they live. . . .
>
> Under the terms of the contract the Union will advise and instruct tenants as to proper maintenance procedures. . . . Perhaps the most important victory for our community, however, is the new sense of hope and power our people have to change things for the better. Stewards, with the help of the Industrial Unions Department, AFL-CIO are being trained in their responsibilities and duties as stewards under the terms of the contract.[8]

Lawndale Community Union

The ideas behind the formation of the Lawndale Community Union were straightforward: people in the neighborhoods needed work, and labor groups were interested in organizing workers. The move from community protests in the form of rent strikes to collective bargaining by tenant organizations was the stimulus for connecting SCLC's organizing center at the Warren Avenue Congregational Church (the Chicago Freedom Movement's West Side headquarters) with the Chicago labor movement at the Lawndale Community Union during the winter and spring of 1966. The idea was to identify large, unorganized employment sectors that could be targeted for organizing campaigns and thus build the bridge between community and labor. With the blessing of national labor leaders Bayard Rustin, Norm Hill, and others, as well as the SCLC leadership, particularly James Bevel, a plan was conceived to open an organizing center in Lawndale, with staff contributed by SCLC and labor groups.

A. Philip Randolph's guiding philosophy was behind this initiative. As Hill recalls, "Randolph's simple but profound credo, which I adopted, was 'at the banquet table of nature there are no reserve seats. You take what you can get and you keep what you can hold. If you can't take anything, you won't get anything. And if you can't hold anything, you won't keep anything. And you can't take anything without organization.'" In 1965 and 1966 Hill was assigned by Jack Conway, executive director of the IUD, to the community union project in Chicago. The IUD's rationale for community unions had been developed by Brendan Sexton, a UAW staff representative based at the union's Detroit headquarters. He believed the skills of trade unionists—how to run a meeting, how to organize, how to fight and file grievances, how to speak, and how to raise money—would make them effective community organizers. The basic idea was to apply these union-learned skills to the building of a community union focused on community concerns and grievances.

The Lawndale Community Union project was directed by Charles Chiakulas, IUD's area director. The immediate director was Ted Black from the UAW. Local labor representatives who had been involved in tenant union organizing and the Chicago Freedom Movement became part of the Lawndale Community Union, notably, Carl Shier and Gil Cornfield. Melody Heaps, who had been responsible for facilitating SCLC's connections with labor, became the Lawndale Community Union's local director.

The plan was to link worker organizations with employment and training opportunities through community organizations. As in the case of the tenant unions, the overarching goal was to develop democratic organizations that would be vehicles for improving members' lives and developing indigenous leadership.

Hospitals were the biggest and fastest-growing unorganized sector of the economy in metropolitan Chicago. Only the University of Chicago Hospital was organized (accomplished by the CIO before its merger with the AFL). Rustin, Hill, Shier, Cornfield, and others developed a game plan to secretly place organizers in many of the major hospitals. The code name for this project was HELP—the Hospital Employees Labor Program. A number of experienced organizers from CORE, SCLC, and IUD obtained jobs in the hospitals, and HELP took significant steps toward implementation. On the eve of the launch of the organizing drive, however, the targeted hospitals recognized a joint Teamsters–Service Employees International Union, thereby thwarting the Lawndale Community Union's efforts.[9] It was assumed that the hospitals had learned of the movement's organizing drive and seized on the opportunity to enter into a quick settlement. Although unionization was supported by all, the model developed by the Lawndale Community Union would have promoted institutional social and economic justice though labor and community organizations. With no possibility of continuing its hospital organizing efforts, the primary program of the Lawndale Community Union fell apart by October 1966.

This setback for the Lawndale Community Union came at a time of mounting pressure on Dr. King and the Chicago Freedom Movement. To be sure, Jesse Jackson's Operation Breadbasket was opening new job opportunities in companies that had previously employed only whites. But the turbulence over the Summit Agreement in late August 1966, which brought the Chicago movement's open-housing campaign to a close, along with the rise of the Black Power approach to tackling racial inequity, undercut the ability to focus on the civil rights–labor partnership.

Furthermore, Lawndale Community Union staff found that their SCLC colleagues had difficulty making the organizational transition from projects that were essentially racial, such as the desegregation of public accommodations in the South, to those that were economic and social in the North. The organizing tactics of the civil rights movement and the labor movement were different. The labor movement was centered on industrial organizing. Organizers went into a plant that made widgets or into a hospital to bargain for better pay and benefits, limited work schedules, and work breaks. Under the vision of the Lawndale Community Union, those tactics would be integrated into a movement that challenged the fundamental economic and social issues surrounding poverty and racial injustice in the North. Desegregation of accommodations and voting rights could be achieved by demonstrations in the South. In the North, decent-paying jobs, the improvement of living conditions in the ghetto, and the ultimate destruction of the slums would require a sustained and complex organizing and political effort.

In addition, there had always been tension between SCLC's open-housing protests and labor's economic organizing strategy. As Melody Heaps recalls, "Our argument was that it was important to have open housing, but far more important was the need to end the slums, the need to bring economic justice and power to the people in the community." There were many people, she adds, "who felt that it really didn't matter if Gage Park was opened up. What mattered was that people couldn't find a decent place to live in Lawndale, that rats are running over kids, that there wasn't a grocery store, that people didn't have jobs. The track of open housing almost worked against the track of economic organizing. Staff and leadership time and resources became diverted. The full focus on the momentous efforts required for tenant and hospital union organizing never materialized."[10]

In the North, the civil rights movement needed the labor movement to redress the racism embedded in economic injustice and political hegemony. As Dr. King stated, "Achievement of these goals will be a lot more difficult and require much more discipline, understanding, organization and sacrifice."[11] In addition, Dr. King's Chicago campaign had to confront social and economic segregation within a community whose African American political leadership had established its own power relationship with city officials and worked to protect it. The Chicago white power establishment had created a political system that allowed some black individuals to succeed and prosper, provided they did not live in white neighborhoods or take away "white" jobs. In the South, blacks could live in close proximity to whites but were forbidden to share in the power.

It was the hope of labor organizers that the partnership created in Chicago and its attendant organizing activities would become a national model for recruiting community residents into large-scale democratic organizations, stimulating economic security, and engendering personal empowerment. One untold story of the labor movement is that it allowed men and women who were often only half-literate to become local and national leaders capable of holding their own, intellectually and emotionally, with Harvard graduates.

With the Summit Agreement on open housing reached by Dr. King and Mayor Daley, growing pressure to address the Vietnam War, and mounting criticism of the nonviolent movement as a means to redress racial grievances, SCLC's work in Chicago began to center around Jesse Jackson's Operation Breadbasket, and resources for organizing on the West Side decreased. The disappointment of those who had envisioned a new kind of movement centered around issues of economic justice was palpable. They had hoped for a different relationship between the labor movement and the civil rights movement—one that would spread like wildfire out of Chicago. As Cornfield recalls, "We were talking about thousands of people to be organized. . . . The potential was so great and so much effort was put into getting it together."[12]

Aftermath

In retrospect, it was probably unrealistic to imagine that a civil rights movement focused on southern segregation and voting rights could be turned into a social and economic movement to change the fundamental structure of poverty in less than two years. The issues raised in the 1960s by the Chicago Freedom Movement resonate today. The Occupy demonstrations in 2011 revealed that the economic chasm between rich and poor, between the powerful and the powerless, still exists. Labor unions are in decline, the fiscal gap is widening, and middle-class economic security is receding. These issues, so critical to a democratic capitalist society, are ones that the Chicago Freedom Movement confronted and perhaps unveiled.[13]

Although SCLC withdrew most of its staff from the tenant organizing efforts by late 1967, local organizing continued into the 1970s. Cornfield and other attorneys continued to work pro bono for tenants who took their landlords to housing court over seriously neglected buildings. Most landlords settled with the tenants, but one, Jack Spring, did not. Cornfield took this case before the Illinois Supreme Court and won. In this landmark case, the court recognized that the obligation to pay rent was contingent on the landlord's maintenance of the property in accordance with building codes—what became known as an "implied warrant of habitability."[14] This ruling represented a monumental shift in landlord-tenant law, giving tenants newly recognized rights and moving landlord-tenant law far beyond its English common-law origins in the Middle Ages.[15]

In December 1966 SCLC, along with the Chicago City Missionary Society, received grant money to form the Community Renewal Foundation for the purpose of enabling nonprofit groups to secure real estate loans at a market rate in order to build affordable housing. The foundation acquired buildings in Lawndale that had been organized by the tenant union. These buildings were renovated and offered as decent housing for the tenants.[16]

When Andrew Young was recently asked about the effort to organize hospital workers, he said, "It didn't work in Chicago, but it did later on in Charleston." He was referring to events that took place in 1969, when SCLC was invited to join a major effort by RWDSU Local 1199 in Charleston, South Carolina, which would eventually become the largest hospital workers' union in America. After 12 employees were fired for union organizing activities, 500 Charleston hospital workers, mostly black women, walked out. SCLC sent some of its field staff—including Billy Hollins, James Orange, Bernard LaFayette, and Andrew Young, who had worked in the Chicago Freedom Movement—to Charleston to mobilize community support for the strike. Coretta Scott King spoke at numerous rallies, telling the strikers and their supporters, "If my husband were alive today he would be right here with you tonight." There were evening rallies in churches, and "thousands of Charleston's black citizens turned out regularly for marches along routes lined with police, state troopers, and National Guardsmen with fixed bayonets." Young reported, "We had a boycott shutting down the town so that nobody was shopping for anything but food and medicine." Young began negotiating with hospital administrators and eventually won most of the strikers' demands. "Once we got to talking to each other," he said, "we worked out very specific things . . . which is what you're supposed to do in nonviolence." This Charleston collaboration of the civil rights movement, the labor movement, and the black community became an example of the kind of collective power we had envisioned. Alvin E. Heaps became president of RWDSU and continued to organize hospital workers across the country.[17]

Gil Cornfield asked Jack Greenberg, head of the NAACP's Legal Defense Fund, to support a Chicago Legal Services Project that would continue to offer legal and other support services to community organizations in Chicago. Melody Heaps was the project's first director, and many of the attorneys involved in the Chicago Freedom Movement served as members of its Board of Directors, including Cornfield and James Montgomery, who would become chief counsel to Harold Washington, Chicago's first black mayor.

Chicago-based labor and civil rights leaders continued their struggle to organize the unemployed, confront poverty, fight for employment opportunities, and bring social justice to the streets of America's towns and cities. After his time in Chicago, Norman Hill was sent to Newark, New Jersey, to build a community union there. SCLC began organizing a Poor People's Campaign and a march on Washington, DC. Dr. King went to Memphis to support striking garbage workers.[18]

Notes

Passages from the testimony of Al Raby to the Robert E. Mann Commission on Low Income Housing, Illinois State Legislature, September 1966, box 4-21, Al Raby Speeches, 1965–1966, CCCO Papers, King Center Library and Archives, are included here courtesy of the King Center Library and Archives.

1. Martin Luther King Jr., "Nonviolence: The Only Road to Freedom," in *A Testament of Hope: The Essential Writings and Speeches of Martin Luther King, Jr.*, ed. James M. Washington (New York: Harper San Francisco, 1991), 58.

2. The United Packinghouse Workers of America later merged with other unions to form the United Food and Commercial Workers. For King's thoughts on and interactions with organized labor, see Martin Luther King Jr., *All Labor Has Dignity*, ed. Michael K. Honey (Boston: Beacon, 2011). For an analysis of King's evolving perspectives on labor and economic justice, see Thomas F. Jackson, *From Civil Rights to Human Rights: Martin Luther King, Jr., and the Struggle for Economic Justice* (Philadelphia: University of Pennsylvania Press, 2007).

3. Milton Derber, *Labor in Illinois: The Affluent Years, 1945–1980* (Urbana: University of Illinois Press, 1989), 230–51.

4. On the packinghouse workers in Chicago, see Rick Halpern, *Down on the Killing Floor: Black and White Workers in Chicago's Packinghouses, 1904–54* (Urbana: University of Illinois Press, 1997), and Cyril Robinson, *Marching with Dr. King: Ralph Helstein and the United Packinghouse Workers* (New York: Praeger, 2011).

5. James R. Ralph Jr., *Northern Protest: Martin Luther King, Jr., Chicago, and the Civil Rights Movement* (Cambridge, MA: Harvard University Press, 1993), 70–72.

6. For an overview, see Gilbert Feldman's testimony in Sol Tax, ed., *The People vs. the System: A Dialogue in Urban Conflict (Proceedings of the Community Service Workshop, Funded under Title 1 of the Higher Education Act of 1965 and Held at the University of Chicago, October 1966–June 1967* (Chicago: Acme Press, 1968), 276–81.

7. Gil Cornfield, interview by Mary Lou Finley and Pam Smith, Chicago, November 2010.

8. Al Raby, testimony before the Robert E. Mann Commission on Low Income Housing, Illinois State Legislature, Springfield, Illinois, September 1966, box 4-21, Al Raby Speeches, 1965–1966, CCCO Papers, King Center Library and Archives.

9. For a brief overview, see Ralph, *Northern Protest*, 72.

10. Melody Heaps, interview by Mary Lou Finley and Pam Smith, Chicago, November 2010.

11. King, "Nonviolence: The Only Road to Freedom," 58.

12. Cornfield interview.

13. On the Occupy movement, see Sarah van Gelder, *This Changes Everything: Occupy Wall Street and the 99% Movement* (San Francisco: Berrett-Koehler, 2011), and Todd Gitlin, *Occupy Nation: The Roots, Spirit, and Promise of Occupy Wall Street* (New York: HarperCollins, 2012). On economic trends, see Robert B. Reich, *Aftershock: The Next Economy & America's Future* (New York: Random House, 2010).

14. *Jack Spring v. Little,* 50 Ill.2d 351 (1972).

15. For further discussion of the dramatic implications of this Illinois Supreme Court ruling, see Anthony J. Fusco, Nancy B. Collins, and Julian R. Birnbaum, "Damages for Breach of the Implied Warranty of Habitability in Illinois—A Realistic Approach," *Chicago-Kent Law Review* 55, no. 2 (1979): 337–56, http://scholarship.kentlaw.iit.edu/cklawreview/vol55/iss2/4 (accessed February 13, 2015). For further discussion of the history of landlord-tenant law and the rise of tenant unions, see chapter 7 by Herman Jenkins.

16. Ralph, *Northern Protest*, 225.

17. Andrew Young, interview by Mary Lou Finley, Atlanta, January 2, 2012; Wendy L. Wilbanks, "Union Power, Soul Power: Intersections of Race, Gender, and Law," *Golden Gate University Law Review* 26, no. 2 (1996): 441–47, http://digitalcommons.law.ggu.edu/ggulrev/vol26/iss2/7 (accessed February 13, 2015); Leon Fink and Brian Greenberg, *Upheaval in the Quiet Zone: A History of Hospital Workers' Union, Local 1199* (Urbana: University of Illinois Press, 1989), 129–58. See also Madeline Anderson's film about the strike, *I Am Somebody* (Icarus Films, 1970).

18. On the broader connections between the civil rights movement and the labor movement in the last year of Martin Luther King's life, see Michael K. Honey, *Going Down Jericho Road: The Memphis Strike, Martin Luther King's Last Campaign* (New York: W. W. Norton, 2007). For a crisp overview, see Michael K. Honey, "Forty Years since King: Labor Rights and Human Rights," *OAH Magazine of History* 22 (April 2008): 18–21.

Part 5

Lessons Learned and the Unfinished Work

20

Nonviolence and the Chicago Freedom Movement

Bernard LaFayette Jr.

It was the summer of 1964, and I had just completed a year of college at Fisk University in Nashville. Hundreds of students from the North were headed south that summer to work on voter registration and Freedom Schools in Mississippi in what became known as Freedom Summer. But I was headed in the opposite direction: north to Chicago. I had been involved in the movement in the South for several years—from the Nashville lunch counter sit-in movement to the Freedom Rides and then to Selma, Alabama, where I'd initiated the voting rights movement there in 1962–1963 as a staff member for the Student Nonviolent Coordinating Committee (SNCC). Now I was ready to move north to lay the groundwork for the next movement.

I'd been invited to come to Chicago for the summer by Kale Williams, executive director of the American Friends Service Committee (AFSC). They deliberately wanted someone with extensive experience working with nonviolence in the South to come to Chicago and experiment with how nonviolence could work in the North. The Reverend Jim Lawson (who had taught our nonviolence workshops in Nashville) had recommended me as well as Glenn Smiley of the Fellowship of Reconciliation, whom I knew from workshops at the Highlander Folk School in Tennessee.[1] My work was to be exploratory, figuring out how nonviolence could be applied to urban problems, and I would be working out of AFSC's Project House on the West Side of Chicago. At the end of the summer I was offered a full-time job as director of AFSC's new Urban Affairs Program.

The South Side of Chicago, where many African Americans had lived for decades, had a large concentration of public-housing projects, such as Robert Taylor Homes. Much of the old housing in those neighborhoods had been torn down to make room for these projects. But the West Side was home to a newer African American community; there were still many tenement buildings in that neighborhood, with people living in overcrowded and neglected slum housing. In many buildings, each apartment had been converted into several tiny living spaces.[2]

At that time, AFSC had a housing program in the suburbs of Chicago. Bill Moyer was working with suburban fair-housing groups to desegregate housing on the North Shore and in the western suburbs. AFSC wanted to get something going to address slum housing on the West Side, so we began to focus on housing problems. For both upper-middle-class African Americans in the suburbs and lower-income and working-class African Americans in the city, the problem was the same: racial discrimination. This discrimination caused overcrowded conditions in the city, one of the key factors in the creation of slums.

Chicago's South Side had an older and more established African American community; as a result, community organizations on the South Side tended to be older and more established as well. There weren't as many organizations on the West Side, so its problems didn't get a lot of attention. Most of the African American people who lived on the West Side were more recent arrivals from the South, especially from Mississippi. In many cases they were joining family members who had already moved north. The jobs in the cotton fields had recently dried up due to the introduction of machinery. One historian noted, "In 1959 there had been 65,000 jobs for hand-picking cotton in the Delta fields. In the main harvesting months of 1966 . . . there were fewer than 3,000 hand pickers in the fields."[3]

When I arrived at AFSC's Project House, Tony Henry, director of the Pre-Adolescent Enrichment Program (PREP), was also there, working with youth. He would bring children from the suburbs to participate in programs with children on the West Side, and then he would take children from the West Side to programs in the suburbs. Although this was his primary job, Tony also began to think about housing issues in the neighborhood. (When Jesse Jackson, who was then a student at Chicago Theological Seminary, told me he needed a job because he had babies to take care of, the only job AFSC had available was working with this children's program, so that was his first movement job in Chicago.)

The Six Steps of a Nonviolent Campaign

As we plunged into organizing on the West Side, we based our work on what we now call the Six Steps of a Nonviolent Campaign, which we had learned during our work in the South: (1) information gathering, (2) education, (3) personal commitment, (4) negotiations, (5) direct action, (6) reconciliation.[4]

Step 1: Information Gathering

We started by looking at all the issues affecting people in the neighborhood, collecting information from the residents. We were looking to identify the conditions that create slums. The most obvious was overcrowding; as mentioned earlier, landlords would divide one apartment into several tiny ones. In addition, city services were curtailed when African Americans moved in. The streets were not cleaned, and rats were everywhere; sometimes babies died after being bitten by rats while sleeping at night. Another issue was lack of access to other neighborhoods in the city based on race, so people were forced to live in these poor conditions. This discrimination created a high demand for housing in West Side neighborhoods. The landlords didn't invest in maintenance, which helped create slums. Most were absentee landlords, and they used their buildings as a source of income and as collateral for loans. Then they would buy other investment properties, rather than spending money to maintain and repair the apartment buildings they already owned. People who were suffering from these conditions felt powerless when it came to demanding services.

Contract buying was another problem related to slum housing. The banks and savings and loans would not loan money for mortgages on the West Side, so people had to buy their houses on contract, which meant they had no equity in the houses until they made their final payments. If they missed a payment, they would often lose the house and everything they had put into it. (See chapter 8 for more on contract buying and the later organizing related to it in North Lawndale.)

Also, there were no recreational facilities for young people on the West Side: no swimming pools and no organized recreational programs for children and youths. This contributed to gang activity. There was violence in the community, and the people were frustrated and afraid.

During this phase, I decided I wanted Jim Bevel to join me in Chicago. He and I had worked together in the South, attending the Reverend Jim Lawson's nonviolence workshops and participating in the student sit-in movement in Nashville, the Freedom Rides, organizing in Mississippi, and the demonstrations in Birmingham. I organized my campaign to recruit Bevel by describing all the terrible conditions the West Siders faced. I tried to convince Bevel that Chicago had pressing problems that needed immediate attention and that there was a real possibility to create a movement for change here. First he would have to make up his mind to come to Chicago; then we would have to make an argument to SCLC that Chicago was the place to conduct a nonviolent direct action campaign in the North.

The residents on the West Side were essentially the same people we had been working with in the South. We were dealing with a lot of people from Mississippi, but in a northern setting. (In fact, Bevel was originally from Itta Bena, Mississippi, a tiny town near Greenwood at the eastern edge of the Mississippi Delta.) So we had an understanding of their culture and the issues and concerns they had brought from the South. They were familiar with the movement and even knew some movement songs! And we knew they had an understanding of exploitation and oppression. They had been tenant farmers, growing up on plantations. They had experienced the violence and racial oppression of Mississippi, particularly economic oppression. They had been paid very little for the work they did on the plantations, and they were often cheated out of what little they should have received. Some people had escaped Mississippi because they had been kept in debt by the plantation owners; others had come because they believed they could make a decent living in Chicago and maybe even send some money back to their families in Mississippi. If they had gone to rural Illinois, they would have been able to survive. They knew how to grow food. But instead, they were on the concrete streets and sidewalks of Chicago.

By the late spring of 1965, Jim Bevel had decided to come to Chicago.

Step 2: Education

In this step, we educated the community about the issues. We shared the information we'd gathered in step 1 and discussed what they could do to make a change. We did this in community meetings with small groups of people and also in mass meetings. We used the mass meetings to convince people they could do something about the problem. At one point we held a mass meeting at the Warren Avenue Congregational Church in East Garfield Park to discuss one question: What is a slum? We wanted to get the people to agree on this. An eleven-year-old girl came up with this definition: a slum is a place where everything is taken out and nothing is put back in. We also collected the addresses of buildings where people were having problems with their landlords. This education of the community eventually led to people being organized into tenant unions.

A crucial part of this step was developing a clear and effective message. We knew from our work in the South that it was important to boil the issue down to something short—preferably three words or less. In Selma it was "The Right to Vote." In Birmingham it was "Public Accommodations." For this movement we decided on "End the Slums."

Step 3. Personal Commitment

This step involves preparing to take action by learning the concepts of nonviolence and preparing oneself spiritually. It often includes specific training to prepare for the suffering one might endure during direct action, and it is designed to overcome fear of the unexpected. Seeking spiritual health and intellectual clarity is necessary to deflect any ideological propaganda that might be directed toward the movement.

Like in the South, we used mass meetings in Chicago to prepare people spiritually for what lay ahead. Why mass meetings? Most often, individuals are the targets of discrimination, abuse, neglect, and violence. When people are alone, they feel like they can't do anything; they don't feel a sense of power that would allow them to stand up to repression. Mass meetings cultivate and engender a sense of collective power—there is strength in numbers. When people don't have to stand alone, this generates a sense of empowerment and a feeling that things can change.

Sharing with a community of people with similar values strengthens and reinforces convictions about the movement and its objectives. And sing-ing—always an important part of mass meetings—is a way to nourish their souls. Music helps maintain high morale and a spirit of hope.

Step 4: Negotiation

In this step, we negotiate with the community power holders who have the ability to make the changes we are seeking. It is the art of bringing together opposing views to arrive at a just conclusion or to clarify the unresolved issues, at which point, the conflict is formalized. Preparation for negotiation includes a thorough understanding of all sides of the issue and the possible alternatives for making a persuasive argument. We began negotiating with landlords, especially Condor and Costalis, which owned many buildings on the West Side, to get them to fix up their buildings.

Step 5: Direct Action

If negotiations are not successful, we move on to direct action. The goal is to return to step 4 from a stronger place, in the hope that the negotia-tions for change can go forward. In the case of the tenant unions, direct action took the form of rent strikes. When the landlord refused to fix the building, the tenants withheld their rent. During this campaign, there were many, many buildings involved in rent strikes on the West Side. At one point, we picketed the house of one of the landlords after a two-year-old boy died when he fell through a broken railing on the back steps of one of their apartment buildings. We discovered where the landlord lived from a West Side woman who worked cleaning houses in his comfortable suburban neighborhood nearby.

Step 6: Reconciliation

The goal of this final step is to reach an agreement to work to solve prob-lems with our opponents. On July 13, 1966, a few days after 30,000 peo-ple gathered for a massive rally at Soldier Field and Martin Luther King led a march of thousands through downtown Chicago to post the movement's demands on the door of City Hall, Condor and Costalis agreed to cooperate with us. Many of their buildings were already on rent strike, but instead of carrying out mass evictions, they signed a collective bargaining agreement with the tenant union. They agreed to repair and rehabilitate the apartments, and they also agreed to a deconversion process to reduce the number of apartments in one building. Sears, Roebuck and Company donated funds to help with the deconversions, and other groups came in to help (for additional information, see chapter 7 on tenant unions). Condor and Costalis later had a demonstration building, showing how they had deconverted these apartments. They became the example and the model.[5]

Another example of reconciliation comes from our earlier campaign against childhood lead poisoning. When we discovered that many of the children in the buildings we were organizing were suffering from lead poisoning due to peeling paint, we wanted to attack the immediate problem and get help for the children. We came up with a solution and developed a program to do something about it. We organized local youths to go door-to-door to collect urine samples from the children for testing, enlisted the support of Presbyterian–St. Luke's Hospital and local scientist David Elwyn, and had discussions with the Chicago Board of Health. Within a matter of months, the City of Chicago began a screening program for childhood lead poisoning (see chapter 13).

Working with our opponents to solve problems is a key part of nonviolent campaigns. Our goal is to end with a process of reconciliation, to repair relationships and go forward together to address the issues.

Principles of Kingian Nonviolence

When we teach nonviolence, we begin with the Six Principles of Kingian Nonviolence. Here, I provide some examples of how we put those principles into practice during the Chicago Freedom Movement.

Principle 1: Nonviolence Is a Way of Life for Courageous People

Dr. King often talked about how the movement was not for cowards. Somehow, we need to find the courage deep within ourselves to confront conflict rather than run away from it.[6]

It took some courage just to *be* on the West Side of Chicago. One evening, after working late at the office, I was walking from Project House down to catch the El—Chicago's elevated train. It was dark, about 7:00 p.m. in the wintertime. I was walking down Kedzie Avenue when I saw a man staggering toward me. When he got up to me, he pulled out a knife, stuck it against my stomach, and asked for my money. I said to him, "I've only got a $5 bill, and I was going to stop at the grocery store and get some milk for the baby. So, I'll split it with you. You've got needs and I've got needs. Don't go anywhere, I'll be right back." As I talked to him, I was backing away. I went into the grocery store and got change for my $5 bill. When I came out, he was looking like he didn't know what was going to happen. Had I called the police? But I said, "Wait a minute, don't run. I've got your money here. Here's your money." And I gave him $2.50. Then I said, "And don't be going around sticking people with knives when you need something. You need to ask for what you want." I ignored the knife and focused on him, rather than on me. I made it known that we were both in the same shape. We didn't have much money, but we both had needs. In the end, I was very thankful that I didn't lose my guts. Nonviolence means having guts!

Here is another example from the Chicago movement that illustrates this principle. When we were marching for open housing in the summer of 1966, we marched into the heart of white neighborhoods. The purpose of the marches was to demand our right to live in those neighborhoods. But the residents felt threatened and were worried about losing their neighborhoods. There were so many of them that they easily could have surrounded us. They were hostile, yelling and waving White Power signs with Nazi symbols. They threw rocks and firecrackers at us. They set our cars on fire. In the South, the violence was more organized—either by local law enforcement, as in Mississippi, or by mobs organized by the Ku Klux Klan, as in Alabama. In Chicago, it was ordinary people reacting to a situation. But like in the South, the police didn't do anything—they had decided amongst themselves that they weren't going to intervene. Despite all this, we went back to the neighborhood and we continued to march, again and again. It takes a lot of courage to persevere, knowing what the reaction is going to be. In the face of violence, you don't back down. When things started to escalate, we didn't leave. Eventually, the

Chicago Police Department changed its mind and decided to protect us, so in the later marches we didn't face the same kind of attacks.

We also trained gang members to be marshals for the marches, walking at the edges of the demonstrations to protect the marchers and ensure that nonviolence was maintained. The gang members had experience with violence, having been in fights with weapons, mostly with knives. They had scars. It took a lot of courage on their part to be marshals, and they did it for a good cause. They had been taught not to retaliate in the nonviolence training we provided for them.

Late in the open-housing campaign, it was announced that there would be a march to Cicero, a suburb just west of Chicago. Cicero was known for its particularly virulent, violent racism. The movement's Agenda Committee, made up of local organizational leaders, met with Dr. King and told him a march to Cicero wouldn't be a good idea. Dr. King replied, "You don't have to convince me." He said he was not anxious to demonstrate in Cicero, where an African American high school student looking for a job had recently been killed while just walking down the street. He stated that we were not looking for a violent confrontation; that was not our goal. We were trying to raise the issue of discrimination in housing where it had the potential to get results. When the Summit Agreement was reached on August 26, the Cicero protest was canceled. However, Bob Lucas of Chicago CORE led about 300 people on a march to Cicero anyway. Unfortunately, the nonviolent discipline broke down, and this created problems.[7]

Principle 2: The Beloved Community Is the Framework for the Future

We should strive to create a community where all people can live together in harmony, with no oppressors and no oppressed, no winners and no losers. We should work for the common good, not just personal gain. The first part of this principle, the "beloved community," calls on us to be inclusive, sharing, trusting, and loving. It is not just an absence of conflict but a positive process in which people attempt to reconcile conflict. The second part of the principle looks toward the future with hope and possibility.[8]

Many philosophers were utopians who portrayed their concepts of the ideal society. Plato described what we know as Plato's Republic; Tolstoy called his version of utopia the Kingdom of God. Martin Luther King Jr. described his ideal society as the "beloved community," a community based on inclusion and love, where all human beings are welcome and respected and equal. For instance, people may be taller or shorter, but that does not eclipse the fact that they are equal. There are some advantages to being tall: a tall person can reach the top shelf, but a short person can get a ladder. And there are things short people can do that tall people can't. In the beloved community, even if you have some physical or intellectual advantage, it is not because of you, so you should not claim any extra credit. Tall people have a responsibility to get things off the top shelf and share; those with an advantage must serve others.

Dr. King described it like this in December 1956, just after the successful conclusion of the Montgomery bus boycott: "The end is reconciliation; the end is redemption; the end is the creation of the beloved community. It is this type of spirit and this type of love that can transform opposers into friends. It is this type of understanding good will that will transform the deep gloom of the old age into the exuberant gladness of the new age. It is this love which will bring about miracles in the hearts of men."[9]

The way you practice the beloved community is that, even though you recognize, for example, systematic forms of discrimination or efforts to deny people equality, you work to change these conditions and these attitudes and you refuse to hate. You exemplify the attitude of forgiveness, putting love into action. Your behavior exemplifies what you expect in return.

In Chicago we put this into practice by reaching out to the white communities that were hostile toward us because of our call for open housing. One night in late July, I went to speak at a Catholic church in Belmont-Cragin, a North Side neighborhood where we were preparing to march for open housing. We wanted to explain how both African Americans and white people would be better off if there were open housing, if the Chicago real estate industry's system of blockbusting—converting neighborhoods from white to African American—could be changed. The church was full, and people were listening and asking questions; we were having a discussion. But then a small group of men drifted in and began walking down the central aisle of the church toward me, apparently intending to have a physical confrontation. The priest who had invited me just stood there. A group of plainclothes policemen stood up at the front of the church and faced them. One of the policemen ushered me out the side door, saying it was time to go.

In spite of these difficulties, we worked with a wide range of community groups and people. We worked with priests and ministers who organized small meetings with white people who were sympathetic to open housing in Southwest and Northwest Chicago neighborhoods. A group called Concerned Citizens for an Open City formed on the Southwest Side in late July and sponsored newspaper ads explaining why open housing would benefit white families as well as African Americans. The following winter, a group on the Northwest Side began to work with the Lawndale Union to End Slums, helping African American families find housing in their Northwest Side neighborhood.

We also worked with groups in white neighborhoods on the West Side. For example, Florence Scala, a leader in the Italian American community on the Near West Side, was very supportive of the movement. She later ran for alderman and received a lot of support and cooperation from the African American community there.[10]

One of the characteristics of the beloved community is that the actions we take must be consistent with its goals; the means must reflect the ends we are trying to achieve. This allows others to see where we are headed by the path we are taking. We believe the beloved community can be achieved globally, because we can see it happening on the local level. It becomes a way of life, not just a strategy.

Principle 3: Attack the Forces of Evil, Not the Persons Doing Evil

Removing a particular individual from office might make a difference, but it typically doesn't solve the problem. The focus must be on understanding the root of the problem that produced the oppressive conditions and then deciding how to change the contingencies that led to the conditions. The forces of evil that surround a person support his or her unacceptable behavior. Therefore, our nonviolent approach is to change the conditions in order to solve the problem.[11]

To attack evil, you have to dissociate the person doing evil from the system. If you can get people to withdraw from the system, then the system cannot stand. A system can't exist unless people on both sides—both the victims of the system and those using the system to their advantage—support it or at least cooperate with it. The strategy in nonviolence, then, is to win people over while challenging the system.

We wanted to end the slums—but how could we do that? We took a leapfrog approach. First, we confronted real estate agents, who were the primary force in the system preserving the slums, because they both owned property and controlled the sale of houses, using a clear pattern of blockbusting. Second, we got the real estate companies to fix up their rental properties and treat people humanely (attacking forces within the slums). We also advocated for rent control: people were paying rents that were beyond their means, which caused a number of evictions. Finally, we worked to get people active in demanding more. That was how we built the tenant unions. Our demonstrations focused on the real estate companies—not the individuals who worked there—because they were the ones doing the discriminating.

Years later, after the movement had an agreement with the City of Chicago, the Leadership Council for Metropolitan Open Communities offered workshops for real estate agents to teach them how not to discriminate. An owner of one of the biggest real estate firms, John Baird, later saw the wisdom of this, and he furthered the goals of nondiscrimination by working with movement activists. Kale Williams, former executive director of AFSC, was executive director of the Leadership Council and led this aspect of the work.

Principle 4: Accept Suffering without Retaliation for the Sake of the Cause, to Achieve the Goal

Accepting suffering is not a popular idea for most people. Most would rather avoid suffering. In the context of nonviolence, this concept has a different meaning. It doesn't mean accepting abuse and punishment with no response. In fact, a response is required. But that response must be consistent with the goals we seek, so that suffering occurs not in a vacuum but in the context of a campaign for change. The first change takes place within the individual who is the object of an attack. If a person who is attacked exhibits no purposeful response, that person could be considered a victim. However, if the person responds not with violence but with the power of nonviolence and as part of a strategy to achieve a more just condition, then that person's suffering becomes a source of strength. Confronting an attacker with courage, steadfastness, determination, and nonviolent resistance creates the potential to reach the conscience of the assailant.[12]

In Chicago we did not face the same kind of suffering we encountered in the South, where we might be beaten at any point and our lives were in danger. But there were some moments. On some of the marches into white neighborhoods on Chicago's Southwest Side, the demonstrators were pelted with rocks and large firecrackers (cherry bombs). The crowds were massive and very hostile. On one of these marches, Dr. King was hit on the head with a rock; other people were injured as well. Because our cars, which were parked in Marquette Park, were set on fire and pushed into the lagoon there, we had to march several miles back to the African American community, all the while being pelted with rocks and firecrackers. The Chicago police were there, but they just stood by while all this happened. The gang members who were serving as marshals did a fantastic job, catching rocks that were aimed at the marchers and never retaliating. Change is the goal. We don't stop because of the suffering. It's temporary, and it may well mobilize more people.

Sometimes it's difficult to maintain nonviolence, and we're not always as successful as we would like to be. You can only do your best under the circumstances. One evening we were marching out of Gage Park, and it was getting dark. Police were helping us move the marchers forward. I was bringing up the rear, along with one of the gang members known to us as Charlie Ghetto. Charlie was slight of build but energetic, and he had taken it upon himself to educate the staff in the ways of the ghetto. He had been to many meetings with us over the months. Behind Charlie and me was a group of about ten or twelve hostile young white guys; they were yelling at us, and one of them said something to Charlie that upset him. Charlie told me he wanted to stay behind. "It's something between me and them. You all go ahead; I'll take care of myself," he said. I stopped the march and I told Charlie, "We're not going to leave without you." I ran to the front and called for LaMar McCoy, a tall, strong guy who had previously been a gang leader but had been with us on the Selma march and was then on the SCLC staff. I asked LaMar to go to the back of the line and talk to Charlie Ghetto. "What I need you to do is to persuade him to come," I said. Ten minutes later, here comes LaMar with Charlie Ghetto tossed over his shoulder, knocked out cold. He had to punch Charlie just once, he told me. Sometimes you have to choose the lesser of two evils. It would have been a greater evil to leave Charlie Ghetto there to face those hostile young men by himself. It also would have been a greater evil to stop the march there past dark and risk being attacked. Charlie believed in nonviolence as a tactic but not as a way of life. When faced with an insult, he reacted in his old, violent way. He had to be saved from his own limited perspective of nonviolence. Thinking back on this, I wonder if I could have talked him out of it myself, but the sun was going down, and time was limited. When I reached my limitations, I turned to somebody who could get the job done, even if it wasn't in the way I had hoped. After it was all over, Charlie thanked me. He said, "I'm glad you didn't leave me." He realized he had used poor judgment and would have been putting the other marchers in danger. It shows that sometimes, you have to take action in the best interests of a person, even if it's not your first choice.

Principle 5: Avoid Internal Violence of the Spirit as Well as External Physical Violence

Sometimes when we use hurtful words, we do internal harm to a person's spirit, inflicting psychological and spiritual violence. Dr. King said the psychological scars of segregation take longer to heal than the physical scars. We also do damage to our own spirits when we allow ourselves to be hateful toward others.[13] And as Dr. King said, a wounded spirit takes longer to heal than a wounded body. Today, we would call this emotional or verbal abuse, and we must avoid it. We've all heard the old adage, "Sticks and stones may break my bones but words will never hurt me." This is not the case. Many people are severely damaged by unkind words. Even when someone just ignores another person and denies his or her existence, this is a kind of violence against the spirit. Sometimes it's self-inflicted, or what we might call internalized oppression. This must be resisted.

It is helpful to have a spiritual base or framework. Dr. King often said that we are all children of God and we are all deserving of respect. Gandhi, drawing on his own faith, said, "All men are brothers" (in the language of his time). As the Quakers would say, there is that of God in every person. Secular humanists often articulate these values in terms of universal human rights. For example, the Universal Declaration of Human Rights, developed by the United Nations in the aftermath of World War II and passed unanimously in 1948, declares that "all members of the human family" enjoy "inherent dignity and equal and inalienable rights."[14]

Several aspects of this principle were important in the Chicago Freedom Movement. First, when we made picket signs for our marches and demonstrations, we never called people nasty names; we always hoped to reach the best in our opponents and win them over to our views. Second, our mass meetings created a sense of unity that was spiritually uplifting; when we sang together, there was a sense of being in tune with one another. This was a source of strength that gave us the will to endure; it also helped overcome any internalized oppression among the people working with us. Third, we trained the gang members in nonviolence so they could serve as marshals for the marches. They did a great job and were able to avoid participating in external physical violence.

The only reason people act violently is because they feel violated. The question is, how can you restore them by your actions? When they strike and your response is love, you are showing them how to behave when they feel violated. You are showing them that there is a choice, another possible response. The only way to bring out the best in others is to reach down and bring out the best in yourself. That is the redeeming factor. When we say that suffering is redemptive, we mean that accepting suffering becomes a strength rather than a weakness. Even when you are broken, physically injured, a nonviolent response brings out the best in yourself, and the broken places heal and become even stronger. You endure breaks, but your resolve is not broken. Your resolve is not dissolved; it is replenished rather than diminished, and that gives you the strength to reach out to others. Leadership makes the difference, and leaders should be trained in nonviolence because that sets the tone for everyone else.

Principle 6: The Universe Is on the Side of Justice

In our struggles, we sometimes can't see the end in sight or recognize the goals that are within our grasp. However, we must maintain faith that no matter how dim the hour, how dark the night, or how cloudy the moment, our goal is reachable. People struggle only when they believe they have a chance of achieving their goals. They don't persevere if they think there's no possibility of success.[15] No matter what we faced, no matter what kind of repercussions there were, we had full confidence that we would reach our goal. As Dr. King often said, the moral arc of the universe is long, but it bends toward justice. Ultimately, we bend that arc because of our hard work and our faith. This is why we have faith: because we are working. We wouldn't be able to work if we didn't have faith.

One of the things that gave us hope in Chicago was organizational unity. There was, for instance, a federation of ministers on the West Side, and there were many collaborating groups that worked together on the tenant unions and the lead poisoning project on the West Side. The Coordinating Council of Community Organizations (CCCO) brought together dozens of Chicago organizations, including the Urban League, CORE, NAACP, and many others. When groups join together, that gives them power and strength.

The fact that we are doing the right thing means that we will get the results, because the end preexists in the means. Justice is affirmed through our actions to achieve a more just society. A colleague of mine, drawing on a spiritual tradition from India, articulates it this way: "grace and self-effort are the two wings of the bird."

Finally, in summing up, I want to say that, contrary to what some people have said, nonviolence *did* work in the North, and it can still work in our communities today, North or South. As in the South, the movement in Chicago brought to the surface the underlying tension, the subtle racism, and made it overt. Before you can solve a problem, you have to see that it exists. The movement in Chicago did that.

The movement also made it clear that the conditions endured by the people in Chicago—the oppression and the poverty and the discrimination—differed only in degree from those in the South. Because there were no signs over the water fountains in Chicago, people did not react in the same way. In Chicago, where there were slums, a high unemployment rate, and overcrowded conditions, oppression was still there. Finally, the Chicago Freedom Movement raised people's awareness so that they could stand up for themselves and fight against the system. This is the necessary first step in bringing about change for people who are oppressed.

Notes

1. On my work in Selma, Alabama, see Bernard LaFayette Jr. and Kathryn Lee Johnson, *In Peace and Freedom: My Journey in Selma* (Lexington: University Press of Kentucky, 2013). On Highlander—now the Highlander Research and Education Center—see Myles Horton with Judith Kohl and Herbert Kohl, *The Long Haul: An Autobiography* (New York: Doubleday, 1990).

2. Robert Taylor Homes was a massive, high-rise public-housing project built in the late 1950s and early 1960s on Chicago's South Side. The buildings have now been torn down as a part of the Chicago Housing Authority's Plan for Transformation. See D. Bradford Hunt, *Blueprint for Disaster: The Unraveling of Chicago Public Housing* (Chicago: University of Chicago Press, 2009), 140–43, 282.

3. Kay Mills, *This Little Light of Mine: The Life of Fannie Lou Hamer* (Lexington: University Press of Kentucky, 2007), 192–93, quoting Mike Higson, "Casualty of the Great Society," *Southern Patriot,* January 1967.

4. Bernard LaFayette Jr. and David Jehnsen, *The Leaders Manual: A Structured Guide and Introduction to Kingian Nonviolence: The Philosophy and Methodology* (Galena, OH: Institute for Rights and Responsibilities, 1996), 79. See also "Six Steps of Kingian Nonviolence," http://positivepeacewarriornetwork .wordpress.com/kingian-nonviolence/6-steps-of-kingian-nonviolence/ (accessed January 26, 2015).

5. James R. Ralph Jr., *Northern Protest: Martin Luther King, Jr., Chicago, and the Civil Rights Movement* (Cambridge, MA: Harvard University Press, 1993), 63–64.

6. LaFayette and Johnson, *In Peace and Freedom.*

7. "Open Housing Pact Okayed in Chicago: Marches Called off by Dr. King in Return for City Promise," *Baltimore Sun,* August 27, 1966, A1. See also "March Ends in Rock Fight," *Chicago Tribune,* September 5, 1966, 1.

8. LaFayette and Johnson, *In Peace and Freedom,* 166.

9. Martin Luther King Jr., "Facing the Challenge of a New Age," in *A Testament of Hope: The Essential Writings and Speeches of Martin Luther King, Jr.*, ed. James M. Washington (New York: Harper San Francisco, 1991), 140. See also Charles Marsh, *The Beloved Community: How Faith Shapes Social Justice from the Civil Rights Movement to Today* (New York: Basic Books, 2005).

10. On Florence Scala, see Carolyn Eastwood, *Near West Side Stories: Struggles for Community in Chicago's Maxwell Street Neighborhood* (Chicago: Lake Claremont Press, 2002), 119–97.

11. LaFayette and Johnson, *In Peace and Freedom*, 167.

12. Ibid.

13. Ibid., 168.

14. Mohandas K. Gandhi, *All Men Are Brothers: Life and Thoughts of Mahatma Gandhi as Told in His Own Words*, ed. Krishna Kripali (Ahmedabad, India: Navajivan Publishing House, 1960). Also see A. C. Grayling, *The God Argument: The Case against Religion and for Humanism* (New York: Bloomsbury, 2013), 180.

15. LaFayette and Johnson, *In Peace and Freedom*, 168.

21

Movement Success

The Long View

Mary Lou Finley

How can we think about the impact of the Chicago Freedom Movement? For many in the United States, poverty is even worse today than when Martin Luther King moved into that slum apartment in North Lawndale. And it is clear that racism is far from over.[1]

In the mid-1960s in Chicago, Dr. King faced both racism and poverty in an intimate way, meeting with those who were most affected, often in that North Lawndale apartment. There, he began to intensify his work against poverty, which profoundly affected African Americans as well as many others, while continuing to work against racism as well. The seeds were sown there for the multiracial coalition that became the Poor People's Campaign that Dr. King was organizing when he was assassinated in Memphis in April 1968. His work was brought to a tragic end long before it was finished.

Dr. King's assassination, as well as the assassination of Senator Robert Kennedy two months later, on the evening of his victory in the California presidential primary, stunned the nation and generated a wave of shock and despair across the civil rights movement and across the United States and the world. In a sense, we have not recovered from it yet.[2]

Still, if we dig deeply into the Chicago movement stories, we can see that its work had a significant impact then and in the years and decades that followed. That is the story we have told in this book. The Chicago Freedom Movement involved many people, and they carried on the work when King's eloquent voice and soulful presence were taken from us.

Further, political forces have been attempting to undermine that progress over the last five decades. We must explore these as well.

It is my sense, however, that we are entering a new era in which the issues raised by Dr. King and so many of his compatriots in the struggle are once again on the public agenda. Burgeoning movements for racial justice, for social and economic justice, and for a living democracy are taking root. Inequality is being acknowledged and debated in the public arena across a broad political spectrum. So far, however, poverty still seems to be hovering in the background, just out of public view for those not caught in the midst of it.[3]

The question remains: how can we assess the success of the Chicago Freedom Movement? When evaluating the impact of any social movement, it is best to take the long view; I would suggest that many have been measuring the Chicago movement's impact with a ruler when a yardstick is called for. Bill Moyer's Movement Action Plan (MAP) model of successful social movements can provide a frame for our exploration of that long view. This model was developed to support activists in their strategizing and organizing work, but it also provides a relevant frame as we look back on the Chicago Freedom Movement and the subsequent efforts to move its agenda forward in the decades that followed.[4]

In the MAP model, successful social movements move through eight stages: (1) normal times, (2) proving the failure of official institutions, (3) ripening conditions, (4) movement takeoff, (5) perception of failure—a movement detour, (6) building majority public support, (7) success, and (8) continuing the struggle. In this chapter I provide a brief overview of key campaigns of the Chicago Freedom Movement as viewed through the lens of the MAP model.[5]

When we think of social movements, we often think of major direct action campaigns with marches, rallies, sit-ins, and other publicly visible tactics. These campaigns can sometimes spark a dramatic "movement takeoff" (stage 4) that puts the issue on the public agenda; suddenly, there is much public discussion about the issue, and the strategies and tactics used in the direct action campaign are often picked up by others and replicated in other locations. The student lunch counter sit-in movement of 1960 is a classic case. I would suggest that the Chicago Freedom Movement's open-housing marches sparked such a takeoff, focusing the nation's attention on housing discrimination. However, the takeoff is not the beginning; a movement takeoff builds on preliminary organizing in smaller, local campaigns and often involves unsuccessful efforts to work through official channels (e.g., public hearings, lobbying, or laws and regulations that prove inadequate to the task).

But more important for our purposes here is the model's suggestion that success generally does not come at the end of movement takeoff; rather, the takeoff sets in motion an array of social forces that begin to build majority public support for the movement's goals (stage 6) and eventually lead to success (stage 7).These social forces involve myriad related organizing efforts as well as a deepening and widening of what Jane Mansbridge and Aldon Morris call "oppositional consciousness": a shift toward more hope and less despair, the generation of more anger and more energy for change as the movement exposes the violations of important values and the unfairness of current social practices and then spurs those suffering and their allies of conscience to act. With all this activity, public opinion begins to shift. And then successes, both small and large, become possible.[6]

The Chicago Freedom Movement was, in fact, several movements (or submovements, in the language of the MAP model) wrapped into one: the open-housing movement, with its marches into white neighborhoods; the end-the-slums movement, which focused primarily on organizing tenant unions but also analyzed the myriad forces that create slums; and economic justice efforts led by Operation Breadbasket's campaigns to generate more and better jobs for African Americans and more opportunities for African American businesses. Other submovements included the organizing of welfare rights groups and the remnants of the schools campaign that rocked Chicago from 1962 through 1965 and led to the collaboration between Martin Luther King's Southern Christian Leadership Conference (SCLC) and Chicago's Coordinating Council of Community Organizations (CCCO). In addition, the organizing against childhood lead poisoning was related to early tenant union organizing and was part of the groundwork for the Chicago Freedom Movement. Finally, out of civil rights activism in Chicago—the Chicago Freedom Movement included—came the growing political power of African Americans in Chicago and the nation. All these organizing efforts were wrapped together in a general antipoverty movement aimed at improving the lives of African Americans and others caught in the poverty and systemic discrimination of the urban North.

If we want to examine the Chicago Freedom Movement through the lens of the MAP model, then we need to treat its various submovements separately. For this discussion, I focus on three key campaigns: open housing, tenant unions, and economic justice (tables 1, 2, and 3 summarize the progression of these issues through the MAP stages). The Chicago Freedom Movement and its Chicago team had a crucial role in some of these changes, while much of the later work was carried on by others, as is often the case when social change happens.

The Open-Housing Movement

The summer 1966 direct action campaign—with its marches through Chicago's white working-class neighborhoods—generated a "movement takeoff" for the issue of housing discrimination. The dramatic—and hateful—responses from residents of these neighborhoods electrified the nation, embarrassed many Chicagoans, and set in motion a range of efforts to address the discriminatory real estate practices that kept African Americans locked in carefully defined neighborhoods.

Why was movement takeoff possible? First, this was essentially an issue of outright, overt discrimination: African Americans were not served by real estate offices when they requested housing in white neighborhoods. This paralleled quite precisely the refusal of service at restaurants and other public facilities in the South. Coming just three years after the Birmingham campaign and the March on Washington and two years after passage of the Civil Rights Act of 1964, it was an extension of the principle of nondiscrimination established by the southern movement and the Civil Rights Act. It is often easier to win related campaigns once a movement has achieved some victories and certain principles—such as nondiscrimination—have been established.

Second, Chicago had passed a fair-housing ordinance in 1963, but testing by activists working with the American Friends Service Committee (AFSC) provided clear evidence that it was not being enforced, thus taking this issue through MAP stage 2: the failure of official institutions.

Table 1. Chicago Freedom Movement: Open-Housing Campaign

MAP Stage	Events
Stage 1: Normal Times (pre-1963)	Chicago Real Estate Board enforces segregated housing Violent attacks on African Americans who move outside black community
Stage 2: Proving the Failure of Official Institutions (1963–1965)	City of Chicago passes fair-housing law; nothing changes AFSC tests real estate offices for discrimination and finds it
Stage 3: Ripening Conditions (1964–spring 1966)	1964: Civil Rights Act passes 1963–1966: AFSC organizes suburban fair-housing groups June–August 1965: North Shore Summer Project—college students work on fair housing July 1965: Martin Luther King Jr. speaks in Chicago and on the North Shore September 1965: MLK's staff begins organizing on slum-housing issues January 1966: Chicago Freedom Movement forms: SCLC + CCCO
Stage 4: Movement Takeoff (summer 1966)	July–August 1966: Open-housing marches August 1966: Summit Agreement on open-housing issues; ACLU files *Gautreaux* discrimination case against Chicago Housing Authority
Stage 5: Perception of Failure (fall 1966 for several years)	September 1966: Cicero march; breakdown of nonviolence After September 1966: Some SCLC staff leave to work in antiwar movement, some leave discouraged; some Chicagoans also discouraged
Stage 6: Building Majority Public Support (fall 1966–present)	1966–2006: Leadership Council for Metropolitan Open Communities attacks housing discrimination on many fronts **[1968: Martin Luther King assassinated]** 1968–1970: Organizing by Contract Buyers League; direct action to save homes 1968–1980s: Anti-redlining movement 1969: *Gautreaux* case to integrate public housing is successful, but CHA refuses to implement
Stage 7: Success (1968–present)	April 1968: Civil Rights Act, including Fair Housing Act, passes 1976: *Gautreaux* case wins in Supreme Court; some public-housing desegregation occurs via Gautreaux housing voucher program 1977: Community Reinvestment Act passes 1988: Strengthened Fair Housing Act passes 1990s: Violence against African Americans who move into white neighborhoods ceases
Stage 8: Continuing the Struggle (1970s–present)	1988–present: National Fair Housing Alliance initiatives 1990–present: National Community Reinvestment Coalition forms

Finally, there had been considerable preparation in Chicago: AFSC's housing program operated by Bill Moyer, Bert Ransom, and Jerry Davis had pioneered the testing of real estate offices to establish discrimination, as well as staging small-scale protests at real estate agents' open-house events. This group was part of the Chicago Freedom Movement. Thus, the movement had already gone through a period of ripening conditions (stage 3) by the time preparations for the summer action campaign were under way.

Movement takeoff, and the Summit Agreement that resulted, was an important local success (in spite of its limitations). However, passage of the Civil Rights Act of 1968, with its fair-housing provisions, did not occur until two years later. This is what the MAP model would predict: success often comes later, after the activists who sparked movement take-off have moved on to other projects; they may barely notice the "belated" victory. This pattern has also been noted by political scientist Sidney Tarrow, who points out that "cycles of contention are a season for sowing, but the reaping is often done in periods of demobilization that follow, by latecomers to the cause, by elites and authorities."[7]

The model also suggests that even when the movement has achieved success on at least some of its goals, this is not the end of the process. The movement needs to monitor and support the implementation of new laws and policies, fight against possible backlash, and continue to press for further improvements: continuing the struggle (stage 8).

One additional note: The MAP model suggests that after a successful movement takeoff, some activists may get discouraged when victory is not immediate. They may either call for more militant tactics or simply drop out, filled with feelings of hopelessness or despair (stage 5—perception of failure). Although some social movements avoid this detour, the Chicago Freedom Movement did not. The march to Cicero by Bob Lucas and others who were disappointed with the Summit Agreement was an example of opting for more militant tactics, and in this case, the participants chose not to maintain the movement's nonviolent discipline. A few discouraged SCLC staffers resigned and moved away from Chicago shortly thereafter. SCLC's Chicago Project director James Bevel felt called to the antiwar movement, and in January 1967 he left Chicago to coordinate the massive Spring Mobilization to End the War in Vietnam in New York City.

Although I would not characterize his move as being motivated by discouragement, it had a similar impact because he moved on.

We can see that the struggle for fair housing has continued in the years and decades that followed. For instance, the work of Chicago's Leadership Council for Metropolitan Open Communities—an explicit outgrowth of the Summit Agreement with Mayor Richard J. Daley—is described by Brian White in chapter 5. It became a model for nonprofit fair-housing groups across the nation, working both locally and nationally to enhance fair housing. The National Fair Housing Alliance was formed in 1988, the same year the federal fair-housing law was strengthened. All these additional efforts have not ended segregated housing. However, with stronger laws, those discriminated against can seek legal redress. And—even in Chicago—attitudes and practices have shifted significantly. By the 1990s, most of the violence directed against African Americans moving into white neighborhoods had ceased. The Gautreaux Program moved thousands of public-housing tenants into "opportunity neighborhoods" located outside the limits of traditional African American neighborhoods, with generally good results. With the help of the Fair Housing Centers developed in the wake of the movement, many middle-class African Americans were able to buy homes in the suburbs, closer to new employment opportunities. As Chester Hartman and Gregory Squires have noted, however, there was also a waning interest in integration in some quarters. Some attributed this to "integration fatigue," while others saw the concentration of African Americans in urban neighborhoods as an important base for enhanced black political power. Others valued the strong social networks and institutional supports, such as churches, in African American neighborhoods.[8]

In spite of the many modest successes, recent evidence indicates that housing segregation and discriminatory lending practices remain serious problems. In the summer of 2014 US housing discrimination was addressed by the United Nations Committee on the Elimination of Racial Discrimination in its periodic review of signatory nations. A "shadow report" prepared for this meeting by the Poverty and Race Research Action Council and the National Fair Housing Alliance documented with extensive evidence that "the government has taken few meaningful steps to reduce racial segregation," particularly in the areas of mortgage lending (subject to many government rules) and lending practices. This lack of action surfaced publicly during the Great Recession of 2008, when it became clear that African Americans and Latinos had been offered less favorable mortgages than their white counterparts in a process labeled reverse redlining. The report also noted inadequacies in "affirmatively furthering fair housing," as required by federal law, and in providing fair-housing protection for racial minorities who were also members of other protected classes, such as the disabled or LGBT (lesbian, gay, bisexual, transgender) community. The report recommended both congressional and executive branch policy changes.[9]

But there is an unquantifiable impact as well. Mark Warren tells one such story. Sixteen-year-old Jim Capraro had grown up in Marquette Park, and one summer day in 1966, as he was getting ready to go on a date for the first time in the family car, he walked out of his house:

> I saw a huge crowd of white people, four or five deep, on the side-walk, going out into the street. There were policemen with batons, holding them off away from the street. People were throwing beer bottles, just hurling them, at something. Across the street there's some big hubbub, and I could see black people. I could also see clergy, who were not black. They all had signs, and the signs said things like, "End Slums" and "Open Housing." . . . People are jeering and yelling . . . and it's terrible. It's ugly. . . .
>
> I don't know that I was there more than half an hour . . . but it was the longest half hour in my life. And it changed my life forever. Kind of an epiphany, I guess. When I went home that night I couldn't sleep. I had this never-ending stream of thoughts. Everything I thought I had learned or was led to believe I thought was a lie. We're not the greatest country in the world. . . . What just happened two blocks from my house? This can't be the best neighborhood. Look at what people do. Look at how they were behaving . . . I got mad. How dare these people do this stuff? This is a democracy! People have a right to say things and march and think of themselves as being equal with everybody else, and in fact be equal to everybody else.[10]

Later, while at college, Capraro heard Black Power advocate Stokely Carmichael speak. Carmichael remarked that white people who cared about
ending racism should work in their own communities. Jim Capraro took
it to heart and went home to Marquette Park. There, he founded the
Greater Southwest Development Corporation and spent forty years of
his life "combating redlining and white flight and working for economic
development and stable racial integration in a neighborhood that had
become a symbol of Northern racism."[11]

The End-the-Slums Campaign and Tenant Union Organizing

The Union to End Slums neighborhood groups, organized in East
Garfield Park, Lawndale, and the Near North Side, focused on organizing tenant unions to address the often abominable conditions in
rental housing in Chicago's black neighborhoods. Because housing
was so scarce in the African American community, many landlords
divided apartments into "kitchenettes"—just one room where whole
families sometimes lived, with one bathroom down the hall shared by
several families. There were rats and roaches and fires. Rent for these
apartments was often as high as the rent for decent housing in white
neighborhoods.

In MAP terms, the end-the-slums campaign and the tenant union
effort were at an earlier stage than other issues. It was not strictly a case
of overt discrimination, although it was grounded in housing discrimination and the resultant lack of choices for African Americans. Thus,
these efforts were unable to ride the coattails of the southern antidiscrimination movement. Although there had been earlier tenant organizing
efforts—we were aware of Jesse Gray's tenant councils in New York City
in 1963–1964, for example—there was minimal organizing in Chicago at
that time to deal with the crisis of slum housing.[12]

The tenant movement, however, had passed through stage 2, failure of official institutions: City of Chicago building inspectors had not
called a halt to the rental of these grossly dilapidated and overcrowded
apartments through the enforcement of city building codes. Thus, we
would consider the tenant union organizing a stage 3 (ripening condi-

Table 2. Chicago Freedom Movement: End-the-Slums Campaign

MAP Stage	Events
Stage 1: Normal Times (1940s–1950)	Poor live in slum housing; black community drastically overcrowded; apartments converted to tiny living spaces such as "kitchenettes" 1944–1946: Some tenant organizing 1947: James Hickman loses four children in an apartment fire started by arson; he is acquitted after murdering the landlord, who confessed responsibility; dramatic public support for Hickman; case calls attention to horrific living conditions and landlord-initiated arson in Chicago
Stage 2: Proving the Failure of Official Institutions (1950s–1964)	"Urban Renewal = Negro Removal" City building inspectors do not enforce building codes in slums More cases of alleged landlord-initiated arson
Stage 3: Ripening Conditions (1963–1966)	1963–1964: Jesse Gray organizes tenant councils, rent strikes in Harlem 1964: CORE and AFSC start small-scale tenant organizing on Chicago's West Side 1964: AFSC staff discover extensive childhood lead poisoning in West Side apartments 1965: Martin Luther King Jr. brings SCLC to Chicago to join with CCCO 1966: King moves into slum apartment in North Lawndale on West Side 1965–1967: West Side SCLC and AFSC staff and others organize tenant unions May 1966: JOIN collective bargaining agreement with Uptown landlords
Stage 4: Movement Takeoff (1966–1970)	July 13, 1966: Collective bargaining agreement with slumlords Condor and Costalis, including the right to withhold rent 1966: Tenant organizing spreads in Chicago, resulting in 45 tenant unions in a few months 1966–1969: Tenant organizing spreads to over 30 cities across the country 1969–1970: National Tenant Organization founded; 600 affiliates in a year
Stage 5: Perception of Failure (1967–1970)	1967: SCLC lessens commitment to tenant organizing; most staff depart, often discouraged **[1968: Martin Luther King assassinated]** 1968+: Collective bargaining tenant unions difficult to maintain for more than a year in privately owned buildings due to the rapid tenant turnover
Stage 6: Building Majority Public Support (1966–1980s)	1966: First community development corporations begin housing rehabilitation 1974: National Low Income Housing Coalition begins 1975: National Housing Institute and *Shelterforce* magazine support tenant organizers

Stage 7: Success (1972–1990s)	1972: National Tenants Organization successfully negotiates new lease for public housing, giving tenants more rights 1972: Illinois Supreme Court rules in favor of tenants' right to habitable dwellings 1972: Uniform Residential Landlord-Tenant Act approved by National Commission; localities begin to adopt its provisions for implied warrant of habitability, repair and deduct, restriction on retaliation against tenants who organize 1986: Chicago adopts new landlord-tenant law
Stage 8: Continuing the Struggle (1970s–present)	Community development corporations continue to expand More state and local governments adopt landlord-tenant laws that protect tenants

tions) effort, experimenting with various ways to tackle the problem and developing creative approaches to it.

As a result of the Chicago Freedom Movement's tenant organizing efforts, the residents of multiple buildings initiated rent strikes. And by July 13, 1966, there was an agreement with one of the largest slumlords on the West Side—Condor and Costalis—a collective bargaining agreement that established the tenants' right to withhold rent and make repairs if the landlord failed to do so in a timely manner, among other rights. At the time, this important victory was somewhat overshadowed by preparations for the open-housing marches, and it didn't receive much public attention. At first, this appears to be the kind of victory we would expect during stage 3: small and local, yet precedent setting. However, as we examine the events that followed, it begins to look more and more like a movement takeoff for tenant rights. For example, others in Chicago and elsewhere picked up on the tenant union idea and attempted collective bargaining with landlords. Tenant unions mushroomed around the country. A national organizing meeting was held in Chicago in 1969, hosted by the Chicago Tenants Union and cosponsored by Jesse Gray's group in New York City. Chicago organizer Tony Henry was chosen as the national organization's executive director. Within a year, the group had more than 600 affiliates.[13]

Important victories started coming to fruition in 1972. That year, the Commission for Uniform State Laws issued new guidelines calling for new landlord-tenant laws that granted tenants important rights, including the "implied warrant of habitability," and defining landlord-tenant law as a form of contract law. In 1972 Chicago Freedom Movement attorney Gilbert Cornfield took one of the West Side tenant cases to the Illinois Supreme Court and won a major victory for tenants' rights, with the court supporting the "implied warrant of habitability." Institutions to deepen and connect the movement arrived in the mid-1970s. In 1975 the National Housing Institute was founded, and it launched *Shelterforce* magazine as a forum for tenant organizers to connect and share strategies. Landlord-tenant law began to change around the nation.

In 1986 a coalition of more than forty Chicago organizations, the Coalition for the Tenants Bill of Rights, pressured the Chicago City Council into passing an ordinance providing tenants with, among other rights, the right to "repair and deduct," a provision strikingly similar to what the Chicago Freedom Movement had been seeking twenty years earlier. Housing conditions in Chicago's poor neighborhoods remain difficult, but tenants faced with poor conditions now have more legal rights, as do tenants in many localities across the nation.[14]

Further, the movement for improved housing conditions for low-income people has had a strong "constructive program," as community groups forged ahead with housing rehabilitation efforts and the construction of new low-income housing, often through community development corporations. Later legislative successes supporting the expansion of low-income housing included federal laws providing low-income housing credits (1986) and requirements for community reinvestment (1977).[15]

Although the housing stock for low-income communities has definitely improved, there is still a disastrously insufficient supply of decent low-income housing, greatly exacerbated by a major decline in the number of units of subsidized public housing. This loss began during the backlash of the 1980s, when President Ronald Reagan drastically cut funding for new public housing. In 1995 HUD abolished its long-standing rule requiring one-to-one replacement for any demolished public-housing apartments. Between 1995 and 2008 the HOPE VI programs to transform public housing into mixed-income communities, combined with the demolition of other public-housing units, resulted in a 12 percent decline in the total number of units of low-income housing, even though the need for such housing continues to mushroom. Resultant family homelessness, virtually unknown in the 1960s, is now wreaking havoc in families across the country, presenting us with a different—but related—crisis.[16]

There were important victories: new rights for tenants throughout much of the nation, and substantial programs to rehabilitate and build low-income housing. But other forces—at least partially coming from an overt backlash—resulted in increased family homelessness. We are ripe for another movement addressing the housing needs of low-income people, one that builds on successes of the past, takes seriously the creation of an adequate supply of low-income housing, stops the destruction of existing low-income housing, and moves beyond homeless shelters as a solution.

The Economic Justice and Antipoverty Movements

The Chicago movement's economic justice focus centered on Operation Breadbasket, directed by the Reverend Jesse Jackson in collaboration with the Reverend Clay Evans (pastor of Fellowship Missionary Baptist Church and in the mid-1960s president of the Baptist Ministers Conference of Chicago and Vicinity). SCLC had been operating successful chapters of Operation Breadbasket in the South since 1962, so there was already an established pattern for how to proceed. Breadbasket began by developing selective buying campaigns to win more and better jobs for African Americans.[17]

Breadbasket's first victory in Chicago came a few months after its February 1966 start, with a commitment from Country Delight Dairy to hire forty-four new African American employees within thirty days. Commitments from four more dairies followed rapidly, and then the campaign moved on to soft drink companies and supermarkets, with many successes there as well. Later victories were often—but not always—won through negotiations rather than selective buying campaigns, although such campaigns were sometimes needed to encourage cooperation.[18]

By November 1966, Operation Breadbasket had expanded its scope to a "broader program to develop a stronger economic base for the black community." As it was negotiating with supermarkets, it added requests to place black-produced products, such as Joe Louis Milk and Parker House Sausage, on the shelves—something that had been surprisingly difficult even in supermarkets in the black community. Further-

Table 3. Chicago Freedom Movement: Economic Justice Campaign

MAP Stage	Events
Stage 1: Normal Times (pre-1964)	Rampant job discrimination against African Americans; extensive poverty
Stage 2: Proving the Failure of Official Institutions (1964)	War on Poverty passes with no jobs program Civil Rights Act outlaws discrimination in employment, but few immediate changes
Stage 3: Ripening Conditions (1963–1967)	August 1963: March on Washington for Jobs and Freedom raises issue 1965 on: Welfare rights organizing in Chicago and elsewhere Spring 1966: Operation Breadbasket has victories with dairies and soft drink companies, with jobs promised for African Americans Fall 1966: Operation Breadbasket expands to win victories for black-owned businesses January 1967: Freedom Budget issued by A. Philip Randolph Institute, with foreword by Martin Luther King
Stage 4: Movement Takeoff (1968)	[1968: Martin Luther King assassinated] Spring 1968: Poor People's Campaign, Washington, DC Jesse Jackson leads marches to Department of Agriculture to demand end to hunger Spring 1968: Operation Breadbasket meetings on Saturdays expand to 3,000 participants 1969: Black Expo builds community support for black businesses; 600,000 people participate the first year 1969: Campaign for jobs in the building trades; 20,000 jobs in Chicago
Stage 5: Perception of Failure (mid-1970s on)	Elite backlash aims to increase inequality—blames the poor; touts trickle-down economics, deregulation Many activists discouraged
Stage 6: Building Majority Public Support (1969 on)	Momentum from 1960s still strong enough to support many new programs, successes 1980s on: Backlash against the poor
Stage 7: Success (1971 on)	Court requires affirmative action plans, setting goals and timetables for hiring women and minorities and for admission to universities 1973: Nixon's CETA—government jobs program during recession 1970s: Many programs to open opportunities; increase in black middle class; expansion of food stamps, earned income tax credit 1990s: Living wage campaigns successful in many cities

Stage 8: Continuing the Struggle (1974 on)	1974 on: Wages no longer increasing 1980s: Deindustrialization and deregulation escalate and result in growing inequality; backlash against affirmative action, unions; family homelessness begins 2005–present: Some states, cities increase minimum wage 2008: Great Recession devastates many poor and middle class 2010 on: New campaigns for wage increases among working poor 2011: Occupy movement calls attention to growing inequality, using the motto, "We are the 99%"

more, noting the difficulties black-owned businesses had in getting loans from white banks, Breadbasket successfully negotiated with the state of Illinois to place some of its funds in black-owned banks. Black Expo, first held in 1969 and repeated for several years thereafter, was a huge success, bringing out 600,000 people its first year and building visibility and community support for black- and minority-owned businesses. Operation Breadbasket spread to other cities and continued to open up opportunities for both African American job seekers and businesses. This work was highly successful and made significant contributions to the economic well-being of the African American community. In 1971 Operation Breadbasket became Operation PUSH; it is now operating as the Rainbow PUSH Coalition and is still working on economic and political issues in the African American community after nearly fifty years. A recent focus of Rainbow PUSH has been increased jobs in high-tech industries for minorities and women.[19]

In MAP terms, we would say that Operation Breadbasket was essentially operating as a stage 3 (ripening conditions) program, winning important local victories and serving as a model for other communities. Breadbasket itself spread at one point to twenty-five communities across the nation. It was one strand among many that fed into the expansion of the African American middle and upper-middle classes in Chicago and across the country. The provisions of the 1964 Civil Rights Act outlawing discrimination in employment, as well as affirmative action programs to remedy past discrimination, began to open up spaces in universities and businesses and also contributed to the expansion of the African American middle and upper-middle classes. In fact, the Operation Breadbasket frame for increasing employment opportunities for African Americans foreshadowed the "goals and timetables" for hiring minorities and women required by affirmative action programs in the late 1960s and, more expansively, in the 1970s and beyond.[20]

The African American middle class began to grow substantially as higher positions in business, government, and other organizations opened up to African Americans. A 2005 Chicago Urban League study by Paul Street documented that, as a group, African Americans earning more than $75,000 a year were growing rapidly: "Between 1970 and 2000 the number of African American Chicagoans receiving an income . . . of $75,000 and above (according to) the 2000 census increased by 13%, while the comparable increase for all Chicagoans was only 1%." This change represents an important component of progress toward economic justice.[21]

However, the situation for the poor is another story. As noted earlier, Martin Luther King increasingly focused on the issue of poverty in the last years of his life. But first, let us backtrack a bit, to 1964, when President Lyndon Johnson declared a War on Poverty and shepherded the Economic Opportunity Act through Congress, launching antipoverty programs across the nation. Thus, beginning in 1964, poverty was no longer a silent, unacknowledged issue (as in stage 1—normal times); it was an issue that official institutions were attempting to address. There were very important dimensions to the antipoverty program that supplied needed resources to the poor: Head Start provided preschool education in a holistic framework, including both health and nutrition components; community health clinics brought health care to many who had been without it in both urban and rural areas; community action programs provided human services and, in some instances, actually mobilized the poor; Medicaid and Medicare, adopted in 1965, were critically important in bringing health care to the elderly and the poor and were a major factor in the decline of poverty among the elderly. However, the War on Poverty did not directly address the causes of poverty; it did not address widespread hunger, and it did not include a jobs program or strengthened income supports for the poor. So, in spite of its many important contributions, I would argue that, in terms of the MAP model, the War on Poverty can be seen as stage 2 (failure of official institutions). The War on Poverty promised change and raised expectations, but poverty and hunger, in both the North and the South, remained.[22]

Operation Breadbasket's work finding jobs in retail industries for African Americans can be considered stage 3 (ripening conditions), with small but important local victories. Dr. King's eloquent articulation of poverty as a problem of justice also contributed. Federal War on Poverty programs provided some social-services jobs, sometimes for the poor, another aspect of stage 3.

Another project of the Chicago Freedom Movement, the expansion of welfare rights, was a parallel effort to attack the economic problems of the poor. The Wider Community Staff meetings held in the fall of 1965 and winter of 1966 brought together two community groups working intensively on welfare rights: the West Side Organization from the African American community, and the JOIN Community Union from the predominantly white Uptown neighborhood. The Kenwood-Oakland Community Organization developed a welfare rights organizing project a short time later. This organizing effort was in its early stages, and participants were just beginning to articulate the issues. Although neither Dr. King's staff nor the CCCO staff were much involved in the welfare unions, welfare issues were definitely on the agenda of the Chicago Freedom Movement. Among the demands Dr. King posted on the door of Chicago's City Hall were "Welfare Demands," stated as follows:

From the Illinois Public Aid Department and the Cook County Department of Public Aid:

(1) Recognition of welfare unions and community organizations as bargaining agents for welfare recipients;

(2) Regular meetings between representatives of the recipients and top department administration;

(3) Institution of a declaration of income system to replace the degrading investigation and means test for welfare eligibility;

(4) Change in the rules and procedures to speed up the issuance of emergency checks and to eliminate withholding of checks pending investigation.[23]

These demands, like a number of others, never made it to the negotiating table (where the focus was open-housing issues), but they represented an early articulation of concerns that stimulated welfare rights organizing to expand. The National Welfare Rights Organization was launched in 1967, with Chicago groups among the founding participants.[24]

Concurrent with the movement in Chicago, Martin Luther King was also working at the national level with A. Philip Randolph and others to develop a "Freedom Budget," introduced to the public on October 26, 1966. In his introduction to the twenty-page summary of the Freedom Budget proposal, Dr. King said:

> The journey ahead requires that we emphasize the needs of all America's poor, for there is no way to merely find work, or adequate housing, or quality integrated schools for Negroes alone. We shall eliminate slums for Negroes when we destroy ghettoes and build new cities for *all*. . . . The Southern Christian Leadership Conference fully endorses the Freedom Budget and plans to expend great attention and time in working for its implementation. . . . We must dedicate ourselves to the legislative task to see that it is immediately and fully implemented. . . . It is a political necessity. It is a moral commitment to the fundamental principles on which this nation was founded.[25]

Congressional hearings on the Freedom Budget were held soon after its release, and King expected to organize national demonstrations in support of it.[26]

I would suggest, then, that the antipoverty movement reached movement takeoff in 1967–1968, nurtured by the Chicago Freedom Movement's earlier stage 3 work, the federal government's War on Poverty, and many other small local initiatives. King's Poor People's Campaign was central to the takeoff and helped place poverty on the national agenda, even though he was assassinated just before it began in earnest in Washington, DC. His death was a major setback to this campaign as well as a national tragedy.[27]

Senator Robert F. Kennedy also played a key role in calling public attention to poverty issues. In 1967, hosted by attorney Marion Wright (now Marion Wright Edelman, longtime director of the Children's Defense Fund) and other civil rights workers in the Mississippi Delta, he visited shacks where children lived with distended bellies and nutritional deficiencies such as kwashiorkor, reminiscent of famine victims on other continents. He was so shaken by the experience that he returned to Washington determined to find a way to feed those families. He immediately told Secretary of Agriculture Orville Freeman to make food stamps available with no co-payment to families with no income. Senator Kennedy's work was also cut short by his assassination on June 6, 1968, just two months after the assassination of Martin Luther King Jr.[28]

In spite of these tragic losses, these efforts built public support for antipoverty initiatives (stage 6) and resulted in several important successes (stage 7) that to this day provide a critical—if far too limited—safety net that we take for granted. Food stamps, now the Supplemental Nutrition Assistance Program (SNAP), began on a small scale in 1967 and has expanded to provide basic sustenance to more than 47 million Americans today. During the Poor People's Campaign in Washington, Jesse Jackson led daily marches to the Department of Agriculture, demanding an expansion of food programs for the poor. The earned income tax credit, initiated in 1975 and expanded since then, provides an income supplement for the working poor, administered as a refundable tax credit, and it is "now lifting over 40 million people out of poverty."[29]

The movements of that era created a climate in which it became the norm to use our democracy to work toward the inclusion of everyone. This applied not only to Democrats but to Republicans as well. For example, during the recession of the 1970s, Republican Richard Nixon signed into law the Comprehensive Employment and Training Act of 1973 (CETA), which provided federal funding to create jobs, most of which were in the public sector and in nonprofit organizations. An antihunger movement in the early 1970s continued the work begun by King's Poor People's Campaign. Local food banks greatly expanded across the country in the early 1970s. These victories added to the earlier successes of the Johnson era: Medicare, Medicaid, Head Start, and the Economic Opportunity Act (War on Poverty).

Underlying these changes of the 1960s and 1970s was a widespread public consensus that government could be used to address pressing problems of the citizenry; that widespread poverty in the richest country in the world was a travesty that we needed to address collectively; and that, in a democracy, it is the government's responsibility to see that the needs of all people are addressed. This is, after all, the point of democracy.

Yet, in spite of all these efforts and more, poverty is still with us. In fact, it is worse in terms of both numbers of poor and their proportion of Americans. What has happened? How could this be?

There have been many shifts in the economy in the last three to four decades. These include the overseas outsourcing of jobs, the marginalization of much employment (what one political scientist calls "the great risk shift"), and the automation or computerization of many jobs, from robots in factories to online plane reservations. The Great Recession of 2008 and beyond has left much of the middle class in a more precarious financial position, with some of them falling into poverty.[30]

But if there were a strong public commitment to ending poverty, I believe these challenges could be addressed. (The government could, for instance, abolish tax breaks for companies that move jobs overseas and establish a federal jobs program similar to Nixon's CETA or Franklin Roosevelt's Works Progress Administration.) The real question, then, is what happened to that public commitment to end poverty?

We usually date the public backlash against the gains of the 1960s and early 1970s from Reagan's election in 1980. Reagan did much to belittle the poor, such as his talk of "welfare queens," a rhetoric aimed at painting the poor as "unworthy" and undermining poverty as an issue of economic justice. His antiunion campaigns further undermined another source of collective support for economic justice.

But Reagan was not acting alone. Even as these programs to ease poverty were being launched in the late 1960s and early 1970s, a backlash was beginning among the business elite, mostly hidden from public view. It has now come to light that by the early 1970s, some of these prominent Americans were nervous about all this change. One well-known political scientist complained of an "excess of democracy." Recently, a memorandum written by Lewis Powell, appointed to the Supreme Court in 1971 by President Nixon, has come to light. In 1971 Powell was chair of the Education Committee of the US Chamber of Commerce. In this "confidential memorandum," he noted that "the American economic system is under broad attack." He went on to argue that "business must learn the lesson . . . that political power is necessary; that such power must be assiduously cultivated; and that when necessary, it must be used aggressively and with determination—without embarrassment and without the reluctance which has been so characteristic of American business."[31] Powell recommended that businesses organize to support the interests of business as a whole, not just their own industries. This call was enormously successful. For example, Jacob Hacker and Paul Pierson note, "In 1971, only 175 firms had registered lobbyists in Washington, but by 1982 2,500 did."[32]

In the spring of 1974, *Business Week* reported on the meeting of an elite business group, where it was argued that the American people's standard of living would have to be lowered. The speaker opined that when profits had been high, business had been willing to "share," but during this era of lowered profits, change would be necessary. In the fall of 1974 a *Business Week* article put it this way: "It will be a hard pill for many Americans to swallow—the idea of doing with less so big business can have more. Nothing that this nation, or any nation has done in modern economic history compares with the selling job that must be done to make people accept this reality."[33]

During this era, other conservative leaders saw the need for "a generation of conservative idea merchants," and funding was found for the American Enterprise Institute and the Heritage Foundation, which set about building public support for conservative ideas. Other policy groups founded in the 1970s to support business-friendly ideas included the Manhattan Institute for Policy Research, the Cato Institute, Citizens for a Sound Economy, and Accuracy in Academia. The American Legislative Exchange Council was founded in 1973 to provide guidance to state legislatures in developing conservative legislation; within a few years, the focus switched to cutting back on regulations affecting businesses.[34] So, when Ronald Reagan was elected president in 1980 and began to say things like "Government is the problem" and "Get the government off our backs," these bodies were ready to supply what he needed to make those arguments.

We have now lived through more than thirty years of this economic backlash and with a neoliberal economics that argues that giving corporations and the wealthy more money will improve economic circumstances for all. We can now see that this is patently untrue. Peter Edelman points out that "the income of the top 1 percent went up a staggering 275 percent between 1979 and 2007, while that of the bottom 20 percent grew just 18 percent in those 28 years. . . . The income of the top 0.1 percent increased a staggering 390 percent."[35]

It is only very recently that economic inequality has returned to the public agenda, aided significantly by the Occupy movement and its heralding of "We are the 99%." However, it is no longer just a small proportion of the population experiencing poverty; many middle-class and formerly middle-class people have become impoverished as the Great Recession eroded jobs, decent income, adequate housing, and financial security. A movement for change is brewing.[36]

We see growing efforts to raise the minimum wage, both nationally and locally. For example, Seattle recently adopted an ordinance to increase the minimum wage to $15 an hour over the next few years, and San Francisco and Los Angeles quickly followed. Anger at the big banks remains a legacy of the Great Recession of 2008, when the economy crashed because of their risky decisions, causing many Americans to lose their jobs and their homes. The rate of growth in credit union membership is the highest it has ever been, a reminder of the Occupy movement's Bank Transfer Day in 2011. In addition, some organizations are calling for student debt relief. These are signs that conditions for change are ripening, that a movement takeoff on matters of economic justice might be imminent.[37]

So, as we review the impact of the Chicago Freedom Movement, we can see an array of contributions in many arenas. This chapter has focused on three dimensions—open housing, tenants' rights, and economic justice—but as the rest of the book makes clear, there were contributions in many other areas as well, with some successes coming many years after the movement itself. However, in many respects, these problems are still with us, albeit in a less publicly recognized form. The successes of the 1960s sparked a dramatic backlash from the business elite, what might be called "powerholder panic." We are still living with the results of these reactions, which succeeded in changing the public dialogue on race and poverty and in bringing structural changes that increased inequality. So as the MAP model suggests, the struggle must continue (stage 8).

Poverty and economic injustice remain the center of the Chicago Freedom Movement's unfinished work. We need to rediscover the language of Martin Luther King, who framed poverty as an issue of economic justice and an essential topic to be addressed in democratic institutions. Peter Dreier provides important guidance when he argues that in addition to working on the local level, we must combine these local campaigns into a federated effort at the national level, because many of these issues are beyond the capacity of local communities to solve. Dr. King and his nonviolence team were masters at this kind of organizing, stimulating and supporting many local efforts, where grassroots engagement happens, while looking for local issues that could be raised to a national level. The nonviolent strategies of the Chicago movement—and our understanding of its long-term impact—can provide important clues as we seek to develop effective strategies for our time.[38]

As this book goes to press, we are seeing promising signs of new movements tackling the myriad issues of our time: from the economic justice issues discussed here to the challenges of climate change and environmental destruction, from racial justice in policing practices and the mass incarceration crisis to the protection of voting rights for all. Movements such as Black Lives Matter, 350.org on climate change, local efforts to raise the minimum wage and fight for higher pay in the fast-food industry, Moral Mondays in North Carolina, and organizing around the student debt crisis are bubbling up across the nation. We are beginning to understand, or perhaps to remember, what Robert Borage observed in a recent issue of the *Nation:* "The great changes in America have . . . been won by citizens' movements that arise outside the national consensus."[39]

In this midst of all this ferment, the time is ripe for taking up the Chicago Freedom Movement's unfinished work.

Notes

An earlier and much abbreviated version of this analysis—aided in its initial development by Bill Moyer—was published as "Success and the Chicago Freedom

Movement," *Poverty and Race*, May–June 2006, 8–12, and reprinted in *America's Growing Inequality: The Impact of Poverty and Race*, ed. Chester Hartman (Lanham, MD: Lexington Books, 2014), 513–19. Used with permission.

The quotation from Jim Capraro was published in Mark Warren, "How White Activists Embrace Racial Justice," in Hartman, *America's Growing Inequality*, 152–53. Used with permission.

1. Although overall poverty rates have decreased, this is largely due to a dramatic decrease in poverty among the elderly. The official rate of poverty among most other adults has increased since 1968; the rate has doubled for eighteen- to twenty-four-year-olds and more than doubled for adults aged twenty-five to sixty-four with less than a high school education. However, this official measure does not take into account noncash benefits that grew out of the 1960s–1970s, such as food stamps (now the Supplemental Nutrition Assistance Program [SNAP]), rent subsidies, and the earned income tax credit. When these safety-net programs are taken into account, poverty rates are considerably lower: between 11 and 15 percent of the total population. Although there are many ways to document the continued existence of racism, here we note that poverty rates are about two-and-a-half times higher for black and Hispanic populations than for the white population. See Sheldon Danziger and Christopher Wimer, "Poverty," in "State of the Union: The Poverty and Inequality Report," special issue, *Pathways: A Magazine on Poverty, Inequality, and Social Policy* (2014): 13–18.

2. Michael Eric Dyson, *April 4, 1968: Martin Luther King, Jr.'s Death and How It Changed America* (New York: Basic Books, 2008).

3. For one example, see the *Progressive*'s special issue on race and racial justice (February 2015). There are numerous reports of the 2014–2015 protests against police killings of African Americans in Ferguson, Missouri; Staten Island, New York; Cleveland; Baltimore; and elsewhere. The names of those killed echo through the news: Michael Brown and Eric Garner, Tamir Rice and Freddie Gray, to name a few. For one account, see David Dante Troutt, "Imagining Racial Justice in America," *Nation*, December 29, 2014, 17–19.

4. Moyer's MAP model drew on his later reflections on the Chicago Freedom Movement, as well as other social movements. It was first published in 1977 in a pamphlet distributed by the Movement for a New Society and widely used by environmental and peace activists in the late 1970s and the 1980s. For a later revision, see Bill Moyer with JoAnn McAllister, Mary Lou Finley, and Steven Soifer, *Doing Democracy: The MAP Model for Organizing Social Movements* (Gabriola Island, BC: New Society Publishers, 2001). See also www.historyisaweapon.com/defcon1/moyermap.html. For an analysis of the Occupy movement, which draws explicitly on the MAP model, see Nathan Schneider, "Breaking up with Occupy," *Nation*, September 30, 2013, 12–18. On Movement for a New Society, see George Lakey, *Powerful Peacemaking: A Strategy for a Living Revolution* (Philadelphia: New Society Publishers, 1987), and Andrew

Cornell, *Oppose and Propose: Lessons from Movement for a New Society* (Oakland, CA: AK Press, 2011).

5. The MAP model is more complex than I can fully articulate in this chapter. For instance, the model suggests that different issues within the same movement travel through the stages at different speeds; as an example, the issue of marriage equality for the LGBT (lesbian, gay, bisexual, transgender) community is at a more advanced stage—with successes in more arenas—than the issue of transgender rights. Issues can also be at more or less advanced stages in different locales, suggesting that each local community proceeds through the stages at its own pace. The stages also need to be seen as suggestive rather than definitive, and the progression is not always linear; an issue can move back to an earlier stage under some circumstances, particularly if a major backlash occurs. Also, although I am focusing here on Chicago's contributions to the larger stream of events, a more complete analysis would include activities in other communities that also fed into, in the words of Vincent Harding, the great river of black struggle that "continually gathered others unto itself . . . with the force of its vision, its indomitable hope." Vincent Harding, *There Is a River: The Black Struggle for Freedom in America* (New York: Vintage, 1981), xix.

6. Jane Mansbridge and Aldon Morris, eds., *Oppositional Consciousness: The Subjective Roots of Social Protest* (Chicago: University of Chicago Press, 2001).

7. Sidney Tarrow, *Power in Movement: Social Movements and Contentious Politics* (Cambridge: Cambridge University Press, 1998), 202.

8. On neighborhood violence, see James Shannon, interview by Mary Lou Finley and Pam Smith, Chicago, May 2012. On the Gautreaux Program, see Leonard S. Rubinowitz and James E. Rosenbaum, *Crossing the Class and Color Lines: From Public Housing to White Suburbia* (Chicago: University of Chicago Press, 2000). On the continued existence of segregated housing, see Douglas S. Massey and Nancy A. Denton, *American Apartheid: Segregation and the Making of the Underclass* (Cambridge, MA: Harvard University Press, 1993). Contemporary complexities of housing desegregation and integration are discussed in Chester Hartman and Gregory D. Squires, eds., *The Integration Debate: Competing Futures for American Cities* (New York: Routledge, 2010). On building black political power, see Al Sampson, interview by Pam Smith and Mary Lou Finley, Chicago, November 4, 2010.

9. See Poverty and Race Research Action Council, National Fair Housing Alliance, et al., *Discrimination and Segregation in Housing: Continuing Lack of Progress in United States Compliance with the International Convention on the Elimination of All Forms of Racial Discrimination* (Washington, DC: Poverty and Race Research Action Council, 2014). Also see John R. Logan and Brian Stults, "The Persistence of Segregation in the Metropolis: New Findings from the 2010 Census," www.s4.brown.ed/us2010/Data/Report/report2.pdf, cited in ibid., 3.

10. Mark R. Warren, "How White Activists Embrace Racial Justice," in *America's Growing Inequality: The Impact of Poverty and Race,* ed. Chester Hartman (Lanham, MD: Lexington Books, 2014), 152–53. See also Mark R. Warren, *Fire in the Heart: How White Activists Embrace Racial Justice* (New York: Oxford University Press, 2010).

11. Warren, "How White Activists Embrace Racial Justice," 153.

12. On the "kitchenettes," see Joe Allen, *People Wasn't Made to Burn: A True Story of Race, Murder and Justice in Chicago* (Chicago: Haymarket Press, 2011), 17–18. Allen also reports that tenant organizing by the Socialist Workers Party in Chicago in 1944–1946 grew to a citywide organization, the Chicago Tenants Union (38–40).

13. Peter Marcuse, "The Rise of Tenant Organizations," in *Housing Urban America,* 2nd ed. (New York: Aldine Publishing, 1980), 52–53.

14. Gregory D. Squires, Larry Bennett, Kathleen McCourt, and Philip Nyden, *Chicago: Race, Class, and the Response to Urban Decline* (Philadelphia: Temple University Press, 1987), 112. See chapter 19 for more on Cornfield's court case and chapter 7 for additional information on tenant unions.

15. See chapter 9 for a recent effort on Chicago's West Side and chapter 8 for a discussion of the Community Reinvestment Act. On housing laws, see Alex F. Schwartz, *Housing Policy in the United States,* 2nd ed. (New York: Routledge, 2010), 84, 103. On constructive programs, see Gene Sharp, *Gandhi as a Political Strategist* (Boston: Porter Sargent, 1979), 77–86, and Michael Nagler, *The Nonviolence Handbook: A Guide for Practical Action* (San Francisco: Berrett-Koehler, 2014), 33–38.

16. Barbara Sard and Will Fischer, *Preserving Safe, High Quality Public Housing Should Be a Priority of Federal Housing Policy* (Washington, DC: Center on Budget and Policy Priorities, 2008), 6, 30, cited by G. Thomas Kingsley, "Taking Advantage of What We Have Learned," in *From Despair to Hope: HOPE VI and the New Promise of Public Housing in America's Cities,* ed. Henry Cisneros and Lora Engdahl (Washington, DC: Brookings Institution Press, 2009), 266.

17. Operation Breadbasket was patterned after Leon Sullivan's program of selective buying developed in Philadelphia in 1958.

18. Gary Massoni, "Perspectives on Operation Breadbasket," in *Chicago, 1966: Open Housing Marches, Summit Negotiations, and Operation Breadbasket,* ed. David Garrow (Brooklyn, NY: Carlson Publishing, 1989), 202–7.

19. Ibid., 207, 224; Matt Day and Jay Greene, "Rev. Jackson: Tech Companies Are 'Boycotting Our Talent,'" *Seattle Times,* December 2, 2014.

20. The intent of affirmative action was, in the words of President Lyndon Johnson, to require federal contractors to take "affirmative action" to "ensure that applicants are employed and that employees are treated during employment, without regard to their race, creed, color, or national origin." It began in 1965 as a requirement for federal contractors and was then strengthened by President

Richard Nixon in 1969. After *Griggs v. Duke Power* (1971), in which the Supreme Court ruled that employer practices having a disparate impact are illegal, many local jurisdictions adopted laws requiring employers to have affirmative action plans. Affirmative action remains controversial, and recent court cases have undermined it as a means of correcting previous discrimination. See http://civilrights.uslegal.com/affirmative-action/history-of-affirmative-action/ and http://civilrights.uslegal.com/affirmative-action/supremecourt-decisions-on-affirmative-action/griggs-v-duke-power-co/.

21. Paul Street, *Still Separate, Unequal: Race, Place, Policy and the State of Black Chicago* (Chicago: Chicago Urban League, 2005), 29.

22. At a White House conference on civil rights on November 18, 1965, A. Philip Randolph and others "challenged the limits of Johnson's Poverty Program." A CORE representative labeled it "advanced tokenism." See Paul LeBlanc and Michael D. Yates, *A Freedom Budget for All Americans: Recapturing the Promise of the Civil Rights Movement in the Struggle for Economic Justice Today* (New York: Monthly Review Press, 2013), 91.

23. "Program of the Chicago Freedom Movement," in Garrow, *Chicago, 1966,* 107.

24. On welfare rights, see Felicia Kornbluh, "Black Buying Power: Welfare Rights, Consumerism, and Northern Protest," in *Freedom North: Black Freedom Struggles outside the South, 1940–1980,* ed. Jeanne F. Theoharis and Komozi Woodard (New York: Palgrave Macmillan, 2003), and Felicia Kornbluh, *The Battle for Welfare Rights: Politics and Poverty in Modern America* (Philadelphia: University of Pennsylvania, 2007).

25. Martin Luther King Jr., foreword to *A "Freedom Budget" for All Americans: A Summary,* by A. Philip Randolph (New York: A. Philip Randolph Institute, 1967), 1, cited in LeBlanc and Yates, *Freedom Budget,* 93.

26. LeBlanc and Yates, *Freedom Budget,* 114–15.

27. For a different analysis, see Chuck Fager, *Uncertain Resurrection: The Poor People's Washington Campaign* (Grand Rapids, MI: William B. Eerdmans, 1969).

28. Peter Edelman, *So Rich, So Poor: Why It's So Hard to End Poverty in America* (New York: New Press, 2012), 8–9.

29. Ibid., 7.

30. For an early account of the outsourcing of jobs overseas, see Barry Bluestone and Bennett Harrison, *The Deindustrialization of America: Plant Closings, Community Abandonment, and the Dismantling of Basic Industry* (New York: Basic Books, 1984). William Julius Wilson's *When Work Disappears: The World of the New Urban Poor* (New York: Vintage, 1997) describes the devastating effects of deindustrialization for Chicago's African Americans. For a description of the marginalization of many workers, see Jacob S. Hacker, *The Great Risk Shift: The Assault on American Jobs, Families, Health Care and Retirement and*

How You Can Fight Back (New York: Oxford University Press, 2006). For analyses prepared for activists, see Chuck Collins and Felice Yeskel with United for a Fair Economy and Class Action, *Economic Apartheid in America: A Primer on Economic Inequality and Insecurity,* rev. ed. (New York: New Press, 2005), and Chuck Collins, *99 to 1: How Wealth Inequality Is Wrecking the World and What We Can Do about It* (San Francisco: Berrett-Koehler, 2012).

31. Michel Crozier, Samuel Huntington, and Joji Watanuki, *The Crisis of Democracy: Report on the Governability of Democracies for the Trilateral Commission* (New York: NYU Press, 1973), 113; Lewis Powell, "Confidential Memorandum: Attack on the Free Enterprise System," August 23, 1971, quoted in Kim Phelps-Fein, *Invisible Hands: The Making of the Conservative Movement from the New Deal to Reagan* (New York: Norton, 2009), 158, 160. Lewis Powell served on the Supreme Court from 1971 to 1987.

32. Jacob S. Hacker and Paul Pierson, *Winner-Take-All Politics: How Washington Made the Rich Richer and Turned Its Back on the Middle Class* (New York: Simon & Schuster, 2010), 117–19.

33. John Carson Parker, "The Options Ahead for the Debt Economy," *Business Week,* October 12, 1974, 120–22.

34. Hacker and Pierson, *Winner-Take-All Politics,* 123; Peter Dreier, "Building a Movement for Fair Lending, Foreclosure Relief, and Financial Reform," in *From Foreclosure to Fair Lending: Advocacy, Organizing, Occupy, and the Pursuit of Equitable Credit,* ed. Chester Hartman and Gregory D. Squires (New York: New Village Press, 2013), 293.

35. Isabel V. Sawhill and John E. Morton, *Economic Mobility: Is the American Dream Alive and Well?* (Washington, DC: Economic Mobility Project, 2007), 3, cited in Edelman, *So Rich, So Poor,* 33. For further discussion, see Edelman, *So Rich, So Poor,* 25–45.

36. See Todd Gitlin, *Occupy Nation: The Roots, the Spirit, and the Promise of Occupy Wall Street* (New York: HarperCollins, 2012). For one example of how formerly middle-class people are coping, see Jessica Bruder, "The End of Retirement: When You Can't Afford to Stop Working," *Harpers Magazine,* August 2014, 28–36; she discusses the plight of men and women in their fifties, sixties, and older living in recreational vehicles and traveling around the country as a seasonal labor force for companies like Walmart and Amazon because they can no longer afford rent or mortgage payments.

37. Gene Falk, "Seattle Ranks No. 1 for Credit-Union Growth," *Seattle Times,* April 20, 2015.

38. Dreier, "Building a Movement for Fair Lending," 298–99. See also Tavis Smiley and Cornel West, *The Rich and the Rest of Us: A Poverty Manifesto* (New York: Smiley Books, 2012), for one effort to enlist the public.

39. Robert Borage, "Occupy and Organize," *Nation,* April 6, 2015, 125.

Epilogue

Nonviolence Remix and Today's Millennials

Jonathan Lewis

[Editors' note: On August 9, 2014, Michael Brown, an unarmed African American teenager residing in Ferguson, Missouri, was shot and killed by police officer Darren Wilson, who resigned from the police force but was never charged with a crime. Occurring just two years after the murder of Trayvon Martin by neighborhood watch volunteer George Zimmerman in Sanford, Florida, this shooting tapped into a powder keg of discontent caused by police brutality, rampant poverty, and massive joblessness—the same circumstances that stimulated the end-the-slums campaign during the Chicago Freedom Movement nearly fifty years ago. Following a brief period of violence and looting in Ferguson, nonviolent organizing took hold and was buttressed by a Department of Justice report that showed widespread racial targeting of African Americans by the Ferguson police and certain government agencies. As this book goes to press, nonviolent organizing in Ferguson, Baltimore, Chicago, and other cities continues. These efforts have fueled a larger national racial justice movement created on Twitter called #BlackLivesMatter. The editors are inspired by this emerging movement led by young activists to confront the deepening social and economic inequality across the country. In this epilogue, thirty-seven-year-old senior Kingian nonviolence trainer Jonathan Lewis offers a fitting conclusion to our book—his personal take on the prospects for nonviolence today and into the future. Lewis was trained by Bernard LaFayette, a chief organizer of the Chicago Freedom Movement. The unfinished work of the movement continues.]

In the weeks following the death of Michael Brown, young people from all over the country parachuted into Ferguson, Missouri, demanding justice. What made Brown's killing different from that of other black men killed by police in recent years is that the officers left this young man's body in the middle of the road for more than four hours, uncovered and exposed to the sweltering sun. The extreme disrespect with which Brown and his family were treated became a rallying cry for basic human rights. It emboldened the #BlackLivesMatter movement that began in the wake of the Trayvon Martin murder case and gave other oppressed groups a foundation from which to demand respect. It wasn't long before Muslim students, for example, started a Twitter feed called #MuslimLivesMatter, following the shooting deaths of three college students by an unknown assailant in early 2015.

Drawing on the revolutionary wave of protests known as the Arab Spring and the uprisings resulting from Trayvon Martin's murder, Ferguson youths made full use of Facebook, YouTube, Twitter, and all manner of social media to send out a call to fill the streets of Ferguson. I was among the many who answered. In Kingian nonviolence, we teach that the first step toward achieving social change is gathering information. I wanted to determine the facts firsthand by listening to the people of Ferguson and understanding what options they saw to address injustice in their community. In the 1960s nonviolence—the training, the preparation, and the practice—was at the center of everything. It was similar to the violinist, to today's master DJ scratchin' records. The workshops begun by Ella Baker and continued by James Lawson, Dorothy Cotton, Diane Nash, C. T. Vivian, Bernard LaFayette Jr., and so many nameless others were echoed in the training given at Black Panther Party headquarters by Angela Davis and Assata Shakur. Today, they are beginning all over again in places like Ferguson, Missouri.

Soon after the killing of Michael Brown, the King Center in Atlanta, under the direction of Bernice King and with the involvement of senior Kingian nonviolence trainer Charles Alphin, a retired St. Louis police captain and advocate of nonviolent community policing, began holding Kingian nonviolence training sessions in Ferguson. They trained 100 high school students, creating a youth team committed to nonviolence.

There were many community meetings in Ferguson, but I found that while the adult church members and the business community attended, there weren't many youths at those meetings, so I went into the community and just hung out in the projects for a day and a half. I talked with the residents of the Canfield Projects and listened to their stories. What I heard from the younger members of the community were calls for economic redevelopment, a yearning for nonviolent action beyond training, nonviolent tools for life, and a more professional police department. And they wanted the elders to let them be themselves. The historic civil rights organizations were also showing up, but some of the local leadership felt their presence was too late.

A new model for organizing social change appeared on social media during this time. It came from young organizers of the rebellion at Tahrir Square in Egypt, and it was based on the intersectionality of ethnicity, religion, and gender. An overwhelming number of these Arab organizers were young women, and their engagement with social media coincided with a shift in the political landscape.[1] This was also the case in Ferguson, where young women refused to be sidelined. For example, Johnetta Elzie's Twitter feed, which had 20,000 followers, became a central repository of daily news related to the protests and ongoing negotiations with government officials.[2] Young activists are using social media to democratize the information flow and mobilize and organize people. They are remixing nonviolence to fit today's context. I often explain this remixed form of nonviolence to youth in this way: I tell them it's our charge to be the P. Diddy (rapper Sean Combs) of today's movement. P. Diddy found some old tracks, remixed them, and threw a hook on it until we couldn't live without it.

Before moving on, I should explain why and how I became part of this new remixed version of the nonviolence movement. When I was a student at the University of Rhode Island in 1999, I stepped into what would become my future. As a child, I always wished I could have worked with Dr. King. My dreams were filled with what it would have been like to stand shoulder to shoulder with him, fighting for justice, changing the world. So when Dr. Bernard LaFayette Jr. came to our campus, I stepped up to the next best thing. I walked up to him with an outstretched hand and said, "I am Jonathan Lewis and I am going to work with you, Dr. LaFayette." To my amazement he welcomed me with open arms, and I began my pilgrimage in nonviolence. From him I have learned the lessons that are least known about the movement: the strategy, the philosophy.

And in my travels around the world with him, I have learned how universal the Kingian nonviolence philosophy really is. In addition to many states in this country, I have conducted Kingian nonviolence training in Colombia, Nigeria, Mexico, and the Middle East. At the end of 2010 I began the Positive Peace Warrior Network, a group focused on empowering youth with the skills of Kingian nonviolence.

The explosion of the Occupy Wall Street movement and violent responses from the police in communities across the country have resulted in outcries for alternatives to violence. Kingian nonviolence is a viable alternative.

To understand why activist-organizers, protesters, and justice seekers converged on Ferguson, Missouri, we must take a look at the conditions that made this suburb ripe for exactly the kind of events we have seen since August 2014. Analyzing the fundamental conditions, policies, and practices of any conflict, rather than reacting to one's opponents or their personalities, is a central component of Kingian nonviolence. Nonviolent practitioners study conditions so they can educate themselves and the community about the problem and develop articulate spokespeople.

In 1970 the population of Ferguson was 99 percent white. By 2014, the latest year for which statistics are available, blacks made up 67 percent of the city's population, and the white population had dropped to 29 percent.[3] Until recently, the city council had only one African American, and most of the police are white. Two major forces contributed to this population shift in Ferguson: loss of affordable housing and joblessness. According to Clarissa Hayward, political science professor at Washington University in St. Louis, the roots of the racial unrest that racks Ferguson—a meeting point of the Midwest, the West, and the South—can be traced back more than a century. "The St. Louis metropolitan area has been an extreme example of racial segregation for 100 years," she notes. Hayward argues that "the practices and politics of St. Louis created the problems that underlie the tension that boiled over in Ferguson."[4]

In Kingian nonviolence we learn that conflict has history. Just as poverty deterred community advancement during the Chicago Freedom Movement nearly fifty years ago, it continues to be the most devastating factor blocking community progress today. We must build an economic foundation that can sustain our youth, instead of burying them in debt for trying to get an education in the richest nation in the world. In my view, a fundamental restructuring of the nation's economy is needed to distribute wealth in a more equitable manner. In the last few years of his life, Dr. King himself was deeply committed to ending poverty and creating an economically just society; this was a major focus of his work during the Chicago Freedom Movement, and it culminated with the Poor People's Campaign he was organizing in 1968.

In a six-part documentary titled *The Mike Brown Rebellion,* filmmaker N Don't Stop interviewed many of those involved in organizing the protests and other actions in Ferguson. One of them was emcee and activist Tef Poe. Neatly dressed in a T-shirt sporting activist slogans and wearing a camouflage cap turned backward, Poe speaks of becoming involved in the movement for justice for Mike Brown. On the night of the shooting, Poe saw tweets by Brown's stepfather talking about the death of his son. Poe went to the street and saw the bloodstains with his own eyes. He and other youths made a personal commitment to confront injustice; they began to organize and gathered in the streets. As they did, members of the St. Louis County Police Department surrounded them. The youths raised their hands, shouting, "Hands up; don't shoot" and "We are peaceful." In Kingian nonviolence, their actions could be understood as part of negotiation—recognizing that the police perceived them as threatening, the protesters offered a compromise and raised their hands, demonstrating their intent to remain nonviolent. Even so, the police, dressed in full riot gear, began to shoot into the crowd that was demanding justice for a young man who had lost his life after being stopped, according to the Ferguson police chief, for jaywalking.

On August 20, 2014, the crowd again pushed back nonviolently on the police as they were being pushed on. Men, women, and teens of all shapes and sizes refused to go home, saying, "If you want peace, then give us justice." In the film, N Don't Stop speaks of the "liberating" feeling of taking even this small action. Confronting injustice and being willing to accept the consequences of those actions are important parts of a nonviolent direct action campaign.

The process of creating the beloved community in Ferguson and other cities experiencing what Dr. King called the "triple evils" of poverty, racism, and militarism will not be easy or quick. But the signs are promising. Activists are in the fight for the long haul, and their demands are being heard. As I write on the eve of the fiftieth anniversary of the Chicago Freedom Movement, I believe we can look to the stories of that movement of five decades ago, coming out of an urban crisis of its own time, as a source of clues and guidance, warnings and inspiration, as we confront the crises of the present.

Before he died, Dr. King spoke of institutionalizing nonviolence. The next step in that process would be to advocate for national and state legislation to make such a program a standard part of each school day. Conflict is the most prevalent problem our society faces today. It's a public health epidemic, so for the health of our nation, we must give our children the tools they need to solve conflict without violence. Some of the architects of our nation saw fit to ensure that certain subjects would be taught to all children: reading, writing, math, science, and history. Why not add nonviolence training as part of a sound system of public education that prepares our citizens to live moral, productive lives? Today's remixed form of nonviolence, I believe, requires a shaking up of the education system. Our educational institutions must inspire young people to become fully functioning citizens. Dr. LaFayette has said that one of the greatest regrets of the civil rights generation's elders is that the citizenship schools did not continue. We need to teach our youths how to be active citizens and powerful people, for education is the most powerful weapon there is. (Read Frederick Douglass's autobiography, and see how reading brought him freedom.)[5]

It is possible for people to choose peace. And this must be a conscious, deliberate choice. Cultures that are built on the shifting sands of violence can be rebuilt on the solid foundation of nonviolence. Communities must constantly shape and prune the infrastructure with the shears of justice and liberty. We can no longer wait for someone else to take the lead. We must all build the beloved community. Let's create the *shantisena* (peace army) right here, everywhere, right now. We have the skills, we have the principles that are still relevant today, we have the practice, and we have the philosophy. The question is, do we have the focused will to achieve the goal?

Notes

1. Cortney C. Radsch, "Cyberactivism and the Role of Women in the Arab Uprisings," in *Women's Voices, Feminist Vision: Classic and Contemporary Readings,* ed. Susan M. Shaw and Janet Lee (New York: McGraw-Hill 2015), 298–307.

2. Matt Pearce, "Women Find Their Voice in Ferguson Protest Movement," *LA Times,* November 22, 2014.

3. "Ferguson (city), Missouri," US Census Bureau website, http:// quickfacts.census.gov/qfd/states/29/2923986.html

4. Puneet Kollipara, "Wonkblog," *Washington Post,* August 18, 2014.

5. Frederick Douglass, *Narrative of the Life of Frederick Douglass: An American Slave, Written by Himself,* 2nd ed. (1845; reprint, New York: Bedford/St. Martin's, 2002).

Acknowledgments

This book is the product of a long journey. It is an outgrowth of the fortieth anniversary commemoration of the Chicago Freedom Movement held in 2006, which all four editors helped plan. And just like the commemoration, it is the product of a highly collaborative effort. We have many persons and institutions to thank, and here we identify some of those who helped produce this volume, while recognizing that many others, not acknowledged here, also had a hand in its making.

Phil Nyden, David van Zytveld, Aparna Sharma, and the crew at the Center for Urban Research and Learning (CURL) at Loyola University hosted our preparations for the fortieth anniversary events, and they have been a wonderful support system over the years. Kale Williams deserves special recognition. A leading figure in the Chicago Freedom Movement, Kale—as a senior scholar in residence at CURL—was a central force in mounting the fortieth anniversary commemoration. Helen Williams, Kale's wife, worked closely with him to keep our planning on track. And the commemoration would not have been so successful without the creative energy of Matthew Stevens and the organizing talents of Malik Nevels and Carmen Rodriguez, who chaired the youth committee for the fortieth anniversary conference. Wynona Redmond generously provided in-kind contributions in her capacity with Dominick's Finer Foods, and the Freedom Singers of Albany, Georgia, as well as many other talented artists, provided inspiring entertainment.

The fortieth anniversary commemoration was an opportunity for many activists in the struggle for civil rights to share their reflections. We have drawn on some of their voices in this volume: James Godsil, Billy Hollins, David Jehnsen, Herman Jenkins, Bernard Kleina, Gary Massoni, Calvin Morris, the Reverend Kwame John R. Porter, Elbert (Bert) Ransom, Don Rose, and Rosie Simpson.

The preparation of this volume led us to interview many other activists and scholars, and their firsthand experiences greatly enriched its content and analysis. We thank them for giving so freely of their time: Mattie

Amaker, Hal Baron, Timuel Black, Malcolm Bush, Edward Byrd, Tiffany Childress, Spencer Cowan, Larry Dixon, Sylvia Fischer, Darel Grothaus, the Reverend Randall Harris, Mia Henry, Billy Hollins, Janice Jackson, David Jehnsen, Lawrence Johnson, Jim Keck, Lorne Cress Love, Bob Lucas, John McKnight, Jack Macnamara, the Reverend Calvin Morris, Aurie Pennick, the Reverend Al Sampson, the Reverend James Shannon, the Reverend C. T. Vivian, Lucki Wilder, and Ambassador Andrew Young. Aldon Morris added important insights that enhanced our understanding of civil rights movements in the North. Melissa Harris-Perry provided important perspectives on youth activism.

We benefited from interviews conducted by James Ralph for an earlier study with the Reverend James Bevel, Jimmy Collier, Alma Coggs, Gordon Groebe, David Jehnsen, Ed Marciniak, John McDermott, John McKnight, Bill Moyer, Al Raby, Edward Vondrak, and Meyer Weinberg. We also drew on interviews of Bill Berry and Nancy Jefferson by Bob Jordan, of Hattie Williams by Olin Eugene Myers, of Tony Henry by Keith Harvey, and of Bill Berry by Kale Williams.

The voices of participants in the Chicago Freedom Movement were made accessible by the transcription and interviewing work of the following students: Damon Hansen, Allegra Malone, Sam Parnell, Connor Williams, and Devon Wright. Scott Bulua, Sam Moog, and Andy Rossmeisl helped develop and maintain a website on the Chicago Freedom Movement, which has been a helpful archive for this book. Seth McClellan shared his tapes of the fortieth anniversary conference, as well as interviews with many veterans of the Chicago movement. We also wish to acknowledge the students, teachers, and staff at the Al Raby School for Community and Environment for their project on the Chicago Freedom Movement, which included interviewing movement veterans.

We are deeply grateful for the efforts and support of those who contributed to the visual representation of the Chicago Freedom Movement in our volume. Ben Meader prepared the maps for this book. Bernard Kleina generously allowed us to use his remarkable photographs of the Chicago Freedom Movement. Johnson Publishing allowed us to republish a number of vintage images from its files, and the Chicago History Museum allowed us to publish one of its images. The Reverend John

Porter shared a personal photograph, and photographer Bob Fitch permitted us to publish an image from his collection of civil rights movement photos now at Stanford University.

Many others helped shape this book. We are also indebted to the librarians, archivists, and research associates at the King Center, especially Elaine Hall and Cynthia Lewis; the Chicago History Museum, especially Peter Alter; the University of Illinois–Chicago; the University of Illinois–Urbana/Champaign; the Illinois Regional Archives Depository—Chicago Branch; and Middlebury College. Chester Hartman helped spur the development of this book when he commissioned articles for a symposium on the fortieth anniversary of the Chicago Freedom Movement for *Poverty & Race*. We benefited from the assistance of the Reverend Janette Wilson, Alanna Ford, John Mitchell, Lynn Adler, Eric Gellman, and Kathleen McCourt. Art Alexander, Marilyn Austin, Don Comstock, Pamela Finley, Suzanna Finley, John Marrs, Gary Massoni, John McKnight, Jacqueline Moorey, Kareen Snider, and Frank Watkins assisted by reading and editing drafts of parts of the book.

We especially want to thank the contributors to this book, who collaborated with us with such commitment, wisdom, and patience and from whom we learned much: Gene Barge, Hal Baron, Sherrilynn Bevel, Jimmy Collier, Gil Cornfield, Melody Heaps, Norman Hill, the Reverend Jesse Jackson, Kimberlie Jackson, Herman Jenkins, Molly Martindale, Christopher Reed, Don Rose, Leonard Rubinowitz, Gail Schechter, the Reverend Al Sharpton, and Brian White. They opened up new perspectives on the Chicago Freedom Movement, which was a complex initiative ignited by the efforts of thousands of people. Any errors of fact or interpretation rest squarely with the editors.

A long-term project such as this one, with editors who live in four different parts of the country, required the financial assistance of a number of institutions. The Field Foundation and the Woods Family Foundation offered essential support. Loyola University provided many kinds of resources for the 2006 conference and assisted us in other ways for which we are very grateful. The Antioch University Seattle funds for faculty development were vital. Jim Ralph benefited from his appointment as a research scholar during an academic leave at the European Union Center at the University of Illinois–Urbana/Champaign. The

Rehnquist Professorship of American History and Culture at Middlebury College provided funding to support many facets of the preparation of this volume.

We also want to thank the University Press of Kentucky for helping us realize our dream of publishing this volume. Our book was improved by two sets of anonymous readers' reports for the press. Bailey Johnson and Iris Law have shown extraordinary patience and have always been quick to respond to our many questions, and Linda Lotz's expert copyediting did much to strengthen the book. We especially tip our hats to our editor, Anne Dean Dotson, for her guidance, inspiration, and patience.

We four editors are thrilled that we finally reached the finish line, but we will always remember the wonderful camaraderie—as well as the many challenges—in preparing this book. Mary Lou Finley is especially grateful for the wisdom, encouragement, and technical support from her daughter, Suzanna Finley, who managed to find time to assist her mother in the midst of planning her own wedding. Bernard LaFayette is deeply grateful to his wife, Kate LaFayette, for her support, technical assistance, and understanding while he toiled in this labor of love to complete our invaluable project. Jim Ralph is especially indebted to his wife, Ophelia Eglene, for helping him stay focused on this project even as they welcomed two children into this world. And Pam Smith warmly thanks her circle of friends and family who were always supportive throughout this seemingly endless project.

Chronology

1942

Congress of Racial Equality (CORE) is founded in Chicago and integrates Chicago
restaurants

1957

Chicago branch of NAACP issues report "De Facto Segregation in the Chicago Public
Schools"
Southern Christian Leadership Conference (SCLC) is formed

1961

Chatham–Avalon Park Community Council (CAPCC) files suit to correct racial
imbalance in Chicago schools

1962

Black parents on Chicago's South Side stage sit-in at Burnside School to protest racial
imbalance
Coordinating Council of Community Organizations (**CCCO**), including Chicago
Urban League, Chicago branch of NAACP, CAPCC, and The Woodlawn
Organization, is formed; teacher **Al Raby is** eventually selected as convener;
predominantly white groups such as American Friends Service Committee (AFSC)
and Chicago Catholic Interracial Council join later
Chicago delegation joins SCLC campaign in Albany, Georgia

1963

CCCO stages massive boycott of public schools
SCLC leads campaign in Birmingham, Alabama
West Side Federation of ministers is founded

1964

Second major boycott of schools is organized by CCCO
Bernard LaFayette is tapped by AFSC to organize on Chicago's West Side
Freedom Summer in Mississippi: college students organize voter registration drives and
run Freedom Schools
Civil Rights Act is signed into law by President Lyndon Johnson on July 2
AFSC anti–lead poisoning project begins

1965

March—Teams from Chicago travel to Selma, Alabama, to support voting rights
movement

June—CCCO leads daily marches against school segregation

July—Martin Luther King and SCLC tour Chicago; King speaks at rallies in Chicago and on Winnetka village green

City of Chicago Department of Health begins its own program to screen children for lead poisoning

CCCO-organized marches from Buckingham Fountain to City Hall call for resignation of Benjamin Willis, superintendent of Chicago public schools

North Shore Summer Project, AFSC's fair-housing project in northern suburbs, is launched

August—Voting Rights Act is signed into law

Watts riot in Los Angeles

Black woman is killed by fire truck on Chicago's West Side, sparking riots

September—SCLC decides to target Chicago for its next campaign; SCLC and CCCO form Chicago Freedom Movement

Fall—James Bevel, program director for West Side Christian Parish and project director for SCLC, is in command of SCLC staffers and Chicago civil rights activists on Chicago's West Side

1966

January—Kickoff of Chicago Freedom Movement

Martin Luther King moves into decrepit apartment on Chicago's West Side to spotlight commitment to end slums

Unions to End Slums begin in East Garfield Park, North Lawndale, and Near North Side

February—Operation Breadbasket is founded in Chicago

Kenwood-Oakland Community Organization is founded, with Jesse Jackson playing a leading role

SCLC-CCCO takes over slum building at 1321 Homan in Lawndale

SCLC works with youth gangs on West and South Sides

April—Operation Breadbasket achieves its first victory: an agreement with Country Delight Dairy and its parent company, Certified Grocers of Illinois

May—Superintendent of schools Benjamin Willis announces his resignation, effective end of 1966

Civil rights leaders express deep concern that the movement is floundering

Chicago Freedom Movement leaders decide to target housing discrimination in summer campaign

June—Protesters march in Mississippi after shooting of James Meredith; "Black Power" rallying cry is shouted

July—Major rally is held in Soldier Field (30,000 people); Martin Luther King posts demands on door of City Hall

Uprising on West Side over shut-down hydrant

Condor and Costalis—a real estate firm—signs collective bargaining agreement with
    West Side tenants of its buildings
Fair-housing testing is followed by small actions, such as picnic in the park and shop-in
Vigils are held at real estate offices in Gage Park neighborhood
Open-housing marches are launched on Southwest Side

August—Fear of racial explosion as whites erupt against fair-housing marchers
American Civil Liberties Union files suit charging Chicago Housing Authority with
    discrimination (*Gautreaux et al. v. Chicago Housing Authority*)
Negotiations are convened to end demonstrations
Summit Agreement is reached, supported by businessmen, church leaders,
    Mayor Richard J. Daley, and city officials, addressing a range of issues
Dr. James F. Redmond succeeds Benjamin Willis as superintendent of schools

September—Dissatisfied activists stage demonstration in nearby Cicero
Protesters, aided by SCLC staffers, demonstrate against urban renewal in Englewood
    area

November—Edward Holmgren is tapped as director of Leadership Council for Metro-
    politan Open Communities (LCMOC), an outgrowth of the Summit Agreement

1967

January—SCLC activists, led by Hosea Williams, organize voter registration campaign

March—Martin Luther King speaks at rally opposing the Vietnam War in Chicago

April 4—Martin Luther King gives his "Beyond Vietnam" speech at Riverside Church,
    New York City

May—LCMOC launches Project: Good Neighbor
Martin Luther King declares no need for more demonstrations

August—National Conference for a New Politics meets in Chicago, hoping to
    nominate Martin Luther King for president and Dr. Benjamin Spock for vice
    president

September—CCCO dissolves, ending Chicago Freedom Movement

1968

February—Contract Buyers League is founded in Lawndale

April 4—Martin Luther King is assassinated in Memphis, Tennessee

April 11—Fair Housing Act is signed into law by President Lyndon Johnson

April–June—SCLC's Poor People's Campaign

August—Democratic Convention is held in Chicago, with major protests and a "police
    riot"

1969

Coalition for United Community Action protests racial exclusion from construction jobs

1974

Passage of Equal Credit Opportunity Act

1975

Passage of Home Mortgage Disclosure Act

1977

Passage of Community Reinvestment Act

1983

Harold Washington is elected mayor of Chicago

1984

Jesse Jackson's first campaign to obtain Democratic Party nomination for president

1986

New landlord-tenant law is established in Chicago

1988

Jesse Jackson's second campaign to obtain Democratic Party nomination for president
Federal Fair Housing Act is reinforced

2006

LCMOC closes down

2008

Barack Obama is elected president of the United States

2012

Barack Obama is reelected president of the United States

Selected Bibliography

Published Sources

Allen, Joe. *People Wasn't Made to Burn: A True Story of Race, Murder and Justice in Chicago*. Chicago: Haymarket Books, 2011.

Anderson, Alan B., and George W. Pickering. *Confronting the Color Line: The Broken Promise of the Civil Rights Movement in Chicago*. Athens: University of Georgia Press, 1986.

Bagley, Edythe Scott. *Desert Rose: The Life and Legacy of Coretta Scott King*. Tuscaloosa: University of Alabama Press, 2012.

Baroksky, Neil. *Bailout: An Inside Account of How Washington Abandoned Main Street while Rescuing Wall Street*. New York: Free Press, 2012.

Benedict, Don. *Born Again Radical*. New York: Pilgrim Press, 1982.

Berry, Brian J. L. *The Open Housing Question: Race and Housing in Chicago, 1966–1976*. Cambridge, MA: Ballinger Publishing, 1979.

Branch, Taylor. *At Canaan's Edge: America in the King Years, 1965–68*. New York: Simon & Schuster, 2006.

Breines, Winifred. *The Trouble between Us: An Uneasy History of White and Black Women in the Feminist Movement*. New York: Oxford University Press, 2006.

Carawan, Guy, and Candie Carawan. *Sing for Freedom: The Story of the Civil Rights Movement through Its Songs*. Montgomery, AL: New South Books, 2007.

Carson, Clayborne, ed. *The Autobiography of Martin Luther King, Jr.* New York: Warner Books, 1998.

Clemente, Frank, and Frank Watkins, eds. *Keep Hope Alive: Jesse Jackson's 1988 Presidential Campaign*. Boston: South End Press, 1989.

Collins, Chuck. *99 to 1: How Wealth Inequality Is Wrecking the World and What We Can Do about It*. San Francisco: Berrett-Koehler, 2012.

Collins, Patricia Hill. *Black Feminist Thought: Knowledge, Consciousness, and the Politics of Empowerment*. 1990. Reprint, New York: Routledge, 2008.

Curry, Constance, Joan C. Browning, Dorothy Dawson Burlage, Penny Patch, Theresa Del Pozzo, Sue Thrasher, Elaine Delott Baker, Emmie Schrader Adams, and Casey Hayden, eds. *Deep in Our Hearts: Nine White Women in the Freedom Movement*. Athens: University of Georgia Press, 2000.

Danns, Dionne. *Something Better to Our Children: Black Organization in the Chicago Public Schools, 1963–1971*. New York: Routledge, 2003.

Dawley, David. *A Nation of Lords: The Autobiography of the Vice Lords*. 2nd ed. Prospect Heights, IL: Waveland Press, 1992.

Diamond, Andrew J. *Mean Streets: Chicago Youths and the Everyday Struggle for Empowerment in the Multiracial City, 1908–1969.* Berkeley: University of California Press, 2009.

Drake, St. Clair, and Horace R. Cayton. *Black Metropolis: A Study of Negro Life in a Northern City.* Vols. 1 and 2. Revised and enlarged edition. New York: Harper & Row, 1962.

Eastwood, Carolyn. *Near West Side Stories: Struggles for Community in Chicago's Maxwell Street Neighborhood.* Chicago: Lake Claremont Press, 2002.

Easwaran, Eknath. *Gandhi: The Man.* Berkeley, CA: Nilgiri Press, 1997.

Edelman, Peter. *So Rich, So Poor: Why It's So Hard to End Poverty in America.* New York: New Press, 2012.

English, Peter. *Old Paint: A Medical History of Childhood Lead-Paint Poisoning in the United States to 1980.* New Brunswick, NJ: Rutgers University Press, 2001.

Evans, Sara. *Personal Politics: The Roots of Women's Liberation in the Civil Rights Movement and the New Left.* New York: Vintage, 1980.

Fager, Chuck. *Uncertain Resurrection: The Poor People's Washington Campaign.* Grand Rapids, MI: William B. Eerdmans, 1969.

Fairclough, Adam. *To Redeem the Soul of America: The Southern Christian Leadership Conference and Martin Luther King, Jr.* Athens: University of Georgia Press, 1987.

Frady, Marshall. *Jesse: The Life and Pilgrimage of Jesse Jackson.* New York: Random House, 1996.

Gandhi, Mohandas K. *All Men Are Brothers: Life and Thoughts of Mahatma Gandhi as Told in His Own Words.* Edited by Krishna Kripali. Ahmedabad, India: Navajivan Publishing House, 1960.

Garrow, David J. *Bearing the Cross: Martin Luther King, Jr. and the Southern Christian Leadership Conference.* New York: William Morrow, 1986.

———, ed. *Chicago, 1966: Open Housing Marches, Summit Negotiations, and Operation Breadbasket.* Brooklyn, NY: Carlson Publishing, 1989.

Giddings, Paula J. *Ida: A Sword among Lions: Ida B. Wells and the Campaign against Lynching.* New York: Amistad, 2008.

Gilliard, Deric A. *Living in the Shadow of a Legend: Unsung Heroes and "Sheroes" Who Marched with Martin Luther King, Jr.* Decatur GA: Gilliard Communications, 2002.

Gitlin, Todd, and Nanci Hollander. *Uptown: Poor Whites in Chicago.* New York: Harper & Row, 1970.

Goldberg, David, and Trevor Griffey, eds. *Black Power at Work: Community Control, Affirmative Action, and the Construction Industry.* Ithaca, NY: Cornell University Press, 2010.

Grimshaw, William J. *Bitter Fruit: Black Politics and the Chicago Machine, 1931–1991.* Chicago: University of Chicago Press, 1992.

Hacker, Jacob S., and Paul Pierson. *Winner-Take-All Politics: How Washington Made the Rich Richer and Turned Its Back on the Middle Class.* New York: Simon & Schuster, 2010.

Halberstam, David. *The Children.* New York: Fawcett Books, 1998.

Hansberry, Lorraine. *A Raisin in the Sun.* 1959. Reprint, New York: Vintage, 1994.

Harris-Perry, Melissa. *Sister Citizen: For Colored Girls Who've Considered Politics When Being Strong Isn't Enough.* New Haven, CT: Yale University Press, 2011.

Hartman, Chester, ed. *America's Growing Inequality: The Impact of Poverty and Race.* Lanham, MD: Lexington Books, 2014.

Hartman, Chester, and Gregory D. Squires, eds. *From Foreclosure to Fair Lending: Advocacy, Organizing, Occupy, and the Pursuit of Equitable Credit.* New York: New Village Press, 2013.

———. *The Integration Debate: Competing Futures for American Cities.* New York: Routledge, 2010.

Hartsough, David, with Joyce Hollyday. *Waging Peace: Global Adventures of a Lifelong Activist.* Oakland, CA: PM Press, 2014.

Helgeson, Jeffrey. *Crucibles of Black Empowerment: Chicago's Neighborhood Politics from the New Deal to Harold Washington.* Chicago: University of Chicago Press, 2014.

Hill, Anita. *Reimagining Equality: Stories of Gender, Race, and Finding Home.* Boston: Beacon Press, 2011.

Hirsch, Arnold R. *Making of the Second Ghetto: Race and Housing in Chicago, 1940–1960.* Cambridge: Cambridge University Press, 1983.

Holsaert, Faith S., Martha Prescod Norman Noonan, Judy Richardson, Betty Garman Robinson, Jean Smith Young, and Dorothy Zellner, eds. *Hands on the Freedom Plow: Personal Accounts by Women in SNCC.* Urbana: University of Illinois Press, 2010.

Jackson, Jesse L. *Straight from the Heart.* Edited by Robert D. Hatch and Frank E. Watkins. Philadelphia: Fortress Press, 1987.

Jackson, Thomas F. *From Civil Rights to Human Rights: Martin Luther King, Jr., and the Struggle for Economic Justice.* Philadelphia: University of Pennsylvania Press, 2007.

Jones, Patrick D. *The Selma of the North: Civil Rights Insurgency in Milwaukee.* Cambridge, MA: Harvard University Press, 2009.

Keating, W. Dennis, and Norman Krumholz. *Rebuilding Urban Neighborhoods: Achievements, Opportunities, and Limits.* Thousand Oaks, CA: Sage Publications, 1999.

King, Coretta Scott. *My Life with Martin Luther King, Jr.* Revised edition. New York: Henry Holt, 1993.

King, Martin Luther, Jr. *All Labor Has Dignity.* Edited by Michael K. Honey. Boston: Beacon, 2011.

————. *Stride toward Freedom*. New York: Harper & Row, 1958.

————. *The Trumpet of Conscience*. 1967. Reprint, Boston: Beacon Press, 2010.

————. *Where Do We Go from Here: Chaos or Community?* Boston: Beacon Press, 1967.

————. *Why We Can't Wait*. New York: Penguin Books, 1964.

Kleppner, Paul. *Chicago Divided: The Making of a Black Mayor*. De Kalb: Northern Illinois University Press, 1985.

LaFayette, Bernard, Jr., and Kathryn Lee Johnson. *In Peace and Freedom: My Journey in Selma*. Lexington: University Press of Kentucky, 2013.

LeBlanc, Paul, and Michael D. Yates. *A Freedom Budget for All Americans: Recapturing the Promise of the Civil Rights Movement in the Struggle for Economic Justice Today*. New York: Monthly Review Press, 2013.

Lewis, John. *Walking with the Wind: A Memoir of the Movement*. New York: Harcourt Brace, 1998.

Mantler, Gordon K. *Power to the Poor: Black-Brown Coalition and the Fight for Economic Justice, 1960–1974*. Chapel Hill: University of North Carolina Press, 2013.

Markowitz, Gerald, and David Rosner. *Lead Wars: The Politics of Science and the Fate of America's Children*. Berkeley: University of California Press, 2013.

Marsh, Charles. *The Beloved Community: How Faith Shapes Social Justice from the Civil Rights Movement to Today*. New York: Basic Books, 2005.

Massey, Douglas S., and Nancy A. Denton. *American Apartheid: Segregation and the Making of the Underclass*. Cambridge, MA: Harvard University Press, 1993.

McAllister, Pam. *This River of Courage: Generations of Women's Resistance and Action*. Barbara Deming Memorial Series: Stories of Women and Nonviolent Action. Philadelphia: New Society Publishers, 1991.

McKersie, Robert B. *A Decisive Decade: An Insider's View of the Chicago Civil Rights Movement during the 1960s*. Carbondale: Southern Illinois University Press, 2013.

Meyer, Stephen Grant. *As Long as They Don't Move Next Door: Segregation and Racial Conflict in American Neighborhoods*. Lanham, MD: Lexington Books, 2000.

Monson, Ingrid. *Freedom Sounds: Civil Rights Calls out to Jazz and Africa*. New York: Oxford University Press, 2010.

Moyer, Bill, with JoAnn McAllister, Mary Lou Finley, and Steven Soifer. *Doing Democracy: The MAP Model for Organizing Social Movements*. Gabriola Island, BC: New Society Publishers, 2001.

Nagler, Michael. *The Nonviolence Handbook: A Guide for Practical Action*. San Francisco: Berrett-Koehler, 2014.

Olson, Lynne. *Freedom's Daughters: The Unsung Heroines of the Civil Rights Movement from 1830 to 1970*. New York: Simon & Schuster, 2001.

Polikoff, Alexander. *Waiting for Gautreaux: A Story of Segregation, Housing, and the Black Ghetto*. Evanston, IL: Northwestern University Press, 2006.

Ralph, James R., Jr. *Northern Protest: Martin Luther King, Jr., Chicago, and the Civil Rights Movement*. Cambridge, MA: Harvard University Press, 1993.

Rauschenbusch, Walter. *Christianity and the Social Crisis in the 21st Century: The Classic that Woke up the Church*. 100th anniversary edition. New York: HarperOne, 2008.

Reed, Christopher Robert. *The Chicago NAACP and the Rise of Black Professional Leadership*. Bloomington: Indiana University Press, 1997.

———. *The Depression Comes to the South Side: Protest and Politics in the Black Metropolis, 1930–1933*. Bloomington: Indiana University Press, 2011.

———. *Knock at the Door of Opportunity: Black Migration to Chicago, 1900–1919*. Carbondale: Southern Illinois University Press, 2014.

———. *The Rise of Chicago's Black Metropolis, 1920–1929*. Urbana: University of Illinois Press, 2011.

Reich, Robert. *Saving Capitalism: For the Many, Not the Few*. New York: Knopf, 2015.

Rivlin, Gary. *Fire on the Prairie: Harold Washington, Chicago Politics, and the Roots of the Obama Presidency*. Revised edition. Philadelphia: Temple University Press, 2013.

Rose, Tricia. *The Hip Hop Wars*. New York: Basic Books, 2008.

Rubinowitz, Leonard S., and James E. Rosenbaum. *Crossing the Class and Color Lines: From Public Housing to White Suburbia*. Chicago: University of Chicago Press, 2000.

Sampson, Robert J. *Great American City: Chicago and the Enduring Neighborhood Effect*. Chicago: University of Chicago Press, 2012.

Satter, Beryl. *Family Properties: Race, Real Estate, and the Exploitation of Black Urban America*. New York: Metropolitan Books, 2009.

Saul, Scott. *Freedom Is, Freedom Ain't: Jazz and the Making of the Sixties*. Cambridge, MA: Harvard University Press, 2005.

Schneidhorst, Amy. *Building a Just and Secure World: Popular Front Women's Struggles for Peace and Justice in Chicago during the 1960s*. New York: Bloomsbury Academic, 2013.

Seligman, Amanda. *Block by Block: Neighborhoods and Public Policy on Chicago's West Side*. Chicago: University of Chicago Press, 2005.

Sharp, Gene, Joshua Paulson, Christopher A. Miller, and Hardy Merriman. *Waging Nonviolent Struggle: 20th Century Practice and 21st Century Potential*. Manchester, NH: Extending Horizons Books/Porter Sargent Publishers, 2005.

Shaw, Susan M., and Janet Lee, eds. *Women's Voices, Feminist Vision: Classic and Contemporary Readings*. New York: McGraw-Hill, 2015.

Smiley, Tavis, and David Ritz. *Death of a King: The Real Story of Dr. Martin Luther King, Jr.'s Final Year*. New York: Little, Brown, 2014.

Smiley, Tavis, and Cornel West. *The Rich and the Rest of Us: A Poverty Manifesto.* New York: Smiley Books, 2012.

Smith, Valerie. *Not Just Race, Not Just Gender: Black Feminist Readings.* New York: Routledge, 1998.

Stiglitz, Joseph. *The Price of Inequality: How Today's Divided Society Endangers Our Future.* New York: W. W. Norton, 2012.

Sugrue, Thomas J. *Sweet Land of Liberty: The Forgotten Struggle for Civil Rights in the North.* New York: Random House, 2008.

Theoharis, Jeanne F., and Komozi Woodard, eds. *Freedom North: Black Freedom Struggles outside the South, 1940–1980.* New York: Palgrave Macmillan, 2003.

Till-Mobley, Mamie, and Christopher Benson. *Death of Innocence: The Story of the Hate Crime that Changed America.* New York: Ballantine Books, 2003.

Travis, Dempsey J. *An Autobiography of Black Politics.* Chicago: Urban Research Politics, 1987.

War Resisters International. *Handbook for Nonviolent Campaigns.* London: War Resisters International, 2009.

Washington, James M., ed. *A Testament of Hope: The Essential Writings and Speeches of Martin Luther King, Jr.* New York: Harper San Francisco, 1991.

Westgate, Michael, and Ann Vick-Westgate. *Gale Force: Gale Cincotta: The Battles for Disclosure and Community Reinvestment.* 2nd ed. Cambridge, MA: Harvard Bookstore, 2011.

Williams, Jakobi. *From the Bullet to the Ballot: The Illinois Chapter of the Black Panther Party and Racial Coalition Politics in Chicago.* Chapel Hill: University of North Carolina Press, 2013.

Wilson, William Julius. *More than Just Race: Being Black and Poor in the Inner City.* New York: W. W. Norton, 2010.

———. *When Work Disappears: The World of the New Urban Poor.* New York: Vintage, 1997.

Wink, Walter, ed. *Peace Is the Way: Writings on Nonviolence from the Fellowship of Reconciliation.* Maryknoll, NY: Orbis Books, 2000.

Young, Andrew. *An Easy Burden: The Civil Rights Movement and the Transformation of America.* New York: HarperCollins, 1996.

Young, Quentin. *Everybody in, Nobody Out: Memoirs of a Rebel without a Pause.* Friday Harbor, WA: Copernicus Healthcare, 2013.

Multimedia Sources

Anderson, Madeline. *I Am Somebody.* Icarus Films, 1970.

Chicago Freedom Movement fortieth anniversary website. http://cfm40.middlebury.edu/.

Hampton, Henry. Eyes *on the Prize II: Two Societies: 1965–1968.* PBS series, *The American Experience.* Blackside, 1990.

McClellan, Seth. *King in Chicago: The Story of Martin Luther King and the Chicago Freedom Movement: A Documentary.* Thorn Creek Productions, 2007.
————. *The New Battle: Martin Luther King [and] the Chicago Freedom Movement.* Thorn Creek Productions, n.d.

Contributors

Gene Barge, also known as Daddy G, is a legendary saxophonist, composer, arranger, and music producer in Chicago. He worked closely with the Reverend Jesse Jackson as one of the original organizers of the Operation Breadbasket Band and later as the band's director. He was a producer for Chess Records and later Stax Records. Beginning in the 1970s he was an actor and appeared in films such as *The Fugitive*. Currently he performs in Chicago with the Chicago R&B Kings.

Hal Baron worked for many years as the research director for the Chicago Urban League and was active in the Coordinating Council for Community Organizations in the 1960s. He served on the Steering Committee for Harold Washington's mayoral campaign in 1983 and later served as Mayor Washington's chief of policy. He is now retired and works with peasant groups in Central America who are striving to improve their communities.

Sherrilynn J. Bevel has engaged in human and community development for more than thirty years. Her work has included directing civic participation and democratization projects, providing technical support, and making presentations in the United States, East Africa, and Europe for various universities and nongovernmental organizations. A PhD candidate in political science at the University of Chicago, she teaches courses in politics, human rights, and nonviolence.

Jimmy Collier was an organizer, songwriter, and musician on the SCLC staff in Chicago. He later worked as a professional musician, rancher, and business executive until his retirement. He appeared in the documentary *Black Roots* and continues to perform music for activist groups and community events. His song "Rent Strike Blues" appears on the album *We Won't Move: Songs of the Tenants' Movement*.

459

Gil Cornfield is a labor attorney and a founding partner of Cornfield and Feldman LLC. He played a critical role in the Chicago Freedom Movement as the chief attorney for the tenant union organizing drive. He also mobilized a substantial team to provide pro bono legal services to tenants for many years after the movement era. He took one tenant's case to the Illinois Supreme Court in 1972 and won—a ruling that greatly expanded the rights of tenants.

Mary Lou Finley served on the staff of the Southern Christian Leadership Conference's Chicago Project in 1965–1966 as secretary to the Reverend James Bevel. She is a sociologist and Professor Emeritus at Antioch University Seattle. She is a contributor to *Chicago, 1966* (1989) and the coauthor with Bill Moyer and two others of *Doing Democracy: The MAP Model for Organizing Social Movements* (2001).

Melody Heaps founded Treatment Alternatives for Special Clients (TASC), a substance abuse and mental health agency in Chicago, in 1976. She is currently TASC's president emeritus and consultant. Heaps began her professional career during the civil rights movement as a community organizer for the Chicago City Missionary Society (now the Community Renewal Society), working at the West Side Organization. She joined the SCLC staff and was the liaison with labor unions and a tenant union organizer during the Chicago Freedom Movement.

Norman Hill has been a trade union and civil rights activist for more than fifty years and served as a leader of the A. Philip Randolph Institute for nearly forty years. During the Chicago Freedom Movement, he was assigned by the Industrial Union Department of the AFL-CIO to work with the movement on labor and civil rights issues. He was staff coordinator of the 1963 March on Washington for Jobs and Freedom, served as program director of CORE, and was a pioneer in the desegregation of public accommodations, including Rainbow Beach on the South Side of Chicago.

Jesse L. Jackson Sr. is a civil rights leader, Baptist minister, and politician who was a candidate for US president in 1984 and 1988. In 1966 he was appointed by Dr. Martin Luther King Jr. to head the Chicago chapter of SCLC's Operation Breadbasket, the economic arm of the movement. Jackson formed Operation PUSH (People United to Save [Serve] Humanity) in 1971 and the Rainbow Coalition in 1984. His influence extended to international matters in the 1980s and 1990s. He currently leads the Rainbow PUSH Coalition and works on economic justice issues.

Kimberlie Jackson is the principal of Community Pro Partners, a community development firm that assists organizations in shaping their environments. She has served in leadership roles in communities from the Midwest to the East Coast, most recently as executive director of the Lawndale Christian Development Corporation, where she led the physical and social revitalization of Chicago's North Lawndale community.

Herman Jenkins is a political geographer, now retired. He held a number of teaching, research, and administrative positions at CUNY and political appointments in the New York State and New York City governments. He was a resident of Chicago's West Side when the civil rights movement began and worked on tenant union issues during the Chicago Freedom Movement. After joining the SCLC field staff, he completed a short fellowship at the Metropolitan Applied Research Center in New York City and helped organize the Newark, New Jersey, leg of the Poor People's Campaign.

Bernard LaFayette Jr. is a longtime civil rights leader, organizer, nonviolence trainer, and university professor. He was director of urban affairs at the American Friends Service Committee in Chicago and a key leader in the Chicago Freedom Movement. He also played an important role in the Selma, Alabama, voting rights campaign as a SNCC staff member and was national coordinator for SCLC's Poor People's Campaign in 1968. He is the author of *In Peace and Freedom: My Journey in Selma* (2013). He served previously as Distinguished Scholar-in-Residence and director of the Center for Nonviolence and Peace Studies at the University of Rhode Island. Currently he is the Distinguished Senior Scholar-in-Residence at the Candler School of Theology, Emory University, Atlanta, and chairman of the board of the Southern Christian Leadership Conference.

Jonathan Lewis is a senior Kingian nonviolence trainer who has worked for more than ten years bringing nonviolence training to a wide range of groups, from the students at Lawndale Community Prep High School in Chicago to former militants in Nigeria; his special focus is training youth.

Allegra Malone is a folk musician and songwriter in Chicago. She also works with children, teaching the arts. She is particularly interested in Chicago's music history.

Molly Martindale worked for the West Side Christian Parish for two and a half years in the mid-1960s, including a year and a half as a member of the joint WSCP-SCLC staff. She later taught English as a second language, worked for environmental consulting firms, and worked in the wetlands regulatory program for the US Army Corps of Engineers.

James R. Ralph Jr. is Dean for Faculty Development and Research and the Rehnquist Professor of American History and Culture at Middlebury College in Vermont. He is the author of *Northern Protest: Martin Luther King, Jr., Chicago, and the Civil Rights Movement* (1993).

Christopher Robert Reed is an American historian known for his expertise on the African American experience in Chicago during the nineteenth and twentieth centuries. Reed is currently Emeritus Professor of History at Roosevelt University in Chicago. He has served on the faculty of Northern Illinois University, the University of Illinois at Chicago, and the City Colleges of Chicago. He is the author of six books, among them *Black Chicago's First Century, 1833–1900* (2005) and *Knock at the Door of Opportunity: Black Migration to Chicago, 1900–1919* (2014).

Don Rose is a political strategist and campaign adviser who has helped elect Chicago aldermen, mayors, and senators since the late 1960s, from Harold Washington to Paul Simon. He was a mentor to David Axelrod, Barack Obama's top campaign strategist. Rose served as press secretary for Dr. Martin Luther King Jr. during the Chicago Freedom Movement.

Leonard S. Rubinowitz is a professor of law at Northwestern University

School of Law, where he teaches Law and Social Change, Criminal Law, Public Interest Practicum, and Urban Housing. His books include *Low-Income Housing: Suburban Strategies* (1974) and *Crossing the Class and Color Lines: From Public Housing to White Suburbia* (coauthored with James Rosenbaum, 2000).

Gail Schechter has been a leader in advocacy for fair and affordable housing, discrimination investigation, tenant and community organizing, public school funding reform, and public policy research and development since 1984. Since 1993 she has served as executive director of Open Communities, the not-for-profit housing, economic, and social justice organization descended from the North Shore Summer Project.

Al Sharpton is a Baptist minister, a civil rights activist, the founder and president of the National Action Network, and the host of MSNBC's *Politics Nation*. In 2004 he was a candidate for the Democratic nomination for president. Sharpton is a protégé of the Reverend Jesse Jackson.

Pam Smith is on the staff of the University of Arizona and previously taught US history at Northern Virginia Community College. Her company, PSmith Consulting, conducted the feasibility study that set the stage for the Chicago Freedom School. A native Chicagoan, she has worked with many youth groups in Chicago and served as a top communications aide to Jesse Jackson in his 1988 presidential bid and to Barack Obama in his primary campaign for US Senate. She was project manager for the Chicago Freedom Movement's fortieth anniversary celebration and is a certified Kingian nonviolence trainer.

Brian White is a community development professional who served in senior staff roles at the Leadership Council for Metropolitan Open Communities from 2000 to 2005. He also founded and operated a Chicago nonprofit community development corporation, served as a national bank Community Reinvestment Act officer, and, most recently, was the first executive director of the Cook County Land Bank Authority. He is a lifelong resident of Chicago.

Index

Civil Rights and the Struggle for Black Equality
in the Twentieth Century

Series Editors
Steven F. Lawson, Rutgers University
Cynthia Griggs Fleming, University of Tennessee

Democracy Rising: South Carolina and the Fight for Black Equality since 1865
Peter F. Lau

Civil Rights Crossroads: Nation, Community, and the Black Freedom Struggle
Steven F. Lawson

Selma to Saigon: The Civil Rights Movement and the Vietnam War
Daniel S. Lucks

In Remembrance of Emmett Till: Regional Stories and Media Responses to the Black Freedom Struggle
Darryl Mace

Freedom Rights: New Perspectives on the Civil Rights Movement
edited by Danielle L. McGuire and John Dittmer

This Little Light of Mine: The Life of Fannie Lou Hamer
Kay Mills

After the Dream: Black and White Southerners since 1965
Timothy J. Minchin and John A. Salmond

Fighting Jim Crow in the County of Kings: The Congress of Racial Equality in Brooklyn
Brian Purnell

Roy Wilkins: The Quiet Revolutionary and the NAACP
Yvonne Ryan

Thunder of Freedom: Black Leadership and the Transformation of 1960s Mississippi
Sue [Lorenzi] Sojourner with Cheryl Reitan

For a Voice and the Vote: My Journey with the Mississippi Freedom Democratic Party
Lisa Anderson Todd

Art for Equality: The NAACP's Cultural Campaign for Civil Rights
Jenny Woodley

For Jobs and Freedom: Race and Labor in America since 1865
Robert H. Zieger